THE DICKENS COMPANIONS
Series Editors: Susan Shatto and David Paroissien

The Companion to *Hard Times*

THE DICKENS COMPANIONS

[1]
The Companion to *Our Mutual Friend*
MICHAEL COTSELL

[2]
The Companion to *The Mystery of Edwin Drood*
WENDY S. JACOBSON

[3]
The Companion to *Bleak House*
SUSAN SHATTO

[4]
The Companion to *A Tale of Two Cities*
ANDREW SANDERS

[5]
The Companion to *Oliver Twist*
DAVID PAROISSIEN

[6]
The Companion to *Hard Times*
MARGARET SIMPSON

THE COMPANION TO

Hard Times

MARGARET SIMPSON

HELM INFORMATION LTD

© Margaret Simpson, 1997

A CIP catalogue record for this book
is available from the British Library.

All rights reserved: No reproduction, copy or
transmission of this publication may be made
without written permission.

No paragraph of this publication may be
reproduced, copied or transmitted save
with the written permission or in accordance
with the provisions of the Copyright Act 1956
(as amended), or under the terms of any licence
permitting limited copying
issued by the Copyright Licensing Agency,
7 Ridgmount Street, London WC1E 7AE.

Any person who does any unauthorised act in
relation to this publication may be liable to
criminal prosecution and civil claims for
damages.

Published in Great Britain in 1997 by
Helm Information Ltd.
The Banks, Mountfield,
near Robertsbridge,
East Sussex TN32 5JY
U.K.

ISBN 1-873403-56-9

Printed on acid-free paper and bound by
Bookcraft Ltd, Midsomer Norton, Bath,
Somerset BA3 4BS

To Gerry

CONTENTS

	page
List of Illustrations	ix
General Preface by the Editors	xi
Acknowledgements	xiii
Abbreviations for Dickens's Works and Related Material	xv
Bibliographical Symbols and Abbreviations	xvi
Introduction	1
A Note on the Text	13
How to Use the Notes	15
The Notes	17
Appendix A: Glossary of Lancashire Dialect Words Used in *Hard Times*	235
Appendix B: Glossary of Slang Terms Used in *Hard Times*	237
Appendix C: Table of Factory Accidents, 1852–4	241
Appendix D: Table of the *Household Words* Articles Relevant to Topics in *Hard Times*	242
Appendix E: Ballads of the Preston Strike, 1853–4	245
Select Bibliography	248
Index	267

LIST OF ILLUSTRATIONS

		page
1	The first serialized page of *Hard Times* in volume 9 of *Household Words*	18
2	Photograph of Sir James Kay-Shuttleworth (c.1862). From Mary Sturt, *The Education of the People* (London: Routledge, 1967)	29
3	Louisa Woolford and Andrew Ducrow performing 'The Swiss Maid and Tyrolean Shepherd'. From A. H. Saxon, *The Life and Art of Andrew Ducrow and the Romantic Age of the English Circus* (Hamden, Conn.: Archon, 1978)	59
4	'Mademoiselle Ella' and Tom Barry the clown at Drury Lane Theatre, London. From the *Illustrated London News*, 26 November 1853	61
5	Part of an Astley's double-playbill for 11 October 1852 (by courtesy of the Board of Trustees of the Victoria and Albert Museum)	63
6	An unsigned portrait of Tom Barry (1842). From Ifan Kyrle Fletcher, 'A Portrait of Thomas Barry'. *Theatre Notebook* 17 (1963) 116–17, pl. 6	65
7	'Billy Button's Journey to Brentford' (1768) (by permission of the Gunnersbury Park Joint Committee)	67
8	Swainson & Birley's 'Big Factory', Preston (1834), drawn by T. Allom and engraved by J. Tingle (by permission of the Harris Museum and Art Gallery, Preston)	80
9	Details of 'the famous nine oils' from a nineteenth-century chemist's label (Museum of the Royal Pharmaceutical Society of Great Britain)	90
10	Andrew Ducrow as 'The Wild Indian Hunter'. From M. Willson Disher, *Greatest Show on Earth* (London: G. Bell, 1937)	94
11	The perch act. From Hugues Le Roux and Jules Garnier, *Acrobats and Mountebanks* (London: Chapman & Hall, 1890)	99
12	The 'Prince of Clowns', Jean-Baptiste Auriol, at Vauxhall Gardens. From the *Illustrated London News*, 9 June 1849	101
13	Photograph of William Ellis. From Ethel E. Ellis, *Memoir of William Ellis* (London: Longmans, 1888)	112

14	Performing dog act. From Hugues Le Roux and Jules Garnier, *Acrobats and Mountebanks* (London: Chapman & Hall, 1890)	120
15	Payment of cotton workers in the Temperance Hall, Preston. From the *Illustrated London News*, 12 November 1853	173
16	Mortimer Grimshaw. From the *People's Paper*, 4 February 1854; reprinted in H. I. Dutton and J. E. King, *'Ten Per Cent and No Surrender': The Preston Strike, 1853–1854* (Cambridge: Cambridge UP, 1981)	176
17	George Cowell addressing factory operatives in the Orchard, Preston. From the *Illustrated London News*, 12 November 1853	178
18	A lace-edged Astley's programme for 28 February 1854 (by courtesy of the Board of Trustees of the Victoria and Albert Museum)	227

GENERAL PREFACE BY THE EDITORS

The Dickens Companions series provides the most comprehensive annotation of the works of Dickens ever undertaken. Separate volumes are devoted to each of Dickens's fifteen novels, to *Sketches by Boz* and to *The Uncommercial Traveller;* the five Christmas books are treated together in one volume. The series will be completed by a General Index, making nineteen volumes in all.

The nature of the annotation is factual rather than critical. The series undertakes what the general editors of the Clarendon Dickens have called 'the immense task of explanatory annotation' of Dickens's works. Each Companion will elucidate obscurities and allusions which were doubtless intelligible to the nineteenth-century reader but which have changed or lost their meaning in a later age. The 'world' of Dickens passed away more than a century ago, and our perceptions and interpretations of his works can be sharpened by our having recalled for us a precise context or piece of information.

The annotation identifies allusions to current events and intellectual and religious issues, and supplies information on topography, social customs, costume, furniture, transportation, and so on. Identifications are provided for allusions to plays, poems, songs, the Bible, the Book of Common Prayer and other literary sources. Elements of Dickens's plots, characterization and style which are influenced by the works of other writers are also identified. When an aspect of the text can be shown to have been influenced by Dickens's own experience this is indicated. The work of Dickens's illustrators is also discussed. Finally, although the Companions do not attempt the work of a modern scholarly edition, material from Dickens's manuscripts and proofs is included when it is of major significance.

The main part of the information in each Companion is arranged in the form of notes presented for convenient use with any edition of Dickens's works. The information is thus placed where it is most relevant, enabling the notes to be used to elucidate a local difficulty, or to pursue the use of a certain kind of material or the development of a particular idea. To facilitate the last purpose, the notes are cross-referenced, and each Companion contains a comprehensive index. The introduction to each Companion traces the major influences and concerns revealed by the annotation and, where appropriate, demonstrates their place in the genesis and composition of the text.

Dickens's vital and imaginative response to his culture is a familiar fact, but the Dickens Companions demonstrate and explore this response more fully and in far greater detail than has ever been attempted. Hitherto, Dickens's works have been annotated only on a modest scale. Many modern editions of the novels contain some notes, but there is not space in one volume for both the text of a novel and a comprehensive annotation of the text. Because most volumes of the Dickens Companions are devoted to a single work, the series can provide the full-scale, thoroughgoing annotation which the works of Dickens require. The completed series will compose a uniquely comprehensive archive of information about Dickens's world, affording the modern reader an unparalleled record of Dickens's concerns and the sources of his artistry. For many kinds of scholar, not merely Dickensians, the Dickens Companions will provide a fundamental tool for future critical and historical scholarship on various aspects of nineteenth-century British culture.

To undertake the 'immense task' of annotation, the Editors have assembled a team of Dickens scholars who work closely together and with the Editors in order to enhance the depth and scope of each Companion. The series is not a variorum commentary on Dickens: it does not consist of a survey or a selection of comments by other annotators and scholars. Previous scholarship is, in general, cited only when it is considered to identify an important piece of information about the historical, literary and biographical influences on Dickens's works.

The annotation in the Dickens Companions is based on original research which derives for the most part from the writing of Dickens's own time, the reading available to him and the books he is known to have read. The annotation is not perfunctorily minimal: a large number of notes are substantial essays and all are written in a readable style. Nor does the annotation consist of narrow definitions of what the reader (in the opinion of another reader) 'needs to know' in order to 'understand' the text. Rather, the annotation attempts to open up the actual and imaginative worlds which provided the sources and the backgrounds of Dickens's works in the belief that what interested, engaged and amused Dickens can hardly fail to interest, engage and amuse his readers. Our largest hope for the Dickens Companions is that the volumes will be read with a pleasure akin to that with which Dickens's own writings are read, and that they will be genuine Companions to both his works and his readers.

The idea of providing each of Dickens's major works with a companion volume of annotation originated with the late Professor T. J. B. Spencer. It is to his memory that the series is gratefully and affectionately dedicated.

1980–95   SUSAN SHATTO
MICHAEL COTSELL

After the publication of five volumes, Michael Cotsell retired from the series as Associate Editor. David Paroissien replaces him as co-editor, pledged to continue with Susan Shatto an annotative enterprise devoted to recovering and illuminating the allusive worlds of Dickens's novels and the culture which gave rise to them.

1997   SUSAN SHATTO
DAVID PAROISSIEN

ACKNOWLEDGEMENTS

I would like to express my gratitude to the many institutions and individuals who assisted me in my work. I am indebted to the library staff of Queen's University, Belfast, especially to Florence Gray of Inter-library Loans. I am also indebted to Queen's University Photographic Unit, and to the staff of the Humanities and Fine Arts Departments in the Central Library, Belfast, for their willing assistance. I wish to thank the Board of Trustees of the Victoria and Albert Museum for allowing me to reproduce parts of the manuscript and corrected proofs of *Hard Times* held in the Forster Collection, and the British Library for access to page proofs in the Dexter Collection. Thanks are also due to the Central Library, Manchester, the Harris Museum and Art Gallery, Preston, the Preston Harris Library, and the Lancashire County Record Office, Preston, for access to contemporary material, newspapers and illustrations of Preston, the Preston strike and the Lancashire cotton industry. I am particularly grateful to the Preston historian Stephen Sartin for his information about the gallery at the Bull and Royal Hotel, Preston, and for his helpful responses to my queries. For invaluable help with many small but time-consuming queries, I would like to thank the following: Museum of the Royal Pharmaceutical Society of Great Britain; the Wellcome Institute for the History of Medicine; the Royal Academy Library; the Development Officer at Westminster School; George Hoare, archivist, Stoll Moss Archives, Theatre Royal Drury Lane; Maria Blyzinsky, Curator of Astronomy, Old Royal Observatory, at the National Maritime Museum; M. A. R. Kennett, Veterinary Librarian at the Veterinary Library at Edinburgh University; the Temple Reading Room at Rugby School; and Margaret MacKeith, Dean of the Faculty of Design and Technology, Preston. For illustrations (Plates 5, 7 and 18) and access to theatrical playbill collections, I would like to thank the Gunnersbury Park Museum; the Theatre Museum, Covent Garden; and the Victoria and Albert Picture Library. I especially appreciate the efforts and assistance of two circus historians, A. H. Saxon and George Speaight – the former for allowing me to reproduce one of his illustrations (Plate 3) and the latter for his provision of the Auriol engraving (Plate 12). In addition, both made enlightening and amusing suggestions for the 'Clown's performing chair' (3.7). I also thank the *Dickens Quarterly* for permission to reprint many of my notes on the circus which were published, in a slightly altered form, in the issue of September 1993.

I am grateful for the advice and encouragement given to me by many Dickens scholars, including K. J. Fielding, David Paroissien, Nancy Metz, Angus Easson and Philip Collins. I am also indebted to John Manning of the School of English at Queen's University, Belfast, for his constructive support, and to Susan Shatto, who redirected my initial analysis of *Household Words* and *Hard Times*, and gave my work meaning and importance.

Many thanks are also due to Edward Leeson and Stas Radosh whose meticulous and painstaking work made the production of this volume possible.

Finally, I wish to express sincere thanks to my understanding parents and to my long-suffering children, Melanie and Russell. Above all, I extend my deepest appreciation to my husband, Gerry, who has been down the Old Hell Shaft with me and survived. To him I owe everything.

The General Editors join with me in expressing my gratitude to the Dickens Society for a generous contribution to help defray the cost of preparing the final version of my typescript for publication.

ABBREVIATIONS FOR DICKENS'S WORKS AND RELATED MATERIAL

1. Works: Major

AN	*American Notes*
BH	*Bleak House*
BL	*The Battle of Life*
BR	*Barnaby Rudge*
C	*The Chimes*
CC	*A Christmas Carol*
CH	*The Cricket on the Hearth*
CHE	*A Child's History of England*
DC	*David Copperfield*
DS	*Dombey and Son*
GE	*Great Expectations*
HM	*The Haunted Man*
HT	*Hard Times*
LD	*Little Dorrit*
MC	*Martin Chuzzlewit*
MED	*The Mystery of Edwin Drood*
MHC	*Master Humphrey's Clock*
NN	*Nicholas Nickleby*
OCS	*The Old Curiosity Shop*
OMF	*Our Mutual Friend*
OT	*Oliver Twist*
PI	*Pictures from Italy*
PP	*The Pickwick Papers*
SB	*Sketches by Boz*
TTC	*A Tale of Two Cities*
UT	*The Uncommercial Traveller*

2. Works: Miscellaneous Writings

Bentley's	*Bentley's Miscellany*
CP	*Collected Papers*
MP	*Miscellaneous Papers*
RP	*Reprinted Pieces*
AYR	*All the Year Round*
HW	*Household Words*

HN	*The Household Narrative of Current Events*
CD	Charles Dickens Edition, 21 vols (1867–[74])

3. Related Material: Basic Sources

BCP	*The Book of Common Prayer*
BPP	*British Parliamentary Papers*
Forster	John Forster, *The Life of Charles Dickens*, 3 vols (1872–4)
HO	*Home Office Papers* (Public Record Office)
Letters	*The Letters of Charles Dickens*, ed. Madeline House and others, Pilgrim Edition. 8 vols to date (1965–)
Letters: Coutts	*Letters from Charles Dickens to Angela Burdett-Coutts, 1841–1865*, ed. Edgar Johnson (1953)
Letters: MDGH	*The Letters of Charles Dickens*, edited by his Sister-in-law and his Eldest Daughter. Vol 1. 1833–1856 (1880)
Nonesuch	*The Letters of Charles Dickens*, ed. Walter Dexter, Nonesuch Edition, 3 vols (1938)
Speeches	*The Speeches of Charles Dickens*, ed. K. J. Fielding (1960, 2nd edn 1988)

BIBLIOGRAPHICAL SYMBOLS AND ABBREVIATIONS

MS	Manuscript
CP	Corrected proofs
< >	Deletion in MS or proof
∧ or ∧	Addition or substitution in MS
∧ OR ∧	Addition or substitution in proof
illegible word	Signifies an unreadable word in MS

INTRODUCTION

The Genesis of the Novel within a Periodical Format

On 25 October 1853, Dickens wrote to Angela Burdett Coutts from Milan describing his travels via the Simplon Pass into Italy. He was pleased to be in Italy again, and to hear and speak the 'delicate' language once more:

> So beautiful too to see the delightful sky again, and all the picturesque wonders of the country. And yet I am so restless to be doing – and always shall be, I think, so long as I have any portion in Time – that if I were to stay more than a week in any one City here, I believe I should be half desperate to begin some new story!!! (*Letters* 7.171)

This extract appears in both the first and second Norton editions of *Hard Times*, under the section 'Dickens' Comments on the Composition of *Hard Times*'. Its inclusion is an erroneous one, since the 'new story' eventually became *Little Dorrit*, within which Dickens drew upon his Alpine and Italian travels of the 1840s and 1853. The distinction has a hitherto unnoticed bearing on our understanding of the creation of *Hard Times* because it supports the notion that the novel was initially an unwanted child which in all probability would not have existed, and certainly not in its present form, had it not been for the flagging circulation of *Household Words*. The unpropitious circumstances of its conception, however, produced a work which challenged Dickens's skills as a novelist and journalist. His illuminating comment in 1852 about the birth of his last child, 'Plorn' (Edward Bulwer Lytton Dickens), could reasonably be applied to *Hard Times*: 'I am not quite clear that I particularly wanted the latter, but I have no doubt that he is good for me in some point of view or other'. A year later Dickens proudly announced that 'there cannot possibly be another baby anywhere, to come into competition with him' (*Letters* 6.629, 7.87). *Hard Times*, the unintentional novel, became, like Plorn, a blessing in disguise.

Dickens's plans after completing *Bleak House* in August 1853 had been 'to be as lazy as [he] could be all through summer' and 'do nothing in that way for a year' (*Letters* 7.288, 453). However, by the time he returned to England from Italy on 11 December 1853, the weekly sales of *Household Words* – usually averaging 40,000 copies – had dropped dramatically. (Apart from *A Child's History of England*, Dickens's last contribution to *Household Words* had appeared on 8 October 1853, two days before he left for Switzerland and Italy.) Some time between mid-December and 28 December it was agreed that Dickens should write a novel for the periodical: 'there is such a fixed idea on the part of my printers and copartners in Household Words, that a story by me . . . would make some unheard-of-effect with it, that I am going to write one' (*Letters* 7.256). The Agreement, drawn up by his partners, Bradbury & Evans, John Forster and W. H. Wills, dated 28 December 1853, consented to pay Dickens £1,000 in two instalments and clearly states that the weekly serialization of Dickens's new tale was 'the personal venture of the four partners . . . with a view to the enlargement of the circulation of Household Words and the consequent enhancement of the value of their several shares' (*Letters* 7.911).

With the first page written on 23 January 1854, Dickens admitted that his 'purpose [was] among the mighty secrets of the world'. Although he had at that date 'the main idea' for the new work, and although he stated after the novel's completion that 'the idea laid hold of me by the throat in a very violent manner' (*Letters* 7.256, 453), the inspiration did not initially come voluntarily. The 'vague thoughts . . . rife within' Dickens months before he had written *Dombey and Son*, or 'the first shadows' and '[v]iolent restlessness, and vague ideas' that had existed long before he put pen to paper for *Bleak House* (*Letters* 4.510, 6.463), were absent when he came to compose *Hard Times*. Seeking ideas for the new novel, Dickens turned to *Household Words*, within whose covers articles by nearly 400 contributors were ingrained with his inimitable watermark.

Dickens's experience of writing a novel in weekly parts began in 1840–1, when *The Old Curiosity Shop* and *Barnaby Rudge* appeared in his weekly periodical, *Master Humphrey's Clock*. He had yet to find an original format for a periodical, and his insistence on using as models the eighteenth-century favourites of his childhood – such as Addison and Steele's *The Tatler* and *The Spectator*, and Goldsmith's *The Bee* – resulted in falling sales of *Master Humphrey's Clock*. His initial intention of writing 'amusing essays on the various foibles of the day' and '[taking] advantage of all passing events' which he would form into 'sketches, essays, tales, adventures [and] letters' was quickly abandoned, and *The Old Curiosity Shop*, started as a short story in the *Clock*, became the sole contents of the periodical. *Master Humphrey's Clock* continued as a vehicle for the weekly serialization of *Barnaby Rudge*, after which it folded. Despite the number of weekly parts for each novel – 40 for *The Old Curiosity Shop* and 42 for *Barnaby Rudge* (compared to 20 for *Hard Times*) – Dickens found the weekly plan constraining and frustrating. While writing an early number of *The Old Curiosity Shop*, he complained to Forster: 'I was obliged to cramp most dreadfully what I thought a pretty idea in the last chapter. I hadn't room to turn'. With *Barnaby Rudge*, he also found himself 'sadly cramped . . . for room' (*Letters* 2.80, 238). It is therefore not surprising, after the expansiveness of *Bleak House*, that when Dickens found himself in his former literary claustrophobia of a weekly serial problems of space and time were his overriding complaints. In February 1854 – several weeks into writing *Hard Times* – he complained:

> The difficulty of space is CRUSHING. Nobody can have any idea of it who has not had an experience of patient fiction-writing with some elbow-room always, and open places in perspective. In this form, with any kind of regard to the current number, there is absolutely no such thing. (*Letters* 7.282)

By April, Dickens was 'in a dreary state, planning and planning the story of *Hard Times* (out of materials for I don't know how long a story)', and three days before he finished he was 'three parts mad, and the fourth delirious, with perpetual rushing at *Hard Times*'. He had not changed his views when he wrote in November 1854: 'the compression and close condensation necessary for that disjointed form of publication, gave me perpetual trouble' (Letters 7.317, 369, 453). Part of the difficulty lay in his insistence on planning *Hard Times* around a monthly format (see his work plan for the first number), even though the novel was never intended for monthly publication. The decision was understandable, since he had up until this time produced all his novels in monthly parts (the weekly parts of *The Old Curiosity Shop* and *Barnaby Rudge* in *Master Humphrey's Clock* were also issued monthly). The imposition of a monthly framework on a weekly instalment which itself is constrained within a miscellany of articles was to be Dickens's greatest challenge to his creative powers. *Hard Times* appeared for twenty weeks in *Household Words* from 1 April to 12 August 1854. Over the period, circulation was four or five times greater than before the novel's serialization (around 70,000–80,000 copies), greatly outstripping the journal's best figures to date (60,000 copies) (Letters 6.64; Buckler, 1950, 200 and note 6).

The common factors of financial exigency and artistic confinement which link *The Old Curiosity Shop* and *Barnaby Rudge* to *Hard Times* are outmatched by the unusual genesis and journalistic environment of the later novel. Unlike *Hard Times*, the two earlier works were already conceived before readership fell in *Master Humphrey's Clock*. Moreover, both *The Old Curiosity Shop* and *Barnaby Rudge* (with the exception of the first two instalments of *The Old Curiosity Shop*) in essence became the periodical. *Hard Times*, with half the amount of instalments, had to be created swiftly and imaginatively by a maturer hand. Its incremental construction within the established journalistic format of *Household Words* shaped the novel's form and content.

'Household Words' and Dickens's Literary and Social Vision

The special nature of *Hard Times* lies in its relationship to *Household Words* and in the journal's vital role in Dickens's literary and social vision. The journal was the culmination of his dream to edit his own magazine, and he saw it both as 'a *good property*' (Letters 6.83) and as an embodiment of his personality and artistic vision that had been shaped by his childhood reading. His aims for the journal are declared in 'A Preliminary Word', the now famous manifesto which opened the first number on 30 March 1850. The journal promised to nurture the 'light of Fancy which is inherent in the human breast' (1.1), and it had no place for a hard, utilitarian mentality. For Dickens, the fanciful, imaginative treatment of all material for *Household Words* was imperative not only as a stylistic rule but also as a perspective on life itself. Consequently, he frequently insisted that contributions which he felt were 'wanting [in] elegance of fancy' be brightened and lightened: 'KEEP "HOUSEHOLD WORDS" IMAGINATIVE! is the solemn and continual Conductorial Injunction' (Letters 6.522, 7.200). Dickens's subeditor, W. H. Wills, was more realistic about some contributions to the journal: 'No one, not even yourself (as you said the other day) can sparkle to order, especially writers who have only an occasional sparkle in them' (Letters 6.850).

The absence of by-lines, together with Dickens's editorial control, ensured that *Household Words* spoke with only one voice. Readers were reminded of this fact in the running headline of each opening: '[Conducted by Charles Dickens]'. It is interesting to note that one of his proposed titles for the journal in 1850 was 'The Household Voice' (*Letters* 6.26). The anonymity of articles in *Household Words* (and in *All the Year Round*), and Dickens's desire for balance and consistency of opinion within the periodical, demanded editorial scrutiny and dedication. He commissioned, revised, overhauled and positioned articles within the weekly numbers, always conscious of the danger of contradiction which not only might compromise his opinions but also suggest to his readers that 'the journal itself [was] blowing hot and cold and playing fast and loose, in a ridiculous way' (*Letters* 7.47). His frequent trips away – either on holiday or on his public reading tours – disrupted the daily editorial duties and the long Thursday-afternoon meetings at the *Household Words* office. Weekly parcels were sent to him by his subeditor, however – some 'in dimensions like a spare bed, containing "doubtful articles" for Household Words, on which decision was necessary to the peace of mind of the writers' (*Letters* 6.147). Yet, despite his strict control and meticulous revisions, articles contrary to his central beliefs about human existence in an industrialized society did occasionally manage to slip through Dickens's 'inky fishing-net' of corrected proofs (Forster 3.19.453–4). For example, Harriet Martineau's pro-manufacturing stance evident in a series of *Household Words* articles published between 1851 and 1852 was antithetical to Dickens's disenchantment with politico-economic doctrine (see note, pp. 145–6).

The intimate relationship Dickens fostered between himself and his readers lay at the heart of the enormous public success of *Household Words*. Percy Fitzgerald, a contributor from 1856 to 1859, remembered with glowing affection both the journal and its 'magician, the gifted Editor himself':

> Anything by Dickens, a letter, a paper, an opinion, was sought out, talked over and devoured, and people were eager to know what he thought on any and every subject. *Household Words*, a mere twopenny journal, was to be found on every table and in every room, in the palace and the cottage.
> (1913, 135)

That the journal should become disseminated throughout British households was one of the hopes Dickens expressed in 'A Preliminary Word': 'to be a comrade and friend of many thousands of people of both sexes, and of all ages and conditions' (1.1). Despite the many articles written especially for the working class, and notwithstanding the numerous discussions and reports about the conditions of the poor, the majority of *Household Words* readers were middle class (Lohrli, 1973, 15–16). This factor determined the nature of the social criticism in *Hard Times*.

The Interdependency of the 'Great Magazine of Facts' and 'Hard Times'

'In some sense', Sylvia Manning commented in 1984, 'all of *Household Words* bears upon *Hard Times*' (10). Although succinctly expressed, her view was not a new one, for previous critics had discussed the correspondence between the journalism and the fiction. K. J. Fielding, for example, suggested that Dickens 'thought of *Hard Times* almost as a work of journalism itself' (1958, 137). Joseph Butwin's extensive analysis proved that 'the original readers were encouraged to see the novel as a form of journalism to be read continuously with *Household Words*', and that in its one-volume form *Hard Times* 'was bound to appear incomplete' (1977, 167, 186). Malcolm Andrews called the process 'a kind of extended "lateral" reading' (1980, 245). In an article about Dickens's journalistic involvement in the campaign for factory safety legislation and his decision to cancel a related passage and footnote on the corrected proofs of *Hard Times* (pp. 143–6), Peter W. J. Bartrip noted that 'the accident articles, dealing with what was basically a northern textile problem, began to appear just before serialization of *Hard Times*' (1979, 19).

The structure, contents and style of *Hard Times* were determined by Dickens's first publishing it within the covers of what John Forster described as 'a great magazine of facts'. Forster discussed this interdependence when he reviewed the novel for the *Examiner* in 1854; and, although he maintained that the concerns of *Hard Times* are more clearly perceptible in the one-volume edition than in the serialized parts, his preference can be used as effectively to argue the reverse (as Butwin and Andrews do): the journalism and the fiction nourished each other.

The countless citations from *Household Words* included in the annotations show that the topics most common to the journalism and the fiction are industrialism, trade unions, political economy, education, divorce and the circus. Throughout the serialization of the novel, Dickens repeatedly echoed a handful of articles on these topics, using them to inspire and enrich the social criticism in his fiction. Often, he arranged for articles and chapters on the same topic to appear in the same issue. In this way, their common concern would be reinforced and, at the same time, he could counterbalance the 'difficulty of space' imposed by the short chapters with extra 'elbow-room' provided by the journalism (*Letters* 7.282). Indeed, the annotations show that for most issues of *Household Words* that contained *Hard Times* Dickens articulated the journal's contents as skilfully as Mr Venus in *Our Mutual Friend* articulates bones (see Appendix D, pp. 242–4).

While reading the serialized text of *Hard Times*, Dickens's contemporaries were constantly invited to adopt a perspective recurrent throughout his fiction: the blurring of the boundaries between the imaginative world and Dickens's view of the real world reflected in the journalism and channelled into *Hard Times*. This perspective is now lost to modern readers, but it can be recalled through the quotation of parallel extracts from *Household Words*. In addition, such citations sensitize the modern reader to the topicality of the fiction.

1. Industrialism: 'Fire and Snow' and 'Sharpening the Scythe'

Informing a variety of the industrial images in *Hard Times* is Dickens's account of the railway journey he made to Birmingham and Wolverhampton in December 1853, a month before he began writing the novel. His observations of the landscape of the 'Black Country', described in 'Fire and Snow' (8.481–3), are often echoed or reworked in *Hard Times*. For example, the references to the express train whirling over the railway arches (book 1, chapter 12), the long line of arches over a landscape of deserted pits near Bounderby's country retreat (book 2, chapter 9), and the 'dismal stories . . . of the old pits' that portend Stephen's fall into Old Hell Shaft (book 3, chapter 6), all owe their inspiration to a single passage from the *Household Words* article (see notes, pp. 78, 139, 191–2, 220). Reminiscences of other 'Fire and Snow' passages appear in Louisa's imaginative response to the fires of Coketown (book 1, chapter 15), in Mrs Sparsit's own railway journey while stalking Louisa (book 2, chapter 11), and in the image of the 'clanking serpents . . . writhing above coal pits' in the introductory depiction of Coketown (book 1, chapter 5). The serpent and savage imagery in this last example also seems indebted to other sources: Dickens's dislike of African 'natives', his knowledge of circus acts which often featured American Indians, elephants and smoke serpents, and the *Household Words* article 'The Northern Wizard', which describes the manufacture of industrial chemicals (8.225–8). (See notes, pp. 150, 207–8, 79.) The blend of fact and fancy in all these images, together with their anthropocentric emphasis on sullenness, darkness, violence, cold, monstrosity and death, provides a clue to Dickens's personal responses to day-to-day life in an industrial environment.

The significance of James Payn's 'Sharpening the Scythe' (9 [1 April 1854] 150–2) to the events of Stephen's fall and rescue has up until now been overlooked. The article, published in the same number as the first three serialized chapters of *Hard Times*, contains many similar features of the scene around the Old Hell Shaft. The concerted speedy efforts of the men, the surgeon, the restorative alcohol, the makeshift litter, and the funeral procession can all be found in the *Household Words* story of scythe-stone cutters and their perilous excavations (see note, pp. 223–4).

2. Trade Unions and Political Economy: 'On Strike'

Many commentators have noticed the correlation between 'On Strike' (8.553–9), Dickens's *Household Words* article on the Preston strike of 1853–4, and the scenes of industrial unrest in *Hard Times*. But some of the novel's subtle but important echoes of the article have not been noticed hitherto, even though it seems likely that they would have been recognized by Dickens's contemporary readers.

Placards and bills were a crucial propaganda tool used by both workers and masters during the Preston strike, and for 'On Strike' Dickens transcribed 'the worst [he] could find' (554). Apparently expecting to confront a crowd of unruly workers, he seems to have been disappointed at their orderliness and at the uneventful scenes he encountered in Preston. A touch of regret at the absence of drama is suggested in 'On Strike' and in his letter to Forster (see note, pp. 217–18).

He found scenes that were more useful to him at Preston's Old Cockpit when he attended a Sunday weavers' delegate meeting there on 29 January 1854. This occasion inspired the description of the 'densely crowded and suffocatingly close Hall' into which Stephen is brought before the members of the United Aggregate Tribunal in book 2, chapter 4 (see note, pp. 174).

Another incident involving bills and the trade union agitator Mortimer Grimshaw was reworked first in 'On Strike' and then in *Hard Times*. It would appear that Dickens loosely based the placard scenes in the novel on both his general observations of the Preston strikers' eagerness to read the varied bills posted throughout the town and on a specific incident he had witnessed concerning an aggrieved Warrington delegate and 'offensive' bills allegedly posted by Grimshaw (see notes, pp.217–18).

The theory of Political Economy which influenced middle-class Victorian attitudes to trade union policy on wage bargaining was a favourite campaigning issue throughout the Preston strike, and was widely discussed in the local and national press, in letters and editorials. Dickens was aware that there were few supporters among these sources and made it clear in 'On Strike': 'I read, even in liberal pages, the hardest Political Economy . . . as the only touchstone of this strike' (554). He himself was unequivocal about Political Economy, describing it as 'great and useful . . . in its own way and its own place'. However, he 'did not transplant [his] definition of it from the Common Prayer Book, and make it a great king above all gods' (553). Dickens's coupling of Christianity and economics in 'On Strike' is not merely reinforced frequently in *Hard Times* – it is central to the novel's critique of industrialized society. Examples of social criticism which appear in the Gradgrindian principle that 'everything was to be paid for' could prove that the 'Good Samaritan was a Bad Economist', and 'if we didn't get to Heaven that way, it was not a politico-economical place, and we had no business there' (book 2, chapter 12; book 3, chapter 8). Elsewhere, the narrator alludes ironically to a popular religious manual, *The Whole Duty of Man*, in his depiction of Bitzer's lack of Christian charity in shutting up his mother in the workhouse (book 2, chapter 1), and Sissy's confusion over her lesson on political economy evokes a biblical response: ' "To do unto others as I would that they should do unto me" ' (book 1, chapter 9). (See notes, pp. 117–18, 163; for a similar echo of 'On Strike', see also note to book 1, chapter 5, pp. 83–4.)

3. Education: 'Rational Schools' and 'Brother Mieth and his Brothers'

The criticism of the misapplication of Political Economy expressed in 'On Strike' influenced how Dickens treated the subject in relation to the educational themes in the novel. For instance, Bitzer's unchristian selfishness about feeding only himself (book 2, chapter 1) reflects Malthusian population theory. The theory formed the basis of a question-and-answer lesson on social economy given by the Utilitarian educationalist William Ellis, and reported in a *Household Words* leading article by Henry Morley and W. H. Wills in 1852, 'Rational Schools' (6.337–42) (see p. 164). The catechistic format of Ellis's lessons was not lost on Dickens, as Sissy's response – ' "To do unto others as I would that they should do unto me" ' (book 1, chapter 9) – reveals. Another educational method used by Ellis to communicate the principles of Political Economy, the object lesson, is mocked in what is perhaps the novel's most memorable scene – Gradgrind's asking Bitzer for his definition of a horse (book 1, chapter 2). Some of Ellis's 'progressive lessons' are reported in detail in 'Rational Schools', and there is no doubt that, in both the criticism of social engineering in *Hard Times* and the characterization of Bitzer, Dickens was influenced by Morley's account.

The article, however, is qualified by the conclusion that the 'imaginative faculty in all these children . . . we assume to be cultivated elsewhere. Such cultivation . . . is no less important to their own happiness and that of society than their knowledge of things and reasons' (341–2). Similarly, at the heart of Dickens's attack on education in *Hard Times* is the recurrent metaphor of cultivation and growth inherent in the book titles 'Sowing', 'Reaping' and 'Garnering'. For instance, Gradgrind's first utterance in book 1, chapter 1, is ' "Plant nothing else [but facts] and root out everything else" '; Tom destroys the roses and 'scatter[s] the buds about by dozens' (book 2, chapter 7); and Louisa exclaims to her father in book 2, chapter 12: ' "what have you done, with the garden that should have bloomed once, in this great wilderness [my heart]" '. A number of *Household Words* articles deployed the planting image to criticize the inadequacies of the educational system in the 1850s (see, for example, 'The Two Guides of the Child', 1.560–1; 'Received, a Blank Child', 7.49–53). And during the serialization of *Hard Times* another *Household Words* article by Morley appeared which contains a favourable account of Morley's boyhood education at a Moravian school where 'the heart was stirred, the soul was roused, the affections were satisfied [and] no check was set upon the fancy' ('Brother Mieth and his Brothers', 9 [27 May 1854] 346). Morley's gratitude is couched in terms of good husbandry:

> When blight was gathering about the budding faculties, those true-hearted Moravians blew the blight away: and wretched indeed might have been the blossom but for them. You pedagogues, who cut and trim your children into shape, you know well enough that if you mend a rosebud with your penknives, you destroy that upon which you cut your mark. Water the roots, let the wind blow, and the sun shine, and the rains fall; remove all that is hurtful, enrich the soil by which the plant is fed, but let the laws of nature take their course. If you know well, that you must act so by a rosebud which you wish to rear into a healthy blossom, why do you act with less care in your treatment of the budding mind and soul? (349)

The dovetailing of Morley's article with two weekly parts of the novel (that is, between book 2, chapter 1, and book 2, chapters 2 and 3) demonstrating the blighted education of Bitzer, Harthouse and Tom functions as a supplement and complement to Dickens's condensed criticism within the confines of the serialized format (also see note, p. 209).

4. Divorce: Eliza Lynn's Articles

What is most striking about the chapters on divorce as they appeared in *Household Words* is how Dickens reinforced his own attack on the marriage laws with articles on the same topic by Eliza Lynn – a regular and highly valued contributor.

'One of Our Legal Fictions', an article by Miss Lynn about Caroline Norton's unrelenting campaign to reform the laws relating to married women's property, appeared in the issue of 29 April 1854, which also contained chapters 9 and 10 of *Hard Times*. Chapter 10 introduces Stephen, Rachael and Stephen's drunken, adulterous wife, and Dickens's chapter plan starts with 'Open Law of Divorce'. Chapter 11, containing Stephen's interview with Bounderby about the impossibility of working people obtaining a divorce, opened the following week's number of *Household Words*.

It is interesting to notice that the serialized text includes some comments on divorce that were omitted from the text of the one-volume edition (see pp. 133 and 135). The remarks, published only in *Household Words* (they are not in the manuscript or in the corrected proofs), are Stephen's criticism of the legal inequalities suffered by women seeking a divorce. His criticism was highly pertinent to Miss Lynn's centrally placed article in the same number, and his comments were also relevant to other articles on the topic that had appeared in the journal from October 1853 (see note, p. 134). Dickens's decision to omit the remarks from the one-volume text suggests an anxiety that they might lose some of their immediacy and topicality when not supported by the other *Household Words* material.

5. The Circus: 'Phases of "Public" Life', 'Behind the Louvre', 'Tattyboys Rents', 'More Dumb Friends', 'Licensed to Juggle', 'Legs', 'Strollers at Dumbledowndeary'

That Dickens mined so many *Household Words* articles for details about the circus in *Hard Times* would seem to indicate not only his personal enjoyment of the circus but also his desire to make the circus a particularly prominent feature of the novel. His reliance on a variety of sources noticeably enriches the characterization in the circus scenes. The affecting and intelligent Merrylegs, for example, descends from an astounding number of 'originals': a performing dog in 'Phases of "Public" Life' (5.229); a dancing Parisian poodle in 'Behind the Louvre' (9.185–8); an abandoned and down-and-out performing poodle in 'Tattyboys Rents' (9.297–304); an article about animal communication, 'More Dumb Friends' (5.124–7); and, finally, from Dickens's having watched performing dogs at a public house in 1849 (*Letters* 7.895) (see notes, pp. 62–4, 232–3).

'Behind the Louvre', together with an article about a street acrobat in Paris, 'Licensed to Juggle' (7.593–4), describes circus acts similar to the strongman, balancing and juggling feats performed by Sleary's artistes in chapters 3 and 6 (see notes, pp. 64 and 98–100). G. A. Sala's witty article, 'Legs' (9 [15 April 1854] 209–12), which appeared in the same number as chapter 6, also mentions tight-rope performers, clowns and acrobats. The narrator's comment in chapter 6 about the lack of modesty exhibited by the mothers of the troupe ('none . . . were at all particular in respect of showing their legs') has parallels in Sala's article, and Sala's belief that character can be deciphered as much by legs as by faces (9.212) is relevant to the characterization of Childers (whose 'legs were very robust, but shorter than legs of good proportions should have been'), to the aptly named performing dog, Merrylegs, and to the description of the Pegasus's Arms (which should have been called the 'Pegasus's legs'). Moreover, chapter 7 of the novel, which opened *Household Words* for 22 April, made reference to Mrs Sparsit's great aunt, Lady Scadgers, who had 'a mysterious leg which had now refused to get out of bed for fourteen years', and to the late Mr Sparsit who was 'chiefly noticeable for a slender body, weakly supported on two long slim props' (see notes, pp. 97, 100). The intercalation of such articles with the chapters was not accidental, of course, but a device Dickens used to help his readers imaginatively merge the worlds of fiction and reality.

Dickens had another skilful way of using *Household Words* articles to enhance the serialized text of the novel and, at the same time, integrate the contents of the weekly numbers. He would include certain factual articles not apparently relevant to the chapters published in the same issue. For example, Sala's account of itinerant actors, 'Strollers at Dumbledowndeary' (9 [3 June 1854] 374–80), is placed between the tenth and eleventh instalments of the novel (where the characterization of Harthouse and Tom is further developed, and when Stephen is ostracized by his fellow-workers and Bounderby). At this point in the story, the circus has wholly disappeared – to return only in the last instalment. But, together with Sissy, who appears intermittently throughout the novel, 'Strollers at Dumbledowndeary' serves as a stand-in for the circus – like Sissy, its inclusion helps to remind readers during these hard-hearted instalments of the circus's vital, imaginative and benevolent influences.

It is a truism to suggest that *Hard Times* is a condensed analysis of the mid-Victorian milieu and that Dickens deftly encapsulated within the double-columned confines of *Household Words* a diversity of contemporary data. Yet even apparently minor details in *Hard Times* contain allusions to the novel's major issues. Three such details that have escaped previous notice concern Mr M'Choakumchild, Mrs Gradgrind, and Louisa and Tom. In book 1, chapter 2, the narrator observes that M'Choakumchild 'had been turned at the same time, in the same factory . . . like so many pianoforte legs'. My note on this image (pp. 49) describes the woodworking process, explains that mechanized turning in the furniture trade was a relatively recent invention, and comments that the image suggests that Dickens shares a contemporary belief that mechanization resulted in standardization, mass-production and poor quality.

The second apparently innocent simile is the comparison of Mrs Gradgrind to a 'feminine dormouse' in book 1, chapter 9. The note (p. 122) cites a *Household Words* article which explains that dormice were kept as domestic pets, and it quotes a French naturalist (whose work was reviewed in *Household Words*) who considered dormice to be 'the emblems of industrial parasites, who spend three-quarters of their time doing nothing, and who make up for their idleness by living upon the labours of others'. This information supports the earlier discussions (in the notes to book 1, chapters 3 and 4) about the Victorian ideology of womanhood and of Mrs Gradgrind as a fictional representation of how the ideology could cause women to become neurotic, idle prisoners in their own homes (pp. 69–70 and 74).

Finally, the note on the description of Louisa and Tom's study as having 'much of the genial aspect of a room devoted to hair-cutting' (book 1, chapter 4) not only hints at Dickens's own enjoyment of barbers' shops but also enriches the characterization of Louisa. The note (pp. 76–7) mentions Dickens's depiction of barbers elsewhere in his fiction – they are invariably sympathetic, lively and sentimental figures – and it quotes two contemporary sources which describe barbers' shops as neat, attractive and sociable places. Taken together, the information reveals the depths of meaning in the narrator's description of the children's study: underlying the atmosphere of study are attractiveness, vitality and affection.

Hard Times was Dickens's only serialized novel in *Household Words*. The journal's successor, *All the Year Round* – significantly more a literary and less a crusading periodical – serialized *A Tale of Two Cities* (1859) and *Great Expectations* (1860–1). Although it can be disputed that these novels, like *Hard Times*, were used as a means to boost weekly circulation figures (A *Tale of Two Cities* opened the inaugural issue of *All the Year Round,* and *Great Expectations* revived the journal's falling sales during the serialization of Charles Lever's lacklustre story, *A Day's Ride: A Life's Romance*), their creation, unlike that of *Hard Times,* was the result of ideas conceived several years before each appeared in *All the Year Round.* When Dickens added the subtitle 'For These Times' to the one-volume edition of *Hard Times,* he not only rooted the novel in its contemporary setting but also pointed to the immediacy of its material. *A Tale of Two Cities* and *Great Expectations* are novels of public and private histories. *Hard Times,* in its original journalistic environment of *Household Words,* was making its own history.

A NOTE ON THE TEXT

The text of *Hard Times* quoted throughout this volume is that of the Penguin edition, edited by David Craig (Harmondsworth, 1969). The Norton Critical Edition (1966; 2nd edn 1990) has not been used because of the problems with the text identified by Joel J. Brattin in a review article, 'Recent Norton Critical Editions'.

Quotations of the variant readings from the autograph manuscript and corrected proofs, and the transcription of the work plans, are based on the author's examination of these materials in the Forster Collection of the Victoria and Albert Museum, London. The author has also examined the page proofs in the Dexter Collection of the British Library, London. Only a selection of the variant readings are quoted or commented on in the annotation.

HOW TO USE THE NOTES

To help the reader locate in the novel the word or phrase quoted in an entry, the notes are presented in this way: the opening phrase of the paragraph which includes the entry is quoted as a guide and printed in italics; the entry itself appears in bold-face type. This system should also help the reader who turns from the novel in search of a note on a particular word or phrase.

Documentation within the notes is kept to a minimum by the use of an abbreviated form of referencing. Works of literature are referred to by their parts: *Vanity Fair* 12; *Past and Present* 3.2; *The Faerie Queene* 2.12.17.14–16; 'The Idiot Boy' 8–10. Frequently cited works of criticism and other secondary sources are referred to by author, part (where relevant) and page: '(Collins 171–2)', '(Mayhew 3.106–7)'. References to infrequently cited sources add the date of publication: '(Sala, 1859, 23)'. Complete details are given in the Select Bibliography.

The notes indicate the divisions of the novel when it was first published in 20 weekly parts in *Household Words* from 1 April to 12 August 1854.

The Work Plans

The notes include transcripts of the sheets of memoranda on which Dickens sketched out his ideas for each weekly number. He folded each sheet once to make two pages, and he referred to the sheets as 'Mems'. In the present volume they are referred to as 'work plans'. To distinguish the pages from each other, the left page is described as the 'number plan' and the right page as the 'chapter plan'.

To help with the difficulties of weekly serialization, Dickens planned *Hard Times* on a monthly-part basis, dividing the twenty weekly instalments into six monthly parts over five months with a double number in the final instalment. In the notes which follow, the work plans are located among the notes to the first chapter of each 'monthly' number: book 1, chapters 1 and 9; book 2, chapters 1 and 7; and book 3, chapter 1.

Appendices

All Lancashire dialect words and phrases and slang words used in *Hard Times* can be found in Appendix A and Appendix B, and are generally not part of the annotation except when they require an extended note.

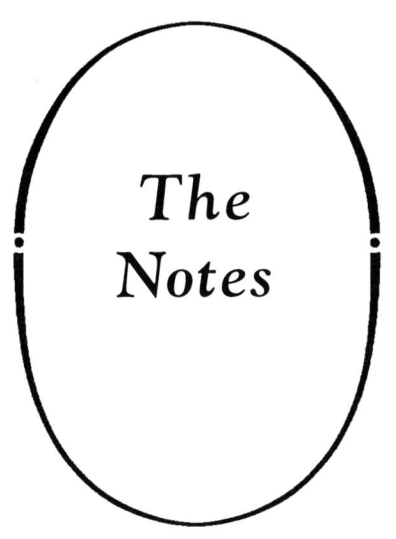

"*Familiar in their Mouths as* HOUSEHOLD WORDS."—SHAKESPEARE.

HOUSEHOLD WORDS.
A WEEKLY JOURNAL.
CONDUCTED BY CHARLES DICKENS.

Nº. 210.]   SATURDAY, APRIL 1, 1854.   [PRICE 2*d.*

HARD TIMES.
BY CHARLES DICKENS.

CHAPTER I.

"Now, what I want is, Facts. Teach these boys and girls nothing but Facts. Facts alone are wanted in life. Plant nothing else, and root out everything else. You can only form the minds of reasoning animals upon Facts: nothing else will ever be of any service to them. This is the principle on which I bring up my own children, and this is the principle on which I bring up these children. Stick to Facts, sir!"

The scene was a plain, bare, monotonous vault of a school-room, and the speaker's square forefinger emphasised his observations by underscoring every sentence with a line on the schoolmaster's sleeve. The emphasis was helped by the speaker's square wall of a forehead, which had his eyebrows for its base, while his eyes found commodious cellarage in two dark caves, overshadowed by the wall. The emphasis was helped by the speaker's mouth, which was wide, thin, and hard set. The emphasis was helped by the speaker's voice, which was inflexible, dry, and dictatorial. The emphasis was helped by the speaker's hair, which bristled on the skirts of his bald head, a plantation of firs to keep the wind from its shining surface, all covered with knobs, like the crust of a plum pie, as if the head had scarcely warehouse-room for the hard facts stored inside. The speaker's obstinate carriage, square coat, square legs, square shoulders,—nay, his very neckcloth, trained to take him by the throat with an unaccommodating grasp, like a stubborn fact, as it was,—all helped the emphasis.

"In this life, we want nothing but Facts, sir; nothing but Facts!"

The speaker, and the schoolmaster, and the third grown person present, all backed a little, and swept with their eyes the inclined plane of little vessels then and there arranged in order, ready to have imperial gallons of facts poured into them until they were full to the brim.

CHAPTER II.

THOMAS GRADGRIND, sir. A man of realities. A man of facts and calculations. A man who proceeds upon the principle that two and two are four, and nothing over, and who is not to be talked into allowing for anything over. Thomas Gradgrind, sir—peremptorily Thomas—Thomas Gradgrind. With a rule and a pair of scales, and the multiplication table always in his pocket, sir, ready to weigh and measure any parcel of human nature, and tell you exactly what it comes to. It is a mere question of figures, a case of simple arithmetic. You might hope to get some other nonsensical belief into the head of George Gradgrind, or Augustus Gradgrind, or John Gradgrind, or Joseph Gradgrind (all supposititious, non-existent persons), but into the head of Thomas Gradgrind—no, sir!

In such terms Mr. Gradgrind always mentally introduced himself, whether to his private circle of acquaintance, or to the public in general. In such terms, no doubt, substituting the words "boys and girls," for "sir," Thomas Gradgrind now presented Thomas Gradgrind to the little pitchers before him, who were to be filled so full of facts.

Indeed, as he eagerly sparkled at them from the cellarage before mentioned, he seemed a kind of cannon loaded to the muzzle with facts, and prepared to blow them clean out of the regions of childhood at one discharge. He seemed a galvanising apparatus, too, charged with a grim mechanical substitute for the tender young imaginations that were to be stormed away.

"Girl number twenty," said Mr. Gradgrind, squarely pointing with his square forefinger, "I don't know that girl. Who is that girl?"

"Sissy Jupe, sir," explained number twenty, blushing, standing up, and curtseying.

"Sissy is not a name," said Mr. Gradgrind. "Don't call yourself Sissy. Call yourself Cecilia."

"It's father as calls me Sissy, sir," returned the young girl in a trembling voice, and with another curtsey.

"Then he has no business to do it," said Mr. Gradgrind. "Tell him he mustn't. Cecilia Jupe. Let me see. What is your father?"

"He belongs to the horse-riding, if you please, sir."

Mr. Gradgrind frowned, and waved off the objectionable calling with his hand.

"We don't want to know anything about

VOL. IX.   210.

---

1   The first serialised page of *Hard Times* in volume 9 of *Household Words*

[DEDICATION]

Inscribed TO THOMAS CARLYLE] Thomas Carlyle (1795–1881) was born in Ecclefechan, Dumfriesshire, but left Scotland in 1834 and moved to 5 Cheyne Row, Chelsea, where he lived for the rest of his life. Carlyle's first important contributions to contemporary social philosophy were his essays 'Signs of the Times' (1829) and 'Characteristics' (1831). His semi-autobiographical *Sartor Resartus* (1833–4; 1838) became one of his most popular philosophical works, and the enormous success of *The French Revolution* (1837) – Dickens's historical source for *A Tale of Two Cities* (1859) – gave Carlyle financial security and literary acclaim. His later works, *Chartism* (1839) and *Past and Present* (1843), articulated for many of his contemporaries the grim social consequences – including revolution – of a laissez-faire society and a dilettante, 'Donothing' aristocracy. Until the publication of his most radical and vehement criticism of society in *Latter-Day Pamphlets* (1850), when he lost many followers, Carlyle's reputation as the 'sage of Chelsea' was unquestioned.

Dickens first met Carlyle in 1840. In his biography of Dickens, John Forster wrote that Dickens's 'Admiration of Carlyle increased with his years; and there was no one whom in later life he honoured so much, or had a more profound regard for' (Forster 1.20.315). During the serialization of *HT*, he told Forster: 'it is impossible for any one to admire [Carlyle] as a great original genius and a most admirable writer, more than I do' (*Letters* 7.332).

It is difficult to be precise about the date when Dickens began to be influenced by Carlyle, but it would appear that from 1844 he integrated Carlylean themes into his work. During the writing of *The Chimes*, Dickens wrote that he 'particularly want[ed] Carlyle above all to see it before the rest of the world, when it is done' and afterwards gave a private reading of the Christmas book to Carlyle and a group of friends in December 1844 (*Letters* 4.209–10; Forster 2.6.137, 2.17.149–50).

Dickens's insistence that Carlyle's presence at the reading was 'indispensable' (*Letters* 4.210) is significant because *The Chimes* serves as the finger-post in Dickens's career, indicating the way he was to proceed with pressing social issues in his later novels. More important for *HT*, *The Chimes* explored in embryonic form the criticisms of a divided, rationalist, utilitarian society based on politico-economic principles that (although voiced by many early Victorian writers) were most notably denounced by Carlyle. This qualification is a vital one, since 'if Carlyle had . . . never written a line about the Condition-of-England Question, it is certain that Dickens would still have belaboured the political economists' (Slater, 1970, 508–9). That is to say, Carlyle's influence 'served to intensify attitudes already held, and sometimes gave them coherent form' (Cazamian, 1973, 325). The coherence of ideas in *HT* owes much to the circulation of Carlylean ideology around the body of Dickens's own brand of social criticism that was based firmly on the current topics of the day.

Dickens acknowledged the novel's debt to Carlyle when he wrote to him from Boulogne on 13 July 1854:

> I am going, next month, to publish in one Volume a story now coming out in Household Words, called Hard Times. I have constructed it patiently, with a view to its publication altogether in a compact cheap form. It contains what

(Friday January 20:^th 1854)

Mr Gradgrind   Stubborn Things

Mrs Gradgrind   Fact

                         Thomas Grandgrind's facts
                            John
                     <George>∧Gradgrind's facts
                     Hard-headed Gradgrind

                     The Grindstone

                     Hard heads and soft hearts

                     <u>The Time Grinders</u>

                     Mr Gradgrind's grindstone

                     <The Family Grindstone>

                     <Hard Times>
                           general
                       The <universal> grindstone

                     Hard Times

                      Heads and Tales
                      Two and Two are Four

                     Prove it!
                     <u>Black and white</u>
                      According to Cocker.
                     Prove it!
                     Stubborn things
                       <Facts are stubborn things>
           <John>   Facts
         <Thomas>   Mr Gradgrind's <grindstone>
         <Thomas   Mr Gradgrind's> grindstone
        The <Thomas>
                   Hard Times

<These real xxxxx days>
   <There's no>   Two and Two are Four.

<No such thing Sir>
                     <Calculations>
  <Extremes meet.>   <according to Cocker>

<Unknown quantities>   <Damaging Facts>

    Simple arithmetic
                     Something tangible
A <mere> matter of Calculation
                   Our hard-headed friend
   A mere question of figures
                     Rust and dust.

[Friday January 20:^th 1854

    Mems: Quantity:

One sheet (16 pages) of Bleak House, will make 10 pages and a quarter of Household Words. <Ten> Fifteen pages of my writing, will make a sheet of Bleak House.

<A line or two more than> A page and a half of my writing, will make a page of Household Words.

The quantity of the story to be published weekly, being about five pages of Household Words, will require about seven pages and a half of my writing.

HARD TIMES.

FOR THESE TIMES.

On 20 January 1854, Dickens wrote to John Forster and enclosed titles for

> the *H.W.* story. . . . It seems to me that there are three very good ones among them. I should like to know whether you hit upon the same.
> 1. According to Cocker. 2. Prove it. 3. Stubborn Things.
> 4. Mr. Gradgrind's Facts. 5. The Grindstone. 6. Hard Times.
> 7. Two and Two are Four. 8. Something Tangible. 9. Our Hard-headed Friend. 10. Rust and Dust. 11. Simple Arithmetic.
> 12. A Matter of Calculation. 13. A Mere Question of Figures.
> 14. The Gradgrind Philosophy. (*Letters* 7.254)

Forster chose 2, 6 and 11; Dickens's 'three very good ones' were 6, 13 and 14. Because both Forster and Dickens had included 'Hard Times' in their choice, the title was decided (Forster 3.2.44–5). Dickens had rejected other possible titles; these included: 'Fact', 'Hard-headed Gradgrind', 'Hard heads and soft hearts', 'The Time Grinders', 'Mr. Gradgrind's grindstone', 'Heads and Tales', 'Black and white', 'Calculations', 'Damaging Facts', 'Extremes meet', 'Unknown quantities' (see work plans).

At a colloquial level the title is resonant of periods of hardship and need, and the phrase was frequently used in folk-songs and ballads throughout the nineteenth century (see Craig, Penguin edn, 1969, 11).

In the one-volume edition of 1854, Dickens added to the title 'FOR THESE TIMES', so placing the novel firmly in its contemporary context and pointing to the topical issues it concerns.

I do devoutly hope will shake some people in a terrible mistake of these days, when so presented. I know it contains nothing in which you do not think with me, for no man knows your books better than I. I want to put in the first page of it, that it is inscribed to Thomas Carlyle. May I? (*Letters* 7.367)

There is no record that Carlyle responded to Dickens's request. The dedication first appeared in the one-volume edition of *HT*, published on 7 August 1854. It was not included in CD (Slater, 1970, 506–26; Oddie, 1972, passim; Goldberg, 1972, passim; Fielding, 1973, 111–18; Ford, 1976, 112–26).

BOOK THE FIRST.

SOWING.

For the one-volume edition, Dickens divided HT into three books entitled 'Sowing', 'Reaping' and 'Garnering', and he also added chapter titles. Reference to the division into three books appears early in the number plans – see Dickens's notes for No. II. Dickens used similar divisions for the rest of his novels, both in volume and serial form, with the exception of MED (see Butt and Tillotson 205).

The titles refer to biblical allusions which use the cultivation of nature as a metaphor for human action. For example, sowing and reaping imagery is utilized in Job 4.8: 'they that plow iniquity, and sow wickedness, reap the same'; in Christ's parables in Matthew 13; and in Galatians 6.7: 'whatsoever a man soweth, that shall he also reap'. A particularly relevant garnering reference is found in Psalms 144.12–13: 'that our sons may be as plants grown up in their youth; that our daughters may be as cornerstones . . . that our garners may be full'.

In 1842, Dickens had used the metaphors in a prologue he composed specially for a play called *The Patrician's Daughter*, by the poet and dramatist John Marston (1819–90). Part of the preliminary draft for the Prologue reads:

> Awake the Present! what the Past has sown
> Be in its harvest garner'd, reap'd, and grown!
> How pride breeds pride, and wrong engenders wrong,
> Read in the volume Truth has held so long,
> Assured that where life's flowers freshest blow,
> The sharpest thorns and keenest briars grow.
> (*Letters*: MDGH 1.78)

In 1868, Dickens omitted the book titles for CD but included running headlines (*Letters* 3.370–1, 377–80).

Book 1, Chapter 1   First weekly part
                                         Saturday, 1 April 1854

THE ONE THING NEEDFUL

The title is a reference to Luke 10.42: 'But one thing is needful: and Mary hath chosen that good part, which shall not be taken away from her'.

In his speech to the Birmingham Polytechnic Institution in 1844, Dickens asserted that 'education – comprehensive liberal education – is the one thing needful, and the one effective end' (*Speeches* 63). At the beginning of January 1854, a few weeks before he started writing *HT*, Dickens qualified this unequivocal view in a letter to the writer and adviser to the Queen, Arthur Helps: 'Sanitary improvements are the one thing needful to begin with; – and until they are thoroughly, efficiently, uncompromisingly made . . . even Education itself will fall short of its uses' (*Letters* 7.236). Helps had written that education was the major force against cholera epidemics. Carlyle often used the biblical phrase. See, for example, *Past and Present*: 'of all the paths a man could strike into, there *is*, at any given moment, a *best path* for every man. . . . to find this path and walk in it, is the one thing needful for him' (3.13).

'*NOW, what I want is, Facts.*

'**NOW, what I want is, Facts.**]   Edward Bulwer-Lytton's 'View of the English Character' (*England and the English*, 1833) describes a certain Mr Bluff as having 'a great love of facts. . . . He does not observe how the facts are applied to the theory; he only wants the facts themselves . . . and the most preposterous of living theorists, always begins his harangues with – "Now, my friends, let us look *to the facts*" ' (1.75–6). For more information about Bulwer's Mr Bluff and Gradgrind, see notes to book 1, chapter 2, p. 34.

Teach these boys and girls nothing but Facts. Facts alone are wanted in life.]   In 1846 a government-funded pupil-teacher and scholarship system was established under the direction of the sociologist, statistician, educationalist and practical Utilitarian, Sir James Phillips Kay-Shuttleworth (1804–77) (Plate 2). Although the new system helped to raise the social status of the teaching profession, the standard of instruction in most schools eight years later was unsatisfactory. Two main factors contributed to the emphasis given to teaching an accumulation of facts – both to candidate teachers and to children. The first was a desire to systematize a formerly unstructured conglomeration of educational establishments and thus advance the cause of popular education. The second stemmed from the nineteenth-century Utilitarian belief that to implant facts was to instil understanding. (For Utilitarianism, see note to book 1, chapter 2, pp. 33–5.)

Early attempts by philanthropists to develop a system of elementary education produced a double-edged sword which simultaneously promoted and retarded the cause of popular education in Britain. The work of the Quaker Joseph Lancaster, together with that of his Anglican rival, the Rev. Andrew Bell, dominated educational philosophy from the 1790s until the 1830s, leaving an indelible mark on the methodologies adopted in nineteenth-century classrooms. Because both funds and teachers were scarce at a time when the numbers of children in school were increasing, Lancaster and Bell were forced to use older children to instruct the younger ones – thus initiating the well-intentioned monitorial system, with its attendant advantages and disadvantages. From this system, the mechanical method of instruction, highly praised at the time, became ingrained as necessary and desirable.

Between 1830 and 1840, many innovative educationalists had looked abroad for

Mem: Write and calculate the story in the old monthly Nº⁰ˢ:

    Mr Gradgrind.   Facts and figures.   "Teach these children nothing but facts. Nothing but facts"

    M'Chaokumchild.   If he only knew less, how much better he might have taught much more!

               Dolly Jupe
                Sissy
              Bitzer – Pale winking boy

Louisa Gradgrind
  Young Thomas

Mrs Gradgrind - or Miss?   Wife or sister?   Wife.

    Any little Gradgrinds?   Say 3.   Adam Smith ⎫
                                    Malthus   ⎬ No parts to play.
                                    Jane   ⎭

                Circus
                   "Horseriding"
                Sleary

The man who by being utterly sensual and careless, comes to very much the same thing in the end as the Gradgrind school?

                Not yet.

(Hard Times. ———————————————— Nº: 1.)

chapter I

"Teach these children nothing but facts."

Chapter II.

Mr Gradgrind   Cole
                                                                            Sissy

          Marlborough House Doctrine   Bitzer

chapter III.

No 1, Weekly   Mrs Gradgrind - badly done transparency, without enough light behind. No not yet - Mr Gradgrind takes Tom & Louisa home "what will Mr Bound say?"   Bounder

                                                                                     Bounderby

chapter IV.

Mr Bounderby, the Bully of humility   Dawn of Bounderby
    Now, Mrs Gradgrind   The children's study   and Louisa.

chapter V.

No 2, weekly   "Let us strike the key note Coketown"

               Take them to Sleary's headquarters –

chapter VI.

No 3 weekly   The Pegasus's arms. The Circus Company. Sissy's father has deserted her. Over-"goosed" -

Chapter VII.

Mrs Sparsit.   without whom Bounderby's glory incomplete.

chapter VIII.

No 4 weekly   Indication of Louisa's marrying Bounderby, bye & bye.

suitable systems which would replace the notoriously defective monitorialism. British institutions on the whole compared unfavourably with their French, German, Dutch and Swiss counterparts, and it was the Continental establishments which greatly impressed the educational reformers of elementary education. Kay-Shuttleworth made several 'Educational Grand Tours' of the Continent (Sturt 89) both as Assistant Poor Law Commissioner and as first Secretary of the newly created Committee of Council, and experimented with foreign concepts successfully at Norwood School and then at Battersea. (See note to book 1, chapter 2, pp. 47–8, for further information about Kay-Shuttleworth and experimental teaching methods.)

Despite their limitations, the monitorial schools were vastly superior to the early charity schools – the 'dame schools' and 'common day schools' – which continued to operate alongside their eventual successors. Reports from the Manchester Statistical Society in the 1830s and from the early school inspectors in the 1840s testify to the appalling conditions of these charity schools and the inadequate and unsuitable teachers. Although Dickens criticized the schools through the characters of Robin Toodle (*DS*), Uriah Heep (*DC*) and the young Smallweed (*BH*), he supported the Ragged School Movement (officially organized in 1844), which catered for the most disadvantaged of the urban poor. He regarded the foundation of ragged schools as a necessary but temporary measure until a national system of education was in place, and he frequently urged his readers not to view these establishments as appropriate substitutes. (See *MP* 17–21 and these *HW* articles: ' "The Devil's Acre" ' 1.297–301; 'What a London Curate Can Do If He Tries' 2.172–6; 'Chips: Small Beginnings' 3.41–2; 'The Metropolitan Protectives' 3.97–105; 'Lambs to be Fed' 3.544–9; 'Little Red Working-Coat' 4.324–5; 'A Sleep to Startle Us' 4.577–80; 'Boys to Mend' 5.597–602; 'Home for Homeless Women' 7.169–75; 'Deaf Mutes' 9.134–8; *Letters* 4.527.)

In the years before the establishment of the Committee of the Privy Council on Education on 10 April 1839, state intervention in educational matters remained minimal. What was needed was a system of inspection not only to supervise and report on the grant-aided voluntary schools, but also to gauge the standard of teaching and make recommendations. In 1839 the new Committee of Council proposed to appoint inspectors and also to establish a national training college – a Normal School – 'in which candidates for the office of teacher in schools for the poorer classes may acquire the knowledge necessary to the exercise of their future profession', and a Model School 'in which children of all ages from three to fourteen, may be taught and trained, in sufficient numbers to form an Infant School, as well as schools for children above seven' (*Four Periods* 179–80).

Unfortunately, however, the liberal form of religious instruction inherent in the plan for a Normal School guaranteed its demise. Any scheme whereby children from different religious backgrounds could be educated together, regardless of the provision made for separate religious teaching, was abhorrent to both Anglicans and nonconformists. Thus, from 1839 until 1846 no national scheme for the provision of qualified teachers existed.

Fortunately, enlightened reformers who had been experimenting throughout the 1820s and 1830s soon revolutionized educational methodology and helped to develop a state-controlled education system. Samuel Wilderspin, for example, who founded numerous infant schools throughout England, believed in 'the approach

2 Photograph of Sir James Kay-Shuttleworth (c.1862). From Mary Sturt, *The Education of the People* (London: Routledge, 1967)

through the heart'. Though his limitations lay in the pedantic catechistic structure of his lessons, his conviction that the playground was as important as the classroom for character-building made him an influential force in primary education. Through the Infant School Society, founded in 1824, Wilderspin's theories spread to most industrialized towns, and by 1826 forty-eight infant schools founded on his philosophy had been established around the country.

In Scotland, Lancaster's system was opposed by Wood's Sessional School (established in Edinburgh in 1824), which advocated the cultivation of a child's understanding. One of the major contributions to English popular education came from the work of a Glasgow merchant, David Stow. His teacher-training school, the Glasgow Normal Seminary (established in 1826), and his Glasgow Educational Society (1834) transformed methods of instruction in the classroom and emphasized, like Wilderspin, the crucial developmental role of the playground – 'the Uncovered School' (Stow, 1839, 4). A significant number of trained teachers from these Scottish institutions were procured by Kay-Shuttleworth for English workhouse schools for pauper children (*Four Periods* 287), and Stow's gallery system was emulated in schools established by Kay-Shuttleworth.

In the early 1840s individual efforts at educational reform were frustrated by inadequate school buildings and equally impoverished teaching. But, in 1846, Kay-Shuttleworth, supported by the Prime Minister (Lord John Russell), proposed a state-funded pupil-teacher scheme which would raise the educational standard, provide a qualitative supply of teachers to the growing number of schools and, through a series of certificated examinations, give teaching a professional status. The gradual implementation of Kay-Shuttleworth's plan marked the beginning of state control of education, and in 1853 the first fully fledged 'Queen's Scholars' issued from the training colleges (see notes to book 1, chapter 2, pp. 48 and 49–50, about M'Choakumchild's training) (Newcastle Commission, *BPP* 1861, vol. 21.1, 20; Adamson, 1930, 126; Smith, 1931, 94–7; Rich, 1933, 38, 75, 26–7; Collins, 1963, 78; Sturt, 1967, 212–13, 70, 124).

Plant nothing else, and root out everything else.] In Carlyle's *Sartor Resartus* (1831), Professor Teufelsdröckh says that his

> Teachers . . . were hide-bound Pedants, without knowledge of man's nature, or of boy's; or of aught save their lexicons and quarterly account-books. Innumerable dead Vocables . . . they crammed into us, and called it fostering the growth of mind. How can an inanimate, mechanical Gerund-grinder . . . foster the growth of anything; much more of Mind, which grows, not like a vegetable (by having its roots littered with etymological compost), but like a Spirit, by mysterious contact of Spirit. . . . (2.3)

These same beliefs were shared by Lord Ashburton in his widely reported speech to elementary schoolmasters at Winchester on 16 December 1853. (The revised text was published as a pamphlet, *Ashburton Prizes for the Teaching of 'Common Things'*, in January 1854, just when Dickens began to compose *HT*.) Ashburton stressed the need for teachers 'to encourage a knowledge of common, household, and familiar things, as an ingredient in the elementary instruction of the poor' (6). He rejected the

> misleading illustration, that in teaching [a] multitude of facts we only scatter seeds over the boy's mind, for the chance of those which are congenial finding root, and flourishing. We do not merely scatter these seeds . . . we force our facts upon the child's memory. . . . So these poor children are crammed with crude, nauseating facts, to the extinction of their natural appetite for knowledge, and the bounteous designs of God are, by the folly of men, rendered of no avail. (18–19)

Ashburton insisted that faculties other than that of memory should be developed, such as the practical and the reflective. (This sentiment had been iterated in 'Lambs to be Fed', *HW* 3.544–9, a criticism of Anglican, Scottish and some private schools.) It is evident that Dickens supported the new movement towards a more practical form of education and was conversant with its philosophy. Ashburton's proposals were given public airing in the press – see the *Times* leader of 28 January 1854 – and provided Henry Morley with a framework for his article 'School-Keeping', *HW* 8.499–504, which confirmed that 'Lord Ashburton's suggestion has gone off like a gun in a rookery and has set every quill flying' (499). Also see Morley's later article about the education he received at a Moravian school which stressed the 'free play of all . . . faculties' ('Brother Mieth and his Brothers', 9.344–9). The article appeared during the serialization of *HT* (Fielding, 1968, 187–94).

The scene was a plain, bare

plain, bare, monotonous vault of a schoolroom]   In the 1820s the National Society, in its recommendations for the building and layout of schools, suggested that the form of a schoolroom 'should be oblong, a barn furnished no bad model, and a good one may be easily converted into a school room'. Benches and desks should be arranged along the side-walls so that the centre could be used for reading or examinations. This model of one large single classroom, sometimes divided for the separate teaching of boys and girls, proved resistant to change, despite the developments in methods of teaching in the first half of the nineteenth century (Sturt, 1967, 125–8).

William Ellis, founder of the Birkbeck schools, cared little about what sort of buildings he procured to promote the teaching of his brand of political economy to children (see note to book 1, chapter 9, pp. 116–17). He was of the opinion that once other schools saw the beneficial results in his model establishments his methods would be readily adopted, and so the pilot schools would no longer be needed. Consequently, Ellis's assistant, John Rüntz, headmaster of the first Birkbeck school opened in 1848, was commissioned to purchase the lease of anything from derelict chapels and burial-grounds to disused halls and old schools. The first purpose-built Birkbeck school, in Peckham, opened on 19 April 1852. It closed down thirty-five years later (Blyth, 1889, 99, 106, 108).

The emphasis was helped by the speaker's square wall of a forehead. . . . The emphasis was helped by the speaker's hair, which bristled on the skirts of his bald head . . . all covered with knobs . . . as if the head had scarcely warehouse-room for the hard facts stored inside.] According to the adherents of the pseudo-science phrenology, Gradgrind's cranial characteristics constitute particular abilities and propensities. Phrenologists believed that they could identify talents and traits by examining the configuration of the skull, and they maintained that phrenology had important practical applications in areas such as medicine, prison reform, criminology, religion and education.

It is likely that Dickens gleaned much of what he knew of the subject from his friend, the phreno-mesmerist Dr John Elliotson, whom he met in 1838 – when interest in phrenology was at its height in Britain and America. While touring America in 1842, Dickens was phrenologized by Lorenzo Niles Fowler in Worcester, Connecticut, and in 1860 he admitted to 'believe in [phrenology], in the main and broadly, as an essential part of the truth of physiognomy' (21 February 1860, *Nonesuch* 3.152). Later, in 'A Little Dinner in an Hour', he stated that he held 'phrenology, within certain limits, to be true; I am much of the same mind as to the subtler expressions of the hand; I hold physiognomy to be infallible; though all these sciences demand rare qualities in the student' (*UT*) (Davies, 1971, passim; see Pèyrouton, 1967, for a reproduction of the phrenological reading of Dickens's head).

Gradgrind's square forehead phrenologically denotes a well-developed 'Organ of Order' whose function is 'to give the desire of physical arrangement, of order and method in relation to physical objects. Classification, generalization and systematizing, in science or philosophy, depend on the reflective faculties' (Combe, 1839, 372). His bump-covered skull confirms one of the basic tenets of phrenology: that the 'outer surface of the head so nearly corresponds to the outer surface of the brain, that the size and form of the latter, are indicated by the size and form of the former' (1839, 24). (See note to book 1, chapter 2, pp. 38–40, with reference to the creation of Bitzer and phrenological observations.)

The speaker, and the schoolmaster

imperial gallons] Imperial weights and measures were appointed by statute to be used throughout the United Kingdom from 1838. Francis Walkingame's *Tutor's Assistant* (c.1850) provides a table of them.

Book 1, Chapter 2   First weekly part
                                                         Saturday, 1 April 1854

MURDERING THE INNOCENTS

From Matthew 2.16–18: King Herod, believing his position was threatened by the birth of Jesus, ordered the slaughter in Bethlehem of all children under the age of 2. One of the feast days in the Church Calendar is Innocents' Day on 28 December. It was formerly the custom on Holy Innocents' Day to whip children and adults as a reminder of Herod's massacre.

THOMAS GRADGRIND, sir.

THOMAS GRADGRIND, sir. A man of realities. A man of fact and calculations. A man who proceeds upon the principle that two and two are four, and nothing over. . . . With a rule and a pair of scales, and the multiplication table always in his pocket, sir, ready to weigh and measure any parcel of human nature] Gradgrind represents Victorian Utilitarianism and its allied science, political economy, as derived from the seventeenth-century and eighteenth-century materialist and empirical traditions. By the time Jeremy Bentham (1748–1832) came to formulate what became the ethical foundation of many areas of nineteenth-century life, he had at his disposal an established theory of morals based on the assumption that all human action is based upon self-interest. His objective was to measure, value and compare 'lots' of pleasure and pain – the 'greatest happiness' principle – and, through an elaborate enumeration, draw scientific conclusions about human springs of action. Thus, by quantifying sensibilities and creating a rational calculus, Bentham could safely dispense with such nebulous abstractions as love, kindness or sympathy.

In 1776 the Utilitarian and economist Adam Smith (1723–90) produced his *Inquiry into the Nature and Causes of the Wealth of Nations*, a work which became the cornerstone of the first independent social science, political economy. Smith's coupling of economic autonomy and self-interest in the production of wealth and in the relations between labour and capital provided the practical basis for a new economic doctrine in Britain. Later political economists such as Thomas Malthus (1766–1834), David Ricardo (1772–1823), James Mill (1773–1836), J. R. McCulloch (1789–1864) and John Stuart Mill (1806–73) also embraced the practical rationalism of Benthamite Utilitarianism which permeated English society throughout the first half of the nineteenth century. Only J. S. Mill attempted to bridge the chasm between mechanistic formulae and the organismal theories espoused by Coleridge and Wordsworth, which stressed the exercise of the feelings (see his *Autobiography*, 7th edn, 1882, 151–2). However, it was the quasi-scientific, statistical approach of Benthamite Utilitarianism to the problems of living in an industrial world which not only facilitated important changes to the legal, administrative and parliamentary systems and initiated sanitary and educational reform, but also provided the rising entrepreneurial middle class with a convenient deterministic equation for the operation of a free-market economy which insisted upon the non-interference of government.

This 'wider Benthamism' which typified the 'spirit of the new age' (Somervell 49) was described by Edward Bulwer-Lytton in two fictionalized illustrations of the English character in 1833 – Samuel Square and Mr Bluff. The two character sketches bear a remarkable resemblance to Gradgrind's overall characterization. Like the square-headed Gradgrind, Samuel Square

> is of a new school of Radicals. . . . He is not a philosopher, but he philosophizes eternally. He liveth upon "first principles". . . . He thinks men have no passions; he considers them mere clockwork. . . . He is of no earthly utility, though he hath walled himself with a supposed utilitarianism . . . he is as dry as a bone. He lives by system; – he never was in love in his life . . . he never feels for anyone – he only reasons with everyone.
> (*England and the English*, 1.5.69–70)

Similarly, the 'eminently practical' Gradgrind (book 1, chapter 3, and book 1, chapter 4) has all of Mr Bluff's qualities:

> Mr. Bluff . . . is the sensible *practical* man . . . he hates both poets and philosophers. He has a great love of facts; if you could speak to him out of the multiplication table, he would think you a great orator. He does not observe how the facts are applied to the theory; he only wants the facts themselves. . . . Looking only at a fact he does not see an inch beyond it, and you might draw him into any imprudence, if you were constantly telling him, "two and two made four." Mr. Bluff is wonderfully English. It is by "practical men," that we have ever been seduced into the wildest speculations; and the most preposterous of living theorists, always begins his harangues with – "Now, my friends, let us look *to the facts*." (1.5.75)

The characterization of Gradgrind also seems indebted to Sir James Phillips Kay-Shuttleworth. In Manchester he helped to found the first Statistical Society (established in 1834) and it was through his work as a social scientist that he entered the field of popular education. With a career already devoted to the Benthamite principles of the New Poor Law (1834), and with a strong conviction in social paternalism, Kay-Shuttleworth approached education with a fixed ideology which guarded against a broader, humanistic form of popular instruction. He fully expressed his views in a controversial speech on 11 January 1854, at the opening of a school for the children of tradesmen in Padiham in Lancashire. The address concentrated on two current issues – education and the then five-month-old strike of cotton workers in Preston. The local reactions to his pronouncements were still acute when Dickens visited Preston on 28 January 1854. In his speech, Kay-Shuttleworth set out his reasons for the introduction into the school curriculum of subjects which had 'an immediate connection with the trades, manufactures, arts, and employments' of the surrounding area, and he argued at length, with reference to the Department of Practical Science and Art (see notes passim to the present chapter), for the systematic cultivation of the arts of design as applied to manufactures. The rest of his address is an attack on the Preston strikers, who had, he said, violated the laws of political economy: 'to understand what are the only true relations of capital and labour involves the study of a class of abstract truths, easily obscured or perverted to an uneducated people' (*Manchester Guardian*, 14 January 1854, p. 9, and 18 January 1854, p. 3). It was this approach that Dickens found wanting, despite his acquaintance with Kay-Shuttleworth and his admiration for some of his work. Dickens especially disliked what he later called 'Kayshuttleworry' – the factuality of Utilitarian educationalists (*Letters* 8.432).

The character of Gradgrind is also indebted to fictional antecedents in Dickens's own works: the statistically dependent political economist, Mr Filer (*The Chimes*), and the proud, rich merchant, Dombey (*DS*). It is also possible that certain elements in the Gradgrind plot were informed partly by those in the story of Mr Bradshaw in Elizabeth Gaskell's *Ruth* (1853) (see Page, 1971, 413). 'Two and Two are Four' and 'A Mere Question of Figures' were two titles considered by Dickens both in his work plans and in his letter to Forster on 20 January 1854. 'A Mere Question of Figures' made Dickens's shortlist of three: see note at p. 21 (Smith, 1923, 242–3; Rubin, 1929, 168; Briggs, 1959, 337; Plamenatz, 1966, passim; Fielding, 1968, 193; Perkin, 1969, 165; Oddie, 1972, 45; Belcher, 1982, 105–9; Flint, 1987, 74; Lux, 1990, 21–5; *Letters* 1.454, 6.164, 7.56, 254).

You might hope to get some other nonsensical belief into the head of George Gradgrind, or Augustus Gradgrind, or John Gradgrind, or Joseph Gradgrind . . . but into the head of Thomas Gradgrind – no, sir!] An ironic allusion to doubting Thomas: 'Except I shall see in his hands the print of the nails, and put my finger into the print of the nails, and thrust my hand into his side, I will not believe' (John 20.25). While George and Augustus were both popular names for boys in the nineteenth century, Dickens's choice of 'George' and 'Augustus' may have come from his working relationship with a frequent contributor to *HW* and *AYR*, George Augustus Sala.

Indeed, as he eagerly sparkled at them

he seemed a kind of cannon loaded to the muzzle with facts, and prepared to blow them clean out of the regions of childhood at one discharge.] Compare Dickens's later description of Henry Thomas Buckle (1821–62), author of the uncompleted *History of Civilization in England* (Vol. 1 [1857], Vol. 2 [1861]): 'Buckle . . . is a perfect Gulf of information. Before exploding a mine of knowledge he has a habit of closing one eye and wrinkling up his nose, so that he seems to be perpetually taking aim at you and knocking you over with a terrific charge' (*Letters* 7.343). A cancelled fragment in MS reads: 'He seemed a powder-magazine of facts whose explosion would disperse their tender young imaginations into dust, atoms never to be gathered together any more; a galvanizing apparatus into the bargain'.

galvanizing apparatus] The Italian physiologist Luigi Galvani (1737–98) was a pioneer in the field of electrophysiology. In 1794 his experiments with frogs led him to the conclusion that bio-electric forces reside within animal tissue. By the 1840s British electricians had invented a variety of electrical techniques and instruments which had cross-disciplinary applications. The 'galvanizing apparatus' here was probably one of the many electrotherapeutic machines widely used in medical practice, particularly for the treatment of nervous disorders. Two types of electricity were employed: ordinary static electricity and galvanic electricity (derived from a battery or an electromagnetic apparatus). Galvanic electricity was used especially in electric shock treatments, which were often administered before public audiences and so became a part of popular culture (Morus, 1992, 34–52). A 'galvanic blasting apparatus' is used to kill a crocodile in 'The Crocodile Battery', *HW* 2.540–3, and a similar device is employed to punish a fakir in 'A Fuqueer's Curse', *HW* 3.310–12. In an article of February 1854, the torpedo fish is described as being 'provided . . . with a sort of galvanic battery, by which it is enabled to arrest, and obtain for food, the more active inhabitants of the deep' ('A Dish of Fish', *HW* 9.17).

'Girl number twenty,' said Mr Gradgrind

'Girl number twenty,'] It was not unusual for schoolchildren to be addressed by a number instead of by their name. Because hundreds of boys and girls might be taught in one room, they were invariably numbered off and allotted to squads of ten to fifteen pupils in order to solve the logistical problem of identification. J. and B. Hammond record that the Manchester Lancasterian School had two masters and one mistress in charge of one thousand 'close-packed children' who were given numbers and divided into monitorial groups of nine or ten. Remnants of the monitorial system were evident long after the major changes introduced by the Council on Education Minutes of 1846 (Hammond, 1930, 171; Sturt, 1967, 24, 31). In *DS* 5, Robin Toodle is 'number one hundred and forty-seven' in the Charitable Grinders' School.

'We don't want to know anything about that

Your father breaks horses] Philip Astley, commonly believed to be the 'father of the Circus', worked as a horse-breaker before setting up a site for his Riding School in 1768. (For a short history of Astley's, see note to book 3 chapter 7, pp. 228–9.)

'Very well, then. He is a veterinary surgeon

a veterinary surgeon, a farrier] Until the end of the eighteenth century veterinary surgeons were called farriers. The new term was not applied until 1796, when the British Army's Board of General Officers needed a title to differentiate human surgeons from animal doctors. Farriery not only embraced animal doctoring and horse-shoeing, but its practitioners also had a general knowledge of horses and other livestock. In 1791 the Veterinary College, London, was founded as the first British institution to teach and prepare students for the practice of veterinary medicine, but the majority of new veterinary surgeons had to fight for recognition and livelihood amongst twice their number of unqualified practitioners. In 1844 a Royal Charter was granted to the Veterinary College of London and to William Dick's Edinburgh Veterinary School; and the corporate body, the Royal College of Veterinary Surgeons, could now start to control and professionalize veterinary practice. In 1848 the RCVS Registration Committee 'revealed that "under the various denominations of horse-doctors, horse-surgeons, farriers, cowleeches, cattle-doctors, castrators, spayers and gelders, charmers, spell-workers, butty-colliers, water-doctors, and various other local appellations, those who gain a livelihood by the practice of the art" far exceeded men who had been to veterinary school'. The Committee estimated that in Britain 1,500 veterinary surgeons were veterinary school graduates, compared to 6,000 unqualified practitioners. The final report to the RCVS Council in January 1852 listed 1,733 names. In 1881 the passing of the Veterinary Surgeons Act legally empowered the RCVS to protect the title of 'veterinary surgeon', thus distinguishing the trained practitioner from the myriad others purporting to be animal doctors (Pattison, 1984, passim).

Give me your definition of a horse.']   Two related teaching techniques which characterized nineteenth-century educational practice were learning by rote and the object lesson. Learning by rote was an established form of instruction which by the mid-nineteenth century had become a major component in oral and textbook lessons. The proliferation of published sets of questions and answers which were to be learnt parrot-fashion not only reflected the contemporary notion that children should commit to memory 'the elements of universal knowledge' but also provided a cast-iron classroom format that survived to the end of the nineteenth century. The best-known work of this kind was Miss Richmal Mangnall's *Historical and Miscellaneous Questions for the Use of Young People* (1800), which went through many editions until the beginning of the twentieth century and served as the model for many other textbooks.

The object lesson was a staple feature of classroom methodology. Its original proponent, the Swiss educator Johann Pestalozzi (1746–1827), had envisaged a system whereby children would be taught 'by *things* rather than by *words* ... the name will be committed to memory ... its origins must be accounted for; its parts must be described ... something of the kind should be attempted ... wherever education is intended to take a higher character than mere mechanical training of the memory'. Misinterpretation of Pestalozzi's original concept reduced the object lesson to a dry verbal exercise, as evidenced by such books for teachers as Elizabeth Mayo's *Lessons on Objects* (1831) and *Lessons on Shells* (1832), and it became further distorted by the inclusion of Latinate phrases and scientific jargon similar to Bitzer's memorized definition. In his report for 1853, Her Majesty's Inspector of Schools, Rev. Henry Moseley, illustrated the misuse succinctly:

> A teacher proposing to give an oral lesson on coal, for instance, holds a piece of it up before his class, and having secured their attention, he probably asks them to which kingdom it belongs, animal, vegetable, or mineral.... Having

> ... extracted that answer which he intended to get from the children, he induces them by many ingenious devices, much circumlocution, and an extravagant expenditure of the time of the school, to say that it is a *solid . . . heavy . . . opaque . . . black . . . friable . . . combustible.* . . . He has shown some knowledge of words but none of *things.* . . . This tendency runs in a notable manner through almost all of the lessons on physical science which I have listened to.
>
> (*Minutes* 1853–4, BPP 1854, Vol. 51.1. 440–1)

A recurrent object lesson at this time was the description of an animal. The Rev. Richard Dawes, Dean of Hereford and the original proponent of the Ashburton movement for the teaching of 'common things' in schools, included in his *Suggestive Hints* (1847) a possible teaching method with this in mind:

> . . . if a cow or horse is mentioned – drawing them into a description of it – a child will perhaps say: A cow is a four-footed animal. Teacher: Yes, but so is a horse; and then will point out something in which they differ. The child will then try again – a cow has got horns, but a horse has not; then the teacher will point out that some cows have no horns, and will lead them on into things, in which the cow and horse really do differ – such as the hoof; the cow having a cloven foot with two hoofs on one foot: what other animals have the same? – difference in the way of feeding; a cow chews the cud – ruminating . . . what difference in their teeth; has a cow front teeth in the upper jaw? a sheep? a horse? etc.
>
> (6th edn, 1853, 1–2)

William Ellis utilized the object lesson to propound the principles of political economy (see note to book 1, chapter 9, pp. 116–17), but Ellis detested the contemporary practice of instilling pointless knowledge. An excellent description of Ellis's object lessons which he believed prepared children for the more advanced questions and answers on the principles of political economy is found in 'Rational Schools', *HW* 6.337–42 (Blyth, 1889, 155; Green (ed.), 1916, 248; Smith, 1931, 129; Collins, 1963, 155; Fielding, 1968, 198; Shatto, 1974).

The square finger, moving here

Bitzer] This character resembles a boy described in a *HW* article of December 1852, 'Rational Schools' (6.337–42), which reports surprisingly favourably on two schools founded by William Ellis (see note to book 1, chapter 9, pp. 116–17). In lessons on political economy given in the first Birkbeck school at the London Mechanics' Institution, a

> little fellow with light flaxen hair . . . was quite a luminary upon all points that were mooted. He made for himself a cushion of his knuckles, and he sat so on the backs of his hands . . . his quick eyes bent on the teacher, and his face gladdened with a smile of intelligent pleasure in the train of reason-

ing that he had evidently mastered. Where others hesitated, he answered boldly and correctly. . . . There was not a question that he did not answer, and there was not one of his answers that was not clearly and correctly given. It was a touch of the very pleasantest comedy, when this imperturbable young philosopher got the class over a difficult case, by suggesting the line of conduct which a capitalist would probably pursue in given circumstances. A young man with his business head – he is eleven years old – and his knowledge of the laws that regulate prices and other matters in the country, ought to be in Parliament. (339)

At the end of the lessons the article predicted that the

little flaxen-headed statesman . . . will, with Heaven's leave, grow up to be a workman skilful, industrious, sober, honest and punctual. We pictured him to ourselves as he will be hereafter, with a square bald head, sitting beside the neatest of wives, and arguing with his eldest son the question, how he shall dispose of certain capital into which a portion of his wages shall have been by that time converted. It is too much to hope that he will ever be Prime Minister. (340)

Another possible source for Bitzer is the civil engineer and parliamentary adviser George Parker Bidder (1806–78). At the age of seven he was given the title of the 'calculating phenomenon' by his father who, aware of the nineteenth-century relish for freaks and curiosities, found it lucrative to give public demonstrations of his son's extraordinary powers. Bidder's ability to answer arithmetical problems which entailed complex calculations led to exhibitions throughout the country. His talents were exercised fully in his parliamentary practice, where he used his skill to 'detect a flaw in some elaborate set of calculations, thereby upsetting an opponent's case, or would support his own conclusions by an argument based on mathematical data, possibly only then put before him' (*DNB*).

The *Annual Register* reported on a calculating boy called Zerah Colburn (1804–39). The 8-year-old American had arrived in England on 12 May 1812 and, to the astonishment of his father's friends, 'succeeded in, raising the number 8 progressively up to the sixteenth power!!! and in naming the last result, viz. 281,474,976,710,656, he was right in every figure' (1812, 508). Bidder and Colburn were cited in phrenological observations which set out to demonstrate pseudo-scientific theories based on the size and development of the skull (see note to book 1, chapter 1, p. 32). Both children were alleged to possess a large 'organ of number' suggested by a 'fullness to the outer angle of the eye, and a little to the side, a very little below the point called the external angular process of the frontal bone' (Combe, 1839, 244). Bitzer's 'cold eyes' and antennae-like lashes, and the characteristic knuckling of his forehead, might have been partly based on Dickens's awareness of phrenological phenomena (see Sloane, 1974). His description of Bitzer obediently regurgitating memorized facts also reflected the general view that such calculating prodigies were not naturally clever. The feats of memory exhibited on 28 June 1840 by a 13-year-old boy, 'Master Bassle', were recounted by Timbs from a report in *The Times*. Bassle could 'name the day of the week on which any day of any month had fallen in any particular year [and] repeat long series of numbers, backwards and forwards'. It was believed, however, that such performances were 'not the result of any natural mnemonic powers, but of a method acquirable by any person in a course of twelve lessons' (Timbs, 1840, 113–14).

Dickens referred to 'the power of a calculating boy' in *NN* (14), and in 1857 he voiced his concern about schools which discouraged 'the bright childish imagination' and produced nothing 'but little parrots and small calculating machines' (*Speeches* 241). Tom Gradgrind is called 'the calculating boy' (book 1, chapter 16). Bitzer, whose 'proceedings were the result of the nicest and coldest calculation' (book 2, chapter 1), has a name suggestive of incompletion (*bits*) and resentment (*bitter*). He is also the product of a long line of similar characters in Dickens's fiction – Rob the Grinder in *DS*, Uriah Heep in *DC*, and Smallweed in *BH* – who, through misdirected education, grow into calculating and self-interested hypocrites.

'Calculate' and 'calculation' were favourite terms of the Utilitarians. In the *Introduction to the Principles of Morals and Legislation* (1789), Jeremy Bentham insisted that

> When matters of such importance as pain and pleasure are at stake, and these in the highest degree ... who is there that does not calculate? Men calculate, some with less exactness, indeed, some with more: but all men calculate. I would not say, that even a madman does not calculate. Passion calculates, more or less, in every man. ... (187–8)

The prototype of the modern adding machine was Blaise Pascal's digital invention (1642–4) which could add and subtract. In 1671 the eminent mathematician Gottfried Wilhelm Leibniz (1646–1716) developed a mechanism called the 'Leibniz wheel', which led to the construction of a more advanced calculating machine that could automatically add, subtract, divide and multiply – in effect, an early form of today's desk calculator. In the nineteenth century, the work on calculating engines pioneered by Charles Babbage (1791–1871) provided all the major elements of twentieth-century computers. His greatest contribution to modern computation was the invention of the Analytical Engine, a project started in 1834 and still in progress when he died in 1871. Dickens had met Babbage on many social occasions and was well acquainted with his work (Goldstine, 1972, 7–9, 20; Dubbey, 1978, 173, 215; Hyman, 1982, 254).

'Quadruped. Graminivorous. Forty teeth, namely

'Quadruped. Graminivorous.] An early example of the nineteenth-century predilection for definitions and the love of etymological memorizing is found in Samuel Wilderspin's pedantic lessons taught in his infant schools in the 1820s:

> To the question 'To what class does a flower belong that has only one stamen?' he gives the following ... answer: 'The class monandria; and those with

two, diandria; with three, triandria; with four, tetrandria; with five, pentandria; with six, hexandria; with seven, heptandria; with eight, octandria; with nine, enneandria; with ten, decandria; with twelve, dodecandria; with twenty, icosandria; with many stamens, polyandria'.

(Smith, 1931, 95–6)

In Dickens's earlier parody of the 'regular education system' in *NN*, according to Mr Squeers, a horse is described as 'a quadruped, and quadruped's Latin for beast, as everybody that's gone through the grammar knows, or else where's the use of having grammars at all?' (8).

The third gentleman now stepped forth.

The third gentleman now stepped forth. A mighty man at cutting and drying . . . always to be heard of at the bar of his little Public-office] Dickens's 'government officer', as revealed in the chapter plan, was originally conceived as a caricature of Henry Cole, Superintendent of the Department of Practical Art, a revamped version of the School of Design. Henry Cole (1808–82), a senior assistant keeper at the Public Record Office from 1838, became a member of the Society of Arts in 1846 and later took over as chairman in 1851 and 1852. At the end of 1851 he was made secretary of the School of Design and in 1852 became Superintendent of General Management to the newly formed Department of Practical Art. From that time, Cole directed public art education for twenty years.

Dickens, who had joined the Society of Arts in 1849, knew Cole well. Of especial interest to them both had been the defects of patent law before the passing of the Patent Act in 1852. Cole's report, *Rights of Inventors*, formed the basis of Dickens's article 'A Poor Man's Tale of a Patent' (*HW* 2.73–5); see *Letters* 5.40, 6.180 and notes. Other articles concerned with Cole's work appeared in *HW*: 'The Adventures of the Public Records' (1.396–9); 'What Is Not Clear about the Crystal Palace' (3.400–2); 'A House Full of Horrors' (6.265–70); and 'Case of Real Distress' (8.457–60).

After 'stepped forth. A' the MS reads: 'bustling, pleasant little gentleman he was'. This, and other cancellations made later in this chapter, deprived the unnamed third gentleman of an amiability and lightheartedness associated with Henry Cole. A jolly family man whose 'imperturbable good temper was never ruffled' (*DNB*), Cole was nevertheless stubborn and authoritative – 'a hyperactive Benthamite civil servant . . . looking for new fields to conquer' (Lubbock). In the sphere of popular education, he stood for utilitarianism in its most rigid form channelled through the doctrines expounded by the Department of Practical Art at Marlborough House. The representation of Cole in *HT* transforms the cheerful but brisk civil servant into a severe, unimaginative exponent of rational aesthetics, so shifting the emphasis from personality to personification (see Fielding 275–6).

The character also exemplifies a new breed of instructor who was by 1854 a familiar visitor to elementary schools. As part of the reorganization carried out by the newly formed Department of Practical Art in 1852, Cole made provision for teachers and pupil teachers in public schools who could not attend classes in Marlborough House to be visited by a trained drawing master and instructed in the use of examples recommended for teaching elementary drawing. By 1854 this scheme was well in place with a formal elementary art course operating in most schools. Furthermore, in 1853 the Committee of Council, with the assistance of Marlborough House, had added a compulsory exercise in drawing as part of each examination, and these examinations were carried out in both the day schools and training colleges. Cole's department also offered to send their own inspectors to visit any school and give advice. Dickens's government officer could be the visiting art master or an inspector from Cole's department testing the children's knowledge on this relatively new branch of primary education (*First Report of the Department of Practical Art*, BPP 1852–3, Vol. 54, 5–6, 10; BPP 1853–4, Vol. 51.1, 24; *Manchester Guardian*, 14 January 1854, 9; Fielding, 1953, 270–7; Bell, 1963, 213; Macdonald, 1970, 157, 228–33; Lohrli, 1973, 231; Briggs, 1988, 78; Lubbock, 1995, 249).

The phrase 'third gentleman' derives from the unnamed minor characters with small speaking parts in Renaissance drama (for example, 'third messenger', 'third gentleman', 'third murderer'). Dickens's association of the phrase with a man of the Arts might possibly have had its source in Lytton's 'Advertisement to the First Edition' of *England and the English*, where he thanked certain correspondents for their help: 'to the taste and critical knowledge of a third gentleman I owe many obligations in the chapter devoted to the survey of the "State of the Arts" amongst us at this time' (1833, viii).

a bolus]   A large pill. In the early nineteenth century, boluses were composed of powders with a suitable amount of syrup, conserve or mucilage. A popular handbook on family medicine, William Buchan's *Complete Domestic Medicine* (1830), mentions several types, including an astringent bolus for violent discharges of blood; a diaphoretic bolus to treat rheumatic complaints and disorders of the skin; a pectoral bolus for colds, coughs and asthma; and a mercurial bolus used as a purge for hypochondriacs (510–11).

To continue in fistic phraseology, he had a genius for coming up to the scratch]   Up until the introduction of the Queensberry Rules in 1867, boxing meant bareknuckle prizefighting which included, in various degrees, wrestling holds and throws. In an effort to give the sport some respectability, the championship boxer Jack Broughton devised rules in 1743 which governed the boxing world until 1839, when the London Prize Ring rules were first applied in a championship fight between James Burke and William Thompson, alias 'Bendigo'. A *HW* article by Dickens and Henry Morley, 'Mr. Bendigo Buster on Our National Defences against Education', employs similar 'fistic phraseology' to emphasize the need for a national system of education (2.313–19). The London rules, revised in 1853, made provision for a ring 24 feet square, bounded by ropes; into the centre of the ring, a mark was introduced called a 'scratch'. At the start of every round, each boxer had to get to the scratch line unaided. If he could not do this by the end of eight seconds, he was declared 'not up to scratch' and thus lost the fight.

an ugly customer.] Pugilist slang for a dangerous opponent. MS and CP initially read 'a glutton', but the reading was altered in proof to 'an ugly customer'.

bore his opponent (he always fought All England) to the ropes, and fall upon him neatly.] The London or All England rules allowed a boxer to use his own weight to press against his opponent and force him up against the ropes.

knock the wind out of common-sense] Floor or defeat an opponent.

he had it in charge from high authority to bring about the great public-office Millennium, when Commissioners should reign upon earth.] A reference to Revelation 20.1–6, when Christ will reign on earth for one thousand years. Henry Cole had been an energetic commissioner on the executive committee appointed in 1849 to conduct the Great Exhibition of 1851.

'Very well,' said this gentleman

Would you paper a room with representations of horses?] The discourse which follows about Victorian taste in art and design is a satiric treatment of the principles laid down by the Department of Practical Art, successor to the School of Design set up in 1837. Under the Board of Trade, the Department of Practical Art was established at Somerset House in 1852 but moved the same year to Marlborough House in Pall Mall.

In his Penguin edition of *HT* (1969), David Craig has argued that the Department of Practical Art is not the object of Dickens's satire here because it 'would not have been exactly a famous target by 1854' (319). On the contrary, in 1852, *HW* published a caustic review by Henry Morley of the new Department's permanent exhibition at Marlborough House ('A House Full of Horrors', 6.265–70) (see notes following).

Henry Cole was the Department's Superintendent of General Management, and Richard Redgrave was Superintendent of Art. Their aims were categorized under three headings: 'General Elementary Instruction in Art, as a branch of national education among all classes of the community . . . Advanced Instruction in Art' and the 'Application of the Principles of Technical Art to the improvement of manufactures, together with the establishment of Museums' (*First Report of the Department of Practical Art*, BPP 1852–3, Vol. 54.2). Cole lost no time in making direct links between his department and the schools. A teachers' training master was appointed to visit the National and Public Elementary Schools and tutor schoolmasters, schoolmistresses and pupil teachers in the art of drawing instruction. This new emphasis towards a universal education in art prompted a call for similar changes in science education, and in October 1853 the Department of Practical Art became the Department of Science and Art, with Cole as its Inspector General, Redgrave as Art Superintendent, and Lyon Playfair as the Department's secretary. It was hoped that 'the better education . . . will have its foundations laid . . . in sound teaching of the fundamental and elementary principles of science: art ought, assuredly, to rest on the principles of science' (*First Report of the Department of Science and Art*, appendix B, 13). This reorganized Department became extremely influential in the field of popular education. As a sign of its greater involvement with the Committee of Council on Education, the Department was placed under the Committee's jurisdiction in 1856 (*First Report of the Department of Practical Art*, BPP 1852–3, Vol. 54.6; for information on all the stages of the National Course of Instruction, see the Report's appendix I, 49–53; BPP 1852–3, Vol. 79.1.22; Fielding, 1953, 270–7; Macdonald, 1970, 159–60, 205–6).

Underlying Dickens's derision of such design reformers as Cole and Redgrave is his criticism of a government-sanctioned department which could control public and private taste in design including the pattern on a tea-cup (see note below, p. 46). It is significant that he connected these fixed principles in art with the classroom not only because the former were now part of elementary instruction in schools, but also because Dickens was aware that regulation in design, as in education, was an insidious form of social engineering. Lubbock, in *The Tyranny of Taste*, suggests that Pugin

> the seminal figure in the Good Design Movement . . . perceived that any artefact, be it a building, a chair or a dinner plate, could be made an object lesson in how we should conduct our lives. . . . [T]he real motif of those involved [in the Arts of Design] was to reshape personal morality by implementing the kind of control over individual consumption about which . . . Pugin had merely written. (247–8)

The arguments which Dickens applies to the Utilitarian nature of practical art he had previously used in relation to the teaching of science. In *The Examiner* of 9 December 1848, he praised an imaginative textbook of science, *The Poetry of Science; or, Studies of the Physical Phenomena of Nature* by Robert Hunt (MP 124–8). And, in HW, Morley's 'Science and Sophy' (8.505–8) commended the English translation of an amusing and instructive French book of science.

'I'll explain to you, then,' said the gentleman

Do you ever see horses walking up and down the sides of rooms in reality – in fact?] In 1849, Richard Burchett, then master in the Class of Form at the Head School of Design, remarked that 'an elephant would not be a proper animal to put upon [wallpaper], particularly a large one – he would be quite out of place on the wall. A trellis covered with pineapples is all right' (Macdonald, 1970, 131, 230).

'And is that why you would put

'And is that why you would put tables and chairs upon them, and have people walking over them with heavy boots?'] The likely source of this interrogation comes from Owen Jones's 'Observations' in the catalogue of the permanent exhibition of ornamental manufactures at Marlborough House – a collection of textiles, ceramics, porcelain and metalwork from the Great Exhibition out of which eventually developed the Victoria and Albert Museum (Fielding 274). Jones was the designer, architect and superintendent of works for the Great Exhibition of 1851, and author of *The Grammar of Ornament* (1856), the most influential illustrated reference-book for Schools of Art in the latter half of the nineteenth century. In his 'Observations' Jones declared that

> There are here no carpets worked with flowers on which the feet would fear to tread. ... We have no artificial shadows, no highly wrought imitations of natural flowers, with their light and shade, struggling to stand out from the surfaces on which they are worked, but conventional representations founded upon them. (*First Report of the Department of Practical Art, BPP* 1852–3, Vol. 54.231)

The catalogue and its contents were scathingly described in Morley's article, 'A House Full of Horrors', where much of the third gentleman's arguments about taste are to be found. Morley reports that a carpet

> is to be considered as a background. Imitations of fruit, shells, and hard substances in relief are improper. Treat the forms of flowers and leaves flatly, as ornaments, and not as imitations, if you please, but in the design painted upon a floor there must be nothing to contradict to the eye the necessary element of flatness. Neither must there be any strongly marked forms or violent contrasts or displays of colour, to take from the floor its character of background to the chairs and tables, and the people who stand over it. (6.269)

Geometrical patterns instead of flower designs were favoured, to give carpets the appearance of flatness.

Fielding suggests that Cole wrote Dickens 'a friendly letter of protest' during the serialization of *HT* (274), which might imply that Cole recognized Dickens's satiric treatment of himself and the Marlborough House doctrine. Dickens replied on 17 June 1854:

> I often say to Mr. Gradgrind that there is reason and good intention in much that he does – in fact, in all that he does – but that he overdoes it. Perhaps by dint of his going his way and my going mine, we shall meet at last at some halfway house where there are flowers on the carpets, and a little standing-room for Queen Mab's Chariot among the Steam Engines. (*Letters* 7.354)

(Fielding, 1953, 270–7; Macdonald, 1970, 178, 247.)

'You are not, Cecilia Jupe,'

Cecilia Jupe,']   MS and *HW* here read 'Mary Jupe', and 'Mary' was allowed to stand in CP. The Christian name, however, does not recur in the novel, nor is it present in

Dickens's work plans or in the one-volume edition. A proposed alternative name for Sissy was 'Dolly'.

'You are to be in all things

You don't find that foreign birds and butterflies come and perch upon your crockery.] Displayed in an anteroom of the museum of ornamental art in Marlborough House were so-called 'Examples of False Principles in Decoration'. In 'A House Full of Horrors' a 'quiet City man' called Mr Crumpet visits the museum and has his sensibilities of taste tested when he finds a butterfly painted on his teacup: 'Butter-fly-inside my cup! Horr-horr-horr-horr-ri-ble!' (270). The room, better-known as the Chamber of Horrors, was part of Henry Cole's plan to induce Victorians 'to investigate those common principles of taste, which may be traced in the works of excellence of all ages'. He readily admitted that the room 'appear[ed] to excite far greater interest than many objects the high excellence of which is not generally appreciated' (*First Report of the Department of Practical Art*, BPP 1852–3, Vol. 54.2, 33).

You must use,' said the gentleman] After 'gentleman' the MS reads 'with a blithe sententiousness peculiar to him,'. Cancelled on CP.

'for all these purposes, combinations and modifications (in primary colours) of mathematical figures which are susceptible of proof and demonstration. This is the new discovery. This is fact. This is taste.'] On 27 November 1852, in an address given by the Art Superintendent, Richard Redgrave set out to illustrate that a knowledge of the laws of colour – and thus an appreciation of 'really good taste' – would be valuable to both manufacturer and trader:

> colours must be arranged together in specific and absolute quantities to be agreeable to the eye. . . . Thus, in arrangements of the primaries, a surface quantity of three yellow requires, to be agreeable to the eye, a surface of five red and eight blue; or three yellow harmonises with its secondary purple as three to thirteen in surface quantity. If, therefore, in any composition these colours were used interchangeably in the ornamental spaces, it must be inharmonious, unless another law is attended to, which is, that a hue of colour diluted with white into a tint, requires a great increase of surface quantity to contrast harmoniously with its complementary full hue. (1853, 78–9)

Redgrave announced that a catechism would soon be available with questions relating to these laws that students in schools associated with the Department 'will be required to answer, and, which will be useful to the public also, in teaching some at least of those simple laws which must govern all tasteful distributions of colour' (79).

'Now, if Mr M'Choakumchild,' said the gentleman

Mr M'Choakumchild,'] The Celtic prefix is indicative of the important influence which colleges like Stow's Glasgow Seminary and Wood's Sessional School in Edinburgh exerted on the shaping of elementary education in Britain. Two Scottish writers in particular may have informed Dickens's choice of name. Both were named M'Culloch. J. M. M'Culloch (1801–83), a clergyman and former headmaster of Circus Place School, Edinburgh, had risen to public success with the publication of school textbooks. His most popular work, *A Series of Lessons in Prose and Verse* (1831), which precluded drama and poetry, was designed to 'store the [juvenile] mind with useful knowledge' (preface). J. R. McCulloch (or M'Culloch) (1789–1864), the economist, was author of the *Dictionary, Practical, Theoretical, and Historical of Commerce* (1832), and other works. Commenting on the education for the poor in *The Principles of Political Economy* (1830), McCulloch believed that 'they should be impressed ... with a conviction of the important truth, that every man is ... the arbiter of his own fortune' (1849 edn, 474).

In 1853, Dickens alluded to this laissez-faire statistician when he described a prospective *HW* article as 'dreadfully literal ... I should have thought the greater part of it written by McCulloch'. And in his article on the Preston strike Dickens called for 'mutual explanation, forbearance and consideration; something that is not to be found in Mr. McCulloch's dictionary, and is not exactly stateable in figures' (*HW* 8.553–9). In 1855, Dickens wrote about McCulloch's free-market economics applied during a Select Committee inquiry into the adulteration of food, drink and drugs: 'We shall never get to the Millennium, sir, by the rounds of that ladder; and I, for one, won't hold by the skirts of that Great Mogul of impostors, Master M'Culloch!' (*Letters* 7.125–6, 687). (For M'Choakumchild's relation to McCulloch's theory of political economy, see book 1, chapter 9, pp. 118–19.)

Although M'Choakumchild closely resembles Dr Blimber (*DS*) in his unimaginative and regimented teaching methods, he is Dickens's fictional prototype of 'the highly certificated stipendiary schoolmaster', Bradley Headstone, and the methodical, rule-orientated Miss Peecher in *OMF* (2.1).

mode of procedure.'] At his Glasgow Normal Seminary, David Stow had devised a 'training system' which he believed was more applicable to the condition of populous towns. He dispensed with monitors and taught children simultaneously through his use of platforms. The 'gallery lesson' became Stow's unique contribution to the development of formative classroom techniques in elementary education. Stow's 'training system' included the provision of a large classroom with a gallery (graduated platforms) at one end to accommodate all the children (around 150) of each department. This simultaneous teaching method for separate age-groups – the Infant and Juvenile departments and School of Industry – was a precursor of class-teaching as opposed to the earlier group/monitorial system with children of every age in one room. Dickens admired Stow's work, and in 1843 called his system 'an excellent one' (*Letters* 3.562–3). In a *HW* article of July 1850, 'A Detective Police Party', Dickens describes a police inspector 'not at all unlike a very acute, thoroughly-trained schoolmaster, from the Normal Establishment at Glasgow' (1.409).

The greatest Continental influence on English teaching methods came from Johann Pestalozzi, who envisaged a teaching method whereby the 'clearness of ideas must have been elaborated . . . before we can assume his capacity to understand the next step – i.e. the definite idea, or . . . its expression in words' (Green, 131). Friedrich Froebel (1782–1852), the German father of the kindergarten movement (which was introduced into England by Johann and Bertha Ronge in 1851), owed much of his progressive methodology to Pestalozzi, and the efforts of Dr Charles Mayo and his sister Elizabeth, founders of the Home and Colonial Infant School Society established in London in 1836, were based on a formalized variation of the Pestalozzian system of object lessons (see note, pp. 37–8). In 1839, Kay-Shuttleworth was especially impressed by the Pestalozzian methods used in the Orphan and Normal Schools of Switzerland and determined to establish his Battersea Training College on these principles. Battersea's other teaching methods derived from Wood's Edinburgh Sessional School, Mülhauser of Geneva, and Wilhelm and Dupois of Paris. All three masters whom Kay-Shuttleworth nominated to help carry out these experimental procedures were past students of Stow's Glasgow establishment. Despite its subsequent shortcomings, Battersea became the model for all future training colleges for the next fifty years. By 1853 there were forty training colleges established as a result of the Battersea experiment (*Four Periods* 338–56; Green (ed.), 1916, 13–14; Smith, 1923, 243; Smith, 1931, 128–30; Rich, 1933, 75; Sturt, 1967, 31, 133–5, 113).

So, Mr M'Choakumchild began in his best manner.

He and some one hundred and forty other schoolmasters, had been lately turned at the same time, in the same factory] M'Choakumchild is the product of the pupil-teacher system (see note to book 1, chapter 1, pp. 25–30). The training programme started with a five-year apprenticeship to a school manager including annual examinations by a school inspector. In school hours the apprentices acted as teachers and received instruction of at least an hour and a half either before or after the school day. Pupil teachers were given a yearly incremental salary conditional upon examination success: £10 at the end of the first year which increased to £20 for the fifth year (*Minutes* 1846, BPP 1847, Vol. 45, 6–7). At the end of the apprenticeship, candidates were presented with certificates which admitted them to sit an examination to become Queen's Scholars. Exhibitions of £20 or £25 were awarded to enable these eligible pupil teachers to enter a training college – a normal school – for a maximum of three years. Certificates of merit were awarded to successful Queen's Scholars at the end of each year's examination, and on completion of the course students became certificated teachers like M'Choakumchild. The first qualified Queen's Scholars graduated from the training colleges in 1853 and 1854.

In an effort to get certificated teachers quickly into the schools, examinations were also offered to students who had already completed a year or more of a training college course, to formerly trained teachers and to heads of schools without formal training. However, as numbers of apprentices steadily increased from eight in 1846 to 1,658 in 1850, a certificated teacher in the 1850s was more likely to be an original product of the new training system. The new system, which produced only several hundred qualified 'Queen's Scholar' teachers in 1853 and 1854, rapidly established a framework in which soaring numbers of students could be trained. In 1854 there were 2,836 certificated teachers employed in Great Britain; by 1859 there were 6,878 (Newcastle Commission, BPP 1861, Vol. 21.1, 638; Adamson, 144; Smith, 1931, 220; Sturt, 189, 193, 197).

turned at the same time, in the same factory, on the same principles, like so many pianoforte legs.] The furniture trade began to adopt mechanization in the 1840s, and turning was possibly the earliest process of mechanical shaping. The piece of wood being turned was kept in motion by means of a steam-engine which replaced the treadle or lever ordinarily operated by the worker's foot. George Dodd lists pillars, posts, legs, knobs and balustrades among the items of furniture mass-produced by the general wood-turner. The present passage reflects a contemporary criticism of mechanization: the machine is associated with mass production, which allegedly results in a lowering of quality and a standardization of design (Dodd, 1854, 18; Edwards, 1993, 19–24, 62–4).

Orthography, etymology, syntax . . . Privy Council's Schedule B] As part of the new teacher-training programme started in 1846, the Committee of the Privy Council on Education set out in detail a list of qualifications required from candidates in each year of their five-year apprenticeship. The schedule was in effect a tentative syllabus, and Dickens wrote to Wills in January 1854 to ask for a copy: 'I want (for the story I am trying to hammer out) the Education Board's series of questions for the examination of *teachers* in schools. Will you get it?' (*Letters* 7.258). Following is a list of the examination subjects for pupil teachers at the end of their fifth (and final) year:

> 1. In the composition of an essay on some subject connected with the art of teaching.   2. In the rudiments of algebra*, or the practice of land surveying* and levelling*.   3. In syntax, etymology, and prosody.   4. In the use* of the globes, or in the geography of the British Empire* and Europe*, as connected with the outlines of English history. In this year girls may be examined in the historical geography of Great Britain.   5. More completely in the Holy Scriptures, Liturgy, and Catechism, in Church of England schools, the parochial clergyman assisting in the examination.   6. In their ability to give a gallery lesson, and to conduct the instruction of the first class in any subject selected by the Inspector.   *General Rules.* – In the subjects marked with an asterisk girls need not be examined, but in every year they will be expected to show increased skill as sempstresses, and teachers of sewing, knitting, &c.
>   In the examinations, the Inspectors will, in each year, observe the degree of attention paid by the pupil teachers to a perfect articulation in reading, and to a right modulation of the voice in teaching a class. A knowledge of vocal music and of drawing (especially from models), though not absolutely required, because the means of teaching it may not exist in every school, will be much encouraged. Every pupil teacher will be required to be clean in person and dress. (*Minutes* 1846, BPP 1847, Vol. 45, 5)

Part of the second year's examination subjects included 'decimal arithmetic, and the higher rules of mental arithmetic. Girls [were] not required to proceed beyond the rule of "Compound Proportion" in this year' (*Minutes* 1846, Vol. 45, 4).

the higher branches of mathematics and physical science, French, German, Latin, and Greek.]   The General Examination of Training Schools for Christmas 1853 contained the following headings: 'Scriptural Knowledge', 'Catechism, Liturgy, and Church History', 'English Grammar, and the History of English Literature', 'History', 'Geography and Popular Astronomy', 'Arithmetic', 'Book-keeping', 'Algebra', 'Higher Mathematics', 'Euclid', 'Mensuration', 'Physical Science', 'Questions in Farming', 'School Management', 'Languages', 'Welsh' and 'Music' (*BPP* 1854, Vol. 51.1, appendix B, 464–84).

He knew all about all the Water Sheds of all the world]   In the training school at Battersea, Kay-Shuttleworth's method of teaching the physical geography of England commenced with a

> description of the elevation of the mountain ranges, the different levels, and the drainage of the country. The course, rapidity, and volume of the rivers are referable to the elevation and extent of the country which they drain. . . . (*Four Periods* 346)

Dickens wrote to Angela Burdett Coutts on 11 July 1856 with reference to the teaching of 'Common Things' in schools and teachers' training colleges. Miss Coutts had just published her *Summary Account of Prizes for Common Things Offered and Awarded by Miss Burdett Coutts at the Whitelands Training Institution*, the introduction to which was rewritten by Dickens. She had visited the Whitelands College with Kay-Shuttleworth in the spring of 1854 to assess its efficiency in industrial training and in the instruction of practical subjects. By July 1855 teachers and pupils at the college were competing for Miss Coutts's prizes. In his letter Dickens commented:

> And I think Shuttleworth and the like, would have gone on to the crack of doom, melting down all the thimbles in Great Britain and Ireland, and making medals of them to be given for a knowledge of Watersheds and Pre Adamite vegetation (both immensely comfortable to a labouring man with a large family and a small income), if it hadn't been for you. (*Letters* 8.160)

During the course of preparation for the second edition of the *Summary Account* in December 1856, Dickens told Miss Coutts: 'I thoroughly agree with you on that point of sending girls to school. There is a vast deal of Kayshuttleworthian nonsense written, sung, and said, on that subject' (*Letters* 8.233–4). A *HW* article of 1854, 'For the Benefit of the Cooks', suggested that 'the teaching of common things . . . should include . . . the economy of the kitchen. To teach the young idea how to cook is to do a great social good' (9.44). An earlier article, 'A Good Plain Cook', bemoaned the deficiencies of an appropriate culinary education for middle-class girls (1.139–41), and 'The New School for Wives' (5.84–9) praised the activities of an evening school for working-class women in Birmingham.

Dickens was clearly in favour of girls' education – albeit one which emphasized a domestic, practical instruction conducive to the comfort of a husband and family in the future. In a speech to the Liverpool Mechanics' Institution in 1844, he praised its members for their involvement in the formation of a girls' school (*Speeches* 55), and he also 'strongly approve[d]' of calls for the admission of female art students to the Royal Academy: 'I think it a capital move, for which I can do something popular and telling, in the Register' (*Nonesuch* 3.101). For discussions on this subject, see Slater, 1983, 323–8, and Collins, 1963, 124–37 (*Letters* 7.559; Fielding, 1968, 191).

If he had only learnt a little less, how infinitely better he might have taught much more!] One of the major criticisms of the training colleges from the early 1850s through to the Newcastle Commission which reported in 1861 was the vast amount of subjects the students had to learn – leaving them little time to develop teaching skills. One inspector's report for 1852 on the schools in the North of England concluded that:

> It is one thing to furnish [pupil teachers] with new information, and to tax the memory with facts; but there is the higher duty of carrying on a systematic mental discipline, which will strengthen the character, and enable the young teacher to appreciate the true uses of knowledge. (*BPP* 1852–3, Vol. 80.2.533).

Her Majesty's Inspector of Schools, Rev. Henry Moseley, proposed that a graduated course of examination for student teachers be considered so that 'by diminishing the number of the subjects of study in successive years, a greater concentration would be obtained on each, and that indefinite and superficial character of the schoolmaster's attainments in *many things* be discouraged, which has hitherto been the cardinal defect and the opprobrium of his education' (*BPP* 1854, Vol. 51.1.453)

He went to work in this preparatory lesson

not unlike Morgiana in the Forty Thieves] In the *Arabian Nights* story of 'Ali Baba and the Forty Thieves', Morgiana, Ali Baba's slave, finds the robbers hidden in oil-jars. She kills them by pouring boiling oil into the containers.

Book 1, Chapter 3   First weekly part
                                                       Saturday, 1 April 1854

A LOOPHOLE

MR GRADGRIND walked homeward

It was his school, and he intended it to be a model.]   The term 'model school' was used to describe an elementary school usually attached to a training college. The aim of the model school was 'to afford [students] for their future guidance a pattern of what a school ought to be' (*Newcastle Report*, 1861, 114). Thus, throughout the Victorian period, the model school exemplified the standard of teaching in the Normal (training) school.

The emphasis placed upon the model school within the training college system left little room for student spontaneity or initiative in teaching methods. However, given the limited intellectual ability of the students and the low standards of instruction and management in elementary schools, it was preferable to prepare future teachers in an ersatz model school than to expose them too soon to the rigours of school life. William Ellis believed that his Birkbeck Schools could become models for other schools to imitate, thereby introducing practical political economy into the general current of popular education for the working classes (Rich, 1933, 78–9; Blyth, 1889, 99, 96).

Not that they knew, by name

Not that they knew, by name or nature, anything about an Ogre.]   Dickens's recent *HW* article, 'Frauds on the Fairies', was written in response to George Cruikshank's edited version of the nursery story of Tom Thumb. The article asserted that 'In an utilitarian age . . . it is a matter of grave importance that Fairy tales should be respected'. Of Cruikshank he wrote that

> he should never lay down his etching needle to "edit" the Ogre, to whom with that little instrument he can render such extraordinary justice. But, to "editing" Ogres, and Hop-o'-my-thumbs, and their families, our dear moralist has in a rash moment taken, as a means of propagating the doctrines of Total Abstinence, Prohibition of the sale of spirituous liquors, Free Trade, and Popular Education. (8.97)

Other articles which stress the importance of fairy-stories for children are: 'A Witch in the Nursery' (3.601–9); 'Little Children' (8.289–93); and 'Case of Real Distress' (8.457–60).

a monster . . . with Heaven knows how many heads manipulated into one, taking childhood captive, and dragging it into gloomy . . . dens by the hair.]   This image appears to be a conflation of one of the labours of Hercules – the fight against the Lernean hydra – and the figure of the Wild Man (*Homo silvestris*) found in Northern European secular art. In classical mythology, the hydra, which ravaged the countryside, had nine heads, one of which was immortal. When Heracles struck off its heads with his club, new ones would grow forth. He finally conquered it by burning away the heads and burying the immortal one under a great boulder. The Wild Man symbolizes lust and aggression, and is commonly represented as covered with long shaggy hair and carrying a wooden club. He is usually portrayed battling a knight and abducting a lady, or fighting monsters or other wild men in the woods.

No little Gradgrind had ever seen

a face in the moon] The fanciful figure of the man in the moon carrying a bundle of sticks on his back – as suggested by the shadows on the moon's surface – is both a nursery tale with biblical origins and a myth common to several countries. Shakespeare and Dante (among others) contain references to the man in the moon. 'Busy with the Photograph' (HW 9.244) reported that astronomers had taken photographs of the moon's surface: 'If we are ever to know what the Man in the Moon is doing . . . the photograph will take a great part in eliciting the information'.

the silly jingle, Twinkle, twinkle, little star] A popular nursery rhyme by Jane Taylor (1783–1824) which first appeared under the title 'The Star' in 1806. The poem (in five verses) begins:

> Twinkle, twinkle, little star,
> How I wonder what you are!
> Up above the world so high,
> Like a diamond in the sky.   (Opie, 1951, 397–8)

dissected the Great Bear like a Professor Owen, and driven Charles's Wain] The Great Bear, or Big Dipper, is the northern constellation *Ursa Major* within which is a group of seven stars, resembling a wagon, called Charles's Wain or the Plough. Sir Richard Owen (1804–92), a friend of Dickens, was a leading anatomist, zoologist and palaeontologist who was at this time the first Professor of Comparative Anatomy and Physiology at the Hunterian Museum. Owen wrote three articles on zoology and natural history for *HW* – 'Poisonous Serpents' (6.186–8); 'Justice to the Hyaena' (6.373–7); 'A Leaf from the Oldest of Books' (13.500–2) – and his work was referred to frequently in many other articles. Forster relates a conversation between Dickens and Owen, probably during a visit Dickens made to Owen on 28 October 1852, about 'a telescope of huge dimensions built by an enterprising clergyman who had taken to the study of the stars' (Forster 2.20.445; *Letters* 6.780).

a locomotive engine-driver.] From 1830 to 1850, British manufacturers enjoyed the monopoly of locomotive design, construction and supply to the rest of the world. In a competition for the fastest locomotive in 1829, George Stephenson's *Rocket* had demonstrated on a mile-and-a-half stretch of new railway between Liverpool and Manchester that acceptable speeds of up to 30 miles per hour could be achieved through locomotion. The Liverpool & Manchester Railway, soon to become the model for other major lines built in the Victorian period, was swift to adopt this form of mechanical traction (using stationary engines only for steep inclines) for its passenger trains. By 1830 the new railway had ten locomotives built by George Stephenson's son, Robert, at his engineering works in Newcastle. With modifications and improvements to the *Rocket*'s original design, Stephenson developed a locomotive which served as a prototype for many engines of the time.

The development of the locomotive, and the introduction, from 1845, of express trains on many lines, gradually increased the speed of railway travel. In 1844, for example, the fastest train service from London to Birmingham took 3 hours 55 minutes at an average speed of 28 miles per hour. The same journey in 1854 was done in three hours at 37.7 miles per hour (Williams, 1968, 18–23; Simmons, 1978, 17–20, 46, 167–8, 176, 271–2).

The speed of locomotives fascinated Dickens, and he frequently associated it with flying, as he does here and elsewhere in *HT*. His account of a rail journey from London to Paris which took eleven hours ('A Flight', *HW* 3.529–33) turns throughout on the image of rapid flight: 'I can fly with the South Eastern, more lazily . . . than in the upper air. I have but to sit here . . . and be whisked away' (529). Dickens expressed his high regard for engine drivers in 'Railway Strikes' (*HW* 2.361–4).

that famous cow with the crumpled horn who tossed the dog who worried the cat who killed the rat who ate the malt]   An accumulative rhyme (first published in 1755), commonly called 'The House that Jack Built', which concludes:

> This is the farmer sowing his corn,
> That kept the cock that crowed in the morn,
> That waked the priest all shaven and shorn,
> That married the man all tattered and torn,
> That kissed the maiden all forlorn,
> That milked the cow with the crumpled horn,
> That tossed the dog,
> That worried the cat,
> That killed the rat,
> That ate the malt
> That lay in the house that Jack built.   (Opie 231)

that yet more famous cow who swallowed Tom Thumb]   In Henry Fielding's burlesque of heroic tragedy, *The Tragedy of Tragedies; or, The Life and Death of Tom Thumb the Great* (1730), Tom Thumb, 'a little hero with a great soul', is devoured by a large red cow (Act 3, scenes 8 and 10). George Cruikshank's version of the story, *Hop o' my Thumb and the Seven League Boots*, appeared in the first number of his *Fairy Library*, a series of four traditional fairy-stories rewritten and illustrated by Cruikshank, published from July 1853 until 1864. Fielding's *Tom Thumb* was performed in the schoolroom at Tavistock House on 6 January 1854 by the children of Dickens and

Mark Lemon, with the 4-year-old Henry Dickens as Tom. The play had been specially 'altered' by Dickens to include 'some capital old Stager dodges and scraps of music' (*Letters* 7.232, 234; Patten, 1992, 29).

To his matter of fact home,

wholesale hardware trade] According to Dodd's *Dictionary of Manufactures* (1869), the term 'hardware'

> is rather absurdly confined to one class of articles which, though certainly hard, are by no means the only kind that deserve the name. Hardware comprises, so far as it is a commercial term, all the commoner useful articles of iron made in Birmingham and South Staffordshire, as well as some of those in copper and brass. . . . Hardware and cutlery are said to comprise: – (1.) Knives, forks, scissors, shears, surgical and anatomical instruments, and other articles of regular cutlery . . . (2.) Anvils, vices, saws, files, edge-tools, cranks, slide-bars, and tools or implements of industry other than agricultural, not wholly composed of iron or steel . . . (3.) Manufactures of German silver, pewter, Britannia metal, papier-mâché, lamps, chandeliers, candelabra, and hardware not specifically described. (165–6)

In 1834, Dickens described Birmingham as 'the town of dirt, ironworks; radicals, and hardware' (*Letters* 1.47).

Stone Lodge was situated on a moor within a mile or two of a great town – called Coketown in the present faithful guide-book.] In 1843, Dickens called Manchester 'this enterprising town, this little world of labour' and 'this great town' (*Speeches* 45–6). He had earlier described Birmingham as a 'great working town' (*PP* 50) and used the same phrase in 1852 about Manchester (*Letters* 6.753). Friedrich Engels' enquiry, *The Condition of the Working Class in England* (1845), contained a section entitled 'The Great Towns' which included factory towns such as Nottingham, Birmingham, Glasgow, Leeds, Bradford, Bolton, Stockport and Manchester (1845). See note to book 1, chapter 5, pp. 77–9, about possible sources for Coketown.

Many middle-class families moved out of the smoky industrial town centres and lived on the outskirts, usually within walking distance from the workplace. Some of Preston's rich bankers and manufacturers did this: for example, the Pedder family, merchants and bankers, lived at Ashton Hall, about a mile from the factories. Social separation was not only desirable as a sign of status and wealth – living a mile or two away from any of the large manufacturing towns was sufficient distance from their unsanitary conditions and pollution (Burnett, 1986, 104–9). Some merchants and mill-owners preferred, like Bounderby, to have both a town house and a residence in the country or along the coast. The prosperous cotton merchants of Liverpool are described in a *HW* article of 1854 as having 'their suburban villas, their marine villas, and their town mansions, on a princely scale' ('Our Sister', 9.473).

The reference to 'the present faithful guide-book' might be read as a ploy to help the novel seem realistic to contemporary readers. But it can also be understood as a joking allusion to the vast number of guidebooks available to mid-century travellers touring the English counties, Ireland, Scotland and Wales. Until the advent of John Murray's popular series in 1836, however, the majority of guidebooks were far from 'faithful'. Murray's contribution to the genre was to provide for the first time detailed, accurate and authoritative information about Britain and other countries. The first edition of Murray's *Handbook for Shropshire, Cheshire, and Lancashire* was published in 1870 (Murray, 1889, 624; Buzard, 1993, 65–77).

A very regular feature on the face

A very regular feature on the face of the country, Stone Lodge was. . . . A great square house, with a heavy portico darkening the principal windows. . . . A calculated, cast up, balanced, and proved house. Six windows on this side of the door, six on that side] It is apt that Gradgrind's home reflects an architectural style opposed to the 'romantic gothic' designs favoured in the nineteenth century. Dickens deliberately portrays Stone Lodge as a classical Georgian dwelling with its emphasis on symmetry, functionalism and, to the Victorian mind, monotony. The contemporary distaste for Georgian architecture was summed up by G. Laurence Gomme at the end of the century, when he commented on the street architecture of London: 'The early years of the Queen were marked by the gloom and incompetence in matters of art which characterized the Georgian period of history. . . . The Georgian spirit of architecture was against art, and declared for so-called utilitarianism, as if utility could exist without the element of art' (1898, 136, 138; Burnett, 1986, 114–15). Also compare the Bradshaws' house in *Ruth* (1853): 'The house was square and massy-looking, with a great deal of drab-colour about the furniture' (17).

Gas and ventilation, drainage and water-service, all of the primest quality.] The prosperous middle class took advantage of every new form of technology – a plumbed water system, improved sewage disposal and gas lighting – which could contribute to domestic health and ease. Gas was the usual form of lighting for the majority of middle-class and upper-class homes in the 1850s. Although gas for cooking had been used commercially from the late 1840s, domestic gas-cookers were rare before 1880. For information about the impact of gas-lighting on industry, see note to book 1, chapter 10, pp. 124-5.

Proper ventilation of homes was a Victorian obsession, since foul smells and a claustrophobic atmosphere were associated with disease-ridden and overcrowded working-class districts in towns (hence Dickens's reference to the 'killing airs and gases' in book 1, chapter 10). The miasmic infection theory (that contagion was possible by breathing offensive-smelling air from decaying animal and vegetable matter and stagnant water) held sway until it was gradually discredited by the general acceptance of the germ theory of disease in the 1870s. In his *Dictionary of Manufacturing, Mining, Machinery and the Industrial Arts* (1869), Dodd expresses the contemporary preoccupation with ventilation:

How to get fresh air into a room, how to get foul air out of it – these are the problems. . . . Sometimes air-holes are made near the floor of a room to admit fresh air; but this occasions a stratum of cold air near the feet, not always either agreeable or healthy. Many sanitary physicians recommend air-holes near the ceiling, if there is an open fire-place to draw down the air so admitted. Perforated air-bricks, perforated zinc or iron sheet, hinged valves connected with air-boxes opening to the outside of the building, perforated panes of glass – these . . . are used to admit air into rooms, or else to afford exit for the impure air. (414–15)

In the 1850s a piped water-supply was expensive, erratic and virtually unknown in working-class inner-city areas, where water was purchased by the bucket from a communal street-pump or -tap at certain times of the day. Before 1860, a piped supply of cold water only was usually restricted to the kitchen, and upstairs plumbing was nonexistent until the 1880s (Burnett, 1986, 99, 214–15; Smith, 1979, 99, 232–3; Wohl, 1983, 61–3, 87–9, 137, 285; Best, 1971, 42).

mechanical lifts] These are dumb-waiters – small lifts or elevators used for conveying food, dishes, etc. from one room or storey of a house to another. (Britain's first domestic lifts, which took the place of back stairs, were installed in flats in Kensington Court in 1884: Hobhouse, 1986, 42.68).

the housemaids, with all their brushes and brooms] There was a range of brushes and brooms specially designed for every conceivable household task: carpet, banister and staircase brooms; long hair-brooms for floors; scrubbing brushes; stove-brushes; furniture brushes; soft brushes for plate; crumb-brushes for the table; and cornice and small dusting brushes. A *HW* article of 1854, 'A Good Brushing' (9.492–5), describes the range of brushes available at the time. A housemaid's day, which began at around 6 a.m., was arduous and full. She was expected to perform many daily household duties including polishing, sweeping, brushing, tidying grates and maintaining the fires, carrying hot water to the bedrooms morning and night, making and turning down the beds, emptying and scalding the chamber-pots and water-jugs, cleaning windows and sewing. Gradgrind is wealthy enough to employ several housemaids. In many such households, a head housemaid would supervise the work of the others and allot specific chores to her junior charges. She herself might only have done light housework and a little sewing (Beeton, 1861, 988–99; Horn, 1975, 63–5).

Everything? Well, I suppose so.

cabinets in various departments of science too . . . the specimens were all arranged and labelled] The fascination for exhibiting collections of rarities in cabinets originated with the private museums of the sixteenth-century aristocracy and clergy – the *cabinets des curieux* in France and the *Wunderkammern* in Germany. The growing interest in natural history and scientific progress, and the recognition that cabinet exhibitions could be a useful educational tool, caused the English antiquarian cabinets that had been in use at the beginning of the seventeenth century to be superseded by larger and more adventurous collections which characterized the first permanent museums (Altick, 1978, 3, 8–10).

the idle legend of Peter Piper]   A tongue-twisting nursery rhyme:

> Peter Piper picked a peck of pickled pepper;
> A peck of pickled pepper Peter Piper picked;
> If Peter Piper picked a peck of pickled pepper,
> Where's the peck of pickled pepper Peter Piper picked? (Opie 347)

He had reached the neutral ground

the neutral ground upon the outskirts of the town, which was neither town nor country]   In 'Locked Out' (HW 8.345) Preston's Marsh had been described as 'a level plain of marshy ground, upon the banks of the Ribble, and below the town of Preston'. In his own article of February 1854, 'On Strike' (written after his visit to Preston), Dickens describes an open-air meeting on another large piece of ground near the centre of the town. This was ' "Chadwick's Orchard" – which blossoms in nothing but red bricks' (8.558). This area had also been a place used for outdoor festivities. Charles Hardwick, the nineteenth-century Preston historian, described

> menageries, circuses, puppet-shows, penny gaff swing-boats, flying-boxes, sword-swallowers, fire-eaters, retailers of Everton toffy [sic], Eccles cakes, and Ormskirk gingerbread, *et hoc genus omnis,* [which] found a spacious and convenient asylum in the then treeless orchard. (*Eliza Cook's Journal,* 11.248)

During the Preston strike, both the Marsh and the Orchard were favourite outdoor venues for mass meetings of the cotton operatives, but after sunset open-air meetings were forbidden, according to a proclamation by Preston magistrates on 19 September 1853 (Dutton and King, 1981, 124).

a wooden pavilion]   Wooden circus buildings were hastily constructed in towns and could be dismantled just as quickly when they had fulfilled their purpose. Travelling circuses frequently transported these structures from one town to another; however, their questionable construction gave rise to many accidents. A HW article of 1854, 'Strollers at Dumbledowndeary', described one strollers' booth as 'a very tumbledown edifice indeed, of old boards and canvas, which have evidently done service in countless grassy patches . . . all over England' (9.376) (Speaight, 1980, 42–3).

A flag, floating from the summit of the temple . . . in an ecclesiastical niche of early Gothic architecture]   Travelling circuses were usually adorned outside with flags, and little Gothic porches served as entrances (Schlicke, 1985, 168). One such archway is used as part of a performance given by Mr Crummles and his company

3 Louisa Woolford and Andrew Ducrow performing 'The Swiss Maid and Tyrolean Shepherd'. From A. H. Saxon, *The Life and Art of Andrew Ducrow and the Romantic Age of the English Circus* (Hamden, Conn.: Archon, 1978)

in *NN* 24. The description of Sleary collecting the money is reminiscent of the introductory chapter to the *Memoirs of Joseph Grimaldi* (1838) in which Dickens remembers

> standing in a body on the platform, the observed of all observers in the crowd below, while the junior usher pays away twenty-four ninepences to a stout gentleman under a Gothic arch, with a hoop of variegated lamps swinging over his head. (9)

Miss Josephine Sleary . . . with her graceful equestrian Tyrolean flower-act.] Louisa Woolford, the unrivalled female tight-rope performer and equestrienne, who reached the peak of her circus career in the 1830s, made her début at Astley's Royal Amphitheatre on 7 April 1828, with her performance of 'The Flower Girl' or 'La Rosière'. In Dickens's sketch, 'Astley's', Louisa is described as going round the ring again 'on her graceful performance, to the delight of every member of the audience, young or old' (*SB* 108). As well as performing solo acts, she later teamed up with Andrew Ducrow – her future husband – to perform equestrian duets such as the variously entitled 'The Tyrolean Shepherd and Swiss Milk Maid', 'The Mountain Maid and Tyrolean Shepherd' and 'The Swiss Milk Maid and Tyrolean Shepherd' (Plate 3). The act was performed at Astley's in 1853. It is possible that Josephine Sleary was based loosely on Louisa Woolford; that the name of Louisa is given to another character in the novel might provide a further link with this female celebrity of Dickens's youth.

Also in 1853, a number of American and British equestrian and gymnastic companies performed at Drury Lane Theatre, London. Among the artistes was a 13-year-old equestrienne called 'Little Ella', whose 'daring exploits in riding and leaping' helped guarantee a profitable production (Plate 4). 'Mademoiselle Ella', the 'American Wonder. . . . the most accomplished Female Equestrian in the World', toured Europe with similar success, and her 'graceful acts of equitation' with 'the young artiste's charms of face and form' drew crowds of male admirers at every venue. In the late 1850s, at a circus in Germany, 'Ella' was discovered to be a man (*Illustrated London News* 23.366; Frost, 1875, 126; Saxon, 1978, 155–6, 220; Speaight, 1980, 105–6; Schlicke, 1985, 158).

very long and very narrow strips of printed bill] In the first half of the nineteenth century, printed playbills for small touring troupes such as Sleary's were rare. Handwritten bills were occasionally seen for itinerant companies performing at local inns or meeting-places. Printed playbills were used, however, when larger travelling circuses appeared in provincial theatres. Crummles's touring troupe is advertised in Portsmouth on 'bills pasted against the walls and displayed in windows', and their bills for a future performance are described as being 'three feet long by nine inches wide' (*NN* 23, 24). Astley's narrow playbills were 9½ inches wide and 30 inches long. The amphitheatre also printed double-bills 10 inches by 15 inches (Plate 5) (Theatre Museum, London; Saxon, 1978, 26).

Signor Jupe] Dickens's early experience of circus clowns derived from watching

4 'Mademoiselle Ella' and Tom Barry the clown at Drury Lane Theatre, London. From the *Illustrated London News*, 26 November 1853

the performances of John Ducrow, younger brother of the famous nineteenth-century equestrian, Andrew. John was the leading Astley clown of the 1820s and 1830s, and according to one circus historian 'was to the circus what Grimaldi [the stage clown] was to the pantomime'. He did not take up his career as clown until 1825, by which time he had gained experience in acrobatics, acting and equestrianism. He incorporated these skills into his comic routines, and despite his short career Ducrow's influence on the style of later nineteenth-century circus clowns was significant. He was still playing the clown at Astley's a month before his death (of consumption) in May 1834. He was thirty-eight years old. Another performer, Tom Barry, may have informed the versatility of Jupe. Barry (Plate 6), an Astley clown from the early 1840s until 1853, had a varied repertoire of skills both verbal and physical. Sometimes known as the 'Celebrated Hibernian Jokist', Barry specialized in playing comic Irishmen in such equestrian pantomimes as 'Harlequin Tam O'Shanter and His Steed Meg'. Dickens would also have seen him perform Barry's favourite farce, 'Billy Button's Ride to Brentford' (see note below, p. 66). Jupe's wide range of acts, however, suggests a conflation of a number of performers – a blend which defies particularization.

The practice of Italianizing English names began early in the nineteenth century. Rope-dancers initially used the Italianate form because many accomplished performers were Italians who had achieved international fame in the eighteenth century. Thomas Frost notes that 'it is worthy of remark that none of the circus performers of the last [eighteenth] century seem to have deemed it expedient to Italianize their names, or to assume fanciful appellations such as the Olympian Brothers, or the Marvels of Peru' (1875, 22–3).

In a *HW* article of 1852, G. A. Sala describes a theatrical public house whose patrons included 'Signor Scapino and his celebrated dog Jowler; Herr Diavolo Buffo, the famous corkscrew equilibrist (from the Danube), and tight-rope dancer; [and] Mademoiselle Smicherini the dancer, with undeniable silk fleshings, and very little else' (5.229). In *NN*, the fashionable dressmaker Madame Mantalini has changed her husband's surname from Muntle, hoping to capitalize on the exotic appeal of the name, since 'an English appellation would be of serious injury to the business' (10) (Disher, 1925, 188–9; Disher, 1937, 114–15; Saxon, 1978, passim).

highly trained performing dog Merrylegs'.] By the 1850s performing dogs were a regular feature of many circus programmes. Their introduction to the ring had been a gradual process which started in the eighteenth century (at Astley's, for example). They eventually achieved fame in such dog dramas as 'The Dog of Montargis', a play first performed at the Royal Circus on 6 October 1814. Other dramas specifically written for performing dogs included 'The Dog of the Château' (1845) and 'The Dog of the Pyrenees' (1845). Their acts were not confined to melodramas alone, and many dogs formed a double-act with their trainer-clown, performing tricks with letters and numbers, or entertaining the audience with their comic antics, or, like Merrylegs, exhibiting their gymnastic skills. Dogs had the dual advantage of being easily trained and of actually enjoying themselves during a performance. This reduced the possibility of ill-treatment by their trainers (see note to book 1, chapter 9, pp. 121–2).

5 Part of Astley's double-playbill for 11 October 1852 (by courtesy of the board of Trustees of the Victoria and Albert Museum)

Dickens had not only seen many performing dogs in circuses and fairs, but he had also enjoyed their acts in the theatrical public houses around London (see *Letters* 7.895). A *HW* article of 1852 describes such a public house where a certain Signor Scapino is 'exercising his celebrated dog Jowler at standing on the hind legs, placing a halfpenny on the counter, and receiving a biscuit instead' (5.229). A week after *HT* began serialization in *HW*, an article entitled 'Behind the Louvre' described a performing poodle, dressed as a 'sergeant of the old guard', entertaining a Parisian crowd (9.187). See also Buffo, the stray performing poodle in 'Tattyboys Rents' (*HW* 9.297–304). Buffo's former master, Monsieur Phillips, who was 'something in the magician, not to say conjuror and mountebank line', had 'one morning suddenly disappeared' (302–3).

Dickens's choice of the name 'Merrylegs' is apt – the clown was often called 'Merry Andrew' or 'Mr Merryman' (see Sala's article 'Strollers at Dumbledowndeary' 9.374–80). In his biography of Dickens, Peter Ackroyd states that Dickens 'in an essay a few months before . . . revealed that in his childhood he had christened a dog with the name of Merrychance' (1991, 735). Ackroyd does not give a source for his claim, and despite considerable research this information cannot be verified (Saxon, 67; Speaight, 1980, 78; Schlicke, 1985, 164).

'his astounding feat of throwing seventy-five hundred-weight in rapid succession . . . thus forming a fountain of solid iron in mid-air] Such acts were commonplace. In 1823, Juan Bellinck, 'the American Indian prodigy and flying rope vaulter', managed to lift a horse while he hung from a slack rope. In 1842 at Batty's new circus, the Olympic Arena, the acrobat Lavater Lee

> vaulted over fourteen horses, threw a dozen half-hundred weights over his head, bent backward over a chair, and in that position lifted a bar of iron weighing a hundred pounds, threw a back somersault on a horse going at full speed, and turned twenty-one forward somersaults, without the aid of a springboard. (Frost, 1875, 104)

Dewhurst the clown, also with Batty's circus, issued his own bill for his benefit night in which he itemized a variety of his performances, including staggering jumps, leaps and dances. During the interval, 'he will *tie his body in a complete knot*. After which he will *walk on his hands*, and carry in his mouth, *two fifty-six pounds weights*' (Frost, 1875, 105; Speaight, 1980, 103).

'Behind the Louvre' describes a 'public exhibitor' who, with one blow, crumbles a large stone into tiny pieces (*HW* 9.188).

Shaksperean quips and retorts'.] Shakespearian clowns were in fashion in the 1850s and, according to Le Roux, were still performing successfully in the circus at the end of the century. Although a clown called Charles Marsh purported to be the first to perfect this art, W. F. Wallett, the self-styled 'Queen's Jester', had a stronger claim, giving speeches similar to those of the fools in Shakespeare. For the first quarter-century of his career, which spanned from 1828 to 1868, Wallett had few rivals, but by the 1850s others gained reputations equal to his (Le Roux, 1890, 278–9; Speaight, 1980, 92).

6   An unsigned portrait of Tom Barry (1842). From Ifan Kyrle Fletcher, 'A Portrait of Thomas Barry'. *Theatre Notebook* 17 (1963) 116-17, pl. 6

MS reads 'Shaksperean witticisms'. The change to 'quips and retorts' might suggest that in Jupe's mélange of skills that of the Shakespearian jester was given a humbler place in his repertoire, and the act restricted to parodies of speeches known to the audience.

The spelling 'Shaksperean' was widely used in the early years of the nineteenth century. Despite Dickens's earlier preference for an alternative spelling (in 1847 he commented favourably about Forster's usage of the 'e' before the 's'), he chose to let 'Shaksperean' stand from MS to CD (*Letters* 5.165).

Mr William Button, of Tooley Street, in 'the highly novel and laughable hippocomedietta of The Tailor's Journey to Brentford'.] This 'whimsical piece of horsemanship' (Frost, 1875, 39) was Philip Astley's adaptation of a popular story which later became the subject of several illustrations (Plate. 7). On 28 March 1768, Brentford was the scene of a famous election fought and won by John Wilkes. The victory was seen as a challenge to the Government, who had recently ousted Wilkes from his seat in the House of Commons for publishing seditious and obscene libels. At the election, thousands of people turned out to vote for the hero of the day. Among the voters, according to the story, was a tailor who had arrived in Brentford after a somewhat clumsy and inept ride on his horse. Astley's adaptation became the first equestran comic act performed at Halfpenny Hatch in July 1768, and his company, under the managership of William Cooke, was still producing a version in their 1853–4 double-bill. The 'Grand Equestrian Comic Pantomime', which ran until 4 March 1854, was announced in the *Illustrated London News* of 24 December 1853 (23.563), and a description of the action appeared on 31 December:

> *Billy Button* receives a letter for his vote, enclosing £10 for his journey to Brentford. After many mishaps with *Stitch'em*, he dresses in his best, and starts for the livery stables. *Billy* tries to mount, but his horse begins kicking, and gallops off. *Billy* calling out for his life. *Goldeye* appears with the Magic Needle. We now find ourselves at the hustings, in Brentford town. Speech making and heads breaking. At this particular moment *Billy Button* arrives. The *Ladies' Favourite* was engaged to take him to the hustings, which he does, and throws him there. (23.599)

The name 'Billy Button', added to the title of the act by Astley in 1807, may have been taken from Samuel Foote's play *The Maid of Bath* (1771), which has as one of its main characters a social-climbing tailor called Billy Button (Belden, 1969, 141–6; Speaight, 1978, 24–5).

Thomas Gradgrind took no heed

House of Correction] The initial impetus behind the building of Houses of Correction came from the example of London's Bridewell. Its opening in 1557 reflected the acknowledgement that steps had to be taken to provide employment for all ablebodied vagrants, whose numbers in London and throughout the country had grown

7 'Billy Button's Journey to Brentford' (1768) (by permission of the Gunnersbury Park Joint Committee)

to unmanageable proportions. By the early eighteenth century all classes of criminal were committed to these 'houses', a practice acknowledged and sanctioned by the legislature in an Act of 1719. The House of Correction and the town gaol became synonymous terms.

Preston's House of Correction, the first of its kind in Lancashire, was built in 1618. A new 'house' was opened in 1790, and it is still used as a gaol. It was originally installed with hand-weaving machines for the male prisoners, and reports of 1806 claimed that the prison was being used as a factory. By 1820, discharged prisoners could leave the House of Correction richer than they would have been on the outside. Despite some adverse contemporary opinion about the dubious punitive nature of the employment the prison continued this practice, even after the introduction of the treadwheel in 1825. For further discussion of Preston's House of Correction and its enlightened prison chaplain, see book 1, chapter 5, pp. 86–7 (Lancashire County Quarter Sessions, 13/4/1820; *Edinburgh Review* 1822, 36.358–9; Holdsworth, 1924, IV.392–8; Paroissien, 1992, 84).

This brought him to a stop.

'Now, to think of these vagabonds,'] By the mid-nineteenth century vagabonds suffered from the inherited prejudice of centuries. With the passing of the Vagrancy Act in 1824, magistrates were allowed to sentence vagabonds, idlers and paupers to one month in prison. Included in the 'vagabond' class were strollers, gypsies, beggars and itinerants. Gradgrind's view of the circus people as idlers and prison fodder is therefore not surprising. A *HW* article of 1851, 'Getting Up A Pantomime', defended performers against such views as Gradgrind's: 'Consider how hard they work, how precarious is their employment, how honestly they endeavour to earn their living. . . . Admit that there is some skill, some industry, some perseverance, in all this, not misdirected if promoting harmless fancy and innocent mirth' (4.296). An earlier article in praise of 'cheap pleasures' criticized the puritanical view that recreation was 'more or less associated with idleness and dissipation. . . . The best words – the mildest definition bestowed by modern Puritans – a large class – upon any sort of amusement is, that it is "a loss of time" ' (3.201; Paroissien, 1992, 88–9).

A space of stunted grass and dry rubbish

Louisa] Dickens's choice of 'Louisa' might have been influenced by the name of an early circus performer, Louisa Woolford (see note at p. 60). He had also used 'Louisa' as a pseudonym in a humorous letter to Forster of 1838 which alluded to a past love-affair between Forster and the poet Letitia Landon. Forster had ended the relationship after alleged, but never substantiated, rumours of Landon's previous lovers (*Letters* 1.422, 488).

peeping with all her might through a hole in a deal board] In 1769, Philip Astley bought deal boards for a fence at his new site in Westminster Bridge Road. Astley's fence had many gaps – as evidenced by the number of people who, rather than pay the sixpence admission, crowded outside every chink between the deal boards (Disher, 1937, 25). A HW article about strolling actors published during the serialization of the novel described children 'oppressed by . . . perpetual want of pence . . . contenting themselves with seeing as much as they [could] of the outside of the show, hopeless of internal admittance' ('Strollers at Dumbledowndeary', 9.374–80).

'In the name of wonder, idleness, and folly!'

'In the name of wonder, idleness, and folly!'] Perhaps an echo of part of the Solemnization of Matrimony in BCP: 'In the Name of the Father, and of the Son, and of the Holy Ghost'.

She was a child now, of fifteen

fifteen or sixteen] MS and CP read 'fourteen or fifteen'.

Would have been self-willed . . . but for her bringing-up.] The Victorian male both feared and detested female wilfulness since it challenged long-held assumptions about the subservience of women and went contrary to the belief that only men were masters of their own destiny (Oppenheim, 1991, 211).

'You! Thomas and you, to whom

the circle of the sciences is open] This image may have been suggested by Henry Morley's HW article, 'School-Keeping', in which an ideal headmaster is advised to 'have a full elementary knowledge of the entire circle of the sciences' (8 [20 January 1854] 499–504, 501). The term also served as the title of a series of science textbooks, *Orr's Circle of the sciences; a series of treatises on the principles of science with their application to practical pursuits*, edited and published by William Somerville Orr during the early months of 1854. The initial series covered 'the mathematical sciences' under three headings: 'Simple arithmetic, algebra, and the Elements of Euclid', 'Planes, spherical trigonometry, series, logarithms and mensuration' and 'Practical geometry'. Later volumes, which appeared between 1854 and 1855, considered 'The principles of physiology' and 'A system of natural history' (Baker, 1977, 78).

'I was tired. I have been tired

'I was tired. I have been tired a long time,'] Louisa's response to her upbringing suggests the early symptoms of severe clinical depression. Throughout the novel, she exhibits a variety of symptoms classified by Victorian medical men as 'nervous complaints'. Depression, in all its forms, was known at the time as 'melancholia', 'shattered nerves', 'broken health', 'nervous exhaustion', 'nervous prostration' or simply 'breakdown'. Later in the century, it was termed 'neurasthenia', a catch-all phrase for a multitude of indefinable symptoms ranging from ennui to total incapacitation. There was much uncertainty and disagreement as to the precise nature and treatment of neurotic disorders, and nineteenth-century doctors frequently conflated depressive illness with hysteria, a psychosomatic condition, and with hypochondriasis, a mild psychological complaint now called hypochondria.

Although Louisa's depression represents the results of a starved imagination, her thwarted nature mirrors the repressed position of women in Victorian society. Victorian ideology decreed that self-willed women were unfeminine, yet it required women in their domestic sphere to be strong and capable (Oppenheim, 1991, passim). (See note to book 1, chapter 4, p. 74, about Mrs Gradgrind's invalidity.)

It was not until the end of the century that some psychiatrists conceded that there might be a causal link between social repression and women's nervous illnesses, although their comments were still coloured by preconceptions about female intellect and the influence of women's reproductive organs on the mind. Nevertheless, practitioners like Henry Maudsley and Charles Mercier both agreed that adolescent girls were deprived of suitable outlets for their heightened emotional and sexual energies: 'Few women', Mercier observed in 1890, 'pass through this period of their development without manifesting signs of disorder . . . at this period, more or less decided manifestations of hysteria are the rule' (from *Sanity and Insanity*, quoted in Showalter, 1985, 131).

The general ennui which permeates *HT* – from the Coketown workers to Louisa, Tom, Mrs Gradgrind, Jupe, and Harthouse – relates to a mood frequently documented in nineteenth-century literature and art, and which many Victorians believed to be characteristic of their age. Carlyle summarized the feeling in *Past and Present* (1843), after his visit to a workhouse: 'Fatal paralysis spreading inwards, from the extremities, in St. Ives workhouses, in Stockport cellars, through all limbs, as if towards the heart itself' ('Midas', 1.1), while other interpretations of what was perceived as a national malaise focused on a lack of religious faith:

> On the whole, these are much *sadder* [sic] ages than the early ones; not sadder in a noble and deep way, but in a dim wearied way, – the way of ennui, and jaded intellect, and uncomfortableness of soul and body. . . . The profoundest reason of this darkness of heart is, I believe, our want of faith.
> (Ruskin, *Modern Painters* 3 (1856) ch. 16, sections 9 and 10)

> predominance of thought, of reflection, in modern epochs is not without its penalties; in the unsound, in the over-tasked, in the over-sensitive, it has produced . . . the feeling of depression, the feeling of *ennui* . . . these are the characteristics stamped on how many of the representative works of modern times!
> (Arnold, 'On the Modern Element in Literature')

(Cook and Wedderburn (eds) 1904, 321–2; Houghton, 1957, 64–5; Neiman (ed.), 1960, 14.)

'What,' he repeated presently

as if Mr Bounderby had been Mrs Grundy.] A censorious character referred to, but never seen, in Thomas Morton's play *Speed the Plough* (1798). The absent Mrs Grundy is constantly upheld in the play as the epitome of respectability and decorum, the stock phrase being 'What would Mrs. Grundy zay?' (3rd edn 1800).

Book 1, Chapter 4   Second weekly part
                                                          Saturday, 8 April 1854

MR BOUNDERBY

He was a rich man: banker

banker, merchant, manufacturer] The majority of private bankers who came from industry and trade viewed their involvement in the banking world as integral to their mercantile concerns. For example, in the Bank Returns to the Inland Revenue on 28 January 1854, the Preston Banking Company, a joint-stock bank, listed among its partners twenty-nine manufacturers and eight merchants (Lancashire Record Office, DDPr. 138/876; Anderson and Cottrell, 1975, 606). For an account of private banks as distinct from joint-stock banks, see note to book 1, chapter 14, p. 146. Dickens's other fictional industrialist, Rouncewell, is a banker as well as an ironmaster (*BH* 63).

inflated like a balloon, and ready to start.] Hot-air balloon ascents had been a popular pastime since the 1780s when the flights of the Montgolfier brothers in Paris and Vincenzo Lunardi in London triggered a ballooning mania which continued throughout the nineteenth century. In the early days of Philip Astley's circus, balloon ascensions were offered as part of the entertainments (see Saxon 22, 280). In his 1836 sketch, 'Vauxhall Gardens by Day' (*SB*), Dickens described an ascent he had watched, and the amusement formed the basis of a *HW* article of 1851, 'Ballooning' (4.97–105). See also Dickens's 'Lying Awake' (6.145–8), and Morley's 'A Call Upon Sophy' (9.174–6), which appeared in the same issue as chapters 4 and 5 of the serialized novel.

A man who could never sufficiently vaunt himself a self-made man.] The Victorian creed of self-help, best-defined by Samuel Smiles in his popular book *Self-help* (1857), stressed the potential of every individual to achieve success and wealth through hard work and perseverance. Its emphasis on personal merit and character – rather than on the wealth and status associated with the upper class – gave the middle class an ethos expressive of their rising influence in nineteenth-century society. However, accompanying the seeming classlessness of the self-help ideology was a desire to climb the social ladder and acquire the respectable trappings of a 'gentleman'. Such pretensions were accommodated by the diminishing power and wealth of the aristocracy – succinctly demonstrated by Dickens in Mrs Sparsit's family history and reduced circumstances and in Bounderby's purchase of a country estate formerly owned by the overspeculative, upper-class Nickits (book 1, chapter 7, and book 2, chapter 7). Firmly allied to its economic equivalent, laissez-faire, the self-help doctrine provided rich industrialists in particular with a moral dimension to individualism and the free-market economy.

Although the Smilesian doctrine preached the superiority of productive and independent lives over material gain – see, for example, Smiles's *Life of George Stephenson* (1857), *Lives of the Engineers* (1861–2) and *Life and Labour* (1887) – the self-help creed in reality was governed by class-consciousness and money. Smiles's optimistic view in 1845 that 'adverse circumstances – even the barrenest poverty – cannot repress the human intellect and character, if it be determined to rise' and that 'knowledge is no exclusive inheritance of the rich . . . but may be attained by all' (*Autobiography*, cited in Dodds, 1953, 132–3), was negated in practice by the prevailing perceptions of the poor. Self-help theory fostered the prejudicial notion that poverty was the result of improvidence and laziness (see Bitzer's comments in book 2, chapter 1). This misconception widened the gap between rich and poor, and hardened the minds of those in the middle class who increasingly controlled the power to alleviate working-class poverty.

The myth of the self-made man is embodied in Bounderby, who invents his own history. He represents the distorted ideals of self-improvement, honesty and humility which Dickens saw as essential to the self-help ethic. In 1869, Dickens remarked: 'Persevere . . . not because self-improvement is at all certain to lead to worldly success, but because it is good and right of itself . . . and . . . it . . . bring[s] with it, its own resources and its own rewards' (*Speeches* 405). Dickens's comments not only reflect his self-determined success but also mirror his resolution of the opposing moral and social forces of self-help. (For an excellent survey of this evolution in Dickens's fiction, see Gilmour 1973.) In 1852, however, Dickens did acknowledge the efforts of certain self-made industrialists 'who have proceeded on the self-supporting principle, and have done wonders with their workpeople', and he admired 'other manufacturers . . . who have awakened to find themselves in the midst of a mass of workpeople going headlong to destruction, and have . . . quite turned [the current] . . . by establishing decent houses, paying schools, savings banks, little libraries, &c.' (*Letters* 6.645). This positive aspect of self-help he portrayed in the characterization of Rouncewell the ironmaster in *BH*.

By 1854, however, Dickens was disillusioned by the hypocrisy and intransigence of manufacturers in the northern industrial towns, and he aimed his attack in *HT* on the 'monstrous claims at domination made by a certain class of manufacturers' (*Letters* 7.320). The shift of perspective is significant, for it suggests that Dickens had finally separated the moral values of self-development (explored later in *GE*) from the version of Victorian self-help which made virtues of riches and status.

Bounderby is related to the self-righteous Alderman Cute and the pompous mammonite Sir Joseph Bowley in *The Chimes*, and both Bowley and Bounderby exemplify Carlyle's 'Man of Business' in *Past and Present*:

> Mark on that nose the colour left by too copious port and viands; to which the profuse cravat with exorbitant breastpin, and the fixed, forward, and as it were menacing glance of the eyes correspond. That is a 'Man of Business;' prosperous manufacturer, house-contractor, engineer, law-manager. (2.17)

Bounderby's unsympathetic and self-satisfied persona is also reminiscent of the reactionary Mr Bendigo Buster in two *HW* articles, 'Mr. Bendigo Buster on Our National Defences Against Education' (2.313–19) and 'Mr. Bendigo Buster on the Model Cottages' (3.337–41). Moreover, Edward Bulwer-Lytton's Mr Bluff (*England and the English*, 1833) might have contributed to Bounderby's 'bluff independent manner' and 'fine bluff English independence' (book 1, chapter 7, and book 2, chapter 7). For Mr Bluff's resemblance to Mr Gradgrind, see note to book 1, chapter 2, p. 34.

In many ways, Dickens's fictional manufacturer is similar to a prominent Preston mill-owner, Thomas Miller, Jnr (1811–65), who, during the Preston strike of 1853–4, became the cotton operatives' fiercest opponent. Owner of Horrockses & Miller, the largest firm in Preston, Miller was the town's wealthiest man, and the cotton operatives believed him to be proud, miserly and tyrannous. As factory master and chairman of the re-established Preston Masters' Association, he lived in a large, double-fronted, porticoed Georgian residence in Winckley Square, an élite area of Preston, and at the time of the lock-out in October 1853 he was purchasing a country house and estate. Miller financed church building during his lifetime and donated land for his project of building a park in his name – Miller Park was completed two years after his death (Houghton, 1957, 184–6; Oddie, 1972, 114; Gilmour, 1973, 71–101; Kovačević, 1975, 35; Dutton and King, 1981, passim; Belcher, 1982, 105–9).

brassy speaking-trumpet] A type of megaphone which was chiefly used at sea, to carry the voice a great distance or to let it be heard above loud noises.

the Bully of humility] Perhaps a reminiscence of lines from Coleridge and Southey's satirical ballad 'The Devil's Thoughts' (1799): 'And the Devil did grin, for his darling sin/Is pride that apes humility'. Mrs Gaskell quoted the lines in *North and South* (1.15) in regard to Mrs Thornton's imperious pronouncements on the study of the classics.

In the formal drawing-room

damp mortar] A damp-proof course was not an obligatory requirement in house construction until 1875 (Marshall and Willox, 1986, 137). Dickens is implying, of course, that Stone Lodge is cold and uninviting, despite all its 'modern' domestic comforts described in book 1, chapter 3.

Mrs Gradgrind, a little, thin, white, pink-eyed

Mrs Gradgrind, a little, thin, white, pink-eyed bundle of shawls, of surpassing feebleness, mental and bodily; who was always taking physic without any effect] Mrs Gradgrind epitomizes the Victorian invalid wife – stereotypically fragile, nervous and intellectually weak. Such women were invariably the products of a total financial and emotional dependence upon their husband, whose authority defined their existence. Deprived of individual will and, in many cases, overcome by enforced domesticity, constant childbearing or boredom, a substantial number of married middle-class women used their 'nervous' incapacitation as a form of escape and often as a powerful tool to manipulate other family members (Showalter, 1985, 130; Oppenheim, 1991, passim). For the prevalence of nervous disorders among Victorian women in general, see note to book 1, chapter 3, pp. 69–70.

Mrs Gradgrind, weakly smiling

like an indifferently executed transparency of a small female figure, without enough light behind it.] Transparencies – scenes painted with translucent paints on calico, linen, or oiled paper, and lighted from behind like stained glass – were used in the theatre for special effects. The French painter and theatrical designer Philippe Jacques de Loutherbourg incorporated the transparency into his shows of brightly illuminated clockwork figures and scenes which he introduced to London in 1781, and in the 1820s pictorial dioramas which featured transparencies were transformed by Daguerre's 'double-effect' technique. The process involved painting a similar scene on both sides of the transparency; spectacular images could then be produced by strategically manipulating the lighting (Altick, 1978, 95, 119, 169–70).

'She kept a chandler's shop,'

chandler's shop] Such a shop originally sold candles and oil for heating and lighting, but by the early nineteenth century it had become more of a general grocer's. Sometimes known as hucksters' shops, they were usually found in the poorest areas of a town and became indispensable to the working women of industrial towns who did not have time to bake at home (Burnett, 1966, 44–5). For a contemporary view of hucksters' shops in Birmingham, see Harriet Martineau's article 'The Miller and his Men', *HW* 4.415–20.

'I was to pull through it I suppose, Mrs Gradgrind.

studying the steeple clock of St Giles's Church, London, under the direction of a drunken cripple, who was a convicted thief and an incorrigible vagrant.] In the early nineteenth century (the time to which Bounderby refers), St Giles's Church (1733), situated between New Oxford Street, Charing Cross Road and Shaftesbury

Avenue, was the centre of a notorious slum, the parish of St Giles. St Giles is the patron saint of the poor and the crippled; but, ironically, the 'rookery' tenements of the parish housed all the outcasts of society – the poor, the crippled, prostitutes and criminals of every kind. Between 1844 and 1847 much of the area was demolished and reconstructed. New Oxford Street, opened in 1847, replaced the squalid narrow courts of Seven Dials, an area described in SB ('Seven Dials'; see also 'Meditations in Monmouth Street'). In 1850 and 1851, Dickens augmented his early knowledge of St Giles's during several visits with Inspector Charles Field to its half-demolished rookery, the model for Tom-all-Alone's in BH (see Dickens's series of HW articles: 1.409–14, 457–60, 577–80; and 3.265–70).

'And Mrs Gradgrind,' said her husband

'I should as soon have expected to find my children reading poetry.'] Reading poetry was an acknowledged Benthamite aversion. Bentham pronounced that 'all poetry is misrepresentation', and J. S. Mill wrote that Bentham's abhorrence of the art stemmed from the belief that 'Words . . . were perverted from their proper office when they were employed in uttering anything but precise logical truth' ('Bentham', 1838, 95).

'Don't tell me that's the reason

'Go and be somethingological directly.'] The Rev. Richard Dawes, in his *Suggestive Hints Towards Improved Secular Instruction*, was wary of the practical application of the 'ologies':

> There may be something of wrongness in some of the *ologies*, as they leave room for the wanderings of fancy, and do not deal in measured quantity as the *ometries* do. Here scientific men may, and perhaps sometimes do, become bold and speculative to a degree which may startle those of a more sober-minded temperament, and who have not paid attention to the subject on which they treat. (6th edn, 1853, 73)

Carlyle's inaugural address as Rector of Edinburgh University in 1866 contained the tongue-in-cheek comment: 'Maid-servants, I hear people complaining, are getting instructed in the "ologies", and are apparently becoming more and more ignorant of brewing, boiling, and baking' (*Critical and Miscellaneous Essays*, 1888, 575).

In truth, Mrs Gradgrind's stock of facts

most satisfactory as a question of figures] Dickens may be referring to Mrs Gradgrind's healthy financial state before she married Mr Gradgrind. All her property after marriage would legally have become her husband's. See note to book 1, chapter 16, p. 151.

she had 'no nonsense' about her. By nonsense he meant fancy]   'Nonsense', in the innocuous, philosophical use of the word, means that which is emotional, vague or elaborate. Plamenatz writes that the utilitarians 'above all men, were determined not to be the dupes of words, and they destroyed more nonsense than any other modern school of philosophers' (1966, 148, 151).

'Stop a bit!' cried Bounderby

one of those strollers' children]   From the seventeenth century, vagabonds, itinerant beggars, pedlars, wandering actors and players were termed 'strollers'. George A. Sala's introduction to his article about a group of strolling actors criticizes an age-old prejudice:

> The strollers. Have not the righteous powers of law, reform, science, and sectarianism been directed for centuries against the strollers? . . . Strollers have been declared rogues and vagabonds by all sorts of statutes: pulpit thunder and quarter sessions lightning have been levelled against them times out of number. No matter; the strollers have a principle of life in them stronger than the whole family of Shallows. (HW 9.374)

So, Mr Bounderby threw on his hat

'I never wear gloves,']   Gloves and mittens, worn both indoors and outdoors, suggested gentility 'indicating that their wearer had no need to use her hands, which must be protected and kept white' (Dunbar, 1953, 81).

Being left to saunter in the hall

the children's study . . . that serene floor-clothed apartment, which . . . had much of the genial aspect of a room devoted to hair-cutting.]   Floor-cloth, such as oilcloth and (from 1860) linoleum, was widely used as a hard-wearing substitute for carpeting. Contemporary accounts of barbers (also called hair-dressers) and their shops suggest that the proprietors were typically talkative, humorous and sharp-witted, and that their shops were attractive, sociable places. *The Complete Book of Trades* (1837) publishes an illustration of 'a Hair-dresser's shop at the present period':

> The display of elegant head dresses on the wax figures . . . the neatness, and in some cases splendour, of the fitting-up of the Hair-dressers' shops, contribute very much to the gaiety of the leading streets of the metropolis.
> (Whittock, et al., 26)

A sketch in *Punch* remarks of barbers and their shops:

They all live in shops curiously adorned with play-bills and pomatum-pots. . . . All are politicians on both sides of every subject. . . . He [the barber] is essentially a social being; company is as necessary to his existence as beards. ('*Punch*'s Information for the People: the Barber', 1 [July–December 1841], 119)

In 'Mr. Weller's Watch' (*MHC*), Sam Weller describes 'a wery smart little [hairdressing] shop vith four wax dummies . . . many hair-brushes and tooth-brushes . . . in the winder, neat glass-cases on the counter, a floor-clothed cuttin'-room up-stairs, and a weighin'-macheen in the shop' (5). A similar barber's shop is presented in *NN* (52) and illustrated by Phiz. For other depictions of hair-dressers' shops as pleasant and relaxing, see *MHC* (3), Poll Sweedlepipe's shop in *MC* (19, 26), and the garrulous barber in 'The Old Couple' (*Sketches of Young Couples*). In the present passage, Dickens's analogy is an early indication of the underlying warmth in the Gradgrind household which will overcome the austerity of a Utilitarian upbringing.

Adam Smith and Malthus] Adam Smith (1723–90), classical economist and author of *An Inquiry into the Nature and Causes of the Wealth of Nations* (1776) which expounded the theory of a laissez-faire economy. The Rev. Thomas Malthus (1766–1834) is principally remembered for his influential thesis on overpopulation, *Essay on the Principle of Population*, which appeared anonymously in 1798 but was later summarized by Malthus under the title *A Summary View of the Principle of Population* (1830). See notes to book 1, chapter 2, pp. 33–4, and book 2, chapter 1, p. 164, respectively.

moist pipe-clay] A fine white kaolin clay used to make tobacco-pipes and fine earthenware, and by soldiers to clean their white trousers ('Pipe-Clay and Clay Pipes', *HW* 4.526–8).

slate-pencil] Because of the high rate of duty imposed upon paper until 1861, slates were the ideal and cheap alternative for schools. In 1853 a dozen ruled, unframed slates, six inches by four, cost 1*s* 3*d* (British and Foreign School Society's sale catalogue, 48th Report, 1853, 141.6).

Book 1, Chapter 5 Second weekly part
Saturday, 8 April 1854

THE KEY-NOTE

COKETOWN, to which Messrs Bounderby

COKETOWN] In 1866, Dickens wrote: 'When I did Hard Times I called the scene

Coketown. Everybody knew what was meant, but every cotton-spinning town said it was the other cotton-spinning town' (*Nonesuch* 3.483). He was giving advice to the actor-manager Charles Fechter, who was producing Dion Boucicault's *The Long Strike* at the Lyceum Theatre. The play used industrial conflict as a backdrop to the domestic squalor of Manchester. Dickens had suggested that it would 'ease the way . . . with the audience, when there are Manchester champions in it, if instead of "Manchester" you used a fictitious name?' (483). Dickens's remarks might imply a distinct correlation between Coketown and Manchester; however, his preceding comments to Fechter about Boucicault's part as an Irish sailor in the play illuminate our understanding of his creation of an industrial landscape in *HT*: 'The very notion of a sailor . . . whose business does not lie with the monotonous machinery . . . is a relief to me in reading the play. . . . I would make him the . . . airiest sailor that ever was seen; and through him I can distinctly see my way out of "the Black Country" into clearer air' (*Nonesuch* 3.482). The interchangeable manner in which Dickens associates the ironworks and coalfields of the Midlands – the Black Country – with the cotton-factories of the North facilitates the notion that Coketown was a coalescent creation.

It is likely that Dickens knew Birmingham rather better than he knew Manchester, but his knowledge of either town was not an intimate one (Collins 653, 655). Dickens's first-hand experience of Birmingham began in the early 1830s as a reporter for the *Morning Chronicle* (*Letters* 1.47). His tour of the Midlands and North Wales in late 1838 took him across the industrial landscape around Birmingham and Wolverhampton 'through miles of cinder-paths and blazing furnaces and roaring steam engines, and such a mass of dirt gloom and misery as [he had] never before witnessed' (*Letters* 1.447). This infernal topography inspired similar scenes in his work: see *PP* (50), *OCS* (44, 45) and *Letters* 2.131–2; *DS* (20) and *BH* (63). Of particular added importance to *HT* is Dickens's *HW* article, 'Fire and Snow' (8.481–3), which describes a railway journey to Wolverhampton in December 1853. All the elements of industrial activity incorporated within Dickens's account are absorbed into the description of Coketown. What Dickens did not include was his positive opinion of Birmingham factories in which he had seen 'such beautiful order and regularity, and such great consideration for the work people provided, that they might justly be entitled to be considered educational too' (*Speeches* 160).

Manchester has a complex role in Dickens's creation of a manufacturing, and essentially northern, town. Dickens was certainly acquainted with Manchester's mills and its 'school' of business ethics: see *AN* (4); *Letters* 1.483–4; *Speeches* 152. As the metropolis of the cotton-towns in Lancashire, Manchester – 'Cottonopolis' – symbolized an industrial, utilitarian ethos which influenced the commercial and social organization of a whole factory district. Despite Dickens's praise of the city (*Speeches* 45–6), he was well aware of the underside of industrial progress. In 1852 he wrote to Angela Burdett Coutts on the day he spoke at the opening of Manchester's Free Library: 'Such a noble effort . . . so wonderfully calculated to keep one part of that awful machine, a great working town, in harmony with the other' (*Letters* 6.752–3). By the time Dickens re-echoed these sentiments in Birmingham at the end of 1853 (*Speeches* 167), numerous workers' strikes for higher wages had occurred during the year in Manchester and throughout England and Wales, with the cotton operatives' campaign for a 10 per cent wage increase at its height in Preston. The sharpened conception of Coketown owes much to Dickens's investigative visit to Preston at the end of January 1854, only days after he started writing *HT*. The cotton-town, with its close association to Manchester, provided the final link in the concatenation of Dickens's previous experience of industrial life (Briggs, 1963, 105; Brantlinger, 1971, 270–85; Fawkes, 1979, 164; Collins, 1980, 651–73; Dutton and King, 1981, 27, 33).

It was a town of red brick

like the painted face of a savage. It was a town of machinery and tall chimneys, out of which interminable serpents of smoke trailed . . . state of melancholy madness.]   Dickens used the same serpent images in 'Fire and Snow' as he made his way by train towards Wolverhampton (*HW* 8.481). A *HW* article of 1853 about the chemical manufacturing industry in Manchester and Glasgow conflates images of savagery and sea-serpents ('The Northern Wizard', 8.226). The images in the present passage are rich in allusions. Savages in general evoked disgust and hatred in Dickens. In 'The Noble Savage' (*HW* 7.337–9) he stated that the 'endurance of despotism is one great distinguishing mark of a savage always. . . . His virtues are a fable; his happiness a delusion; his nobility, nonsense' (339). Serpent and monster images were frequently associated with the railway, and painted savages, smoke serpents and elephants were all features of the circus. Serpents of smoke also featured in firework displays (*Dickensian* 67.130; Steig, 1971, 147; *HW* 8.45–8; *Illustrated London News* 23.518; Saxon, 1978, passim; Schlicke, 1985, 179–80).

It had a black canal in it, and a river that ran purple with ill-smelling dye]   Water pollution caused by manufacturing processes was one of the major concerns of the *Inquiry into the State of Large Towns and Populous Districts* in 1844. The rivers and canals of Manchester and Salford not only served as conduits for drainage and sewerage from Bolton, Bury and Rochdale, but they also received the effluent from numerous dams and weirs erected by paper-mills, dyeworks, chemical works, tanneries and logwood-mills (*Appendix to the Second Report of the Commissioners for Inquiring into the State of Large Towns and Populous Districts*, BPP 1845, 18.95–7). In 1845, Engels reported on these polluted conditions and described Manchester's River Irk as 'a narrow, coal-black, foul-smelling stream, full of débris and refuse' (89). The factories of the Yorkshire woollen industry also polluted their waters (see 'The Great Yorkshire Llama', *HW* 6.252).

Edwin Chadwick's investigations and publication of his *Report on the Sanitary Condition of the Labouring Population of Great Britain* (1842) helped to make the general public aware of the problems and led to a series of Royal Commissions and Acts during the 1840s and 1850s. The most important of these were the Towns Improvement Clauses Act (1847), the Public Health Act (1848) and the Metropolitan Interments Act (1850). Dickens was an indefatigable proponent of sanitary reform, and from 1849 (motivated by the work of his brother-in-law Henry Austin, a civil engineer who had become Secretary to the General Board of Health in 1848) he actively supported measures for a badly needed sewage-disposal system for London (see *Letters* 5.564 n, 710–11; *Speeches* 104–10, 127–32). More than a score of *HW* articles by

8 Swainson & Birley's 'Big Factory' Preston (1834), drawn by T. Allom and engraved by J. Tingle (by permission of the Harris Museum and Art Gallery, Preston)

Dickens, Morley, Horne and others wholly or partly focused upon London's water pollution or drew attention to the need for sanitary reform in general.

vast piles of building full of windows]   A typical Lancashire cotton-mill is described by George Dodd:

> It is a brick building of vast length and height, with as many windows as there are days in a year, or perhaps more. Dull are the bricks, unadorned are the windows, and monotonous the whole appearance of the structure. (HW, 1853, 6.501)

The article goes on to relate the 'great process' of mechanized cotton-manufacturing:

> The cotton is conveyed in its bag, perhaps to one of the upper floors, and it travels downwards from floor to floor, as the order of processes advances; a "devil" tears the locks of wool asunder; a "scutcher" blows away all the dirt; a "carding-machine" lays all the fibres parallel; a "drawing machine" groups them into slender ribbons; a "roving machine" slightly twists them into a soft spongy cord; a "mule" or a "throstle" spins the roving into yarn; and men and women, boys and girls, tend on the machines while all this is being done.... All the real labour is performed by machines. (501)

Dodd called it 'a mistake to suppose ... that factory labour reduces the factory workers to mere machines: their duties require much quickness, delicacy, and discrimination' (501).

The biggest cotton-factory in Preston was Swainson & Birley's Fishwick Mill, known locally as 'The Big Factory'. Built in 1823, it had 7 storeys of spinning-blocks, was 158 yards long, 18 yards wide, and had 660 windows constituting 32,500 panes of glass (Plate 8). The largest Preston firm and employer, however, was Horrocks, Miller & Co., which had ten mills and employed 2,000 workers in 1847 (Dutton and King, 1981, 11–12; Morgan, 1990, 16).

It contained several large streets all very like one another, and many small streets still more like one another ... the counterpart of the last and the next.]   James Kay (later Kay-Shuttleworth) observed in 1832 that

> Prolonged and exhausting labour, continued from day to day, and from year to year, is not calculated to develop the intellectual or moral faculties of man. The dull routine of a ceaseless drudgery in which the same mechanical process is incessantly repeated, resembles the torment of Sisyphus – the toil, like the rock, recoils perpetually on the wearied operative.
> (*The Moral and Physical Condition of the Working Classes*, 22)

Regimented rows of back-to-back buildings with three shared walls, and windows and doors only at the front, were the speedy 'architectural' response to the rapid increase in the population of industrial towns (Burnett, 1986, 70–7).

the same as yesterday and tomorrow, and every year the counterpart of the last and the next.] Hebrews 13.8: 'Jesus Christ the same yesterday, and today, and forever'.

These attributes of Coketown

comforts of life which found their way all over the world] The Janus-faced nature of cotton manufacture – it gives pleasure to the well-to-do but misery to the working class – is a point frequently made in *HW* articles. In 'Lancashire Witchcraft', manufactured cotton is sent to Liverpool 'where ships are always ready to sail to all parts of the world', but 'on a cold, raw, dark December morning, hundreds and thousands of women, slipshod in mind and body, may be dimly seen amidst the murky gloom of fog and smoke, slinking along toward the many factories' (8.550–1). In 'Spitalfields', Dickens observed: 'It is difficult to reconcile the immense amount of capital which flows through such a [silk-weaving] house as this . . . with the poignant and often-repeated cry of poverty that proceeds from this quarter' (3.26). For other articles concerned with the history, supply, manufacture and reputation of cotton, see: 'Food for the Factory' (2.225–9); 'British Cotton' (5.51–4); 'Chip: The Crimes of Cotton' (6.188–9); 'Wallotty Trot' (6.499–503); 'The Power Loom' (7.440–5); 'A Manchester Warehouse' (9.268–72); and 'Our Sister' (9.471–4).

You saw nothing in Coketown

If the members of a religious persuasion built a chapel there . . . they made it a pious warehouse of red brick, with sometimes . . . a bell in a bird-cage on the top of it. The solitary exception was the New Church; a stuccoed edifice with a square steeple over the door, terminating in four short pinnacles like florid wooden legs.] The early chapels of nonconformist groups were built with restricted budgets and were functional in design. Many denominations used the cheap and available material of the industrial town – red brick – and produced church buildings virtually indistinguishable from their urban surroundings. The architectural dullness of the dissenting chapels also owed much to the imitation of 'Commissioners' Churches' – Anglican churches built quickly and cheaply with State grants from 1818, in response to a growing urban population. By 1851, 2,529 new churches, mostly in the Gothic style, had been built by the Church of England. They had 'a peculiar drabness about them . . . a lack of vitality, as if their designers had driven themselves to a task for which they had no heart'. One of their main considerations was 'how to get two thousand people into a presentable rectangular box, with galleries, at so much a sitting' (Summerson 315–16). By the mid-nineteenth century, nonconformists were in the process of trying to create an architectural identity – 'Dissenting Gothic' – separate from the Established Church.

The 'New Church' which Dickens describes is built in the 'decorated' or 'florid' style, considered the purest Gothic form. Thomas Rickman's 'Commissioners' Church', St Peter's in Preston, is an architectural example. The building, still known as St Peter's, is now part of the University of Central Lancashire. The

New Church – or New Jerusalem Church – formed in 1787 was an esoteric nonconformist body whose doctrines were based on the religious writings of the theologian and philosopher Emanuel Swedenborg (1688–1772). Of the fifty New Jerusalem churches in England and Wales by 1851, most were found in the industrial districts of Lancashire and Yorkshire. At the only New Jerusalem church in Preston, built in 1843, a hundred members attended morning service on 30 March 1851. By the late 1860s, there were seventy 'Swedenborgians' in Preston and approximately the same number of Sunday scholars: 'The church is not well attended; hardly half of it is occupied except upon special occasions' (Hewitson, 1869, 58). It is unlikely that Bounderby, who thinks Stephen Blackpool is trying to 'floor the Established Church' (book 2, chapter 8), would agree to be married in a New Jerusalem church, as he does in book 1, chapter 16. It is possible that Dickens inadvertently confused dissenting Gothic church architecture with the similar economical Gothic style of the 'Commissioners' Churches' (*BPP* 1852–3, (89), xciv–xcvii, 76, 95–7; Hewitson, 1869, 51, 55–60; Summerson, 1953, 314–17; Norman, 1976, 124; Binfield, 1977, 145–8; Hill, 1981, 118–19; Howell and Sutton, 1989, ix).

a pious warehouse of red brick]   Dissent was often associated with trade and the red-bricked industrial North, where trade flourished. The early Victorian functional brick chapels became symbolic of a spiritual dearth and inhumanity which many saw as an inevitable result of factory life (Cunningham, 1975, 68–89).

the lying-in hospital]   Lying-in hospitals were charitable teaching institutions sponsored by local ladies' committees and clergymen. In London alone, twenty such establishments existed in 1843, and throughout the century their numbers increased all over England. The strict exclusion rules enforced at most lying-in hospitals – no unmarried pregnant women, no first pregnancies (to preclude the possibility of an unwedded conception), no childless women or women with a deformed or diseased child, no complications during delivery, such as fever or sepsis – provided them with sustained healthy hospital statistics and ensured a firm moral framework necessary to maintain and attract middle-class subscribers. Despite their claims of low death rates, lying-in hospitals were reputed to be run by ' "raw country boys" and uncouth apothecaries', which added to the perils already inherent in childbirth at this time (Smith, 1979, 34–40).

what you couldn't state in figures, or show to be purchaseable in the cheapest market and saleable in the dearest]   A reference to the empirical science of political economy and its universal laws of supply and demand. The associated science of statistics provided utilitarian political economists with a convenient, quantifiable answer to every socio-economic problem and satisfied the obsession with classification and measurement. The growth of statistical science is exemplified by the number of associated societies set up in the early 1830s: for example, a statistical office was founded at the Board of Trade in 1832, the Royal Statistical Society began in 1833, and Manchester established a statistical society in 1834. In Dickens's article on the Preston strike, he said that 'into the relations between employers and employed . . . there must enter something of feeling and sentiment . . . something which . . . is not exactly stateable in figures; otherwise those relations are wrong and rotten at the core' (*HW* 8.553). This echoes Carlyle's remarks in *Chartism* (1839):

> How is [the labourer] related to his employer; by bonds of friendliness and mutual help; or by hostility, opposition, and chains of mutual necessity alone? . . . The labourer's feelings, his notion of being justly dealt with or unjustly; his wholesome composure, frugality, prosperity . . . how shall figures of arithmetic represent all this? ('Statistics', ch. 2)

For information about Dickens's distrust of statistics and government blue books, see note to book 1, chapter 15, pp. 147–8 (Smith, 1970, 23; Oddie, 1972, 121; Flint, 1987, 2–3).

The words 'or show to be purchaseable in the cheapest market and saleable in the dearest' do not appear in MS or CP. They are in *HW* and in the one-volume edition.

was not, and never should be, world without end, Amen.] From the 'Gloria' in the BCP: 'Glory be to the Father, and to the Son: and to the Holy Ghost; *Answer*. As it was in the beginning, is now, and ever shall be: world without end, Amen.'

No. Coketown did not come out

gold that had stood the fire] Compare Seneca: 'Gold is tried by fire, brave men by affliction' (*De providentia*).

Who belonged to the eighteen denominations? Because, whoever did, the labouring people did not.] The number of religious denominations had increased steadily throughout the first half of the century and continued to do so for the next fifty years: there were 244 registered sects in 1890. The proliferation of sects and the corresponding erection of churches were responses to changing class and political structures brought about by industrialization. Up until 1850, it was assumed by Anglican clergymen and many nonconformists that urban workers only required access to religious worship in order to become church-going Christians, but the findings of the 1851 Census of religious worship in England and Wales, published in 1854, confirmed a high degree of working-class non-attendance among all denominations, and the Census report proposed new approaches to the problem. Significantly, it recognized that the provision of more churches 'must produce comparatively small results' given that the 'absence from religious worship is attributable *mainly* to a genuine repugnance to religion itself'. Despite the building of new churches and chapels 'the masses of the population, careless or opposed, will not frequent them' (Hempton, 1987, 182; BPP 1852–3, Vol. 89.clxi).

Of particular importance was the report's identification of four major causes of working-class infidelity: the maintenance of social divisions (through the pew rent system) within what was perceived by the working population as middle-class religious institutions; the apathy of churches towards the social problems of the poor; a belief that ministers were in part driven by financial self-interest; and the alienation resulting from poor and overcrowded housing conditions. The chief proposal of the report was to bring the gospel to people in 'their own haunts' through '*aggressive* Christian agency' such as the adaptation of rooms in working-class areas for services, and 'street-preaching . . . for the terrible emergency' (clxii).

The success of the experimental ragged churches and dissenting services specifically organized for workers in halls and lecture-rooms was proof 'that multitudes will readily frequent such places, where . . . there is a total absence of all class distinctions, who would never enter the exclusive-looking chapel' (clix) (*BPP* 1852–3, Vol. 89 *Census of Great Britain, 1851. Religious Worship. Report and Tables*; Inglis, 1973, 1–20, 118; Hempton, 1987, 177–96).

there was a native organization in Coketown itself, whose members were to be heard of in the House of Commons every session, indignantly petitioning for acts of parliament that should make these people religious by main force.]   A major part of the Sabbatarian crusade to sanctify Sunday in order to prevent a national decline in Christian observance involved the presentation of numerous petitions to Parliament by Sunday observance organizations. The campaign was led by the Society for Promoting the Due Observance of the Lord's Day, popularly known as the Lord's Day Observance Society (LDOS). Founded in 1831, this middle-class Anglican society became the prominent pressure group for Sabbath legislation. A Sabbatarian bill of 1836 aimed 'to Promote the Better Observance of the Lord's Day' and attempted to prohibit all forms of Sunday travel except for church attendance, impose penalties on those hiring carriages or trading on the Sabbath, suppress Sunday recreations and close all licensed establishments. Opposed to such legislation, Dickens published his pamphlet *Sunday Under Three Heads. As It Is; As Sabbath Bills Would Make It; As It Might Be Made* (1836). The Bill was defeated (see later note to this chapter, p. 88).

From 1850, *HW* published many articles criticizing the LDOS campaign to stop postal collections and deliveries on Sundays, prohibit recreation, labour and trading, prevent the opening of galleries and museums, and promote temperance; see: 'The Sunday Screw' (1.289–92); 'Chips: Sabbath Pariahs' (1.378–9); 'Cheap Pleasures.– A Gossip' (3.201–3); 'Whole Hogs' (3.505–7); 'Sunday Morning' (6.81–4); 'The Bottle of Hay' (9.69); 'Tattyboys Rents' (9.297–304); 'It Is Not Generally Known' (10.49–52); 'Sunday Out' (10.73–7); 'Sunday Tea-Gardens' (10.145–8); 'Bullfrog' (10.333–6); and 'The Great Baby' (12.1–4) (Pope, 1978, 44–71; Wigley, 1980, 34–7, 42–3, 64–6).

Then, came the Teetotal Society, who complained that these same people *would* get drunk]   Dickens frequently castigated the temperance movement for its confusion of personal moral failure with the ills of society, and he criticized its relative indifference to the need for alternative forms of recreation in poor and overcrowded industrial districts. In 'Gin-Shops' (1835) he argued that if 'Temperance Societies would suggest an antidote against hunger, filth, and foul air . . . gin-palaces would be numbered among the things that were' (*SB*). He reiterated these views in a full exposition of temperance misconceptions in 'Demoralisation and Total Abstinence' (*Examiner*, 27 October 1849) and continued his campaign in *HW* (see previous note).

In the history of temperance societies, Preston is notable for being the place where working-class teetotallers first declared the pledge of total abstinence as a prerequisite for membership to the temperance movement – thus distinguishing themselves from the traditional middle-class moderationists who proscribed only excessive drinking. As the teetotal crusade took hold in the towns, the moderates diminished in number, and by the late 1840s teetotalism and temperance were interchangeable terms (Walmsley, 1892, 2, 6; Harrison, 1971, 116–20, 127–46; Shiman, 1988, 9–23).

no inducement, human or Divine (except a medal)] New temperance members advertised their conversion by wearing badges and regalia, and by carrying flags and banners in teetotal processions (Harrison, 1971, 129, 132, 155; Shiman, 1988, 143).

the chemist and druggist . . . showing that when they didn't get drunk, they took opium.] Before the first Pharmacy Act of 1868, opium was freely available over the counter at chemist's shops, chandler's shops and in street-markets. The drug was cheap and came in the form of pills, lozenges, powders, and opium-based syrups for children, but the most popular form with the working class was tincture of opium or laudanum (opium diluted with alcohol or water). Laudanum was used to treat many ailments (headaches, rheumatism, insomnia, colds, coughs, diarrhoea), and to alleviate the symptoms of lethargy, depression and heavy drinking. Thomas De Quincey's revelations in 1821 about Manchester cotton operatives taking opium as a cheap substitute for ale or spirits raised the question of popular opium-eating for stimulant purposes, and the numerous commissions of the 1830s and 1840s into public health and child employment concentrated on the potential moral problems inherent in the drug's 'recreational' use. Attempts to regulate the availability of opium in the 1850s were generally ineffective, and the campaign continued up to the Pharmacy Act of 1868 (*BPP* 1857, 12.13, 32–3, 64; Berridge, 1978, 446–8; Berridge and Edwards, 1981, *passim*). Also see the many articles in *HW*: 'Protected Cradles' (2.108–12); 'Poison Sold Here!' (2.155–7); 'Household Crime' (4.277–81); 'The Wonders of Mincing Lane' (5.273–6); 'An Opium Factory' (6.118–20); 'Opium, chap. i: India' (16.104–8); 'Opium, chap. ii: China' (16.181–5).

Then, came the experienced chaplain of the jail, with more tabular statements . . . showing that the same people *would* resort to low haunts . . . where they heard low singing and saw low dancing . . . a tip-top moral specimen.] A reference to the Rev. John Clay (1796–1858), Chaplain of the Preston House of Correction from 1821. He issued influential annual tabulated prison reports from 1824 until 1857, several of which appeared in the governmental blue book for 1836. In 1851, Clay sent Dickens some of his reports, which, according to Dickens's reply, 'required no other commendation more . . . than [Clay's] own character, experience and earnestness' (*Letters* 6.264–5). However, Clay's report for 1850 included comments similar to those used satirically by Dickens:

> The preponderance of evil over good! – It may be seen in a thousand deposits in the pawn shop for one in the savings bank, in a thousand revellers in drink

and debauchery on a Saturday night – not one of whom attends the worship of God the next day! And this is permitted, – sanctioned; – Mammon and Moloch, – the greed of gain, – 'the lusts of the flesh,' – dancing rooms, singing rooms, beer-houses, and brothels . . . are all doing their appointed work, and no law interposes.

(Clay, 1861, 534)

Giving evidence before a Select Committee on Public Houses and the Sale of Beer in 1853, Clay, a champion of the Temperance Movement, was asked if 'prisoners ascribed their ruin to other places, such as concert-rooms, saloons, and casinos'. He replied: 'The adult prisoners ascribe their ruin to the beerhouses and public-houses; the young ones . . . to the concert-room and dancing-room' (*BPP* 1852–3, 37.369).

Clay's decision to send his reports to Dickens may have been influenced by Dickens's views on the 'separate system' which he had witnessed in the Eastern Penitentiary near Philadelphia in 1842 and later criticized when it was introduced experimentally at Pentonville Prison (see *AN* (7) and 'Pet Prisoners', *HW* 1.97–103). Clay wrote to a friend in 1854: 'I see that Mr. Dickens, in *Hard Times*, has a laugh at my "tabular statements," and also at my credulity. He is not the only man I have met with who prefers to rely on his own theories and fancies rather than on well ascertained facts' (Clay, 1861, 620). Clay is mentioned sometimes favourably and sometimes critically in several *HW* articles: 'Lambs to be Fed' (3.544–9); 'It Is Not Generally Known' (10.49–52); and 'The Great Baby' (12.1–4).

bought fresh butter] The cheap alternative to fresh butter was 'firkin' butter, that is, butter put into small half-hundredweight casks with added salt (Dodd, 1856, 302–3). A *HW* article claimed that England produced 'the best butter in the world. . . . We eat all we make, and then look round for more – for the best we can get' ('Butter', 6.345).

Mocha coffee] Because of the high import duty on coffee, the working class drank a mixture of coffee and duty-free chicory. Moreover, with coffee at 1s 4d per pound and chicory at 4d, fraudulent grocers frequently added undeclared amounts of chicory and other ingredients such as roasted corn, potato-flour, beans and burnt sugar to pure coffee (Dodd, 1856, 418–19).

the old nursery fable]

> There was an old woman, and what do you think?
> She lived upon nothing but victuals and drink:
> Victuals and drink were the chief of her diet,
> And yet this old woman could never keep quiet.
>
> She went to the baker, to buy her some bread,
> And when she came home, her old husband was dead;
> She went to the clerk to toll the bell,
> And when she came back her old husband was well. (Opie 430)

Is it possible, I wonder, that there

That there was any Fancy in them demanding to be brought into healthy existence . . . some relaxation . . . some recognized holiday . . . which craving must and would be satisfied aright, or must and would inevitably go wrong] Pre-industrial, cyclical and community-based recreations had no place in an urban environment where industrialists considered working-class leisure unproductive, economically wasteful, and potentially dangerous to social order and morality. The regulation of factory workers' time, the scarcity of available open spaces for entertainments, and the disappearance of recognized holidays in the working year forced the work-weary to find relief in gambling and excess drinking. In 1854, English workers could expect two national holidays a year – Christmas Day and Good Friday. Notwithstanding the extension of free time – especially the 'short Saturday' introduced by the Ten Hours Act of 1847 – for many workers a holiday of more than a day was rare. This was considered 'a national misfortune' in a *HW* article of 1853 ('Holiday Times', 7.329–32), and a later article stated that 'Sunday in England must perforce be taken as a holiday, as we have scarcely any other holidays during the long year' ('Sunday Out', 10.73).

Dickens's early fiction attests to his belief that amusements are a necessary and functional part of people's lives (see, for example, *SB*, *PP*, *NN* and *OCS*), and after 1850 he often articulated these views in *HW* and *AYR*: see 'A Preliminary Word' (*HW* 1.1–2) and 'The Amusements of the People' (*HW* 1.13–15, 57–60).

Regular theatre visits by factory operatives were commonplace after 1853, especially on Saturday nights, although the theatres stayed open most nights during the week. While, in the northern theatres, drama, variety shows and the occasional large circus were enjoyed by all social classes, many factory workers in the cotton-towns of Lancashire resorted to the public houses which, by the 1850s, provided variety acts, bands and space for dancing. In the 1850s and 1860s, the larger entrepreneurial public houses extended and added music-halls. Less adventurous entertainments existed in smaller pubs – such as the 'Free and Easies', which included some piano-playing and singing, and were popular from the 1840s onwards. For workers under 25, the singing-saloons (which ranged in quality and reputation) were regular meeting-places.

Some of the dubious amusements that competed with the musical entertainments included Chalk Farm fair, held at Easter and Whitsuntide, which attracted a 'fighting, screeching, yelling, blaspheming crowd', and fairs held outside a prison during a public hanging. Other 'corrupting influences' included betting shops, horse races and prize-fights ('Open-Air Entertainments', *HW* 5.165–9; 'Betting Shops', *HW* 5.333–6; 'The Sporting World', *HW* 6.133–9; 'Piping Days', *HW* 10.197; Smith, 1970, 38, 69–73, 104–5, 158; Malcolmson, 1973, 15; Bailey, 1978, 3–4, 14, 81; Walvin, 1978, 9; Hopkins, 1979, 29; *Letters* 5.644–5, 651–4).

The words 'That there was any Fancy in them demanding to be brought into healthy existence instead of struggling on in convulsions?' and 'some relaxation, encouraging good humour and good spirits, and giving them a vent – some holiday, though it were but for an honest dance to a stirring band of music' were added on CP. In *HW*, after 'some', Dickens added 'recognised'.

'This man lives at Pod's End

Pod's End]   A humorous allusion to the cotton pod, which protects the fragile fibres inside until the cotton is ready to be picked.

'Gin,' said Mr Bounderby.

Gin]   Gin was a mainly lower-class drink obtainable for a penny a glass at establishments variously called 'gin palaces', 'gin-shops' or 'ginneries'. For the poor, the brightly decorated 'palaces' were inviting havens from their dark and miserable homes. Dickens observed in *SB* that, although gin-shops 'are to be met with in every second street, they are invariably numerous and splendid in precise proportion to the dirt and poverty of the surrounding neighbourhood' ('Gin-Shops').

'Dear, no sir! It's the nine oils.'

It's the nine oils.']   A veterinary medicine for horses, nine oils was used by circus performers as a surgical dressing because they considered it the most effective treatment for bruises. The ingredients are: 'Train oil 23 lb., oil of turpentine 6 lb., oil of bricks 1 lb., oil of amber 1 lb., spirit of camphor 2 lb., Barbadoes tar 7 lb., oil of vitriol 2 oz' (Henry Beasley, *Druggists General Receipt Book*, 4th edn, 1857, 86). Although nine oils was essentially an embrocation for animals, a chemist's label from around 1830 confirms its general application for humans (see Plate 9). (Correspondence with the Museum of the Royal Pharmaceutical Society of Great Britain.)

'It's what our people always use

'They bruise themselves very bad sometimes.']   Bruises and falls were a daily part of circus life, and more serious injuries were not unknown. Wallett relates a first night with Holloway's Amphitheatre, Sheffield, in which a 'twelve-horse entree' went disastrously awry when 'five of the twelve riders were *hors de combat*. Two of the clowns were much hurt, one having three fingers broken.' He later recalls another incident in the 1840s at Batty's circus in Manchester when a rider fell off his horse, dislocating his shoulder. Wallett's opinion was that 'as a rule clowns, acrobats, gymnasts, and the like are bad riders' (1870, 29–30, 70).

THE FAMOUS NINE OILS

Discovered by the Franciscan Monks

Cures Rheumatics, Sprains, Bruises, Lumbago and Neuralgic Pains

DIRECTIONS: Rub the liniment well into the parts affected two or three times a day, previously taking the bath

9 Details of 'the famous nine oils' from a nineteenth-century chemist's label (Museum of the Royal Pharmaceutical Society of Great Britain)

Book 1, Chapter 6   Third weekly part
                                     Saturday, 15 April 1854

SLEARY'S HORSEMANSHIP

The name of the public house

The name of the public house] A cancelled fragment on the verso of a folio of the MS reads: 'The name of the public house was The First and Last, implying that'. The allusion means that this particular public house is the first one seen going into the town and the last one on the way out. See also Revelation 1.11: 'I am Alpha and Omega, the first and the last'.

the Pegasus's Arms] The description of this tavern seems to be based on several actual taverns. The Grey Horse and Seven Stars was an old Preston pub in Fishergate, only a few yards from the Bull Inn and Royal Hotel in Church Street, where Dickens stayed during his visit to the town in January 1854. The tavern's original name, the White Horse, was changed because the smoke and soot of factory chimneys had turned grey the inn's statue of a horse. Part of the description of the Pegasus's Arms might derive from Sala's account of a 'theatrical "public"' and its thespian characters in *HW* 5.229–30 (see notes to book 1, chapter 3, p. 62). During the early composition of *DC* in 1849, Dickens invited Mark Lemon to visit a similar establishment by the Thames where 'performing dogs go at night. I think the travestie may be useful to me, and I may make something out of such an expedition' (*Letters* 7.895).

'Pegasus' was a familiar name in the circus world. Andrew Ducrow, the most celebrated of all the circus equestrians, had a horse called Pegasus, and the name was used generically to describe any accomplished steed. When the Royal Circus, Blackfriars Road, London, first opened in 1782, the exterior sported on its roof a statue of a winged Pegasus – only a slight deviation from Astley's horse and rider atop his partially covered arena at Westminster Bridge Road (Speaight, 1980, 35; Sartin, 1988, 40, 49). Pegasus is the winged horse of Greek mythology who caused the fountain Hippocrene to spring forth on Mount Helicon, the home of the Muses, and so release the waters of poetic inspiration.

The Pegasus's legs might have been more to the purpose; but, underneath the winged horse upon the sign-board, the Pegasus's Arms was inscribed in Roman letters. Beneath that inscription again . . . the painter had touched off the lines:] The practice of identifying houses by signboards goes back to ancient Rome, where many streets acquired their names from signs. Taverns, too, had their own symbol (the bush), and stories were painted on the inns to serve as exterior decoration. At a later date, Roman craftsmen used the insignia of their particular trade to identify their houses. In England, in the Middle Ages, local coats of arms or crests were added to signboards over doors and inns to attract business, and painted verses were common. The verse beneath the inscription of the

Pegasus's Arms comes from a signboard of the Malt Shovel Inn, High Street, Chatham, Kent, only a short distance from the house where Dickens's parents lived from 1817 to 1821 (Larwood and Hotten, 1866, passim; Langton, 1883, 203–4; Gadd, 1940, 85).

They walked in; and Sissy

The white night-cap, embellished with two peacock's feathers and a pigtail bolt upright] There were as many varieties of clowns' costume as there were clowning acts, and Dickens chooses Jupe's pieces of costume carefully to suggest a specific blend of dress consonant with the clown's position in Sleary's circus. Jupe's night-cap is suggestive of the court fool's 'tasselled cap' worn by Wallett. The clown's pigtail comes from the old mummers' plays which formed one of the main entertainments of rural communities up until the twentieth century. The stock character of the plays was a drunken dupe who evoked ribaldry and abuse (as does Jupe). An engraving in the *Illustrated London News* of 1853 shows the clown Tom Barry at Drury Lane Theatre sporting an erect pigtail at the back of his head (Plate 4). Peacock feathers were used decoratively or as a prop in the act (balancing a peacock's feather was a common trick in a clown's repertoire) (*Illustrated London News*, 23.460; Disher, 1925, 189; Craig (ed.), 1969, 322; Speaight, 1980, 94, 92).

'Father must have gone down

the Booth] Sissy means the circus, but the term also applied to a covered stall at a market or a fair. George Sala refers to strollers at 'Dumbledowndeary' erecting a booth on a suitable patch of grass (*HW* 9.376).

Before Mr Bounderby could reply

Newmarket coat] Originally a double-breasted riding-jacket, taking its name from the Newmarket race-course, this long, close-fitting tail-coat, cut away above the waist, was the precursor of the morning-coat (*OED*). Although the Newmarket coat seems to be Childers's usual outdoor dress, what became known as 'jockey acts' developed from equestrians performing in jockeys' costumes. Andrew Ducrow presented an early riding spectacular in 1824 called 'Le Jockeis anglais, aux courses de Newmarket', and in 1843 the famous French equestrian Tourniaire appeared as the 'English Jockey' for one of his horse acts (Saxon, 1978, 123; Speaight, 1980, 55, 59).

smelt of lamp-oil, straw, orange-peel, horses' provender, and sawdust] Up until the late 1860s, circuses used either candles or gaslight for illumination, and tenting companies used naphtha-flare lamps – a dangerous but effective practice which involved the dripping of oil over a hot burner. Eating fruit – especially oranges – at the theatre or circus was standard practice, particularly among the 'half-pricers' who filled the ring during the stage-plays. Disher entitled the first part of the opening chapter of his *Greatest Show on Earth* 'Romance Scented with Oranges'. His nostalgic account involves all the senses, including 'that smell. Stables were in it with a whiff of ammonia exuded by lions; and many oranges. All the sights and sounds together were not as exciting as that smell' (1937, 4). Also note the description in 'Town and Country Circus Life': 'there is always uppermost a strong perfume of damp sawdust, wet litter, and horse-breath, with a faint indication of bad drainage and other horrors' (AYR 6.182) (Speaight, 1980, 45–6).

a most remarkable sort of Centaur, compounded of the stable and the playhouse.] Childers's appearance epitomizes the dual nature of the circus at this time. Stage entertainments such as burlettas, melodramas and pantomimes, as well as displays of horsemanship in the ring, were staple attractions in any one programme. This distinctive blend gave rise to many travelling circuses performing in local theatres throughout the country, some of which were adapted in order to suit the performances (Saxon 19, 21).

Mr E. W. B. Childers] The name given to this equestrian and *voltigeur* would have produced some laughter from Dickens's contemporary readers. A horse called 'The Flying Childers' had been billed to appear at Astley's during the seasons of 1853 and 1854. The name had been given to the first great thoroughbred racehorse, bred in 1715, by a Colonel Leonard Childers of Doncaster. 'Childers' thus became synonymous with excellence, speed and pedigree, even giving its name to an inn at Melton Mowbray in the nineteenth century (Larwood and Hotten, 1866, 175; Longrigg, 1972, 55).

his daring vaulting act as the Wild Huntsman of the North American Prairies] The performance described is a combination of two famous acts – 'The Wild Indian Hunter', a pantomime on horseback also called 'Le Chasseur Indien' (Plate 10), and 'Le Bouquet de l'Amour, ou Les Jeux de Zéphyre et de Cupidon', otherwise known as 'Cupid and Zephyr'. Both acts were devised by Andrew Ducrow some time between 1818 and 1824 while he was performing in France; and, like the majority of his equestrian productions, they were imitated by many circus companies for decades afterwards. Dickens's mixture of the adventurous West and the mythical world – with Master Kidderminster magically changing from a huntsman's son into a cherub-like Cupid – can be substantiated in fact. An equestrian scene in 1828 depicted a brave but compassionate Indian chief who finished the sketch with his 'grand attitudes' – a representation of 'The Flying Mercury' (Schlicke, 1988, 158–9). Similar acts were billed from July to December 1853. During the weeks of 18 July and 5 December, for example, 'The Indian of the Far West or the Wild Horse of the Prairie' was performed at Astley's, and the American equestrian Eaton Stone was giving his interpretation of the act at Drury Lane Theatre in October. Appearing at Astley's between 10 September and 10 December was a burlesque entitled 'Jupiter's Decree and the Fall of Phaeton' (*Illustrated London News* 23.366; Saxon, 1978, passim).

a diminutive boy with an old face] The heyday for child performers was the early part of the nineteenth century, when numerous 'infant' acts appeared. Saxon lists

10 Andrew Ducrow as 'The Wild Indian Hunter'. From M. Willson Disher, *Greatest Show on Earth* (London: G. Bell, 1937)

some titles encountered around the first decade of the century, names which were used repeatedly for different performers: 'Infant Prodigy', 'Infant Hero', 'Infant Rossignol', 'Infant Phenomenon', 'Infant of Hope', 'Infant Equestrian', 'Infant Hercules', 'Child of Promise'. Many 'infants' assumed these roles well into their teenage years. Crummles's daughter, Ninetta, another 'infant phenomenon' (based on the child actress Jean Margaret Davenport), is claimed by her father to be 10 years old but 'had moreover been precisely the same age . . . certainly for five good years' (*NN* 23). A number of such children were still in evidence in the mid-century and beyond, appearing in equestrian melodramas such as the one Sleary describes in book 3 chapter 7, 'The Children in the Wood'. An 'Infant Phenomenon' is mentioned in a *HW* article of 1851 written by Dickens. Moreover, in his letters Dickens recurrently refers to the newest baby in his own household as 'the Infant Phenomenon' ('Our Watering Place', *HW* 3.433; Saxon, 1978, 25).

white bismuth, and carmine]   Bismuth is a tin-white metal used chemically in the arts and in medicine. Carmine is a red or purplish-red pigment found in cochineal. Both substances were used as cosmetics (*OED*).

of the Turf, turfy.]   'The first man is of the earth, earthy: the second man is the Lord from heaven' (1 Corinthians 15.47).

'You see, my friend,' Mr Bounderby put in

you are the kind of people who don't know the value of time.']   The Victorian emphasis on 'time thrift' – a notion central to a manufacturing and mercantilist economic base – had its antecedents in the Puritan–Calvinistic ethos of the sixteenth century. The doctrines of predestination and individual election made time a precious commodity to be used wisely and productively for the glory of God. Idleness in any form – especially popular amusements – was considered a profligate waste of time. The coupling of nascent capitalism and Calvinist morality was the spur which served to control time and reshape workers' lives. The harnessing of labour insisted on the ownership of time:

> Those who are employed experience a distinction between their employer's time and their "own" time. And the employer must *use* the time of his labour, and see it is not wasted: not the task but the value of time when reduced to money is dominant. Time is now currency: it is not passed but spent. (Thompson, 1967, 61)

It is no coincidence that Josiah Wedgwood, during the reorganization of his Etruria pottery works in 1780, drew up plans for a basic clocking-in system to promote punctuality and efficiency (McKendrick, 1961, 41–2; Buckley, 1966, 5–9; Thompson, 1967, 56–97; Hobsbawn, 1968, 66–7; Brailsford, 1991, 17–20, 48–50).

'*Kidderminster, stow that!*'

'Kidderminster] There is an obvious pun alluding to Kidderminster's age. Moreover, William Wallett, the Shakespearian jester, had built a permanent circus at Kidderminster, Worcestershire, in the mid-nineteenth century. Perhaps a more subtle allusion is being made to a famous ringmaster at Astley's, John Esdaile Widdicombe (1787–1854), who was the epitome of sartorial elegance and seemingly perpetual youth. Although unnamed in 'Astley's' (*SB*), Widdicombe would seem to have been the model there for the ringmaster with 'his polished boots, his graceful demeanour . . . and the splendid head of black hair' (107).

'*Offered at the Garters four times*

'Offered at the Garters. . . . Missed his tip at the banners . . . and was loose in his ponging.'] Garters (narrow bands) and banners (bordered cloths held horizontally) are jumped across by an equestrian (Plate 4). If a performer fails to do this, he has 'missed his tip'. The expression 'loose in his ponging', according to Childers, means 'bad in his tumbling', although 'ponging' could apply to any aspect of the performance, since 'pong' is circus slang meaning 'to perform'. 'Ponging' can also be defined as 'talking'. Dickens would have picked up pieces of circus slang from the early 1830s onwards, but on 20 February 1854 he asked Mark Lemon to

> note down and send me any slang terms among the tumblers and circus-people, that you can call to mind? I have noted down some – I want them in my new story – but it is very probable that you will recall several which I have not got. (*Letters* 7.279)

For all slang terms used in *HT*, see Appendix B, pp. 237–40.

'*We'd have had a young gentleman*

bespeak] Also called a 'ben'. A theatrical word for a benefit performance in which the money would be kept by the actor or circus performer (Hotten).

'*Ay! I mean,' said Mr Childers*

goosed] Hissed at by the audience. According to Hotten, continued 'goosing' 'generally end[ed] . . . in the play or the players being "damned" ' (60).

'*His joints are turning stiff*

Cackler] Or a 'cackling-cove' (Hotten): an actor or performer who has a speaking part. Childers's criticism about earning one's living as a 'cackler' was a view shared by many, both within the circus fraternity and among the audiences of the day. Shakespearian jesters like Wallett presented the audience with recitations and wordy Shakespearian addresses and speeches – an act which for a circus could be boring, hence the need for performers to be all-rounders (see Frost, 1875, 185; Disher, 1937, 209).

'Very well,' said Bounderby.

Dick Jones of Wapping] Wapping, in Stepney, East London, is a dockland area which Dickens had visited since childhood. In *DS* Captain Cuttle's lodgings are in this area (9), and it is a crucial backdrop to the action in *OMF*.

'Jupe sent his daughter out on an errand

a bundle tied up in a handkerchief] MS reads 'belcher handkerchief', which became in CP '<dark> handkerchief'. The handkerchief referred to was a large cheap cotton neckerchief worn exclusively by men of the lower classes. The belcher (normally blue with white spots) was named after the famous pugilist Jim Belcher (1781–1811). Bill Sikes wears a grubby belcher handkerchief round his neck (*OT* 13).

'Because those two were one.

those two were one. Because they were never asunder.] 'Those whom God hath joined together let no man put asunder' (Solemnization of Matrimony, *BCP*).

with their legs wider apart than the general run of men, and with a very knowing assumption of being stiff in the knees. This walk . . . was understood to express, that they were always on horseback.] Sala's 'Legs', the concluding article of the *HW* number in which this chapter of *HT* appeared, deals exclusively with the many neglected aspects of these limbs – in their practical use, in fashion and in the definition of character:

> There are as infinite varieties of expression in legs as in faces, and I wait with impatience for the day when some learned man shall give to the world an elaborate commentary on all the legs he has met with: the long and the short, the thick and the thin, the bandy and the bow, the in-kneed and the out-toed.
> We are told that we can tell a man by the company he keeps; why not by the legs that take him into that company? (9.212)

'I never apprenticed? I was apprenticed

I was apprenticed when I was seven year old.']   Childers's apprenticeship is late by all accounts. 'Peter Paterson' states that

> The artists of the Circus, in most instances, fulfil a long bondage of gratuitous labour – fourteen years generally, and in some cases twenty-one. Their fathers and mothers being in "the profession" before them, they commence their studies at perhaps two years of age.
> ('Town and Country Circus Life', AYR 6.184)

Andrew Ducrow appeared as an 'Infant Wonder' from the age of 3, and his second wife, Louisa Woolford, was billed at the age of 9 as 'the greatest Wonder of the present Age', having spent her early childhood on stilts, on the tight rope, and acquiring equestrian skills. Circus apprenticeships were, however, informal procedures which remained non-contractual. Apprenticing in both trades and professions was a legally binding practice with all 'trainees' formally indentured. Hence the implication of Gradgrind's comment which prompts Childers's speedy retort. Early apprenticeships and the itinerant nature of circus life left many performers uneducated, hence Jupe's wish for Sissy not to be apprenticed and to receive some formal education. See also the note about child performers, this chapter, pp. 93–5 (Speaight, 1980, 48; Saxon, 1978, 154).

'When Sissy got into the school

as pleased as Punch.]   In the 'Punch and Judy' puppet-show, Punch is always singing or smiling with self-satisfaction.

Meanwhile, the various members of Sleary's company

The father of one of the families was in the habit of balancing the father of another of the families on the top of a great pole]   This act was gaining popularity in the middle of the nineteenth century and was known as 'à la Perche' (Plate 11). The performer balances a pole 24–40 feet in length either on his shoulder or from a pouch attached to a belt around the waist or forehead. Another acrobat climbs up the pole and does head stands and other balancing tricks from the top. A variation of the perch act involves a 'break-away' ladder balanced on the sole of a recumbent performer's foot.

Circus historians are unable to determine the date of the first performance of the perch act, but the acrobat Lavater Lee had incorporated it in his repertoire in 1849. Dickens may have seen it performed by the 'Brothers Siegrist' at Astley's in October 1852 (Plate 5) or at the Drury Lane Theatre in early 1853. Three London circuses had presented the act throughout that year (Theatre Museum, London; Speaight, 1980, 69).

Two varieties of the perch act, one with a break-away ladder.

11 The perch act. From Hughes Le Roux and Jules Garnier, *Acrobats and Mountebanks* (London: Chapman & Hall, 1890)

the father of a third family often made a pyramid of both those fathers] The 'Egyptian Pyramids' or 'La Force d'Hercule' was one of Philip Astley's early acts and obviously one of his favourites – he called his house Hercules Hall.

all the fathers could dance upon rolling casks, stand upon bottles, catch knives and balls, twirl hand-basins, ride upon anything, jump over everything, and stick at nothing. All the mothers could (and did) dance . . . and perform rapid acts on bare-backed steeds] The balancing acts Dickens describes were perfected in the 1830s by a French clown-acrobat, Jean-Baptiste Auriol (Plate 12). According to Disher: 'He would dive through fireworks . . . march, drill, and fire his musket while balancing on the tops of a dozen wine bottles' (1937, 173). 'Licensed to Juggle' (*HW* 7 [20 August 1853] 593–4) may also have influenced Dickens's choice of juggling acts. The article relates the fortunes of an ex-London street-performer who does tolerably well on the Champs Élysées in Paris. His previous accomplishments in London were 'to balance a scaffold pole upon his chin, to whizz a slop-basin round upon the end of it, and to imitate fire-works with golden balls and gleaming knives' (593).

none of them were at all particular in respect of showing their legs] The implication that the mothers were relatively lacking in modesty is supported by Sala:

> Legs have fallen to the province of mountebanks, tight-rope dancers, acrobats, and ballet girls. From neglect they have even fallen into opprobrium; and we cannot find a baser term for a swindling gambler than to call him a "Leg". (*HW* 9.210)

Le Roux informs his readers that

> a well-to-do manager, who thinks of marrying his daughter in the *bourgeoisie* – or even in the aristocracy – hesitates to exhibit the young girl in the seminudity of tights. He is afraid of alarming the future husband. . . . Apparently, in a circus, a woman's virtue is in inverse proportion to the length of her skirts; the riding habit is suspected, whilst muslin petticoats soar above all scandalous aspersions. (173, 175)

and one of them, alone in a Greek chariot, drove six in hand into every town they came to.]

> The "parade", or grand entrée, which always takes place in each town, is the cause of what may be called "a profound sensation," especially if the day be a genial one. Then the company shine out resplendent in tinsel and gold, and spangles and feathers, and glass and zinc diamonds. There are, besides, crowns and tiaras, and rich silk and satin dresses. In the grand entrée, as it is called, all is couleur de rose; private woes or sorrows, general to the company, are hidden for the moment, and on blood chargers, curveting and prancing, decorated with magnificent trappings, may be seen the more prominent heroes and heroines of the heathen mythology. The parade may be described as the per-

12 The 'Prince of Clowns', Jean-Baptiste Auriol, at Vauxhall Gardens.
From the *Ilustrated London News*, 9 June 1849

oration advertisement, which puts the keystone on the gaudy bills that have hitherto served to whet curiosity.

('Town and Country Circus Life', AYR 6.185)

They all assumed to be mighty rakish and knowing, they were not very tidy in their private dresses] This echoes Dickens's remarks in 'Astley's' about the performers off-stage having

> an indescribable public-house-parlour swagger, and a kind of conscious air, peculiar to people of this description. They always seem to think they are exhibiting; the lamps are ever before them. That young fellow in the faded brown coat, and very full light green trousers, pulls down the wristbands of his check shirt, as ostentatiously as if it were of the finest linen, and cocks the white hat of the summer-before-last as knowingly over his right eye, as if it were a purchase of yesterday. (SB 108–9)

There were, however, 'tip-toppers' in the profession – performers who could earn £50 or £60 a week, or ones who had achieved success overseas. They dressed somewhat differently from men 'of lower grade': 'you may meet one wearing a sealskin coat, unbuttoned, and displaying beneath a crimson velvet vest, crossed by a heavy chain' (Frost, 1875, 284).

the combined literature of the whole company would have produced but a poor letter on any subject. Yet there was a remarkable gentleness and childishness about these people . . . deserving . . . of as much respect . . . as the every-day virtues of any class of people in the world.]

> They are, as a class, a light-hearted set, not remarkable for providence, but bearing the vicissitudes of fortune to which they are so liable with tolerable equanimity, showing a laudable desire to alleviate each other's failings, without exhibiting a greater tendency to vice than any other class. There is not much education among them, as I have before indicated, and they are not much addicted to literature of any kind. This seems to arise, not from any deficiency of natural aptitude for learning, but from their wandering lives and the early age at which they begin to practise the feats by which they are to be enabled to live. (Frost, 1875, 286)

Last of all appeared Mr Sleary

Mr Sleary: a stout man as already mentioned, with one fixed eye and one loose eye, a voice (if it can be called so) like the efforts of a broken old pair of bellows, a flabby surface, and a muddled head which was never sober and never drunk.] Sleary bears a close resemblance to Jack Clarke, whose family became a household name in the circus of the nineteenth century. A noted equestrian from 1815 and a proprietor of his own circus by 1825, Clarke travelled with his company around the eastern, southern and western counties of England and was to be found at all the London fairs up until 1840. Charles Montague confirms that Clarke, like Sleary, had a 'gruff asthmatic voice', and in his *Recollections* Montague relates a conversation he had with Clarke:

> 'I've jutht given three performanthes in Reading, and lortht nearly two hundred poundth by them. It'th a fact, thir. . . . I made my calculathonth that the firtht evening'th performanth would produth a hundred poundth, and the nectht two nightth we thood take at leatht fifty poundth a night; that'th two hundred poundth in all, thir. Well, you'd thearthely believe it, thir, but we only took twenty-thickth!' (1881, 90–1)

Also incorporated into Sleary's characterization is Clarke's mixture of generosity and quick temper – Clarke 'would shout at his audience and brandish a stick at them if they misbehaved, and the boys delighted in teasing him'. Although Wallett's memory of Clarke was of 'a man of violent passions' who 'indulged in the strongest expletives', his more beneficent qualities caused him to be remembered with affection and warmth (Speaight, 1980, 48; Wallett, 1870, 64). The links between Crummles, the theatrical manager in *NN*, and Sleary are also evident (22, 30).

one fixed eye and one loose eye] Dickens has used this description before in his fiction. Newman Noggs has 'two goggle eyes whereof one was a fixture'; Zephaniah Scadder's '[t]wo gray eyes lurked deep within this agent's head, but one of them had no sight in it, and stood stock still'; and Captain Bunsby has 'one stationary eye in the mahogany face, and one revolving one, on the principle of some lighthouses' (*NN* 2; *MC* 9, 21; *DS* 23). Dickens may have had in mind *Hamlet* 1.2.11: 'With an auspicious and a dropping eye'.

'What thall it be, Thquire

Thall it be Therry?] Sleary's sherry may have been one of the many imitation sherries, or 'horrible mixings': 'cheap London sherries. . . . very "curious" indeed – mere doctors' draughts, in fact, made up according to certain swindling prescriptions' ('Sherry', *HW* 18.511; see also Dodd, 1856, 482–7; Jeffs, 1961, passim; Freeman, 1989, 104, 101–2).

'Don't thay nothing, Thquire.

glath of bitterth.'] Bitters are alcoholic liquors impregnated with the extract of gentian, quassia, wormwood, orange-peel, etc., and used as stomachics or anthelmintics (*OED*). According to 'The Chemistry of a Pint of Beer', 'Wormwood, quassia, and other bitters, may . . . be employed in lieu of hops, without poisoning the consumer' (*HW* 2.498–502; see also 'Constitutional Trials', *HW* 5.423–6).

Here his daughter Josephine

her dying desire to be drawn to the grave by the two piebald ponies] Such a funeral request had been made by the Astley clown John Ducrow (brother of Andrew). When he died in 1834, his hearse was led to the graveyard of Old Lambeth Church, London, by his two favourite performing ponies (Disher, 1937, 116).

'At the thame time,' said Sleary,

Emma Gordon, in whothe lap you're a lyin' at prethent, would be a mother to you, and Joth'phine would be a thithter to you.] Wilkie Collins's unsuccessful novel, *Hide and Seek; or, The Mystery of Mary Grice*, started in January 1853 and published in June 1854, concerns the search for the parentage of an illegitimate deaf mute called Mary, better-known as Madonna. As part of the unravelling of the heroine's mysterious history, book 1, chapter 3, of the novel (written in 1853) describes Madonna's childhood experiences in a travelling circus where she has been brought up by acrobats and animal trainers. It has been suggested that Dickens modified the story and used it as a model for Sissy's early life, and that *HT* is 'the earliest of Dickens's works that shows any borrowing from Wilkie'. On 22 July 1854, Dickens told his sister-in-law, Georgina Hogarth, that he thought *Hide and Seek* was 'the cleverest Novel [he had] ever seen written by a new hand' and called it 'a very remarkable book'. Collins dedicated his novel to Dickens (*Letters* 7.376, 335; Davis, 1956, 153).

'Good-bye, my dear!'

I with your father hadn't taken hith dog with him; ith a ill-conwenienth to have the dog out of the billth. But on thecond thoughts, he wouldn't have performed without hith mathter] Highly trained dogs could attract large audiences, but success was also dependent on the strong attachment formed between animal and trainer. Le Roux relates the tragic death of a little mongrel 'dog-clown' who had broken its back during a performance: months later, its master 'still wept when he mentioned the poor clown, whom he had cherished with human friendship' (114).

Book 1, Chapter 7   Fourth weekly part
Saturday, 22 April 1854

MRS SPARSIT

MR BOUNDERBY being a bachelor

Mr Bounderby's car] Dickens's chapter plan included 'Bound', 'Bounder' and 'Bounderby'. A 'bounder' in the 1850s was a four-wheeled cab or trap. The modern definition of 'bounder' as a cad or an objectionable person did not gain currency until around 1889 (*OED*).

For, Mrs Sparsit had not only seen different days

Mrs Sparsit had not only seen different days, but was highly connected.] Compare *As You Like It* (2.7.120): 'True is it that we have seen better days'. Dickens's repeated mocking references to Mrs Sparsit's aristocratic pretensions allude to the prevalent middle-class obsession with genealogy at this time. From the beginning of the nineteenth century, growing public interest in family pedigree as a definition of social and political status was cultivated by such publications as John Debrett's *Peerage* (1802), which went through fifteen editions, and Burke's *Peerage* (1826), published annually from 1847. For ordinary people, the ability to trace ancestral stock was facilitated by the establishment of the Public Record Office in 1838. However, the irresistible attraction of aristocratic lineage gave rise to a thriving market in so-called genuine heraldic arms and impressive but spurious family genealogies (personal correspondence with Nancy Metz).
    Although Dickens frequently satirized those who claimed social status through what were in many cases dubious ancestral lines – see, for example: the story of 'The Baron of Grogzwig', in *NN* (6); the 'ancient origin' of the Chuzzlewit family related in *MC* (1); and the pride in her Welsh genealogy displayed by Mrs Woodcourt in *BH* (17) – Dickens himself used an unauthorized family crest which he claimed was his father's: 'a lion couchant, bearing in his dexter paw a Maltese cross. I have never adopted any motto, being quite indifferent to such ceremonies' (5 April 1869, *Nonesuch* 3.717; see also *Letters* 2.139–40; Cotsell, 1986, 27).

Hebrew monetary transactions] A euphemism for cash borrowed from Jewish money-lenders at high interest rates. Traditionally, Jews had the monopoly of the money-lending business from early Christian times, when the practice was considered sinful. Henceforth, Jewish money-lenders in general acquired an unwholesome reputation which was still prevalent in the nineteenth century.

Insolvent Debtors Court] The Court for the Relief of Insolvent Debtors dealt with the affairs of insolvent non-traders, before it was abolished in 1861. Prior to that date, only traders could declare themselves bankrupt and so benefit from the bankruptcy laws. Insolvent individuals faced imprisonment for debt since 'it was open to any creditor to imprison his judgment debtor and keep him in prison till his debt was paid' (Holdsworth 13.377). This practice was abolished by the Debtors Act of 1869. Dickens's many references to the Insolvent Debtors' Court and imprisonment for debt (SB, PP, DC, LD) can be attributed to the experiences of his father, who appeared before the court in 1824 and was then imprisoned for three months in the Marshalsea Debtors' Prison (Yate-Lee and Wace, 1887, 8; Holdsworth, 13. 376–8, 15 (1965), 97–100; Woodward, 1962, 472).

The late Mr Sparsit, being by the mother's side

Calais] Because of its proximity to the coast of England, Calais became a haven for those fleeing from creditors or from the law. Dickens frequently passed through Calais on his way to and from his many visits to the Continent, so he knew the Channel port well. In LD he called it 'a low-spirited place' and described the difficulties of passengers disembarking from a packet steamer on to the pier 'where all the French vagabonds and English outlaws in the town (half the population) attended to prevent their recovery from bewilderment' (2.20). The Veneerings in OMF, after becoming bankrupt, retire to Calais and live off the proceeds of Mrs Veneering's diamonds (4.17). Dickens's mixed feelings about Calais are expressed in 'The Calais Night Mail' (UT).

the Coriolanian style of nose and the dense black eyebrows] This aspect of Mrs Sparsit's classical features alludes to the proud hero of Shakespeare's Roman tragedy *Coriolanus*, and underlines her pseudo-aristocratic snobbery and dislike of the working class. She is later likened to the imperious mother of Coriolanus, Volumnia (book 2, chapter 1), the name given to the aristocratic but impoverished spinster cousin of Sir Leicester Dedlock in BH.

If Bounderby had been a Conqueror

here she is at a hundred a year . . . keeping the house] The most prestigious position for a female domestic was that of housekeeper. According to the size of the household, she supervised the domestic staff, ordered provisions, was responsible for the household linen and china, directed operations in the stillroom and kept accounts. Mrs Sparsit is of the more 'genteel' class of housekeeper, authoritative and dauntingly efficient, and her salary is handsome indeed. The average annual wage for a housekeeper ranged from £20 to £45 (Beeton 8, 22–3; Horn, 1975, 53–7, 76, 184–5).

Nay, he made this foil

They made him out to be the Royal arms, the Union-Jack, Magna Charta, John

Bull, Habeas Corpus, the Bill of Rights, An Englishman's house is his castle, Church and State, and God save the Queen, all put together.] All the things which denote British patriotism, civil rights or the British national character. The Royal Arms are borne by the sovereign of the United Kingdom. Dickens's reference is to the design introduced on the accession of Queen Victoria in 1837: a shield divided into quarters, with the lions of England in the first and last, the lion and tressure of Scotland in the second, and the Irish harp in the third. The Union Jack, the small flag flown by ships, is the national banner of Great Britain and Ireland. Magna Charta (or Carta) is the Great Charter of the liberties of England, extorted in 1215 from King John, under pressure from the barons. John Bull, the nickname for a typical Englishman, derives from a collection of pamphlets, *The History of John Bull* (1712), which advocated the cessation of the war with France. The writ of Habeas Corpus, an old common-law right embodied in the Magna Carta, was enforced by the Habeas Corpus Act of 1679. The main provisions of Habeas Corpus prevent people being imprisoned merely on suspicion and make it illegal to imprison a person for an indefinite time without trial. The Bill of Rights, enacted in 1689, embodied the rights of Parliament and citizens, and restored the monarchy to its constitutional position after the Revolution of 1688. 'A man's house is his castle' is one of the English common-law rules explained and defended in the *Institutes* (1628–44) of the legal author Sir Edward Coke. 'Church and State' most often occurs in the description of the roles of the sovereign: as well as being head of state, the sovereign is also the head of the Anglican Church, which became the Established Church of England under an Act of Parliament in 1532. Finally, 'God save the Queen' is the British national anthem. The words and music are attributed by some to Dr John Bull (d. 1628), and by others to Henry Carey (d.1743).

Bounderby's form of nationalism is reminiscent of Bendigo Buster's misdirected patriotism in 'Mr. Bendigo Buster on our National Defences against Education': 'England, as a nation, don't trouble herself much about the education of the masses; something like forty-five out of a hundred of 'em can't read and write. That's why I'm partial to my country, and shout "Rule Britannia," with a will' (*HW* 2.313).

Princes and Lords may flourish or may fade,/A breath can make them, as a breath has made] From Goldsmith's *The Deserted Village* (1770):

> Far, far away thy children leave the land.
> Ill fares the land, to hastening ills a prey,
> Where wealth accumulates and men decay:
> Princes and lords may flourish, or may fade;
> A breath can make them, as a breath has made. (50–4)

'I'm not going to take him at once

he is to finish his educational cramming before then . . . if he knew how empty of learning *my* young maw was, at his time of life.'] Compare *Measure for Measure* 3.2.20–2: 'Do thou but think/What 'tis to cram a maw or clothe a back/From such a filthy vice'.

At the time when, to have been a tumbler in the mud of the streets, would have been a godsend to me, a prize in the lottery to me, you were at the Italian Opera.] Mayhew records the experiences of a crossing-sweeper who also works as a tumbler at night:

> We're always sure to make money if there's mud – that's to say, if we look for our money and ask; of course, if we stand still we don't. . . . At night-time we tumbles – that is, if the policeman ain't nigh. We goes general to Waterloo-place when the Opera's on. . . . It's no good tumbling to gentlemen *going* to the Opera; it's when they're coming back they gives us money. (2.496)

The Italian Opera was Her Majesty's Theatre in Haymarket. Opened on 9 April 1705 as The Queen's Theatre, it was established as an opera-house in 1711. In 1837 the theatre became known as Her Majesty's Theatre, Italian Opera House, in recognition of Queen Victoria's accession to the throne. It retained the name 'Italian Opera House' until Covent Garden took over the title in 1847. However, Londoners of the 1850s would still have referred to Her Majesty's as the Italian Opera (personal correspondence with George Hoare, archivist, Stoll Moss Archives, Theatre Royal Drury Lane; MacKeith, 1986, 15).

a prize in the lottery] Lotteries were in operation from the sixteenth century until the Government outlawed them in 1826 on account of widespread fraud and illegal side-gambling by lottery contractors. During that time, however, lotteries were used to raise revenue for the construction of Westminster Bridge in 1739 and the British Museum in 1753. The Drury Lane Theatre was showing an 'afterpiece' called 'The Lottery Ticket' in March 1850, and a playbill for Astley's of 29 March 1852 advertised their production of 'The Lottery Ticket' as a 'Laughable Farce' (Playbill Collection, Theatre Museum, London).

a link to light you.'] A hand-held torch or light carried by 'linkboys' to light up the street for pedestrians. This practice became rarer with the introduction of gas lighting, first used on the streets of London in 1807 and found in most major towns and cities by the mid-nineteenth century (Woodward, 1962, 49).

'Egad, ma'am, so was I,' said Bounderby

A hard bed the pavement of its Arcade used to make] The Royal Opera Arcade, which runs from Pall Mall to Charles II Street, opened in 1817 as a covered entrance to the east side of Her Majesty's Theatre. However, the arcade was out of the way from any busy traffic routes or streets, and so the shops inside tended to cater for theatre-goers. Apart from shops now lining both sides of the arcade, the building remains unchanged from the original design by John Nash and George Repton. It is unlikely that Bounderby slept in the arcade since there are gates at either end and these were probably locked at night. For Dickens's description of Burlington Arcade, see 'Arcadian London', *UT* 16 (MacKeith, 1985, 82; 1986, 97–8).

May Fair] A fashionable area of London whose perimeters include Oxford Street, Park Lane, Piccadilly and Regent Street. Its name derives from the annual fair which took place in its Brook Field from 1660 until the end of the eighteenth century, when the fair was suppressed as a public nuisance. Between 1700 and 1750, plans were drawn up to turn the fields of Mayfair into a select area for aristocrats and wealthy gentry, and by 1800 the district had been transformed into the most expensive and desirable residential part of London (Timbs, 1868, 564–5; Piper, 1980, 51).

'I shall have the satisfaction of causing

You will be reclaimed and formed.] Reclamation and the 'formation of habits of firmness and self-restraint' (*Letters* 4.554) were Dickens's primary objectives for the inmates of Urania Cottage, Shepherd's Bush – Angela Burdett Coutts's home for 'fallen' and destitute females. From 1846 until 1854, Dickens was heavily involved in the management of Urania Cottage, establishing a system of re-education and reformation that would prepare the young women for colonization and 'improve them by education and example' (*Letters* 5.208, 178).

'About the Fairies, sir, and the Dwarf

the Dwarf, and the Hunchback, and the Genies,'] All from one of Dickens's favourite storybooks, *The Arabian Nights' Entertainments; or, The Thousand and One Nights*. HW articles about dwarfs, giants, fairy- and ghost-stories, folk-lore, superstitions and comic-books appeared several weeks before and throughout the serialization of HT (see Appendix D). For earlier HW articles which emphasize the necessity of fairy-stories for children, see note to book 1, chapter 3, p. 52.

Book 1, Chapter 8 Fourth weekly part
Saturday, 22 April 1854

NEVER WONDER

Now, besides very many babies

a considerable population of babies] This paternalistic attitude towards the working class was criticized by Margaret Hale in Mrs Gaskell's *North and South* (1854–5): ' "my informant . . . spoke as if the masters would like their hands to be merely tall, large children . . . with a blind unreasoning kind of obedience" ' (1.15).

Body number three, wrote leaden little books for them] Probably Harriet Martineau's *Illustrations of Political Economy*, a series of didactic short stories written between 1832 and 1834 to demonstrate the efficacy of a laissez-faire economic system. Two of the stories deal with industrial conflict – *The Hill and the Valley* (1832) and *A Manchester Strike* (1833). There is an interesting similarity between HT and the latter tale, which tells of a father and his daughter who leave the factory to become professional entertainers. As in HT, the vivacity of the performers' lives is compared to the dreary industrial town (Melada, 1970, 49–58; Smith, 1973, 161; Kovačevič, 1975, 123).

transported] See notes to book 2, chapter 5, p. 185 and p. 186.

There was a library in Coketown

There was a library in Coketown, to which general access was easy. Mr Gradgrind greatly tormented his mind about what the people read in this library: a point whereon little rivers of tabular statements periodically flowed into the howling ocean of tabular statements] Dickens had in mind the Manchester Free Library, opened on 2 September 1852 with Dickens as one of its guest speakers. In his speech, Dickens praised 'this great free school . . . starting upon its glorious career with twenty thousand volumes of books – knowing no sect, no party, no distinction – nothing but the public want and the public good' (*Speeches* 152). For the library's first annual report, the librarian, Edward Edwards, an early pioneer of public libraries, compiled tables for every month of the previous year, showing the various demand for books in each library department. The tabulated report formed the basis of a HW article entitled 'Manchester Men at Their Books' (8.377–9), published five weeks before Dickens started writing HT. The article reported that the reference section and lending library were used by all social classes; however, the lending library was mainly frequented by working men and women. It was also found that each book in the literature section, 'including poetry and fiction, essays, literary history, and encyclopaedias', was read fifteen times on average per annum; books on theology and philosophy, nine times; history and biology books, eight times; scientific works, seven; and every book on law, politics or commerce was read twice a year. The article continued:

> There is a fine earnestness about all this. Then there is something very natural and amusing in the results of the librarian's notes as to the books most in request in each department. The reference library is crowded in the evening by working men; and their great delight and refreshment appears to consist in an escape from routine life to dreams of romance or peril, in relieving the monotony of toil with tales of battle, shipwreck, or adventure. In a word, the imagination, even in Manchester, refuses to be crushed. The pleasure book most read, during the first six months after the library opened, was – the Arabian Nights. The weary warehousemen, mill-hands, and shopkeepers spent their evenings with Haroun al Raschid. The next

best books for them, after the Arabian Nights, appear to have been Ivanhoe, Robinson Crusoe, and the Fortunes and Misfortunes of the Famous Moll Flanders. (8.378)

In the present paragraph, Dickens criticizes those aspects of the library system that help him to make his point. The tabulated library report was Dickens's springboard from which he could, in the novel, make a more general attack upon those who were concerned about working-class reading habits – an invidious concern conditioned by Utilitarian and religious principles.

Before the Public Libraries Act of 1850, which enabled town councils to erect rate-supported libraries, the provision of reading material for the working classes was made chiefly through circulating libraries, book clubs, church-based village libraries, occasional book collections in factories and, initially, mechanics' institute libraries. All had their shortcomings. The libraries of the mechanics' institutes soon reflected their Utilitarian and middle-class bias, imparting to workers useful but selective knowledge, especially that which concerned machines and industrial processes.

It was from 1840 that Dickens became involved with mechanics' institutes, raising funds for them through his public readings and speeches (for his favourable views about the libraries of the Manchester Athenaeum, and the mechanics' institutions in Liverpool and Leeds, see *Speeches* 46, 54, 83). He was an ardent advocate of their aims but could see that their original purpose – to act 'as secondary schools for adults' – had been subsumed by middle-class financial and social control, so gradually alienating their working-class membership. Dickens expressed his misgivings on this point in his speeches and letters (see, for example, *Letters* 7.230–1, 253). See also his account of the Chatham mechanics' institute library in 'Dullborough Town', *UT* 12.

Village libraries, run by the local clergy, were in effect channels for indoctrination through religious works and tracts and tame secular writings. Similarly, those mill-owners who provided reading matter on their premises were prone to censor 'unsuitable' literature. However, an eclectic range of working-class book clubs existed, partly as a response to the partisan nature of other libraries, and partly as a genuine attempt to enable working people to acquire an education (Collins, 1955, 115–27; Altick, 1957, passim; Gilmour, 1967, 207–24; *Letters* 7.230–1 and notes).

Many *HW* articles included information and comment on the provision of books and papers for workers. See 'Free Public Libraries', 3.80–3; 'The Labourer's Reading-Room', 3.581–5; 'Birmingham Glass Works', 5.32–8; 'The Babbleton Book Club', 6.129–33; 'Accommodation for Quidnuncs', 8.88–91; and 'Lancashire Witchcraft', 8.549–51. The whole paragraph about the Coketown library is not in MS but was added by Dickens in CP.

common men and women!]   The sentence 'Facts and figures were not always all sufficient for them as they would have been for good machines.' was added on CP.

after fifteen hours' work]   The 1853 Factory Act, which amended the ineffective 1847 Act, secured a 10½-hour day and 'short Saturday' for all adult workers. This marked a victory for the Ten Hours Movement which had begun in the early 1830s.

13 Photograph of William Ellis. From Ethel E. Ellis, *Memoir of William Ellis* (London: Longmans, 1888)

Dickens might have had in mind here the long working day of the Spitalfields hand-loom weavers, for in a *HW* article, 'Spitalfields', 3.25–30 (written by Dickens and Wills), one weaver complained about 'leaning for'ard . . . for fifteen or sixteen hours at a stretch' (28). The image of the weaver bending over his loom may have informed Dickens's description of Stephen 'bent over his loom' at book 1, chapter 11.

They took De Foe to their bosoms, instead of Euclid, and seemed to be on the whole more comforted by Goldsmith than by Cocker.] *Robinson Crusoe* (1719) by Daniel Defoe and *The Vicar of Wakefield* (1766) by Oliver Goldsmith were two of Dickens's favourite novels. (See the autobiographical chapter 4 in *DC*.)

Euclid] The Greek mathematician (c.300 BC) who established the principles of geometry. The 1853 Christmas examinations of candidates for Queen's Scholarships, and the General Examination of Training Schools, included in their list of subjects a test paper on 'Euclid' (*Minutes* 1853–4, *BPP* 1854, 51.1, appendix A and B). A *HW* article of November 1853 had defended 'harmless fictions' for children against the early teaching of Euclid's Elements (8.291).

Cocker] Edward Cocker (1631–75) was the author of *Cocker's Arithmetic* (1678), which went through one hundred editions. The *Arithmetic* became a standard textbook, and its popularity gave rise to the phrase 'according to Cocker', meaning 'in accordance with established rules' or 'according to what is correct'. The familiar phrase was the first on Dickens's shortlist of titles for the novel. An ironic allusion to the 'Gospel according to Cocker' appeared in a *HW* article of 1853, 'In and Out of Jail', 7.241–5.

'No, Loo; I wouldn't hurt you.

at first.] After these words in MS, and cancelled on CP, is the sentence 'I should be a fool indeed, as well as a brute, to hurt the person I love.'

Jaundiced] In Tom's sense, meaning 'sullen', 'melancholic', 'languid'. In the Victorian age, jaundice was thought to be a somatic disease which was triggered by depression, fright or anger. Dickens had made much play of the word and its associations in *BH* (see Shatto, 1988, 32).

'Nonsense!' said Mrs Gradgrind

combustion, and calcination, and calorification] In chemistry, all processes concerned with the production of heat.

                                    Man of Nº: 1? - <u>Not yet.</u>

                    Law <u>of Divorce</u>

John   Prodge   ?

Stephen   ?

                                            Mill Pictures.

   George   ?

      old Stephen?

                        Stephen   Blackpool

                                            Rachael

            Turtle and Venison & a gold spoon.   " That's what the

             Hands want Sir!   –

            Bounderby's mother?   Yes

Bitzer's father & mother?   No.

children grow up and Louisa married

  Carry on Tom - Selfish - calculations all go to Nº 1.

  Carry on Louisa - Never had a <childh> child's belief or a child's fear

  Carry on Sissy - Power of affection

      Republish in 3 books   ?

                        1.   Sowing

                          2.   Reaping

                            3.   Garnering

(Hard Times. ———————————————————————— N°: II)

Weekly N°: 5   chapter IX.

Present Sissy in her simple & affectionate position - low down in the school - no arithmetic ⎯⎯ Interests Louisa
                              ⎯⎯ Tells her story

chapter X.

Open Law of Divorce.   Stephen Blackpool and Rachael
            (Wolverhampton black ladder)
                    Find his bad wife at home "Come awa' from th' bed! 'Tis mine! Drunk agen? Ah! why not?"

Weekly N°: 6
                        Chapter   XI.

    Mill Picture ⎯⎯ Interview with Bounderby and Mrs Sparsit.   "I mun 'be ridded o'her. How? Law to punish me. What law to help me!"
Goldspoon

chapter XII.

    Bounderby's mother
                ⎯⎯ Mill Picture
                              Stephen <xxx> goes home, wrathful

Weekly N° 7   Chapter XIII.

"Quiet and peace were there. Rachael was there, sitting by the bed."
        Poison bottle. "Thou hast saved my soul alive"

chapter XIV.

children grow up.   Time, a manufacturer. Passes them through his
    mill.
        ⎯⎯ Time for Mr Gradgrind "to talk to" Louisa ⎯⎯ Tom   )

Weekly N°: 8
                        Chapter   XV.

    Scene between Mr Gradgrind & Louisa, in which he communicates Bounderby's proposal.
                Force of Figures - Bounderby accepted

chapter XVI.

Mrs Sparsit.   Great intelligence conveyed to her. / To keep the bank
                Happy pair married
                            ⎯⎯ And Bounderby's speech

Book 1, Chapter 9   Fifth weekly part
Saturday, 29 April 1854

SISSY'S PROGRESS

By the eighteenth century the concept of individual progress through life, often depicted satirically within the picaresque framework of a journey, was a central preoccupation of many writers (see Defoe's *Moll Flanders* (1721), Swift's *Gulliver's Travels* (1726), or Fielding's *Jonathan Wild* (1743) and *Tom Jones* (1749)), and the ironic use of the word 'progress' to suggest deterioration and regression was well established. For example, William Hogarth's two series of satirical paintings, *A Harlot's Progress* (1732) and *A Rake's Progress* (1735), are a parodic allusion to John Bunyan's Christian allegory, *Pilgrim's Progress* (1678).

The wretched ignorance with which Jupe

after eight weeks of induction into the elements of Political Economy] James Kay-Shuttleworth had long espoused the teaching of political economy to the working class (see *Four Periods* 63, 366); however, the leading proponent and pioneer of the teaching of political economy in schools was the Utilitarian, William Ellis (1800–81) (Plate 13). Ellis began his educational work in 1846 by giving a series of lessons to boys in a British and Foreign school on what he termed 'social economy', and by offering financial assistance to the Chartists' 'National Association for Promoting the Political and Social Improvement of the People' for a day school in their National Hall in Holborn which opened two years later. He is best-remembered for establishing and funding the Birkbeck schools, named after George Birkbeck (1776–1841), who founded the London mechanics' institute for the advancement of adult education (1824). The first Birkbeck school opened in the institute at Southampton Buildings, Chancery Lane, on 17 July 1848. Between 1849 and 1852, five more schools were established in different districts of London. Students were charged a fee of sixpence a week, paid in advance.

Ellis taught political economy under such terms as 'elementary social science', 'economic science', 'social science', 'social economy' or the 'science of conduct', and introduced children to its elementary laws through a graduated series of oral lessons designed in the manner of Socratic questioning (see Ellis, 1888, 3–4). This coupling of politico-economic theory with elementary popular education (the focus of Dickens's criticism of social engineering in *HT*) stemmed from the Victorian belief in working-class education as an instrument of control. Ellis believed that a working man who felt that he laboured only to produce goods for the privileged classes would see his life as

> a succession of disappointments and sorrows – perpetual discontent, at one time smouldering, at another bursting forth into complaint and remonstrance

... combinations and strikes; exhaustion of savings ... future lower wages, bitterness of spirit, and domestic wrangling, or torpor of despair; dwellings bare of food and furniture; sickness and desolation.

(*Progressive Lessons* xii–xiii)

Ellis thus perceived his systematic indoctrination of political economics in schools as the only Utilitarian course of action: 'no other subject of school instruction will afford such scope for training children in correct habits of reasoning' (xxi).

Many schools in Scotland and England adopted Ellis's methods and used his textbooks, and some received financial help or teachers trained at Ellis's establishments, or both. By 1854 a school inspector's report stated that lessons on the principles of political economy were taught 'with great clearness' to working-class children in the London schools inspected for that year (*BPP* 1854–5, 42.394; *Progressive Lessons in Social Science*, 1850, xv; Ellis, 1888, 48–9, 51; Blyth, 1889, 72–3, 82, 92, 111–17; Kelly, 1957, 201; Gilmour, 1967, 207–24).

In 1852, *HW* published an on-the-spot report of the Birkbeck school in the London mechanics' institution and the day school established by Ellis in Holborn. 'Rational Schools' (6.337–42) describes what Ellis called his 'vitalized object lessons' and reports in detail some of his progressive lessons in social economy. The article's overall approval of Ellis's methods is tempered by a reservation about the broader educational needs of pupils: 'The imaginative faculty in all these children, and also ... their religious principles, we assume to be cultivated elsewhere ... no amount of political economy ... will or can ever do without them' (341–2).

Dickens thought that political economy was 'a great and useful science in its own way and its own place' but he 'did not transplant [his] definition of it from the Common Prayer Book, and make it a great king above all gods' (*HW* 8.553). In December 1854 he reiterated this opinion:

> My satire [in *HT*] is against those who see figures and averages, and nothing else – the representatives of the wickedest and most enormous vice of this time – the men who ... will do more to damage the real useful truths of political economy, than I could do (if I tried) in my whole life.
>
> (*Letters* 7.492)

'To do unto others as I would that they should do unto me.']   This is the answer to the question in the Catechism 'What is thy duty towards thy Neighbour?': 'My duty towards my Neighbour, is to love him as myself, and to do to all men as I would they should do unto me' (*BCP*). See also Matthew 7.12.

On 28 January 1854 the *Preston Guardian*, a local newspaper sympathetic to the factory workers who were on strike in the town, reported the views on political economy promoted by one of the strike leaders, George Cowell:

> When the working classes begin to want more money, they are taunted about their ignorance. These political economists, however, will fail to convince you that 18s a week is preferable to 20s. ... Political economy! What is it? The doctrine of buying cheap and selling dear – a doctrine utterly irreconcil-

able with the divine precept "Do unto others as you would that they should do unto you." The sooner we can rout political economy from the world, the better it will be for the working classes of this country.

(Quoted in Dutton and King, 1981, 55–6)

Dickens was in Preston on 28–30 January 1854.

In *Utilitarianism* (1861), John Stuart Mill declared that in 'the golden rule of Jesus of Nazareth, we read the complete spirit of the ethics of utility. "To do as you would be done by," and "to love your neighbour as yourself," constitute the ideal perfection of Utilitarian morality' (24).

Mr Gradgrind observed, shaking his head

blue book] A blue book is a published parliamentary report, in a blue paper cover, containing factual and statistical information gathered from evidence taken during a governmental inquiry (see note to book 1, chapter 15, pp. 147–8, about Dickens's attitude towards blue books and statistics).

There had been so little communication

like a piece of machinery which discouraged human interference] One of several allusions to the many factory accidents which took place daily in the mills. Other references are found in book 1, chapter 11, and book 2, chapter 1 (see note to book 1, chapter 13, pp. 143–6).

'I am almost ashamed,' said Sissy

Mr M'Choakumchild was explaining to us about Natural Prosperity.'] Sissy's innocent substitution of 'Natural' for 'National' is an ironic jibe at those who used axiomatic natural laws to introduce what they believed were 'natural', laissez-faire economic laws. William Ellis's *Progressive Lessons* (first published in 1850) were designed for this purpose (Gilmour, 1967, 216–17).

'Yes, Miss Louisa, I know it was, now.

I thought it must be just as hard upon those who were starved, whether the others were a million, or a million million.] Sissy's constant regard for the minority in M'Choakumchild's statistical propositions is Dickens's attack on the Benthamite 'principle of utility' – what Bentham later called the 'greatest happiness principle'. The Utilitarian theory of the greatest happiness of the greatest number failed to take into account the corresponding unhappiness of the smaller number. The Benthamite political economist J. R. M'Culloch noted that it is not required of the economist, that his theories should square with the peculiarities of particular persons.... He has to deal with man in the aggregate.... He is... to apply himself to discover the sources of national wealth and universal prosperity, and the means by which they may be rendered most productive. (1849, 15–16)

'Yes, Miss Louisa – they always remind me

And I find ... that in a given time a hundred thousand persons went to sea on long voyages, and only five hundred of them were drowned or burnt to death. What is the percentage?] Dickens mocks William Ellis's tendency to create economic propositions out of personal tragedy and death. Compare part of lessons 51 and 55 from Ellis's *Progressive Lessons in Social Science* (1850):

> If all the parties insured at a life-office were to die before the payment of a second year's premium, what would be the consequence to the office, and what to the holders of the policies?
> If all the ships insured at a marine insurance-office were to be lost, what would be the consequence to the office, and what to the insured? (51.60–1)

> When men, in the full vigour of their producing powers, are cut off by death before they have had time to effect much saving, what will become of their wives and families? ...
> ... If an insurance company grant life policies and make a profit after compensating the families of the insured who die prematurely, who are the losers, so far as money or the money's worth is concerned?
> In what respects are the families of the four who die worse off than the families of the ninety-six who survive? (55.66)

Apart from his work in the field of education, Ellis's successful management of the Indemnity Mutual Marine Assurance Company (Lloyd's) earned him the title of the 'Father and the King of Underwriters' (Gilmour, 1967, 217; Ellis, 1888, 1).

'Nothing, Miss – to the relations

'Nothing, Miss – to the relations and friends of the people who were killed.] 'Modern Human Sacrifices', a *HW* article of 11 February 1854, echoed Sissy's sentiments and called for compensation to surviving relatives of preventible shipwrecks:

> Life at sea is held too cheaply, and the amount of misery and vice created yearly among people left destitute by sailors' deaths is very great indeed. A charge for their benefit upon shipowners would produce more stringent precautions than are now used for the safety of our seamen; and such a charge

14 Performing dog act. From Hughes Le Roux and Jules Garnier, *Acrobats and Mountebanks* (London: Chapman & Hall, 1890)

would be covered by marine insurance. . . .
. . . though it be natural and right that we should feel much pity for the distress of mind suffered by a captain, who, though tender-hearted, has by a foolhardy or thoughtless course, caused the drowning of a number of his fellow-creatures, yet the sorrows of a thousand must overweigh the sorrows of the one. An imprudent captain who forfeits human life . . . must answer for it and suffer for it. (8.564)

'Did your father love her?'

an interest gone astray like a banished creature, and hiding in solitary places.] These lines may allude to the words of the creature in Mary Shelley's *Frankenstein* (1818): 'am I not alone, miserably alone? You, my creator, abhor me . . . your fellow creatures . . . spurn and hate me. The desert mountains and dreary glaciers are my refuge' (10).

'O very much! They kept him

whether the Sultan would let the lady go on with the story, or would have her head cut off before it was finished.'] A sultan in one of the *Arabian Nights* stories married a new wife each day and then had her beheaded the following morning. In order to gain a reprieve from this fate, Scheherazade, his latest wife, told the sultan a story every night, but left it unfinished so that she could resume the following night. One thousand and one nights passed until the Sultan realized that he was in love with Scheherazade and consequently made her his wife for ever.

'Father, soon after they came home

told Merrylegs to jump up on the backs of the two chairs and stand across them – which is one of his tricks.] In his *Acrobats and Mountebanks* (1890), Le Roux provided an illustration of a similar act (Plate 14): with its tail held firmly between its clenched teeth, the dog has three of its legs balanced over two chairs (130).

Then he beat the dog, and I was frightened, and said, "Father, father! Pray don't hurt the creature who is so fond of you! . . . and father lay down crying on the floor with the dog in his arms, and the dog licked his face.'] On the whole, nineteenth-century animal trainers respected and loved their charges as their own children, but force was sometimes used on both circus animals and children in order to obtain obedience. For instance, Andrew Ducrow's father and trainer often thrashed his son, and made him 'crouch under his chair like a dog' at public houses after performances. Le Roux was of the opinion that the threat of the whip or a blow, the promise of a lump of sugar, and practice were the 'triple forces' which guaranteed an animal-trainer's success (111). The possibility of severe brutality was greatly diminished by the inherent ability of dogs to learn quickly and to cope with new and demanding tricks. (Le Roux, 1890, 110–11; Saxon, 1978, 40–1; Speaight, 1980, 87, 68.)

This observation must be limited

Mrs Gradgrind . . . would come a little way out of her wrappers, like a feminine dormouse] In Victorian times dormice were frequently kept as household pets. A *HW* article of 1853, 'Domestic Pets', referred to dormice as 'Croquenoix' and described them in terms similar to that of Mrs Gradgrind:

> In winter their sleep is so sound that respiration is suspended, and they are cold and death-like. Many a poor Croquenoix has been thrown out of the window by his capturer, under the impression that the vital spark had departed, while Croquey was only slumbering a little more profoundly than usual, and enjoying a complete escape from the troubles of the world. (7.253)

Another article, three months later, contained an account of the second edition of Alphonse Toussenel's *L'Esprit des bêtes* which attempts to describe the human characteristics of animals. 'Dormice', Toussenel argues, 'are the emblems of industrial parasites, who spend three-quarters of their time doing nothing, and who make up for their idleness by living upon the labours of others' (*HW* 7.568).

Book 1, Chapter 10   Fifth weekly part
Saturday, 29 April 1854

STEPHEN BLACKPOOL

I ENTERTAIN a weak idea

the English people are as hard-worked as any people upon whom the sun shines. I acknowledge to this ridiculous idiosyncrasy, as a reason why I would give them a little more play.] This passage echoes Dickens's comments in a letter to Charles Knight, representative of the Society for the Diffusion of Useful Knowledge:

> I earnestly entreat your attention to the point (I have been working upon it, weeks past, in Hard Times). . . . The English are, so far as I know, the hardest-worked people on whom the sun shines. Be content if, in their wretched intervals of pleasure, they read for amusement and do no worse. They are born at the oar, and they live and die at it. Good God, what would we have of them! (17 March 1854, *Letters* 7.294)

Knight had complained that his *Weekly Volume* series had not been a success because of the working class's predilection for fiction (see note on libraries at book 1, chapter 8, pp. 110–11). Dickens's 'weak idea' was 'a glimmering suspicion', in 'Nobody's Story', that 'labouring people of whatever condition . . . [are] in need of mental refreshment and recreation' (*HW* 8.35, Christmas 1853).

In the hardest working part of Coketown

where Nature was as strongly bricked out as killing airs and gases were bricked in . . . pressing one another to death] Two weeks before this chapter appeared in *HW*, Dickens published an article about slum conditions, 'The Quiet Poor', by Henry Morley. The article describes St Philip's, Shoreditch, a district in Bethnal Green where the 'summer heat lifts out of the filthy courts a heavy vapour of death, the overcrowded rooms are scarcely tenantable [and] . . . The air everywhere indeed is stifling, but within doors many of the cottages must be intolerable' (9.202). Dickens was 'affected . . . deeply' by 'The Quiet Poor' and thought 'it absolutely impossible that it could have been better done' (*Letters* 7.313–14). See notes to book 1, chapter 3, pp. 56–7, and book 1, chapter 5, p. 81, for information on ventilation and contagion theory, and working-class housing respectively.

generically called 'the Hands', – a race who would have found more favour with some people, if Providence had seen fit to make them only hands, or . . . only hands and stomachs] This well-known synecdoche had been similarly interpreted by Dr Thomas Arnold (1795–1842), headmaster of Rugby School from 1828:

> A man sets up a factory and wants hands. I beseech you to observe the very expressions that are used, for they are all significant. What he wants of his fellow creatures is the loan of his hands – of their heads and hearts he thinks nothing. These hands are attached to certain mouths and bodies which must be fed and lodged; but this must be done as cheaply as possible. . . . But further, these hands are attached to reasonable minds and to immortal souls. The mouths and bodies must be provided for, however miserably, because without them the hands cannot work; but the minds and souls go utterly unregarded. Is this any other than a national crime? (cited in Evers, 1939, 36)

Similar sentiments appeared in the *Special Report by the Directors to the Proprietors of Price's Patent Candle Company* which Dickens had read in May 1852 and considered 'a very remarkable document indeed' (*Letters* 6.681, 701–2). One of the directors pointed to

> the great evil and intense temptations to which the uncared-for children of our English factories are necessarily exposed when herded together in hot contaminating crowds, and regarded, as the very term 'hands' so generally applied to them itself suggests, rather as so many mere component parts of the machinery than as human beings. (32)

forty years of age.] Life expectancy for the working class in many manufacturing towns was often below twenty years. By the late 1840s, Preston had the highest death rate in Britain. In a 'life table' for Preston around 1849, Anderson shows that 47 per cent of children died under 5 years old, 56 per cent of adults died before the age of 25, and only three-fifths of those over 25 lived until 50 years of age. Two out of five reached the age of 60. Stephen may have been considered old despite his added hardships (Anderson, 1971, 34, 203).

A rather stooping man, with a knitted brow

power-loom weaver] In 1787, Edmund Cartwright invented the power-loom, which was faster than the hand-loom and produced smoother cloth. By Cartwright's own admission, his first loom 'was a most rude piece of machinery' (Baines, 1835, 230), and it took many more refinements by others before power-loom weaving could be extensively introduced into cotton-mills. At the end of 1845 the northern manufacturing districts of Lancashire, Yorkshire and Northumberland and Durham had 142,950 fully operative looms, 138,720 of which were for cotton manufacture (Chapman, 1904, 27–32). For an account of Cartwright's power-loom and his other inventions, see 'The Power-Loom', *HW* 7.440–5.

As a 40-year-old male power-loom weaver, Stephen was an exception throughout the cotton industry. By mid-century, the majority of factory weavers were women, and the average age of both male and female cotton workers was between 20 and 30 years (Lowe suggests it was considerably younger: see 'Locked Out', *HW* 8.346). A number of factors – ranging from low wages to physical deterioration – often led older operatives, especially men, to take up other forms of employment (Anderson, 1971, 26–9; Dutton and King, 1981, 14, 19).

The lights in the great factories

The lights in the great factories, which looked, when they were illuminated, like Fairy palaces] For the hundreds of windows in large factories, see note to book 1, chapter 5, p. 81. The factories were lit by gas, which was first used commercially in 1792 when the inventor and steam pioneer William Murdock (1754–1839) lit his house and offices at Redruth in Cornwall. In his *Dictionary of Manufacturing, Mining, Machinery and the Industrial Arts*, George Dodd recorded that

> In 1802 he [Murdock] illuminated the Soho factory of Boulton and Watt in the same way. In 1803 he lighted up two of the cotton-mills at Manchester with gas. In 1812 Mr. Winsor lighted some of the streets of London with gas, and from that year the gradual extension of the system all over the civilised world may be dated. (1869, 143)

There were several reasons why gas was a suitable source of light in factories. The depletion of tallow and whale-oil imports as a result of the Napoleonic Wars precipitated the need for a relatively cheap and safe form of illumination. As a result of the extension of work into the night and the additional incentives of reduced insurance premiums for those mills which used gas-lighting, manufacturers recognized the economic advantages of gas. For domestic gas usage, see note to book 1, chapter 3, pp. 56–7 (Woodward, 1962, 49). 'Fairy palace' was the description often applied to the Crystal Palace, the vast building constructed from cast iron, wrought iron and glass that was built to house the Great Exhibition of 1851. See, for example, the *HW* articles 'Fairyland in Fifty-four' (8.313–17) and 'Plant Architecture' (9.130). See also 'The Private History of the Palace of Glass' (2.385–91) and 'Three May-Days in London. iii. The May Palace (1851)' (3. 121–4).

travellers by express-train]   The first line to run express trains was the Great Western Railway in 1845, when it operated two express locomotives from London to Exeter at an average speed of 43 miles per hour; for further information, see note to book 1, chapter 3, pp. 53–4 (Simmons, 1978, 46).

the bells had rung for knocking off for the night]   Factory bells summoned operatives to work and rang intermittently throughout the day to denote breaks and the resumption of labour. Engels wrote that the 'despotic bell calls [the operative] . . . from his bed, his breakfast, his dinner' (193).

clattering home]   'Mere lads in barragon jackets, and lasses considerably under twenty, pattering about in their neat little clogs (a distinguishing mark of the factory lass), form an overpowering proportion of the operative population' ('Locked Out', *HW* 8.346).

'Yet I don't see Rachael, still!'

Rachael]   In the Bible, Rachael is the younger daughter of Laban, who has to wait fourteen years before she can marry Jacob. Jacob, who had served seven years for Rachael's hand, is given instead Leah, her older sister, because of Laban's insistence that 'It must not be so done in our country, to give the younger before the firstborn'. Another seven years has to be served for Rachael (Genesis 29.16–28). 'Rachael' was a popular Christian name in the eighteenth and nineteenth centuries.

'I thought thou wast ahind me, Rachael?'

ahind me]   Unlike Mrs Gaskell, who used her years of first-hand knowledge of Lancashire dialect to enrich the portrayal of northern working-class life in her fiction, Dickens used a popular eighteenth-century book as his primary source for the regional dialect in *HT*. His source was *A View of the Lancashire Dialect* (1746) by 'Tim Bobbin' (the pseudonym of John Collier). Dickens owned the 1818 edition (Stonehouse, 1935, 111). Almost all of the dialect words and phrases in *HT* can be found in Bobbin's glossary (see Appendix A, pp. 235–6). Some time before mid-June

1854, during the serialization of HT, Dickens had also read 'with uncommon pleasure' (*Letters* 7.357) the Rev. William Gaskell's *Two Lectures on the Lancashire Dialect* (1854). Although Gaskell's *Lectures* contain words that occur in the novel ('dree', 'fro', 'fra', 'skrike o' day', 'mun', 'brig', 'een' – all found in Bobbin), it is unlikely that Dickens had read the *Lectures* before he embarked on the speech of Stephen and, to a lesser degree, that of Rachael. (For an analysis of Dickens's use of dialectal forms in HT, see Brook, 1970, 125–30; see Ingham, 1986, 522–3, on Dickens's textual alterations to regional forms in order to accord with those found in Bobbin's glossary.)

Stephen's dialect does not reflect the degree of familiarity with Northern speech forms that is shown, for example, in *Mary Barton* (1848) and *North and South* (1854–5), but Dickens nevertheless deploys it as effectively as Mrs Gaskell as a marker of social division. Especially through his interviews with Bounderby (book 1, chapter 11, and book 2, chapter 5) and in his valedictory speech in book 3, chapter 6, Stephen serves as the mouthpiece of industrial hardship, suffering and alienation. The function of his Lancashire dialect as a thematic carrier is further emphasized by Dickens's exploitation of middle-class prejudices about non-standard spoken English which, in the nineteenth century, was associated with ignorance and moral inferiority (Mugglestone, 1995, chapters 3, 6). The questionable dialectal verisimilitude which Dickens achieved is redeemed by his wider intentions in using the Lancashire dialect (Page, 1973, 62–5; Ingham, 1986, 518–27; Mugglestone, 1995, 69, 108–9, 258).

'Never fret about them, Stephen,'

'Let the laws be.'] The chapter plan for the present chapter notes 'Open Law of Divorce'. Rachael ironically reinforces Bounderby's views about the marriage laws (see book 1, chapter 11), and her comments are also reminiscent of those in Eliza Lynn's *HW* article, 'One of Our Legal Fictions', which criticizes the attitude of many Victorians about legal reform: 'men stand by and say, "It is useless to complain. The laws must be obeyed. It is dangerous to meddle with the laws!" ' (9.260).

'Yes,' he said, with a slow nod or two.

Let everything be. Let all sorts alone.] A possible allusion to the economic doctrine of laissez-faire, which is based upon the premise that society is better off if markets – for land, labour, capital and commodities – are allowed to operate free of state interference. The principle reflected Victorian individualism, which dominated every aspect of nineteenth-century life, especially the industrial world. Manufacturers could thus claim that, because 'natural' or free laws of supply and demand regulated wages, there was little point in workers combining or striking for higher pay. The Lancashire cotton operatives who campaigned in 1853–4 for a 10 per cent wage increase were well aware of the mill-owners' views. One of the many songs written during the dispute, which centred on Preston (see Appendix E, pp. 245–7), included the chorus:

> So we've put by the reed-hook and the comb,
> And hung up the shuttle on the loom;
>> And we'll never be content
>> Till we get the ten per cent.,
> In spite of the 'let well alone.'
>> (*Preston Guardian*, 18 March 1854)

Carlyle attacked this economic principle in *Chartism* (1839): 'That self-cancelling Donothingism and *Laissez-faire* should have got so ingrained into our Practice, is the source of all these miseries' (7).

Dickens demonstrates the pervasive nature of laissez-faire in Victorian society by reiterating Stephen's remarks in different contexts throughout the novel: Louisa's resigned comment 'Let it be so', in accepting Bounderby's proposal of marriage at book 1, chapter 15; the negligent Harthouse philosophy, 'What will be, will be' at book 2, chapter 2; Stephen's reply, 'So let be', to Slackbridge's accusations at book 2, chapter 4, and his wise advice to Bounderby that 'lettin alone will never do't' in labour relations at book 2, chapter 5; Sissy's loving hand upon Louisa's neck at book 3, chapter 1 – 'Let it lie there, let it lie', and Dickens's closing words to his readers, 'Let them be!' (Dutton and King, 1981, 83; Crouzet, 1990, 105).

They had walked some distance

the favourite undertaker (who turned a handsome sum out of the one poor ghastly pomp of the neighbourhood) kept a black ladder, in order that those who had done their daily groping up and down the narrow stairs might slide out of this working world by the windows.] The removal of the dead from the constricted space of working-class houses often necessitated the use of a strengthened black-painted slide:

> The ladder . . . was set up against the window, and a basic coffin, or 'removal shell', was hauled up, loaded, and then lowered down the incline aided by ropes threaded through handles affixed to the angled sides of the shell at the head end (for bodies have always been transported feet first).
> (Note by Paul Schlicke, *HT*, World's Classics edn, 1989, 416–17)

Dickens's chapter plan includes the insertion '(Wolverhampton black ladder)'.

Dickens often spoke out on behalf of the reform of funeral practices. He was repulsed by the unscrupulous methods through which undertakers and myriad middlemen could cash in on the process of burial, and was horrified at the indulgent expense of 'the "black job"' in the name of Victorian gentility ('Trading in Death', *HW* 6.241–5). The poor were also caught up in these pretentious funeral customs and subscribed to burial clubs or guilds (many officers of which were undertakers) in order to avoid the indignity of a pauper's funeral. Abuses of this benefit system were frequent and, with a high rate of infant mortality, the death of children especially provided lucrative returns:

> Soon after a child is born it is entered on the books of as many burying clubs as the parents can command funds to pay for. . . . And the investment may always be made a profitable one. The hapless child has to be killed by exposure, by neglect, and worse treatment, to give these unnatural parents a claim upon the several societies of which they have enrolled their infant a member, to the extent in all, perhaps, of 30, 40, or even 50.
>
> (*Catholic Weekly Instructor*, 1845, cited in Rowell, 1970, 52)

During the debates on the Metropolitan Interments Bill passed in 1850, numerous articles appeared in *HW* concerned with burial-grounds, funeral practices and costs of undertaking: 'Heathen and Christian Burial' (1.43–7); 'From the Raven in the Happy Family' (1.241–2); 'Address from an Undertaker to the Trade' (1.301–4); 'City Graves' (2.277); 'Trading in Death' (6.241–5); see also 'Medicine Men of Civilization' (*UT*). In his Will, Dickens directed that he himself 'be buried in an inexpensive, unostentatious, and strictly private manner' (*Nonesuch* 3.799; Pike, 1966, 354).

She went, with her neat figure

in his innermost heart.] After 'heart' MS reads:

> It may be one of the difficulties of casting up and ticking off human figures by the hundred thousand that they have their individual varieties of affection and passions which are of so perverse a nature that they will not come under any rule into the account.

The passage was cancelled in CP.

Such a woman! A disabled, drunken

but so much fouler than that in her moral infamy] One of the first suggestions that Stephen's wife is an adulteress. For further allusions, see notes to book 1, chapter 11, p. 131, and book 1, chapter 13, p. 140.

Book 1, Chapter 11   Sixth weekly part
                                                    Saturday, 6 May 1854

NO WAY OUT

So many hundred Hands

So many hundred Hands in this Mill; so many hundred horse Steam Power. It is known, to the force of a single pound weight, what the engine will do] Dickens may have had in mind the comments made by Leonard Horner, Inspector of Factories, in his report for the half-year ending 31 October 1853:

> In the twelve months ending on the 31st of October last, 113 new mills have been built or set to work (not included in the preceding statements of 1851 and 1852) having an aggregate engine-power of 3,195 horses; and additions to the power of existing factories have been made, amounting to 1,049 horses; and thus, after deducting 350 horses, on account of mills that from various causes have been given up during the year, there remains a gross increase for last year of 3,894 horses, requiring not less than 15,600 additional hands. (*Reports of Inspectors of Factories*, BPP 1854, 19.270)

the National Debt] Britain's national debt, begun during the reign of William III (1689–1702), steadily increased chiefly as a result of the War of American Independence (1775–83) and the French Revolutionary Wars (1793–1815). In 1850 the National Debt stood at £804 million; five years later the figure had fallen to £789 million (Knight, 1851, 641; *Encyclopaedia Britannica*).

Supposing we were to reserve our arithmetic for material objects, and to govern these awful unknown quantities by other means!] Dickens reiterated these sentiments four years later in a speech to the Institutional Association of Lancashire and Cheshire in Manchester:

> Do not let us, in the midst of the visible objects of nature, whose workings we can tell off in figures, surrounded by machines that can be made to the thousandth part of an inch, acquiring every day knowledge which can be proved upon a slate or demonstrated by a microscope – do not let us, in the laudable pursuit of the facts that surround us, neglect the fancy and the imagination which equally surround us as part of the great scheme. (*Speeches* 284)

The day grew strong, and showed itself

the Smoke-serpents, submissive to the curse of all that tribe] Genesis 3.14: 'And the Lord God said unto the serpent, Because thou hast done this, thou art cursed above all cattle, and above every beast of the field; upon thy belly shalt thou go, and dust shalt thou eat all the days of thy life'.

Stephen Blackpool in the parlour.

netting at the fire-side, in a side-saddle attitude, with one foot in a cotton stirrup.] Netting was a popular form of Victorian decorative needlework using linen, silk or cotton thread. Favourite articles included fine mesh purses and embroidered linen, antimacassars and handkerchiefs. For work on large or coarse pieces of mesh, the tension required to make the knots was achieved by slipping a loop of string under the foot, which provides an anchor for the foundation loop (Brittain, 1979, 186).

'Now, you know,' said Mr Bounderby

turtle soup and venison] These were expensive dishes served only in the best taverns or reserved for special occasions, civic functions and banquets (Freeman 271). Bounderby's hyperbole seems to derive from the statement of a certain conservative and patriotic Mr Snoady in Dickens's *HW* article about a fine London tavern, 'Lively Turtle' (2.97–9). Mr Snoady constantly reminds his readers how extravagant but how deserving he is to have a tureen of turtle soup, a pint of punch and a tender steak, and repeats the phrase 'We are all very comfortable as we are . . . leave us alone!' Another article described a civic dinner at London's Mansion House as 'gorgeous. For four ecstatic hours, we ate and drank. I felt all turtle and venison' ('Chips: Corporation Dreams', 7.512–13).

'I ha' coom,' Stephen began

I were married on Eas'r Monday] This would not have been a statutory day off for Stephen. Christmas Day and Good Friday were the only established public holidays prior to the Bank Holidays Act of 1871 which added Easter Monday, Whit Monday, the first Monday in August, and 26 December (if a weekday). However, given that the time-scheme of the novel shows that Stephen would have married about 1835–6, many concessions for fairs, wakes and local holidays were made at that time, regardless of resistance by manufacturers. Local fairs were sometimes held on Easter Monday (see note to book 1, chapter 5, p. 88) (Smith, 1970, 189; Walvin, 1978, 6–7).

Several details of Stephen's marriage correspond to details of Dickens's marriage. Dickens was married on 2 April 1836 – an Easter Saturday. Moreover, Stephen, like Dickens, was in his forties, had married eighteen years before and had experienced increasing unhappiness with his wife, as Dickens had done, for different reasons, in his own marriage to Catherine. Dickens had also witnessed the turbulent marital relationship between his younger brother, Frederick, and his wife Anna (*née* Weller) whom he married against Dickens's advice (see *Letters* 5.400–1) on 30 December 1848. Anna left Frederick on 15 June 1854 and returned to him on 1 January

1855, but owing to Frederick's mounting debts and suspected adultery – and taking advantage of the new Divorce Act of 1857 – Anna petitioned for a legal separation in 1858. They finally separated in 1859 (*Letters* 7.361 and note; Kaplan, 1988, 422).

nineteen year sin]   At book 1, chapter 13, it is eighteen years.

She were a young lass]   The word used for 'she' in Lancashire dialect is 'hoo'. The Rev. William Gaskell, in his *Two Lectures on the Lancashire Dialect* (1854), remarked that 'Every one who has lived but a short time in the county, must be well aware what is the word used for "she" ' (22). Dickens would have known this dialect form (Bobbin lists it in his glossary: see Appendix A), but opted for a certain clarity in Stephen's speech which would be accessible to his wide readership (see note to book 1, chapter 10, pp. 125–6).

'I have heard all this before,' said Mr Bounderby.

'She took to drinking]   Before 'took' *HW* reads: 'found other companions,'. Perhaps another veiled allusion to Mrs Blackpool's infidelity.

played old Gooseberry.']   Played the devil; upset or spoilt; defeated without delay. The fact that Bounderby already knows of Mrs Blackpool's past behaviour avoids the explicit mention of her adultery. That the term 'old Gooseberry' also applies to an unwanted chaperon of two lovers indicates a further nuance in Bounderby's remarks. Stephen's wife's 'moral infamy' (book 1, chapter 10) is confirmed later by Bounderby's description of the three stages required for Stephen to obtain a divorce *a vinculo matrimonii* – adultery was the sole ground for full dissolution of marriage (Hotten; *Dictionary of Historical Slang* 1972).

'I ha' coom to ask yo, sir

how I am to be ridded o' this woman.']   Evolving cultural forces gave rise to changes in divorce law in the nineteenth century. In the 1820s and 1830s there was a general dissatisfaction with the fragmented nature of the legal machinery ill-equipped to meet the judicial needs of a growing industrial nation and, after 1832, an enfranchised middle class. The acceptance of Benthamite legal theory, which called for an integrated system 'which so orders society as to maximise its utility', led to a commission in 1824 concluding that ecclesiastical courts were inefficient and anachronistic. The privileged political position of the Anglican Church was attacked by the strong nonconformist lobby and by growing numbers of people with more liberal and secular views about marriage and divorce. For example, the influential Law Amendment Society (1844) championed the abolition of church jurisdiction over matrimonial affairs. Secular intervention was demonstrated by an Act in 1836 which introduced a civil ceremony by public registrars. To compound matters, the less rigid divorce laws in Scotland brought Scottish and English jurisdictions into conflict, serving to highlight the inadequacies and inequalities inherent in English legal administration.

The appointment of a Royal Commission in 1850 to look into the law of divorce was a major step towards change. The commissioners' recommendations of 1853 included the complete transfer of all matrimonial cases then heard by the church courts to new civil courts that would also be commissioned to grant divorces *a vinculo matrimonii* ('from the bond of marriage') previously only possible by an Act of Parliament. They also proposed to maintain the distinction between divorce *a mensa et thoro* ('from bed and board') and divorce *a vinculo matrimonii*. Divorces *a vinculo* would be granted for adultery only, and generally on the suit of the husband. A wife, however, could apply for divorce *a vinculo* 'in cases of aggravated enormity, such as incest or bigamy'. Grounds for divorce *a mensa et thoro* would be adultery, gross cruelty, or wilful desertion (BPP 1852–3, 40 (1604), 22). In June 1854, a month after Stephen's interview with Bounderby appeared in HW, Lord Chancellor Cranworth submitted a divorce bill to the House of Lords based substantially on the 1853 proposals. After a second reading on 13 June 1854, the bill was withdrawn owing to lack of agreement about an appropriate and professional tribunal. Two similar bills were introduced in 1856 and 1857, and on 28 August 1857 the Matrimonial Causes Bill received the royal assent. For the legal procedures and costs involved prior to the 1857 Divorce Act, see note below at pp. 135–7 (Graveson and Crane, 1957, 11; James, 1973, 272; Holcombe, 1983, 12–13; Horstman, 1985, 47; Shanley, 1989, 34–5; Stone, 1992, 353–4).

'What do you mean?' said Bounderby

You took her for better for worse.']   From the Solemnization of Matrimony: 'to have and to hold from this day forward, for better for worse, for richer for poorer, in sickness and in health, to love and to cherish, till death us do part'.

'He wishes to be free

much dejected by the immorality of the people.]   It was a common assumption among the middle class that accessibility to a cheaper and simpler tribunal for matrimonial causes would have a deleterious effect on the morality of the poorer sections of society.

'I do. The lady says what's right.

I ha' read i' th' papers that great fok . . . are not bonded together for better for worse . . . but that they can be set free . . . an marry ower agen.]   Stephen's case, and his later comments to Bounderby, reappear in Dickens's 'The Murdered Person', a HW article of 11 October 1856:

The most profligate of women, an intolerable torment, torture, and shame to her husband, may nevertheless, unless he be a very rich man, insist on remaining handcuffed to him, and dragging him away from any happier alliance. . . . Out of this condition of things among the common people . . . aggravated, in cottages and single rooms, to a degree not easily imaginable by ill-assorted couples who live in houses of many chambers, and who . . . can keep clear of each other and go their respective ways – vices and crimes arise which no one . . . can fail often to trace, from the Calendars of Assizes, back to this source.(14.290)

In the HW text of HT, after 'wrongs' Stephen says: 'than is suffered by hundreds an' hundreds of us – by women fur more than men – they can be set free for smaller wrongs'. This textual change, and a similar, later deleted, reference (see this chapter, p. 135), reflect the special relationship between HT and the journalism which surrounded it in HW. A week before this chapter opened the 6 May issue of HW, an article entitled 'One of Our Legal Fictions' (by Eliza Lynn) had appeared as the concluding piece in the periodical. The article was based on the celebrated Norton divorce case and called for reform in the laws relating to married women's property. In 1836, Caroline Sheridan Norton (1808–77) separated from her husband, who had legally taken their three children away to a secret location and filed a suit for 'criminal conversation' ('crim. con.') against the Prime Minister, Lord Melbourne, accusing him of adultery with his wife. (A 'crim. con.' suit was heard in a civil court after a person, normally a man, had obtained a decree of divorce *a mensa et thoro* in the ecclesiastical court.) Norton's suit was dismissed, but his wife's name suffered irreparable damage; moreover, because an unsuccessful petitioner in a 'crim. con.' action could not go on to the third (parliamentary) stage towards divorce *a vinculo matrimonii*, the Nortons were legally bound to each other for life.

Mrs Norton began her first campaign to reform the law by publishing three pamphlets: *The Natural Claim of a Mother to the Custody of Her Children as Affected by the Common Law Right of the Father* (1837); *The Case of the Hon. Mrs Norton* (1838); and *A Plain Letter to the Lord Chancellor on the Law of Custody of Infants* (1838). Her close friends Lord Lyndhurst and Thomas Noon Talfourd, Serjeant-at-Law, urged her cause in Parliament, and in 1839 the Infant Custody Act was passed. In August 1853, Mrs Norton was back in court fighting over the validity of a financial deed of separation signed by her husband and herself. This case exposed the anomalous position of separated married women who were still legally bound by the common-law principle of coverture ('covered' by their husbands in all contracts, debts, and a few criminal laws). All property which belonged to a woman at the time of marriage was afterwards regarded as the husband's; thus she was legally non-existent and, like criminals, the mentally ill, and minors, she was 'excluded from many civil, and all political rights in England' (Cobbe, 1868, quoted in Dennis and Skilton, 1987, 148). Ultimately Mrs Norton was defeated by the coverture rules, but she used Lord Cranworth's forthcoming Divorce Bill (tabled in June 1854) as a motive for publishing a pamphlet called *English Laws for Women in the Nineteenth Century* (1854) – Eliza Lynn's source for 'One of Our Legal Fictions' (HW 9.257–60). Dickens had written a lengthy report for the *Morning Chronicle* of 23 June 1836 on the Norton v. Melbourne 'crim.

con.' case, aspects of which he used in the Bardell v. Pickwick trial (*PP* 34), but he did not meet Mrs Norton until 1837.

Dickens's decision to publish 'One of Our Legal Fictions' in *HW* a week before he published the present chapter lent support to Caroline Norton's fight and brought to public attention the wider issues involved in the campaign for reform. It is significant that Stephen's two parenthetical remarks about the injustice to women can only be found in *HW*. Such particularized comments in the fiction which uphold views found in the surrounding journalism are ultimately more forceful and immediate if sustained within a topical reportorial framework. Dickens's chapter plan for chapter 10 of *HT* starts with 'Open Law of Divorce'. Eliza Lynn's centrally positioned article between chapters 10 and 11 'opened' the issue out into the journalism but fed it back into the novel the following week. Other related articles had appeared in *HW* from October 1853: see Dickens's 'Things That Cannot Be Done' (8.121–3) and Eliza Lynn's 'Rights and Wrongs of Women' (9.158–61), which was published the same week as the opening chapters of *HT*. See also later articles: 'A Legal Fiction' (11.598–9) and 'Marriage Gaolers' (13.583–5) (*Letters* 1.153; Holcombe, 1983, 53, 58, 62–3; Shanley, 1989, 23–6; Poovey, 1988, 51–2; Chedzoy, 1992, 232–7).

they has rooms o' one kind an another in their houses . . . and they can live asunders . . . they ha' gowd an other cash, an they can say "This for yo, an that for me," an they can go their separate ways.] In October 1857, Dickens arranged to have a bedroom, bathroom and dressing-room at Tavistock House made into two separate rooms – one for himself and one for Catherine. He wrote: 'I want the recess of the doorway between the Dressing-Room and Mrs. Dickens's room, fitted with plain white deal shelves, and closed in with a plain light deal door, painted white. . . . The sooner it is done, the better'. Dickens formally separated from his wife in May 1858. After the separation, he set Catherine up in a small house in Gloucester Crescent, Regent's Park, and paid her £600 a year for life (*Nonesuch* 2.890; Kaplan, 1988, 375; see also Tomalin, 1990, 116).

'If I do her any hurt, sir

'If I do her any hurt, sir, there's a law to punish me?'/'Of course there is.'] Bounderby's swift affirmative responses to Stephen's questions are somewhat misleading. Marital cruelty, desertion, bigamy, adultery and illegitimacy were commonplace in the nineteenth century and extremely difficult to detect among the poorer classes. Bigamy and cruelty amounting to bodily harm were criminal offences, but the expense of legal proceedings and the acceptance of physical violence within marriage resulted in few prosecutions. Those who were convicted for extreme brutality to their wives could receive a short prison sentence of six months. Convicted bigamists could expect months of hard labour or transportation. Many such cases were the result of the complicated and costly legal process involved in obtaining a full divorce (see note below at pp. 135–7) (Stone, 1992, 142–3, 198).

Although Dickens acknowledged that the cause of much violence within marriage was largely due to marital breakdown (see 'The Murdered Person', *HW* 14.289–

91), he was unequivocal in his views about the leniency of the legal system towards the ill-treatment and exploitation of wives by their husbands. In a *HW* article of 1853, 'Things That Cannot Be Done', he castigates the inadequacy of the law in its punishment of such malefactors:

> It is true that an ill-conditioned friend of mine, possessing the remarkably inappropriate name of Common Sense, is not fully satisfied on this head . . . he says to me, "Will you look at these cases of brutality, and tell me whether you consider six years of the hardest prison task-work (instead of six months) punishment enough for such enormous cruelty?" . . . It is true, I say, that my ill-conditioned friend does twit me . . . but it is enough for me to know, that for a man to maim and kill his wife by inches – or even the woman, wife or no wife, who shares his home – without most surely incurring a punishment, the justice of which satisfies the mind and heart of the common level of humanity, is one of the things that cannot be done. (8.121)

'Hem! There's a sanctity

There's a sanctity in this relation of life,']   The established ecclesiastical practice of only granting divorce *a mensa et thoro*, which barred the separated couple from remarrying, was a reflection of the belief in the sanctity of marriage. One commissioner, Lord Redesdale, took the scriptural position in his statement to the Divorce Commission in 1853, and rejected the proposal that divorce *a vinculo matrimonii* should be granted on other grounds than adultery (BPP 1852–3, 40 (1604), 23–4).

'No no, dunnot say that, sir.

I read in th' papers . . . how th' supposed unpossibility o' ever getting unchained from one another, at any price, on any terms, brings blood upon this land, and brings many common married fok to battle, murder, and sudden death.]   'Battle, murder, and sudden death' echoes the Litany in *BCP*: 'Good Lord, deliver us. From lightning and tempest; from plague, pestilence, and famine; from battle and murder, and from sudden death.' Stephen's remarks were reiterated by Dickens in 'The Murdered Person' (*HW* 14.289–91): 'out of . . . the impossibility of relief . . . vices and crimes arise which no one with open eyes and any fair experience of the people can fail often to trace, from the Calendars of Assizes, back to this source' (290).

After 'married fok' *HW* reads: '(agen I say, women fur of'ener than men) to battle, murder, and sudden death.' This is the second reference – in *HW* only – to the disadvantaged legal position of married women in matrimonial causes (see earlier note p. 133).

'Why, you'd have to go to Doctors' Commons

'Why, you'd have to go to Doctors' Commons with a suit, and you'd have to go

to a court of Common Law with a suit, and you'd have to go to the House of Lords with a suit, and you'd have to get an Act of Parliament to enable you to marry again, and it would cost you . . . from a thousand to fifteen hundred pound. . . . Perhaps twice the money.'] English laws relating to separation and divorce remained unchanged from the Reformation until the nineteenth century, when the Divorce Act of 1857 enlarged if not equalized the rights and responsibilities of spouses. Exclusive jurisdiction of all matrimonial matters was exercised by the ecclesiastical courts of the Church of England, which assiduously applied canon law, established before the Reformation and incorporating Roman Catholic legal practices. Canon law insisted on the Christian tenet of the sanctity and indissolubility of marriage, and its legal remedies in matrimonial causes reflected the sacramental nature of wedlock. This religio-legal stance consistently formed the basis of controversy from the time of the Reformation up until the parliamentary debates on the divorce bill in the 1850s.

Church courts heard four kinds of matrimonial suit: nullity (in cases of incest, physical or mental incapacity, or marriage without parental consent to someone under 21 years of age); jactitation of marriage (a petition to obtain a decree of perpetual silence against a person who publicly made a claim to a marriage – this type of suit had virtually disappeared by the late eighteenth century); restitution of conjugal rights; and divorce *a mensa et thoro* (granted on the grounds of adultery or extreme physical cruelty. It was in effect a judicial separation since neither spouse was allowed to remarry). These narrow ecclesiastical definitions provoked constant demands for change in canon law. From the eighteenth century up to 1857, the standard legal practice to obtain a 'full' divorce was for the petitioner firstly to have a decree of divorce *a mensa et thoro* granted in the ecclesiastical court. Following a successful outcome, the second step was for the husband to issue proceedings in a common-law court for damages against his wife's alleged lover. Only after a man could prove that 'criminal conversation' (adultery) had taken place would damages be assessed and awarded. Finally, for a divorce *a vinculo* (from the bonds of marriage), a private bill had to be presented to the House of Lords, and if it survived a third reading the bill then went to the House of Commons. Royal assent was given only after the success of these three actions. This expensive process ensured that parliamentary divorce was the privilege of wealthy men and that divorce with the right to remarry was a remote possibility for the majority of the population.

This labyrinthine legal procedure was highlighted by a bigamy case which appeared before Justice William Maule at Warwick Assizes on 1 April 1845. Justice Maule's sarcastic speech in sentencing the bigamist, Thomas Hall, 'a poor man not possessed of a farthing', to four months' hard labour was widely circulated in various forms throughout the 1850s. One version was given by Lord Campbell in the House of Lords on 13 June 1854 as an illustration of the 'anomalous and preposterous state of things' which led to injustice and inequality before the law:

> The prisoner said, the case was really one of great hardship; his wife was not only an adultress, but she lived with another man, and as she had taken another husband, he thought he might take another wife. "But," said the Judge, "your course ought first to have been to bring an action against

your wife, to be tried before a judge and jury; and then . . . you ought to have instituted a suit in the Ecclesiastical Court to obtain a divorce *a mensâ et thoro*; and . . . you should then have petitioned the House of Lords for a divorce . . . and then, having obtained the sanction of one branch of the Legislature, you ought to have carried your Bill to the House of Commons, and asked them to concur in it . . . you would then have had to obtain the Royal assent; and if you had succeeded . . . all this might have been accomplished for 1,000*l*." "My Lord," said the man, "I never was worth 20*l*. in all my life, and I have not now a single farthing."

(3 *Hansard* 134, 14–15)

Bounderby's account strikingly resembles Lord Campbell's version, one Dickens would have known at this time. The cost of a parliamentary divorce was mentioned in a *HW* article of 1850, 'A Visit to the Registrar-General', which describes a register office wedding: 'They are bound man and wife at the small charge of seven shillings altogether, with a degree of certainty which nothing but an Act of Parliament price one thousand pounds can undo' (2.237–8) (Graveson and Crane, 1957, 5–6; Stetson, 1982, 7; Horstman, 1985, 4–5, 32–3; Shanley, 1989, 17; Poovey, 1988, 54–6; Stone, 1992, passim. For a nineteenth-century account of the history of divorce in England, see *BPP* 1852–3, 40 (1604), *First Report of the Commissioners Appointed by her Majesty to Enquire into the Law of Divorce*, 1–12).

Doctors' Commons] The Consistory Court of London, the most important and largest canon-law court in England, together with the Court of Arches which heard appeals from all ecclesiastical courts, was popularly known as Doctors' Commons. These courts dealt with the bulk of matrimonial cases in England, and by the nineteenth century the Consistory Court in Doctors' Commons was the major channel through which petitioners nationwide could make their case for separation. When jurisdiction over matrimonial business and probate was transferred from the ecclesiastical to new civil courts in 1857, Doctors' Commons was dissolved. Dickens worked as a freelance shorthand writer in Doctors' Commons (situated near St Paul's Cathedral) from 1830 to 1832, and his early disdain for the institution is expressed most clearly in a sketch called 'Doctors' Commons' (*SB*); other references to it are scattered throughout the novels (Holcombe, 1983, 15; Bentley *et al.*, 1988, 76; Stone, 1992, 33, 43–4).

'There's no other law?'

'There's no other law?'] When the Married Women's Property Bill began its second reading in June 1868, Dickens fully supported it but expressed his pessimism about its success:

The Bill will not pass, we know very well; but would it not be wise and just to take away any such opportunity of setting right some little item in the wrong that springs up under our law of marriage and divorce? Grant what we are told of bishops, priests, and deacons about sanctity of marriage, indissolubility of marriage tie, etc., etc. Grant that such things must be for the general good, cannot we . . . help the weak and injured party?

Reverse the case, and take a working man with a drunken woman saddled on him as long as he lives. If he must not be able to divorce himself – for the general good surely the "general good" should in turn punish the woman.

(4 June 1868; Nonesuch 3.653)

Although the bill was passed in the Commons and referred to a Select Committee, it was withdrawn on account of lack of parliamentary time (Shanley 69).

'Pooh, pooh! Don't you talk nonsense

not your piece-work] That is, 'none of your business'. The expression refers to a system of wages where workers are paid by the piece. The practice had been customary in the old domestic spinning and weaving industries when workers and dealers came to a mutual arrangement about different rates for different pieces. When the traditional weavers and jenny-spinners moved into the early factories, they tried to retain the piece-work method with some success, although it is likely that some were paid time-wages instead. With the gradual adoption of piece-rate price-lists from the mid-1840s, this dual system of payment was maintained. The lists became increasingly influential in standardizing rates of work throughout the cotton industry, and by the 1850s spinners and weavers considered it imperative to have them. For example, one demand of the strike of Lancashire factory operatives which eventually centred on Preston during 1853–4 was 'an equalization or standard list of prices' to regulate their future earnings. Throughout the 1850s and 1860s in Lancashire successive weaving lists appeared for plain cloth, fancy cloth, fine goods and satin. However, many were liable to alter or become obsolete according to prevailing conditions and mechanistic improvements in the industry (Ashworth, 1854, 10; Chapman, 1904, 262–72).

Book 1, Chapter 12   Sixth weekly part
Saturday, 6 May 1854

THE OLD WOMAN

It was not the touch he needed most

the touch that could calm the wild waters of his soul, as the uplifted hand of sublimest love and patience could abate the raging of the sea] The allusion is to the miracle of Jesus, who 'rebuked the winds and the sea; and there was a great calm' (Matthew 8.23–6). There is also the implication of a 'lucky touch' which Stephen deserves at this time. In *BH* 32, Mr Guppy gives Tony Jobling a ' "lucky touch" on the back'. Dickens summed up the meaning of this superstition in *LD* 1.18: '[Mr Chivery] had . . . given his boy what he termed "a lucky touch", signifying that he considered such commendation of him to Good Fortune, preparatory to his that day declaring his passion and becoming triumphant.'

'By Parliamentary, this morning. I came forty mile

By Parliamentary]   Under section VI of the 1844 Railway Act it was 'expedient to secure to the poorer class of travellers the means of travelling by Railway at moderate fares, and in carriages in which they may be protected from the weather'. The fare for third-class passengers was not allowed to 'exceed one penny for each mile travelled'. The Act authorized all passenger railway companies to provide at least one parliamentary train per day each way except Christmas Day and Good Friday (7 & 8 Vict. 1844, 643–4).

No, no; they didn't follow him there

Divine Right]   The notion that monarchs were chosen by God and not by the will of the people originated from the Old Testament, in which kings are called the Lord's anointed because they were believed to be God's earthly representative.

She was gone by and by

over the arches near]   By the mid-nineteenth century, railway viaducts were ubiquitous features of the English landscape, spanning rivers, valleys and roads. Some were immense: the Welwyn Viaduct of the Great Eastern Railway, opened in 1850, was 519 yards long and 100 feet high, with 40 arches, each spanning 30 feet (Klingender, 1947, 211).

Machinery slackened; throbbing feebly

their tall chimneys rising up into the air like competing Towers of Babel.]   Genesis 11.4–9 describes the attempted construction of the tower of Babel, where the confusion of languages is said to have taken place. The term 'tower of Babel' is associated with the concept of disorder, incoherence and turmoil, but it can also mean 'a visionary scheme' (*OED*).

O! Better to have no home

O! Better to have no home in which to lay his head, than to have a home and dread to go to it] Reminiscent of Tennyson's *In Memoriam* (1850): ' 'Tis better to have loved and lost/Than never to have loved at all' (27.15–16). The lines originally appeared in William Congreve's *The Way of the World* (1700): 'Say what you will, 'tis better to be left than never to have been loved' (2.1).

Book 1, Chapter 13   Seventh weekly part
                                        Saturday, 13 May 1854

RACHAEL

'And next, for that I know

"Let him who is without sin among you, cast the first stone at her!"] John 8.7: 'He that is without sin among you, let him first cast a stone at her'. Rachael's allusion to the biblical adulteress further confirms Mrs Blackpool's infidelity. Her words also foreshadow Stephen's impending 'martyrdom': Christ's apostle, Stephen, is stoned to death in Acts 7.58–60.

The wounds of which she had spoken,

The wounds of which she had spoken, seemed to be about the neck of the self-made outcast. . . . She steeped a piece of linen in a basin, into which she poured some liquid from a bottle, and laid it with a gentle hand upon the sore.] Mrs Blackpool's sores may be the manifestation of the primary stage of syphilis, since the throat is one possible site for the development of syphilitic ulcers or chancres. Venereal sores were treated with mercurial ointments and antiseptic solutions, the most favoured of which was hydrargyri perchloridum, commonly known as corrosive sublimate. Dressings and lotions were prepared with either water or glycerine and could be used as an eye lotion, an antiseptic for syringing ears, and as a local treatment for gonorrhoea, gleet and syphilitic ulcers and skin diseases. Other forms of mercurial treatment for syphilis included oral preparations, vapour baths ('moist fumigation') and, from the 1820s, hypodermic injection. Mercury compounds were highly toxic, hence Stephen's initial reaction to the letters on the bottle ('POISON'), his haunted dream and Rachael's later comments when she pours the liquid into the fire. For Dickens's textual change, see note below, p. 142 (Parker, 1854, 17; Martindale, 1884, 147, 328–9; Goldwater, 1972, 224; Baird, 1977, 408).

He had a violent fit of trembling

she looked as if she had a glory shining round her head.] 'Glory', a word dating from the seventeenth century, is another term for a halo or aureole – a circle of light surrounding the head or the whole figure of the Saviour, the Virgin, or one of the Saints.

He closed his eyes, more to please her

he dreamed a long, troubled dream.] Stephen's dream incorporates many of Dickens's progressive theories about the psychological nature of dreams, expressed three years before in a long letter to a contributor of *HW*, Dr Thomas Stone. Stone's proposed article, 'Dreams' (*HW* 2.566–72), was radically rewritten to incorporate Dickens's knowledge of contemporary dream theory and his enlightened observations on the subject (see *Letters* 6.276–9). Dickens was familiar with all the recent developments in dream research and had in his library the following works which reflected the decisive movement away from the conjectural, superstitious analyses of dreams towards more scientific interpretations: John Abercrombie's *Inquiries Concerning the Intellectual Powers and the Investigation of Truth* (10th edn, 1840); Robert MacNish's *Philosophy of Sleep* (1840); and Dugald Stewart's *Elements of the Philosophy of the Human Mind* (1843). Dickens also owned a copy of Dr John Elliotson's *Human Physiology* (1840) in which a section, 'Dreaming', concerns phrenological dream theory (Stonehouse, 1935, 5, 42, 77, 105). For an authoritative account of Victorian perceptions of dreams and Dickens's selective application of contemporary theories in his work, see Bernard (1981).

He thought that he, and some one

but she was not Rachael, and that surprised him, even in the midst of his imaginary happiness . . . he recognized among the witnesses some whom he knew to be living, and many whom he knew to be dead] It was Dickens's belief that there is some conscious and reasoning part of the brain which is aware that we are dreaming:

> I cannot help thinking that this observant and corrective speck of the brain suggests to you, "my good fellow how can you be in this crowd, when you know you are in your shirt?". It is not strong enough to dispel the vision, but is just strong enough to present this inconsistency. (*Letters* 6.279)

In 'Lying Awake' (*HW* 6.145–8), Dickens wrote: 'Perhaps, with no scientific intention or invention, I was illustrating the theory of the Duality of the Brain; perhaps one part of my brain, being wakeful, sat up to watch the other part which was sleepy' (145). The sense of self which Stephen experiences within his dreaming state was noted in 'Dreams': 'it is remarkable . . . that we always preserve the consciousness of our own identity' (*HW* 2.568).

the shining of a tremendous light.]   This may be a reminiscence of Dickens's *HW* article of 1850, 'A Child's Dream of a Star', in which a boy dreams that a shining star opens up to reveal the road to heaven (1.25–6). The article has a significant bearing on Dickens's use of a guiding star at Stephen's death (see note to book 3, chapter 6, p. 222).

one line in the table of commandments]   The sixth commandment: 'Thou shalt not kill' (Deuteronomy 5.17).

They stood in the daylight before a crowd so vast . . . and they all abhorred him. . . . He stood on a raised stage . . . and hearing the burial service distinctly read, he knew that he was there to suffer death. In an instant what he stood on fell below him, and he was gone.]   Compare the bodysnatcher William Burke's recurring dream before he was convicted and sentenced to hang in 1829: 'he imagined himself going to be executed, and his chief anxiety was how he should comport himself on the scaffold before the assembled multitude, whose faces he beheld gazing up and fixed upon him' ('Dreams', *HW* 2.571). Dickens was convinced that everyone has dreams that contain common elements: 'We all fall off that Tower – we all skim above the ground at a great pace and can't keep on it . . . [we all try] to break some Thraldom or other, from which we can't escape' (*Letters* 6.278–9; Dickens reiterated these features in 'Lying Awake', *HW* 6.145–6).

Out of what mystery he came back

a mortal fear of one particular shape which everything took.]   The identity of this shape was made ambiguous by Dickens's cancellation in CP of a phrase that originally concluded the next paragraph. Following the words in the published text, 'was the shape so often repeated', Dickens cancelled '– the bottle with the cautionary word Poison.'

With her woful eyes, so haggard and wild

the woman he had married eighteen years before.]   In his first interview with Bounderby, Stephen said that he had been married nineteen years (see book 1, chapter 11). Dickens himself had been married eighteen years on 2 April 1854.

All this time, as if a spell were on him

as if a spell were on him, he was motionless and powerless]   A reference to mesmerism or 'animal magnetism', a phenomenon developed from the doctrine of the Viennese physician Franz Anton Mesmer (1734–1815). The process was pioneered in England by Dickens's close friend Dr John Elliotson (1791–1868), who ardently believed that mesmerism could be used as a way to alleviate pain in surgical procedures and that it had a place in the treatment of disease and nervous disorders, especially epilepsy. Elliotson's mesmeric experiments were witnessed by Dickens in 1838 and 1840, and from 1842 Dickens practised mesmerism himself – first on his wife and later on Madame de la Rue, whom he met in 1844 on his visit to Genoa (Kaplan, 1975, passim). Elliotson also propounded a phrenological dream theory with which Dickens was familiar (see p. 141).

As she looked at him, saying 'Stephen?'

put an end of her shawl to his lips.]   Stephen's gesture is mentioned four times in thirty-two lines, giving emphasis to Rachael's angelic and healing qualities. Compare Matthew 9.20–2:

> And, behold, a woman which was diseased with an issue of blood twelve years, came behind him, and touched the hem of his garment: For she said within herself, If I may but touch his garment, I shall be whole. But Jesus turned him about, and when he saw her, he said, Daughter, be of good comfort; thy faith hath made thee whole. And the woman was made whole from that hour.

'I am, as I have told thee, Stephen

there is a deep gulf set.]   Rachael is referring to the biblical story of the beggar Lazarus and Dives, the rich man – the gulf that exists is between Dives in Hell and Lazarus in Heaven (Luke 16.26). In *Mary Barton* (1848), John Barton used the same parable in relation to the chasm between the rich and the poor in society: ' "We are their slaves as long as we can work; we pile up their fortunes with the sweat of our brows; and yet we are to live as separate as if we were in two worlds . . . as separate as Dives and Lazarus" ' (1).

'Thou changest me from bad to good.

an a' the muddle cleared awa'.]   After 'cleared awa' ' the MS contains a fragment which was not cancelled in CP but which was not published in *HW* or subsequent editions of the novel. The CP read:

> Thou'st spo<k>ken o' thy little sisther. There agen! Wi' her child arm tore off afore thy face!"
> She turned her head aside, and put her hand ∧up∧ to her eyes.
> "Where dost thou ever hear or read o' *us* – the like o' *us* – as being otherwise than onreasonable and cause o' trouble? Yet think o' that. Government gentlemen comes down and mak's report. Fend off the dangerous machinery, box it off, save life and limb, don't rend and tear human creeturs to bits in a Chris'en country! What follers? Owners sets up their throats, cries out, 'Onreasonable! Inconvenient! Troublesome!' Gets to Secretaries o' States wi' deputations,

and nothing's done. When do *we* get there wi' *our* deputations, God help us! We are too much int'rested and nat'rally too far wrong t' have a right judgment. Hap∧p∧ly we are; but what are they then? I' th' name o' th' muddle in which we are born and live and die, what are they then?"

"Let such things be, Stephen. They only lead to hurt; let them be!"

"I will, since thou tell'st me so. I will. I pass my promise."

Dickens added a footnote in CP referring the reader to the article 'Ground in the Mill' (the note was cancelled before publication). The article, by Henry Morley, appeared in HW on 22 April 1854 (chapters 7 and 8 of HT opened the number) and was one of a series published from 1854 until 1856 on factory accidents and mill safety regulations (see note to book 2, chapter 1, p. 158, about manufacturers' reactions to the enforcement of factory legislation). 'Ground in the Mill', based on the *Reports of the Inspectors of Factories* for the half-year ending 31 October 1853, is a graphic account of industrial fatalities and injuries suffered because of insufficient or non-existent fencing of mechanical gearing (see Appendix C, p. 241) in contravention of section 21 of the 1844 Factory Act (see 7 Vict. cap. 15). A representative sample of factory accidents was described in 'Extracts from Reports of Certifying Surgeons' appended to the inspectors' reports. The list included such examples as:

An adult	Climbed to the top of his machine to put the strap on the drum; his smock wrapped round the shaft.	Both arms torn out of the shoulder joints, abdomen lacerated, the intestines protruded, both legs broken, head contused, and *death*.
A young person	Playing with a shaft, above some bags of wool, her slip got fast to the shaft.	Left arm torn out at the shoulder joint, right arm fractured, and contusion of head.

(BPP 1854, 19.369)

'Ground in the Mill' contained these examples together with the majority of cases cited by the certifying surgeons. In Dickens's unpublished passage, the amputated arm of Rachael's sister would appear to have been suggested by one of the injuries suffered by the 'young person' on the surgeons' list – Morley's 'factory girl' in the article. It is possible that Dickens saw the Reports and Appendices a month before Morley's article was published. In a letter of 24 March 1854 to his subeditor, Dickens – writing with 'the strongest feeling of indignation and horror' about the issue – asked 'to have the subject to which the accompanying papers (just received) refer, done *at once*. Will you let Morley know that I shall feel greatly obliged to him if he will write a little paper on it for our immediate publication' (*Letters* 7.297).

It would appear that – in keeping with the allusory nature of the novel – Dickens decided to include less specific references to industrial injuries (see book 1, chapter 11; book 2, chapter 1; and Stephen's fate in the disused coalpit in book 3, chapter 6). However, the unpublished passage would have explained Stephen's stance against the United Aggregate Tribunal (book 2, chapter 4) and his later comments to

Bounderby at book 2, chapter 5. Dickens also changed his mind about the cause of death of Rachael's sister. The reader is told later that she died at home of 'sickly air' (book 3, chapter 6).

The controversy surrounding factory legislation continued to be promoted in *HW* throughout 1855 with the publication of five more articles by Morley ('Fencing with Humanity' 11.241–4; 'Death's Cyphering Book' 11.337–41; 'Chips: Deadly Shafts' 11.494–5; 'More Grist to the Mill' 11.605–6; and 'Two Shillings per Horse-Power' 12.130–1). The articles prompted Harriet Martineau to write a retaliatory, pro-manufacturers pamphlet, *The Factory Controversy; A Warning Against Meddling Legislation* (1855), published in Manchester by the National Association of Factory Occupiers. (Morley described this group as 'the National Association (for the Protection of the Right to Mangle Operatives)' (*HW* 11.495).) As part of her attack, Martineau criticized *HT* as one example of 'how conspicuous has been Mr. Dickens's proved failure in the department of instruction upon which he spontaneously entered', and she held Dickens responsible for the 'unscrupulous statements, and objectionable representations' of the *HW* articles (*The Factory Controversy* 36–7). An unrepentant reply by Dickens and Morley, 'Our Wicked Mis-statements', *HW* 13 [19 January 1856] 13–19, marked the last of the factory accident pieces in the periodical. The controversy also concluded Harriet Martineau's friendship with Dickens. Her last article appeared in *HW* on 13 January 1855 – she had contributed fifty-three pieces of work to the journal from May 1850.

This bitter dispute and final estrangement between Dickens and Harriet Martineau has a significant bearing on Dickens's modified views of the industrial system and on his strained five-year working relationship with a contributor whose brand of political economy Dickens detested and vehemently attacked in *HT*. K. J. Fielding and Anne Smith, who provide a comprehensive assessment of the subject, observe that

> It is remarkable that Dickens did not foresee from the first that there was a risk in inviting [Harriet Martineau] to be a contributor, and it is not less surprising that she should have agreed to become one in spite of knowing very well from his earlier works that as soon as either of them touched on political economy they were bound to be in fundamental disagreement.
>
> (1970, 414–15)

Although both Dickens and Harriet Martineau had a high regard for industrialization, by the mid-1850s Dickens's pride in 'the progress of mankind' ('A Preliminary Word', *HW* 1.1) was tempered by serious doubts about its dehumanizing effects and the misapplication of politico-economic theory to people's lives. Dickens's strong misgivings are evident in his article about the Preston strike:

> "I believe" . . . "that into the relations between employers and employed, as into all the relations of this life, there must enter something of feeling and sentiment; something of mutual explanation, forbearance, and consideration. . . ." ('On Strike', *HW* 8.553)

Harriet Martineau, however, consistently favoured the interests of the manufacturer, and in her series of twelve HW articles which appeared in 1851 and 1852 on a number of industrial processes she manifests a form of political economy which Dickens considered 'a mere skeleton unless it has a little human covering and filling out . . . and a little human warmth in it' (HW 8.558). The distanced and impersonal treatment of factory operatives in the articles is matched by a warmth for the interests of the manufacturers and their stand against 'legislative meddlings' (4.557). Thus, by 1854, an already wide chasm existed between Dickens's consistently humanistic view of industrialization – strengthened by recent events in Preston and by the campaign for factory safety legislation – and Harriet Martineau's perspective, firmly entrenched in political economy. It is this division which lies at the heart of the novel's meaning (Fielding and Smith, 1970, 404–27).

thou hast saved my soul alive!'] Ezekiel 18.27: 'when the wicked man turneth away from his wickedness that he hath committed, and doeth that which is lawful and right, he shall save his soul alive.' This is also one of the opening sentences at Morning and Evening Prayer (BCP). Dickens's chapter plan includes the quotation.

Book 1, Chapter 14   Seventh weekly part
Saturday, 13 May 1854

THE GREAT MANUFACTURER

Time passed Thomas on

Time passed Thomas on in the mill. . . . Time, sticking to him . . . passed him on into Bounderby's Bank] Tom is likened to an article moving through stages of a mechanized manufacturing process.
    Private banks had been steadily decreasing in number from the late 1830s. The Bank Reform Acts of 1826 and 1833 had made provision for the establishment of joint-stock banks, and up until the Bank Charter Act of 1844, which slightly curtailed their growth, joint-stock concerns proliferated. By 1844 there were over 100 joint-stock banks in England and Wales, compared to 273 private banks. When the 1844 regulations were repealed in 1857, only 157 private banks were in operation. With the extended facility of limited liability to banks in 1862, almost every new bank formed in the 1860s was a limited company. Thus, in the mid-1850s, a private bank faced strong opposition from share-based joint-stock banks (Anderson and Cottrell, 1975, 598–615; Crouzet, 1990, 323–30).

Book 1, Chapter 15   Eighth weekly part
Saturday, 20 May 1854

FATHER AND DAUGHTER

ALTHOUGH Mr Gradgrind did not take

Blue Beard] In the story of Blue Beard, often referred to by Dickens, a rich man disfigured by a blue beard marries six wives who all mysteriously disappear. His seventh wife, Fatima, becomes curious and discovers the room containing the bodies of her predecessors, but she herself is saved from death when her brothers arrive and kill Blue Beard. Although the story became well known in Britain through the first English translation in 1729 of Charles Perrault's *Contes du temps passé* (1696), similar stories are found in other countries (*Oxford Companion to English Literature*, 4th edn).

blue books. Whatever they could prove . . . they proved there, in an army constantly strengthening by the arrival of new recruits. In that charmed apartment, the most complicated social questions were cast up, got into exact totals, and finally settled] Although blue books had been in evidence from the beginning of the nineteenth century, it was not until the 1830s that they became important sociological sources for reformers and novelists alike. The proliferation of parliamentary and statistical society reports during the 1830s, 1840s and early 1850s – on sanitation, health, education, employment and conditions in mines and factories, the state of large towns and populous districts, prisons and the treatment of prisoners – provided valuable documentation of human suffering and degradation brought about by rapid industrialization. Notwithstanding their unconscious debt to these numerous reports, writers such as Dickens and Carlyle utilized blue-book data in order to criticize its methodology and subsequent assumptions about the ills of society. Like Carlyle, who remarked in *Chartism* that 'you might prove anything by figures' (ch. 2), Dickens was not against blue-book statisticians *per se*, but 'against those who see figures and averages, and nothing else' (30 December 1854, *Letters* 7.492). He had succinctly illustrated his belief ten years earlier in *The Chimes*, in which he drew on his knowledge of exploited seamstresses and milliners, set out in the *Second Report of the Children's Employment Commission* (1843), and subtly interwove their experience into Trotty Veck's emotional nightmare of Meg, to contrast with the dry tabular pronouncements of the political economist Mr Filer. Furthermore, in 1851 he had praised the 'first valuable reports' of sanitary reformers Edwin Chadwick and Dr Southwood Smith, 'strengthening and much enlarging [his] previous imperfect knowledge' about the spread of disease (*Speeches* 128–9). *BH* is also a testament to the increased awareness of society as an organic whole, revealed in blue books. Nevertheless, Dickens's early association of blue books and statistical reports with political economy and Benthamite ideology fostered a life-long suspicion of tabulated investigations (see, for example, the Statistics section of the 'Full Report of the First Meeting of the Mudfog Association', *The Mudfog Papers* (1837), and his attack in *OT* on the New Poor Laws). *HW*, itself a periodical full of factual information, reflected Dickens's ambivalence to blue books and statistics. In his announcement of the HW monthly supplement, *The Household Narrative*, Dickens described the proposed annual volume of HN as 'a complete Chronicle of all that year's events, carefully compiled, thoroughly digested, and systematically arranged for easy reference; presenting a vast mass of information that must be interesting to all' (1.49) (Brantlinger, 1977, 26–32; Smith, 1980, 156–7; Flint, 1987, 5).

As if an astronomical observatory should be made without any windows] The Old Royal Observatory at Greenwich (1675) was founded by Charles II and designed by Sir Christopher Wren.

In the mid-nineteenth century the observatory attained a distinguished reputation under the direction of George Biddell Airy, the seventh Astronomer Royal. During his term in office (1835–81), he established a Magnetic and Meteorological department (1840), introduced the Altazimuth (1847) which could make more frequent lunar observations, and erected the Great Transit Circle (1851), which constituted the chief instrument of the observatory at that time. Other contemporary observatories included one in Kew Gardens (1768) which was used for 'magnetic, photoheliographic, spectroscopic, and meteorological observations' (Thorne, 1876, 259–61, 394, 494; Maunder, 1900, 102–23). For a contemporary account of the Magnetic and Meteorological department at Greenwich, see 'Greenwich Weather-Wisdom', HW 1.222–5.

could settle all their destinies on a slate, and wipe out all their tears with one dirty little bit of sponge.] Compare Cassandra's words in Aeschylus, *Agamemnon*:

> This is the state of man: in prosperous fortune
> A shadow, passing light, throws to the ground
> Joy's baseless fabric: in adversity
> Comes malice with a spunge moisten'd in gall,
> And wipes each beauteous character away:
> More than the first this melts my soul to pity.
> (trans. Robert Potter)

The comment may also allude to the Christian mysteries of the Revelation, when all the souls called to heavenly glory shall have their robes washed 'white in the blood of the Lamb' and when God 'shall wipe away all tears from their eyes' (Revelation 7.14, 17; Szirotny, 1968, 421–2; Wheeler, 1979, 67).

To this Observatory, then: a stern room

To this Observatory, then . . . with a deadly-statistical clock in it] Dickens's association of astronomical enquiry with time is reminiscent of Carlyle's pronouncements in *Past and Present*:

There is no longer any God for us! God's Laws are become a Greatest-Happiness Principle, a Parliamentary Expediency: the Heavens overarch us only as an Astronomical Time-keeper; a butt for Herschel-telescopes to shoot science at, to shoot sentimentalities at. (3.1)

'Father,' said Louisa, 'do you think

'Father,' said Louisa, 'do you think I love Mr Bounderby?'] The following conversation between father and daughter reveals Gradgrind's failure to comprehend Louisa's emotional needs and hints strongly at her future unhappy marriage. A *HW* article which concerns the life of the artist Philip Roos, 'The Cankered Rose of Tivoli' (9.314–17), follows this serialized number of the novel (including Louisa's marriage to Bounderby in chapter 16). The story of Roos' wife – her miserable life with him and estrangement from her father – is a reminder of the breakdown of relationships taking place within the fiction.

'Why, my dear Louisa,' said Mr Gradgrind

tangible Fact] One of the proposed titles for the novel was 'Something tangible'.

You are, we will say in round numbers, twenty years of age; Mr Bounderby is . . . fifty.] Louisa is thirty-one or thirty-two years younger than Bounderby (see book 1, chapters 3 and 4). When Dickens first met Nelly Ternan in 1857, he was 45 years old and she was 18.

MS reads 'nineteen years'. Corrected on CP to 'twenty years'.

I find on reference to the figures, that a large proportion of these marriages are contracted between parties of very unequal ages, and that the elder of these contracting parties is, in rather more than three-fourths of these instances, the bridegroom.] According to the 1851 Census figures for England and Wales, the number of husbands aged between 50 and 55 years who had wives aged between 19 and 25 was 436 out of a total of 274,892 husbands enumerated. Moreover, comparing the equality and disparity of ages for 'Great Britain and Islands in the British Seas', the Census Report observed that 'the number of cases in which the husband and wife were born in the same year is considerable'. It was true, however, that most husbands were older than their wives: 'at every period of life the proportion of wives older than their husbands is much less than the proportion of husbands older than their wives'. For example, in England and Wales, the number of men aged between 50 and 100 who married women of 15 to 30 years was 3,708. The comparative figure for women of the older age groups who married young men was 296 (BPP 1852–3, 88, Part I, xxxvi–xxxviii, ccxiv). An amusing exception to these statistics is Mrs Sparsit, who was fifteen years older than her husband (book 1, chapter 7).

the Calmucks of Tartary] The Kalmucks, or Kalmyks, are a nomadic Mongol people who inhabit a stretch of land running from west of the Volga river along the north-west coast of the Caspian Sea.

From the beginning, she had sat looking at him

until the last trumpet ever to be sounded shall blow even algebra to wreck.] The allusion is to the seventh angel, who sounds the last trumpet, in Revelation 11.15.

'There seems to be nothing there

when the night comes, Fire bursts out] The image may be a recollection of an extended passage in Dickens's recently published *HW* article, 'Fire and Snow'. When night falls on the furnaces of Wolverhampton, 'darkness shall set off the fires'. Later 'the fires begin to appear':

> In all this ashy country, there is still not a cinder visible; in all this land of smoke, not a stain upon the universal white. A very novel and curious sight is presented by the hundreds of great fires blazing in the midst of the cold dead snow. They illuminate it very little . . . but, generally the fire burns in its own sullen ferocity, and the snow lies impassive and untouched. . . . Sacrificial altars . . . abound. Tongues of flame shoot up from them, and pillars of fire turn and twist upon them. Fortresses on fire, a whole town in a blaze.
> (21 January 1854, 8.482–3)

'It is short, no doubt, my dear.

the average duration of human life is proved to have increased of late years.] The gradual improvement in national health from the 1840s to the end of the century was reflected in the average life-expectancy rates. In 1841 the figure for England and Wales was 40.2 years (for men and women considered together); in 1911 it had risen to 51.5. Greater longevity, however, did not apply across the whole population (see note to book 1, chapter 10, p. 124), and in the 1850s there was still a vast variation in life-expectancy between the middle and working classes (Wohl, 1983, 5–6, 329).

Book 1, Chapter 16   Eighth weekly part
Saturday, 20 May 1854

HUSBAND AND WIFE

On his way home, on the evening

smelling-salts. . . . I'll have the skin off her nose]   The chief constituents of this restorative for fainting and headaches are carbonate of ammonia and scent.

Mr Bounderby sat looking at her

with the points of a stiff, sharp pair of scissors, she picked out holes for some inscrutable ornamental purpose, in a piece of cambric.]   This is a form of cutwork which is the basis of needlepoint lace. The technique involves using very sharp embroidery scissors to cut holes in strong fabrics which do not tend to fray – cambric, good linen, flannel and silk (Brittain, 1979, 281).

'Yes, sir?' returned Mrs Sparsit. 'I hope you may

work-box]   A box containing needlework tools and materials.

'Sir,' rejoined Mrs Sparsit

eating the bread of dependence]   A variation of many similar biblical phrases such as 'to eat the bread of sorrows' (Psalms 127:2), 'they eat the bread of wickedness' (Proverbs 4:17) and 'She . . . eateth not the bread of idleness' (Proverbs 31.27).

she might have said the sweetbread, for that delicate article . . . was her favourite supper]   Veal and lamb sweetbreads were a particular delicacy in the nineteenth century: veal sweetbreads were seasonal from May to August, and lamb sweetbreads from Easter to Michaelmas (Beeton 357, 431).

Meanwhile the marriage was appointed

settlements were made]   Before the Married Women's Property Act (1870), under the common-law principle of coverture all property belonging to a wife before marriage automatically became her husband's. In exceptional cases, a rich father would create a trust for his daughter to give her economic independence within marriage (Shanley, 1989, 8–9, 15).

The Hours did not go through any of those rosy performances, which foolish poets have ascribed to them at such times]   In the *Iliad* and elsewhere in Greek and Roman mythology, the hours (Horae) are personifications of atmospheric moisture: they open and close the gates of Olympus, create and disperse the clouds, and govern the seasons and human life. 'Rosy performances' alludes to the depiction of the Hours in classical and Renaissance art and literature as carrying fruit and flowers. Also, they are the attendants of Aurora, described in Homer's *Odyssey* as the 'rosy-fingered dawn', an image that recurs in Shakespeare and the eighteenth-century poets.

So the day came, as all other days come

when they were united in holy matrimony, they went home to breakfast]   During most of the nineteenth century, marriages in church without a special licence could be performed only between the hours of eight o'clock in the morning and midday. For this reason, a 'breakfast' was the usual form of celebration following the wedding:

> The etiquette of wedding breakfasts varies considerably in good circles. . . . The "breakfast" is more properly a luncheon, as soup, *entrées*, game, etc., may be provided, and champagne often supplies the place of coffee and tea which do not appear. . . . Towards the conclusion of the meal . . . [t]he bride's father proposes the health of the pair, the bridegroom responds. . . . and other toasts follow. At the conclusion of the breakfast, the bride retires to assume her travelling-dress, her adieux are then made, and she proceeds to the travelling-carriage with the bridegroom. (*The Etiquette of Modern Society: a guide to good manners in every possible situation*, 1882, 41)

There was an improving party assembled

bottoms]   That is, 'ships', in which the imported champagne, port and sherry would have travelled. (The 'bottom' is the part of the hull below the water-line.)

the calculating boy]   For this possible allusion to George Parker Bidder, see note to book 1, chapter 2, pp. 38–40.

Shortly after which oration, as they were going

Lyons]   Lyons was the European centre of silk manufacture, the production of which was greatly enhanced by the introduction of a loom invented by Joseph-Marie Jacquard (1752–1834). The Jacquard loom, which was the first to weave figured fabrics, was patented in 1804 and became the early prototype of the automatic loom. It was introduced into England in the 1820s. In a speech given by James Kay-Shuttleworth on 11 January 1854, the French were praised for their superiority in this field:

Thus the Jacquard loom, by which the beautiful figured silks and stuffs of Lyons were woven was worked, not in vast fabrics like our factories, but in the separate houses of the weavers. This invention is remarkably characteristic of French genius and skill. (*Manchester Guardian*, 18.1.1854, 3)

Dickens did not need Shuttleworth's pronouncements about Lyons to decide to send Bounderby and Louisa there on a working honeymoon. He had visited Lyons in July 1844 and wrote to his friend, the artist Count D'Orsay: 'Were you ever at Lyons? That's the place. It's a great Nightmare – a bad conscience – a fit of indigestion – the recollection of having done a murder. An awful place!' (*Letters* 4.170). In *PI* Dickens reiterated his distaste for Lyons:

> Every manufacturing town, melted into one, would hardly convey an impression of Lyons as it presented itself to me: for all the undrained, unscavengered qualities of a foreign town seemed engrafted, there, upon the native miseries of a manufacturing one; and it bears such fruit as I would go some miles out of my way to avoid encountering again.
> ('Lyons, the Rhone, and the Goblin of Avignon')

BOOK THE SECOND.
REAPING.

REAPING]   See Galatians 6.7: 'for whatsoever a man soweth, that shall he also reap'.

Book 2, Chapter 1   Ninth weekly part
                                                  Saturday, 27 May 1854

EFFECTS IN THE BANK

The wonder was, it was there at all.

They were ruined, when they were required to send labouring children to school]   Manufacturers were required by the 1844 Factory Act to produce a weekly certificate from a schoolteacher as evidence that a factory child had attended school for at least three hours in a working day. Factory inspectors could annul certificates if they deemed a schoolteacher unfit to instruct children, and they were bound to name an alternative school within two miles of the factory before such an annulment could take place (7 *Vict.* Cap. 15, XXXVIII–IX). In his inspection of schools attended by factory children in Lancashire and Yorkshire, factory inspector Leonard Horner found the majority of schools he visited

> under the pressure of severe poverty: the teachers most inadequately remunerated; books and other school materials deficient in quantity – torn and defaced; scanty, ill contrived furniture; and very often the poor children in a state of bodily suffering, and even of danger to their health, from bad ventilation or imperfectly finished rooms. (*BPP* 1854, 19.266)

chopping people up with their machinery]   For a discussion of factory accidents, see note to book 1, chapter 13, pp. 143–6.

they need not always make quite so much smoke.]   The Towns Improvement Clauses Act (1847) stated that

> every fireplace or furnace constructed after the passing of the special Act, in order to be used within the limits of such Act in the working of engines by

steam, or in any mill, factory, dyehouse, brewery, bakehouse, gaswork, or in any manufactory whatsoever . . . shall be so constructed as to consume the smoke arising from the combustibles used in such fireplace or furnace.
(10 & 11 Vict. Clause 108, Cap. 34)

Some manufacturers had installed equipment before the 1847 Act in an effort to counteract the clouds of coal smoke which hung over their towns (Mrs Gaskell based the character of John Thornton, in *North and South* (1854–5), on such benign employers.) Despite the 1847 Act, however, smoke pollution from factories was still a major problem in the majority of cities and towns in England in the 1850s. Thornton succinctly explained the position for Manchester – Mrs Gaskell's Milton:

> It was an immediate outlay, but it repays me in the saving of coal. I'm not sure whether I should have done it, if I had waited until the act was passed. At any rate, I should have waited to be informed against and fined, and given all the trouble in yielding that I legally could. But all laws which depend for their enforcement upon informers and fines, become inert from the odiousness of the machinery. I doubt if there has been a chimney in Milton informed against for five years past, although some are constantly sending out one-third of their coal in what is called here unparliamentary smoke.
> <div style="text-align: right">(1.10; <i>HW</i> 10 [7 October 1854] 182)</div>

A *HW* article of December 1853, 'Locked Out', reported that during the Preston strike of 1853–4 'instead of being thick and smoky' the atmosphere of Preston was 'as clear . . . as the air upon Hampstead Heath'. When 'in full work' Preston is 'different from many other manufacturing towns. It is surrounded by agriculture – a smoky island in the middle of an expansive cornfield' (8.345). The Preston historian Charles Hardwick insisted, however, that Preston was an exception to other manufacturing towns because of its elevated position, good drainage, and the sea and mountain breezes: 'That melancholy mixture of smoke and fog, which . . . enshrouds many of our modern "hives of industry" in semi-darkness at noon day, is seldom seen at Preston, except in a very diluted condition' (1857, 427).

Whenever a Coketowner felt he was ill-used . . . he was sure to come out with the awful menace, that he would 'sooner pitch his property into the Atlantic'.] An allusion to manufacturers' resentment and constant flouting of factory legislation. In a joint reply to Harriet Martineau's attack on Dickens's treatment of the factory accident controversy in both *HT* and *HW*, Dickens and Morley deal with Martineau's statement that 'the issue . . . to which the controversy is now brought, is that of the supersession of either the textile manufacturers, or the existing factory law. The two cannot longer co-exist':

> This is one of those remarkable predictions of which we are beginning, by a very long national experience, to understand the value. If the cry be not ridiculous enough in the form just quoted, how does it look thus . . . . "It seems to be agreed by the common sense of all concerned who have any common

Mrs Sparsit's life at the Bank?   <u>Yes.</u>

    Bitzer, Light Porter   <u>Yes</u>

     Tom's progress   <u>Yes</u>

      Louisa's married life - <u>Dawn of knowledge of her immaterial</u>

          <u>Self - Too late</u>   <u>Scarcely yet.</u>

       Man dropped in Nº: 1   ?   Yes.   Percy Harthouse
                                                              Jem
                                                              James

       A Sunny day in coketown   <u>?</u>   Picture ?   <u>Yes.</u>

         Popular leader   ?   <u>Yes.</u>

           Lover for Sissy ?   <u>No. Decide on no love at all.</u>

            Sissy and Rachael to become acquainted ?   <u>No.</u>

(Hard Times.)   Nº: III.

Weekly Nº: 9.

chapter XVII.

Fire buckets

Mrs Sparsit & Bitzer - Bank description

/ Introduce Mr James Harthouse
                         ___ "Ugh - You - Fool!" said Mrs Sparsit

Weekly Nº: 10

Chapter XVIII.

James Harthouse's antecedents.
    / Bounderby explains Coketown.   "And now you know the place
        / Sees Louisa for the first time   _____ and Tom.

Chapter XIX.

Tom goes home with James Harthouse to smoke.   — Genteel demon
/ Tom shews him everything   — and had better have drowned himself

Weekly Nº: 11

chapter XX.

Working mens' meeting.   Slackbridge the orator
       Stephen won't join, and is sent to Coventry

chapter XXI.

Scene at Bounderby's /
       Stephen's exposition of the Slackbridge question
"Ill-conditioned fellow - your own people get rid of you - well then. I'll get rid of you too"

Weekly Nº: 12

chapter XXII.

Bounderby's old mother again - and Rachael.

/ Scene at Stephens. Louisa

             And Tom (with his Bank scheme)
                     In the dark

Morning picture, of Stephen going away from Coketown
           Out of the coal ashes on to the country dust.

sense, that our manufacturers must cease, or the factory law ... must give way." We believe it was Mr. Bounderby who was always going to throw his property into the Atlantic, and we have heard of Miss Martineau's clients being indignant against Mr. Bounderby as a caricature. And yet this looks very like him! ('Our Wicked Mis-statements', *HW* 13 [19 January 1856] 15–16)

See note to book 1, chapter 13, pp. 143–6.

the Home Secretary] Lord Palmerston (1784–1865) was Home Secretary from 1852 until 1855, apart from a brief period out of office during December 1853. On 21 February 1854 he had been faced with an angry deputation of manufacturers protesting against a Factory Inspectors' circular of 31 January, which, at Palmerston's insistence, had ordered that every shaft be fenced regardless of height or shape. Palmerston retreated in the face of such opposition, and a second letter was circulated on 15 March 1854 suspending the requirements of the original order. It was not until January 1855, as a consequence of a change in Home Office policy, that manufacturers had to comply fully with factory safety legislation.

The Preston strike of cotton operatives in 1853–4 also highlighted Palmerston's equivocal attitude. On 21 November 1853 he received a memorial from the Preston power-loom weavers which related the origins of the strike and set out the workers' case in the dispute. Palmerston was also informed of the weavers' earlier proposals for reconciliation, either by direct talks with their employers or by arbitration, both of which were rejected by the Masters' Association. The weavers assured Palmerston that he would find them 'always prepared to adopt any reasonable course calculated to promote the peace of the country, and the happiness and social well being of its Inhabitants' (*HO* 45/5128E, 45). Palmerston's response to the weavers, widely publicized at the time, was disappointing. He claimed that as a member of the Government he possessed no power to interfere in the dispute, and he proceeded to tell the memorialists that labour was a commodity, that strikes were the cause of 'many and great' evils, and that the politico-economic laws of supply and demand must be allowed to operate. However, in January 1854, via a series of private arrangements, Lyon Playfair, of the Department of Science and Art, agreed to investigate the relations between the Preston manufacturers and their workers. After discussions with a Burnley manufacturer and editors from the regional papers, Playfair reported that the overall belief was that the strike was coming to an end. Palmerston considered that further participation was not necessary (see Dutton and King, 1981, chapter 8, for a full discussion of Palmerston's political motives in secretly initiating tentative government mediation).

However, the Coketowners were so patriotic

and it increased and multiplied.] Reminiscent of Genesis 9.1: 'And God blessed Noah and his sons, and said unto them, Be fruitful, and multiply, and replenish the earth'.

The streets were hot and dusty

There was a stifling smell of hot oil everywhere . . . the mills throughout their many stories oozed and trickled it.] The regular oiling of mechanical couplings and mill-gearing not only created an unpleasant odour in the already hot and humid environment of the spinning-blocks, but it also carried a high degree of risk. Quite apart from the dangerous process of lubricating inadequately fenced machinery, the workers' constant contact with oil gave rise to what was later diagnosed as 'mulespinner's cancer', an occupational disease caused by a worker stretching over a barrier to piece together broken ends of yarn, so pressing oily workclothes against the skin. Moreover, the combination of machine oil and water (from the constant steaming of the atmosphere to work the delicate yarn) produced slippery conditions which forced many spinners to work barefoot (*Old Yarns Respun*, 1991, 6; Appleby, 1994, 59–60).

the breath of the simoom] A hot and suffocating sand-wind which blows across the Asiatic and African deserts periodically during spring and summer (*OED*).

The measured motion of their shadows on the walls . . . for the shadows of rustling woods] Compare Dickens's comments when he visited one of the Preston mills which had stayed open for most of the lock-out from 15 October 1853 until 9 February 1854:

> Four hundred people could find employment in it; there were eighty-five at work, of whom five had "come in" that morning. They looked, among the vast array of motionless power-looms, like a few remaining leaves in a wintry forest. ('On Strike', *HW* 8.558)

Drowsily they whirred all through

the sun itself . . . rarely looked intently into any of its closer regions without engendering more death than life.] 'The Quiet Poor' (*HW*, 1854) observed that in one poor district of Bethnal Green the 'summer heat lifts out of the filthy courts a heavy vapour of death, the overcrowded rooms are scarcely tenantable. . . . The air everywhere indeed is stifling, but within doors many of the cottages must be intolerable'. The minister of the parish, although 'truly a Christian gentleman . . . has his body to maintain alive, and dares not remain too long in the poison bath of his unsewered district during the hot summer days' (9.202).

the eye of Heaven] The sun. This was a favourite Shakespearian image. Compare, for example, *King John* 4.2:

> . . . to be possess'd with double pomp,
> To guard a title that was rich before,
> To gild refined gold, to paint the lily,
>   . . . or with taper-light

To seek the beauteous eye of heaven to garnish,
Is wasteful and ridiculous excess. (9–16)

See also *The Comedy of Errors* (2.1.16), *Love's Labour's Lost* (5.2.375), *Titus Andronicus* (2.1.130) and *The Rape of Lucrece* (356).

Mrs Sparsit sat in her afternoon apartment

Office-hours were over]   Opening hours for the Bank of England were from nine to four daily (see 'The Old Lady in Threadneedle Street', *HW* 1 [6 July 1850] 337–42).

Mrs Sparsit was conscious

the Bank Dragon, keeping watch over the treasures of the mine.]   Here and in the next paragraph, Mrs Sparsit is likened to the dragon Ladon who guards the golden apples in the garden of the Hesperides. For her comparison to another guardian beast in Greek mythology – the griffin – see note to book 3, chapter 2, p. 211.

What those treasures were, Mrs Sparsit knew

secrets that if divulged would bring vague destruction upon vague persons . . . she reigned supreme . . . over a locked-up iron room with three locks]   The Stock Offices in the Bank of England contained

> records of the Dividends that are, and have been, and of the Dividends unclaimed. Some men would sell their fathers into slavery, to have the rummaging of these old volumes. . . . These are the books to profit by. (*HW* 1.341)

The bank's Storeroom, where new notes were kept, contained a number of large iron safes with double locks attached. Two storekeepers each had a key to his own particular safes (1.339).

light porter]   An employee required to do only light duties. The light-haired Bitzer carries out the varied tasks of bank messenger, waiter and security guard.

laid his head every night]   In 'The Old Lady in Threadneedle Street' 'two of the Senior Clerks sit up in turn every night, to watch over her [the Bank of England]; in which duty they are assisted by a company of Foot Guards' (*HW* 1.342).

a truckle bed, that disappeared at cockcrow]   A low bed running on truckles (corded, grooved wheels) or castors, which was usually pushed underneath a 'standing' bed when not in use. In houses where servants' quarters were scarce, it was usual for the kitchen maid or maid-of-all-work to sleep in a truckle bed under the kitchen table.

Bitzer and his bed are well matched: 'to truckle' means to submit from an unworthy motive, to act with servility (OED).

wafers] Small coloured discs made from flour mixed with gum or gelatine. When moistened they were used for sealing letters or for receiving the impression of a seal (OED).

'Merely going on in the old way, ma'am.

Uniting, and leaguing, and engaging to stand by one another.'] Dickens's contradictory depiction of trade unionism reflects his ambivalent attitude towards workers' combinations. The attitude was shared by many of his contemporaries. The equivocal notions evolved from the history of the unions' struggle for recognition in an industrialized society governed by the laws of supply and demand. From the late eighteenth century, the nascent factory system had effected a radical change in the relationship between masters and men. The old guilds which had accommodated the interests of both skilled journeymen and masters could not survive in an industrial society, and other forms of separate combination were necessary for the preservation of workers' rights. With the increasing adoption of laissez-faire economics (which in effect disposed of traditional wage regulation), combinations were viewed by employers and government as being anarchic and politically dangerous. Thus, in many trades, legislative steps were taken to outlaw them. Nevertheless, clubs, associations and trade societies furtively flourished – often within friendly societies which had acquired legal status in 1793 by the Friendly Societies Act. Under their aegis, funds legitimately used for workers' life insurance, sickness and unemployment benefits could also be diverted to provide pay during strikes.

The ineffectual Combination Acts of 1799 and 1800 – a reaction by the Government against fears of revolution during the war with France – were repealed in 1824. However, in 1825, after a series of militant strikes organized by the newly liberated trade unions, the Combination of Workmen Act was introduced which severely limited the legal concessions made to combinations the previous year. From 1825 until the 1860s, trade unionism defiantly grew and developed outside the legal constraints placed upon combinations to confine their dealings only to matters of wages, prices and hours of work. Between 1829 and 1834, several attempts were made to establish general unions, but these all proved short-lived. During the 1830s the steady formation of small craft unions and larger district societies gave the worker a more trustworthy and supportive base than the general unions could guarantee. A milder and limited form of confederation of trades appeared in 1845 with the establishment of the National Association of United Trades for the Protection of Labour. This body sought to combine autonomous unions only for the purpose of industrial arbitration and parliamentary lobbying on the workers' behalf. The Association remained active up until the mid-1860s, but its influence waned considerably from 1851. By the 1850s the trade union movement had striven to rid itself of its militant image and to exhibit a commitment to self-help, moderation, social improvement and respectability. The early union resistance to industrial change was generally replaced by a willingness to work within the established system. The difficult task for trade unionists in the mid-nineteenth century was to convince their middle-class opponents that their values were not dissimilar to their own.

Unfortunately, the old Luddite image of unionism remained uppermost in the Victorian mind. This had much to do with the industrial unrest of the 1830s and 1840s, and the turbulent decade of Chartist activity until 1848. Thus, the widely held misconception that all working-class combinations must be revolutionary, dictatorial and physically violent disfigured the emergent face of unionism in the 1850s. Additionally, the clash with politico-economic theory which condemned wage bargaining as disadvantageous to other groups of poorer workers morally marred trade-union policy in the eyes of many middle-class observers. Such views proved especially detrimental to the engineering union, the Amalgamated Society of Engineers, during their strike of 1852 (see note to book 2, chapter 4, pp. 175–7). Significantly, when the cotton operatives of Preston were locked out on 15 October 1853, the workers received a sympathetic (if not supportive) response from the press and public alike. This crucial modification of opinion, initially triggered by the mill-owners' intransigence during the dispute, demonstrated a growing awareness that unions and combinations had a role to play in industrial relations.

Many novels of the 1840s and early 1850s concerned with trade-union activity tended to reflect the old, but persistent, image of rebellion and secret rituals: see, for example, Dickens's BR (1841), Disraeli's *Sybil* (1845), Mrs Gaskell's *Mary Barton* (1848), Charlotte Brontë's *Shirley* (1849) and Charles Kingsley's *Alton Locke* (1850). The portrayal of the union in HT, however, is indicative of society's changing perception of working-class protectionism: it was simultaneously condoned and condemned (Pelling, 1963, passim; Brantlinger, 1969, 37–52; Fraser, 1974, 43, 54–9, 75–6, 185–6, 200–1; Hopkins, 1979, 39–41; Pimlott and Cook (eds), 1982, 15–18; Evans, 1983, 164–5).

'Being united themselves, they ought

'Being united themselves, they ought one and all to set their faces against employing any man who is united with any other man,'] The Preston Masters' Association was considered one of Lancashire's most formidable employers' unions. Its strength had been proved in the unsuccessful spinners' strike of 1836, and it is likely that the association was influential during the years of depressed trade between 1846 and 1848 when short-time working and wage reductions were endemic throughout the county. (Dutton and King, 1981, 86–7, state that there is no direct proof of its role at that time; however, James Lowe, a contemporary commentator on the Preston strike of 1853–4, reported that the association, revived secretly on 18 March 1853, had been dormant since 1847.)

The Manchester Spinners and Manufacturers' Association was formed on 7 July 1853 in response to a rash of strikes by the city's mill-workers for an increase in wages. As a protective measure against workers' unions and with a view to standardizing piece-work lists within the whole cotton industry, the Manchester organization agreed to establish local employers' associations which in turn would unite as a central federation. Little is known of the operations of the umbrella association during the industrial strikes which eventually centred on Preston in August 1853, but it would appear that the Preston Masters' Association had adequate autonomous power of its own, with an iron determination to break down trade-union influence over their workforce – a factor which became more important than the wages dispute itself. In an issue of the *Preston Guardian* published three weeks after the start of the Preston lock-out on 15 October 1853, this shift of emphasis was recognized – as was the hypocrisy of the masters:

> the masters have clearly no reason to dictate to the operatives. They themselves "combine;" they have their "Masters Association," their corresponding and peripatetic secretaries, their bonds of agreement, and their five-thousand pound penalties for breaches of contract; and it is an error to say that all this is but an act of self defence, for a union of masters existed prior to the present general combination of the operatives, although . . . it was less active, compact, and conspicuous than at present. In our opinion, therefore, the masters take untenable ground when they demand a dissolution of the operatives' union as an indispensable condition to the re-opening of their mills, unless they accompany this demand with an intimation that they themselves are prepared to abandon their "association," and to allow each of their body to deal with his workmen according to his own judgment and circumstances.
>
> (5 November 1853)

In his Preston article, 'On Strike', Dickens noted the obvious flaw in the masters' association's stance and called the lock-out 'a grave error'. He stated that the workers had 'a perfect right to combine in any lawful manner' and that combination 'may . . . be a protection to them' (*HW* 8.554) (Lowe, 1860, 214; Dutton and King, 1981, passim).

He held the respectable office of general spy

buy it for as little as he could possibly give, and sell it for as much as he could possibly get]   A reference to the politico-economic doctrine of buying in the cheapest market and selling in the dearest.

it having been clearly ascertained by philosophers that in this is comprised the whole duty of man – not a part of man's duty, but the whole.]   MS and CP have instead: 'but to err is human, and this was his solitary error'.

the whole duty of man]   An allusion to a popular religious manual, *The Practice of Christian Graces; or, The Whole Duty of Man laid down in a plain and familiar way . . . With Private Devotions for several occasions*, published anonymously in 1659 but probably written by Richard Allestree. The work was popularly referred to as *The Whole Duty of Man* and went through numerous editions in the seventeenth and eighteenth centuries; eight editions were published in the nineteenth century.

'I am sure we are constantly hearing ma'am

I don't want a wife and family. Why should they? ... If they were more provident, and less perverse.... They would say, "While my hat covers my family," ... "I have only one to feed, and that's the person I most like to feed." '] Bitzer's pronouncements stem from the Malthusian notion of the different ratios between population and subsistence: 'that the power of population is indefinitely greater than the power in the earth to produce subsistence for man' (Malthus, *Essay*, 1798, 71). In his *Summary View* (1830) Malthus identified two checks – 'preventive' and 'positive' – which, in the case of population increasing faster than food supply, must operate as certainly 'as that man cannot live without food':

> there is no reason whatever to suppose that anything besides the difficulty of procuring in adequate plenty the necessaries of life should either indispose [a] greater number of persons to marry early, or disable them from rearing in health the largest families. But this difficulty would of necessity occur, and its effect would be either to discourage early marriages, which would check the rate of increase by preventing the same proportion of births, or to render the children unhealthy from bad and insufficient nourishment, which would check the rate of increase by occasioning a greater proportion of deaths; or, what is most likely to happen, the rate of increase would be checked, partly by the diminution of births, and partly by the increase of mortality. (243)

During a lesson on social economy given by William Ellis, and reported in 'Rational Schools', a teacher asks the question:

> "If we were all educated, all civilised and working hard, pulling together to increase the wealth of us all – what effect would that have, or would it have any effect, do you think, in increasing or lessening the number of mouths we have to feed?"

A boy replies 'that there would not be quite so many of us: because'

> "If men were intelligent and prudent they would not often marry till they knew beforehand how they were to feed and educate their children."
>
> (HW 6.341)

Dickens criticized this form of social engineering in his satirical portrait of Mr Filer in *The Chimes*. See also 'Chip: A Lesson in Multiplication', *HW* 9 [10 June 1854] 398, about the rise in population.

'If you please, ma'am, the gentleman

entered the board-room in the manner of a Roman matron going outside the city walls to treat with an invading general.] Volumnia, the mother of Coriolanus, entreated her son outside the Roman walls to spare the city from his invading army (*Coriolanus* 5.3).

'Humph!' thought Mrs Sparsit

like the Sultan who put his head in the pail of water] In the *Turkish Tales* (1708) is the story of an Egyptian sultan who needed to be convinced about a passage from the Koran which stated that Muhammad could see 'all things in the seven Heavens, in Paradise, and in Hell' and 'held ninety thousand Conferences with God' in the space of time between an earthen pitcher of water being overturned and before the water was spilt. A 'great Doctor in the Law' duly directed the sceptical sultan to plunge his head into a tub of water and draw it up again immediately. During those seconds the sultan relived past experiences and was 'seized with many melancholy reflections upon his former and his present state of life'. The story is recounted by Addison in the *Spectator* 2, no. 94 (18 June 1711), 71–3 (Easson, 1973, 63; see also Svilpis, 1991, 177–8).

'Assuredly,' said the stranger. 'Much obliged to you

one of the working people; who appeared to have been taking a shower-bath of something fluffy] A fine fluffy dust was produced by the carding process, a stage of manufacture which prepared raw cotton for spinning into yarn (see note to book 2, chapter 5, p. 185). The dust was inhaled by the carding-room operatives and many suffered respiratory disorders, such as weaver's or carder's cough – an asthmatic condition that invariably led to chronic lung disease such as emphysema and caused numerous premature deaths. It was the early study of the inhalation of cotton fluff in 1827 which led the young Dr James Kay (later Kay-Shuttleworth) to his famous indepth investigation published in 1832 as *The Moral and Physical Condition of the Working Class Employed in the Cotton Manufacture in Manchester* (Appleby, 1994, 59).

Bessy Higgins is a victim of the carding-room disease in Mrs Gaskell's *North and South* (1854–5): 'They say it winds round the lungs, and tightens them up. Anyhow, there's many a one as works in a carding-room, that falls into a waste, coughing and spitting blood, because they're just poisoned by the fluff' (1.13; *HW* 10 [14 October 1854] 208).

The shower-bath was a lounge or hip bath with an overhead water-tank supported on legs. The water was pumped from a bucket and forced up one of the supporting legs which served as a pipe. One early shower-bath contained a small circular bath about the same size as its water-tank. Partakers of a cold shower were warned that 'nearly freezing water from a Shower Bath produces a feeling somewhat akin to what might be imagined to result from a shower of red-hot lead; the shock is tremendous, and the shower, if continued for any length of time, would assuredly cause asphyxia' (Wright, 1960, 174). Some Victorian hotels had shower-baths (Dickens enthused about one when staying at the Albion Hotel, Broadstairs, in July 1849), and shower-baths were one of the treatments offered at hydropathy establishments

(*Letters* 5.568, 574 and note, 583, 6.316; Turner, 1967, 149–50, 181; see also 'Malvern Water', *HW* 4.67–71).

Book 2, Chapter 2   Tenth weekly part
                                              Saturday, 3 June 1854

MR JAMES HARTHOUSE

THE Gradgrind party wanted assistance

the Graces]   In Greek mythology, the Charites (called Gratiae by the Romans): the three daughters of Zeus – Aglaia, Thalia and Euphrosyne – who represented charm, beauty and happiness.

Among the fine gentlemen not regularly belonging

his (and the Board of Directors') view of a railway accident, in which the most careful officers ever known . . . assisted by the finest mechanical contrivances ever devised . . . had killed five people and wounded thirty-two]   The common occurrence of railway accidents was brought to the attention of the House of Lords in February 1854, when railway companies were criticized for their self-interested management and their rivalry at the expense of public safety. The problem lay in the half-hearted implementation of the 1844 Railway Act which, for the first time, regulated passenger services and gave a future option for government ownership of new lines. A Railways Board had also been set up in 1844 to inspect and investigate railway accidents. Government interference was minimal, however, not only as a result of the belief in free competition, but also because of the substantial investments in railways made by MPs (over 100 MPs in the 1850s had vested interests in the railways). Thus, like the flouting of factory safety legislation by manufacturers, the directors of railway companies in many cases refused to acknowledge liability for the frequent incidence of fatalities and injuries on their lines (Evans, 1983, 117, 288).

   The Household Narrative (1854, 44) reported that in Great Britain and Ireland, for the half-year ending 30 June 1853, 148 people were killed and 191 were injured on all passenger railways open for public traffic (there were 7,512 miles of open railway at that date). A *HW* article of 1851, 'Need Railway Travellers Be Smashed?' (4.217–21), addresses the indifference of government and railway directors to the introduction of a new signalling apparatus which would eradicate 'the most dangerous and frequent class of railway accidents, rendering those points along a line which now are the most dangerous – sidings, stations, and junctions – the points at which an accident will be least likely to occur' (217). The article concludes that we, as travellers, having found out the existence of an invention which promises to lessen our risk of life and limb on railway lines, expect that this invention shall be fairly tested by the railway companies, and . . . If Mr. Whitworth's [the inventor's] plan be good, no Board of Directors ought to fear the small expense attendant upon its adoption. The money lost by calamities on a line, if put against this outlay, may seem something less; we do not know how that may be. But, may we be allowed to hint, that the loss of credit which follows upon every casualty, is, perhaps, also to be considered; and that the more or less of public confidence may not be inoperative on the value of a railway share?

Now, this gentleman had a younger brother

had tried life as a Cornet of Dragoons, and found it a bore . . . and got bored everywhere. . . . I wonder you don't go in for statistics.' Jem . . . went in. He coached himself up with a blue book or two] Harthouse represents the type of young man, usually upper-class, who has not been trained for any particular profession or calling, has spent time travelling on the Continent and then has drifted into a series of fruitless careers. His characterization owes much to Carlyle's 'Idle Dilettantism' (*Past and Present*, 3.1), evident later in the figures of Henry Gowan (*LD*) and Eugene Wrayburn (*OMF*). The 'Gospel of Dilettantism' produces 'a Governing Class who do not govern, nor understand in the least that they are bound or expected to govern. . . . Accordingly the impotent, insolent Donothingism in Practice and Saynothingism in Speech . . . is altogether amazing' (3.3).

The topical problem of placing such young men in a suitable occupation was discussed somewhat ironically in the *Times* of 27 January 1854 through the reflections of a fictional patron:

> We have not much interest with peers, so he shall be secretary to an MP. There is not much trouble involved in the pursuit. It is astounding, after three months' manipulation of blue books, how intensely wise a man may appear in the eyes of those who do not affect that class of literature.
>
> (Quoted in Oddie, 1972, 57)

A Cornet of Dragoons is an officer in a cavalry troop. To 'go in' is a term in cricket: each member of the team which is batting 'goes in' when he takes his place on the field of play to try to score runs.

'Don't be too sure of that,' said Bounderby.

you see our smoke. That's meat and drink to us. It's the healthiest thing in the world in all respects, and particularly for the lungs. If you are one of those who want us to consume it, I differ from you.] This was one of the requirements of the Towns Improvement Clauses Act of 1847. See note to book 2, chapter 1, pp. 154–5. 'Meat and drink' is an idiomatic expression derived from Romans 14.17: 'For the

Kingdom of God is not meat and drink; but righteousness, and peace, and joy in the Holy Ghost.'

'I am glad to hear it,' said Bounderby.

it's the best paid work there is.]   The average pay for weavers – of which over 60 per cent were women – was 10–12s per week (15s for specialized work). Spinners – virtually all male – earned from £1 to £2 weekly ('Lancashire Witchcraft', *HW* 8.551; Dutton and King, 1981, 14).

From the mistress of the house, the visitor

household gods]   From *lares* and *penates*, the classical Roman tutelary deities of the household. In private worship in Roman houses, crowned images of the *lares* were placed in a shrine to which offerings were made at meal-time, while images of the *penates* stood in the atrium, where a perpetual fire burnt in their honour.

'This, sir,' said Bounderby, 'is my wife

She has lots of expensive knowledge, sir, political and otherwise.]   After 'otherwise.' the MS reads: 'Would do no discredit to Parliament if she could get there.'

'I have not so much as the slightest

There's an English family with a charming Italian motto. What will be, will be.]   The Italian proverb, 'Che sarà sarà' – the family motto of the Russells. The Harthouse philosophy is synonymous with the doctrine of laissez-faire (see notes to book 1, chapter 2, pp. 33–4, and book 1, chapter 10, pp. 126–7).

Mr Bounderby, who had been in danger

blue coaching]   Studying information from parliamentary blue books.

In the evening, he found the dinner-table

had eaten in his youth at least three horses under the guise of polonies and saveloys.]   Types of highly seasoned sausage which usually contained pork. However, horsemeat was frequently added to give the sausage firmness (*OED*; Freeman 27). 'The Cattle-Road to Ruin' describes the horrors of a London horse slaughter-house situated near the largest sausage factory in the metropolis: 'the diseased bullocks . . . are taken to the sausage machine, to be advantageously mixed with the choppings of horse-flesh (to which latter ingredient the angry redness of so many "cured" sausages, *saveloys*, and all the class of *polonies* is attributable)' (HW 1.327). In an article later that year, 'Mr. Booley's View of the Last Lord Mayor's Show', Dickens cynically reports that, in parading an elephant,

> an animal so well known for its aversion to carrion, and its liking for clean provender, the City of London . . . avowed its determination to seek out and confiscate all improper human food exposed for sale within its liberties, and particularly to look, with a searching eye, into the knackers' yards, and the sausage trade. (2.219)

Betsy Prig, in MC, has 'nothink to say to the cold meat' at the Bull Inn, 'for it tastes of the stable' (25), and as Tom and Ruth Pinch stroll through Covent Garden Market they spot 'white country sausages beyond impeachment by surviving cat or dog, or horse or donkey' (40). See also 'Bound for the Great Salt Lake' in which 'Down by the Docks, you may buy polonies, saveloys, and sausage preparations various, if you are not particular what they are made of besides seasoning' (*UT*).

Book 2, Chapter 3 Tenth weekly part
Saturday, 3 June 1854

THE WHELP

He could do no less than ask Tom up

a rarer tobacco than was to be bought in those parts] According to Dodd (1856), the finer tobaccos originated in the Middle East:

> Of the various sorts of tobacco best known in London, Virginia is a strong common kind . . . Cuba and Columbia tobaccos are mostly used for cigars . . . Turkey, Levant, and Persian tobacco are more delicate in flavour and higher in price. (449)

James Harthouse continued to lounge

as if he knew himself to be a kind of agreeable demon who had only to hover over him, and he must give up his whole soul if required.] An allusion to the sixteenth-century legend dramatized in Marlowe's *Dr Faustus* (1604) and Goethe's *Faust* (Part 1, 1808; Part 2, 1832). In the story, a wandering magician sells his soul to the

Devil in return for worldly power or pleasure. Dickens would have known both dramatic versions. The phrase 'agreeable demon' may be a reference to the bad angel in *Dr Faustus*. In Marlowe's play, Dr Faustus is visited by a 'Good Angel' and an 'Evil Angel'. The Evil Angel's offer to Faustus 'of honour and . . . wealth' proves to be more persuasive than the Good Angel's plea to 'think of heaven and heavenly things' (1.5.20–3).

'He did though,' said Tom, shaking his head.

as flat as a warming-pan] Colloquially, 'flat' means inexperienced, dull or silly. A warming-pan was a long-handled covered pan of brass or copper which was filled with hot coals and placed between the bedclothes to heat a bed (Hotten; OED).

The whelp went home, and went to bed.

might have gone down to the ill-smelling river that was dyed black . . . and have curtained his head for ever with its filthy waters.] John Boucher, the victim of trade-union tyranny in *North and South* (1854–5), is found lying face-down in a discoloured stream used for dyeing purposes (2.11; HW 10 (30 December 1854) 471). See note to book 1, chapter 5, pp. 79–81, about pollution of rivers and canals.

Book 2, Chapter 4 Eleventh weekly part
Saturday, 10 June 1854

MEN AND BROTHERS

The words 'Am I not a man and a brother?' were inscribed on a Wedgwood cameo issued in 1786 which depicted a kneeling negro slave in chains. In 1823 the phrase became the motto of the Anti-Slavery Society. Throughout the anti-slavery campaign, from the late eighteenth century to the Abolition of Slavery Act in August 1833, similarities were drawn between African and West Indian slaves and industrial workers of the northern towns in England. Social reformers grasped the opportunity to criticize the blinkered view of many abolitionists who ignored the conditions of factory hands on their own industrial doorstep. In 1830, Richard Oastler, who became a spokesman for the Ten Hours Bill, wrote to the *Leeds Mercury* about 'Yorkshire Slavery':

> Thousands of our fellow creatures . . . are at this very moment existing in a state of slavery *more horrid* than are the victims of that hellish system, *colonial*

slavery. . . . The very streets which receive the droppings of an Anti-Slavery Society are every morning wet by the tears of innocent victims at the accursed shrine of avarice, who are compelled, not by the cart whip of the negro slave driver, but by the equally appalling thong or strap of the overlooker, to hasten, half-dressed, *but not half-fed,* to those magazines of British infantile slavery – the worsted mills in the town and neighbourhood of Bradford!

(Quoted in Hopkins, 1990, 57)

During the Preston strike and lock-out of 1853–4, many speeches to the workers incorporated the language of oppression and slavery. On 10 December 1853, at the height of the dispute, a prominent strike-leader, George Cowell, addressed the assembled workers as ' "My dear slaves" (in allusion to a placard, headed "Cowell and his Slaves" which appeared upon the walls of the town during the week)' (*The Times*, 12 December 1853; see note, pp.177–9 and Plate 17). Similarly, at a large open-air gathering of cotton operatives on 12 March 1854, one Warrington delegate exclaimed that for 'too long have [the people] been sunk in the depths of degradation and slavery. Too long have we borne the proud man's contumely and the rich man's oppression' (*Preston Guardian*, 18 March 1854).

'OH my friends, the down-trodden operatives

'OH my friends, the down-trodden operatives of Coketown! . . . the slaves of an iron-handed and a grinding despotism! . . . the hour is come, when we must rally round one another as One united power, and crumble into dust the oppressors] Compare the fervent rhetoric of one of the main leaders of the Preston strike, Mortimer Grimshaw, on whom Dickens's Slackbridge is modelled:

All we want is, the right to live by our labour – to be paid that which is our due – to enter the mills free men and free women. . . . What we claim is, the right to be masters of ourselves – to resist all petty tyranny and oppression – to hold the right of private judgment, and to speak the free sentiments of our minds. And so far we intend to be masters. . . . (Cheers.) Men and women of Lancashire! now is the time to free yourselves from the iron grasp of your oppressors!

(*Preston Guardian*, 18 March 1854)

Dickens listened to Grimshaw at a delegates' meeting of 29 January 1854 and used much of what he heard for his report on the Preston strike and also for Slackbridge's provocative language. In 'On Strike' (*HW* 8.553–9), Gruffshaw (Grimshaw) speaks to the workers 'in hot blood. . . . O my friends, but it is fit and right that you should have the dark ways of the real traducers and apostates, and the real un-English stabbers, laid bare before you'. In Dickens's article, however, Gruffshaw is quickly silenced by the chairman, an Oldham operative; Dickens remarks: 'Preston has not the strong relish for personal altercation that Westminster hath. Motion seconded and carried, business passed to, Gruffshaw dumb' (557). Grimshaw did not have a monopoly on vitriolic oratory. A Warrington delegate addressed the workers as the 'sons of toil':

> If the operatives of Preston are subjugated, if the iron grasp of oppression sink them in the dust, what will *your* fate be ere a few more years have rolled away? . . . While we have been disunited, our oppressors have gathered strength. While we have been bickering, they have knitted themselves firmer and firmer together. It teaches us this – that if we wish to exercise our power, now is the time to lay the foundation of that power.

The delegate concluded with a verse of poetry which called for all 'toiling, bleeding slaves' to unite and 'proclaim your will' (*Preston Guardian*, 18 March 1854). For more information about the characterization of Slackbridge, and Dickens's views of professional agitators, see note below, pp. 177–9.

One united power] This might allude either to the attempts to establish general trade unions (see note to book 2, chapter 1, p. 161), or to the short-lived and impractical scheme for a Labour Parliament, conceived by the Chartist, Ernest Jones, in November 1853. As a means of successfully ending the Preston lock-out, Jones envisaged a 'mighty delegation from all trades [to] assemble in the centre of action, in Lancashire, in Manchester, and remain sitting until the victory is obtained' (*People's Paper*, 12 November 1853, quoted in Dutton and King, 1981, 59).

Mortimer Grimshaw was a fervent supporter of Jones's plan and advocated its implementation at every opportunity. As Grimshaw was to discover, many were wary of compounding Chartist politics with wage-demands. At a contentious delegate meeting of 29 January 1854 – one which Dickens attended for a short period (reported in 'On Strike', *HW* 9.556–7) – three Manchester delegates associated with the Labour Parliament and supported by Grimshaw wished to address the people, but they were overruled after a show of hands. The Manchester representatives were 'compelled to depart without performing their errand, the nature of which did not transpire' (*Manchester Guardian*, 1 February 1854).

Grimshaw did, however, get a positive response on 11 March 1854, when he addressed a huge outdoor gathering of Blackburn and Preston workers:

> He said they were assembled that day to re-inaugurate the labour movement. And he believed it was possible at the present time, not only to concentrate the veritable working classes of this country into one mighty union, but that by discretion and a proper course of procedure, they should be enabled to enrol under their banners all who were depending upon wages for a livelihood.
>
> (*Preston Guardian*, 18 March 1854)

15 Payment of cotton workers in the Temperance hall, Preston. From the *Illustrated London News*, 12 November 1853

'Good!' 'Hear, hear, hear!'

the densely crowded and suffocatingly close Hall]   This was the Temperance Hall, Preston, otherwise known as the old Cockpit, described by Dickens in 'On Strike'. The building was designed as an amphitheatre for cock-fighting. By the early 1830s the hall functioned as a forum for numerous orators on radical, political and social issues; however, its main use from 1832 to 1852 was as a permanent meeting-place for the Temperance Society. The Temperance Hall, none the less, remained the venue for mass meetings of workers and delegates during times of industrial depression and disruption, especially during the Preston strike and lock-out of cotton-factory workers from September 1853 until May 1854 (Walmsley, 1892, 1–3; Dutton and King, 1981, passim).

During Dickens's stay in Preston in 1854, he visited the old Cockpit twice – once to attend a crowded weavers' delegate meeting on Sunday morning (a regular weekly feature in Preston throughout the strike), and again on Monday to observe the distribution of relief payments to the striking operatives. Dickens commented on his first visit to the hall that it

> was hotter than any mill or factory I have ever been in; but there was a stove down in the sanded pit, and delegates were seated close to it, and one particular delegate often warmed his hands at it, as if he were chilly. The air was so intensely close and hot, that at first I had but a confused perception of the delegates down in the pit, and the dense crowd of eagerly listening men and women (but not very many of the latter) filling all the benches and choking such narrow standing-room as there was. (HW 8.556)

An engraving of the Preston Temperance Hall appeared in the *Illustrated London News* on 12 November 1853 (Plate 15). The plate, which depicts the weekly payment of strike money to the factory workers, accurately shows the tiered circular seating and the large calico crown on a pole which, to Dickens, was 'strongly suggestive of May-day' (8.556).

Good! Hear, hear! Hurrah!

that in this belief, right or wrong (unhappily wrong then), the whole of that crowd were gravely, deeply, faithfully in earnest]   Compare Dickens's comments in 'On Strike' about the striking cotton operatives of Preston:

> I wanted to see with my own eyes . . . how these people acted under a mistaken impression, and what qualities they showed, even at that disadvantage, which ought to be the strength and peace – not the weakness and trouble – of the community. (HW 8.555)

Dickens was impressed by the workers' earnestness and perseverance, and believed 'that their mistake is generally an honest one, and that it is sustained by the good that is in them, and not by the evil' (8.557).

'But, oh my friends and brothers!

United Aggregate Tribunal] The development of trade unionism within the cotton industry in Lancashire was an intermittent yet ultimately successful process. The mule spinners were by far the most effective in formally organizing themselves into local associations and were especially skilful in mustering financial support during strikes through a delegate network which operated from branch to branch in the manufacturing towns. By 1853 the district societies had formed the Amalgamated Association of Cotton Operative Spinners. The weavers' associations had been organized on a casual and short-term basis. An attempt at federation had been made in 1840 with the formation of the General Association of Power Loom Weavers of Great Britain and Ireland, but after the unsuccessful Plug Plot riots and general strike of 1842 it disappeared, only to emerge briefly during the industrial depression of 1846–8.

Trade-union activity was revived and refined during the strike of cotton operatives for a wage-increase of 10 per cent which eventually centred on Preston from September 1853 until May 1854. Separate committees were quickly set up for spinners, weavers and carding operatives, and delegates from each were commissioned to deliver subscriptions to the union meetings, oversee the management of the strike funds and generally supervise the course of events during the campaign. Substantial funds also came from the spinners' Amalgamated Association and from the Amalgamated Committee of Trades and Factory Operatives, set up on behalf of the Preston craft societies in August 1853. The independence of the different committees was matched by a unity of purpose which made the organizations collectively very efficient and resistant, for a time, to the lock-out imposed by the manufacturers on 15 October 1853.

The operatives' justification for a union was articulated in a memorial sent by the Preston weavers to Lord Palmerston on 21 November 1853:

> we had no thought of combination or Union, it has been called into existance [sic] by the natural sympathy that always has and will exist amongst men if they believe their fellow creatures suffering in a righteous cause, we have had no reasons yet shewn that our demands were unreasonable, therefore this has caused us to throw around our suffering brethren the shield of protection and act in union and concert against future acts of despotism. This is the real cause of our organization which at present exists not formed to dictate but to assist by pecuniary aid those who have been thrown out of employment for soliciting their just claims. (HO 45/5128E)

Whilst it is evident throughout the novel that Dickens drew upon his knowledge and views of the Preston strike, his depiction of the operatives' union and union solidarity also stemmed from the perceived role played by the prestigious Amalgamated Society of Engineers (ASE) during the engineers' strike and lock-out of 1852 (see Murphy, 1978, 242–66, for a revaluation of the dispute). The strike issues of the abolition of systematic overtime and piece-work were overshadowed by the more interesting call for the dismissal of unskilled labourers who manned the self-acting machines. For the duration of the lock-out, the influential middle-class newspapers,

"THE TEN PER CENT, AND NO SURRENDER!"

16 Mortimer Grimshaw. From the *People's Paper*, 4 February 1854; reprinted in H. I. Dutton and J. E. King, *'Ten Per Cent and No Surrender': The Preston Strike, 1853–1854* (Cambridge: Cambridge UP, 1981)

especially *The Times*, sustained this emphasis and portrayed the ASE as tyrannical and relentless (Pelling, 1963, 46–8; Fraser, 1974, 20, 29, 200; Murphy, 1978, 242–66; Dutton and King, 1981, 17–19, 61–5).

Slackbridge, the orator, looked about him

Slackbridge, the orator] Slackbridge is based upon one of the main agitators of the Preston strike, a former weaver called Mortimer Grimshaw (Plate 16) – Dickens's 'professional speaker', Gruffshaw, in 'On Strike' (*HW* 8.553–9). Known as the 'Thunderer of Lancashire', Grimshaw (who came from Great Harwood, about twelve miles north-east of Preston) was an experienced radical campaigner who first entered the wages dispute in March 1853, when he addressed weavers in Stockport at the start of the agitation. His notoriety throughout Lancashire for delivering strident and aggressive speeches had been gained the previous year through his political activities in Royton, near Oldham (see Dutton and King, 1981, 46). At the outset of industrial unrest in the spring of 1853, Grimshaw was a full-time agitator who had no intention of returning to his trade. The Lancastrian historian Charles Hardwick, in 'Lancashire Stump Oratory and Reminiscences of the Labour Battle. By a Prestonian', described him as a big man,

> very much marked with the small-pox. He was well known by his white hat which, I suppose, he wore after the fashion of Hunt and Cobbett, to indicate the depth of his 'Radical' propensities. As John Bright plants his elevated fist firmly in advance, whilst eloquently expounding the doctrines of the Peace Society, so Mortimer Grimshaw advocates liberty to the oppressed 'factory slaves' with a dogmatical invective ... more worthy of a Russian despot than an English patriot. I do not assert that he is insincere. Maliciously impugning an adversary's motives is the height of folly to my mind, and the worst of all arguments. He appears to me to be an enthusiast, and that the warmth of his feelings, when excited, overpowers his judgement.
> (*Eliza Cook's Journal*, 19 August 1854, pp. 258–9)

The manufacturer Henry Ashworth, a fierce opponent of the strike, did not hesitate to express his feelings about Grimshaw:

> the less that is said [of him] the better. We have heard it alleged, that every wild and violent sentiment which was uttered during the Preston strike came from his lips.... In his speeches we find the perfection of mob oratory.... We must add, that his talents had failed to secure him honour in his own country, for when on one occasion, he was selected by the committee to fill a gap at a meeting of the Warrington operatives, by whom he was well known, they 'struck' against him, and threatened to break up the meeting if he was permitted to speak. (Ashworth, 1854, 28–9)

Grimshaw had also been cautioned by other delegates to moderate his excessive lan-

17 George Cowell addressing factory operatives in the Orchard, Preston. From the *Illustrated London News*, 12 November 1853

guage at meetings. Dickens observed one such public reprimand at a weavers' meeting on 29 January 1854 (see note above at p. 171).

Grimshaw's hot-headedness was tempered by the calm and resolute figure of George Cowell, a respected Preston teetotal weaver and, arguably, the supreme leader of the Preston campaign (Plate 17). Given the name 'Cowler' in a *HW* article of 10 December 1853, he is described as

> the chosen of the people; rightly or wrongly, they hold him in great regard. His appearance is very much in his favour, for he wears the look of a straightforward honest man; a smile plays round his mouth as he steps forward with the air of a man sure of his audience; but the feverish and anxious expression of the eyes tells of sleepless nights and of constant agitation.
>
> ('Locked Out', 8.346)

Although Grimshaw and Cowell embraced similar political causes – such as Chartism, the Ten Hours Movement and, to a lesser extent on Cowell's part, Ernest Jones's Labour Parliament – it was the antithetical characteristics of the two men which proved to be their greatest strength throughout the strike. Cowell was, nevertheless, representative of the majority of strike leaders, who discouraged violence and who conducted an orderly campaign which gained them public respect and sympathy. Such recognition was cultivated by the national press, principally *The Times*, whose erstwhile role in tarnishing the image of the engineers' union and its leaders during the strike of 1852 had been decisive (see note above at pp.175–7).

Dickens's contempt for agitators, especially professional outsiders, was unyielding (see 'Railway Strikes', *HW* 2.361–4, and 'On Strike', *HW* 8.553–9). In 1852 he blamed the striking engineers for 'trusting their affairs to contentious men' (*Letters* 6.580), and in a letter of December 1854 he reiterated his disdain but acknowledged the veracity demonstrated by agitators during the Preston strike (*Letters* 7.485).

Dickens did not differentiate between the demagogic outsider, Grimshaw, and the restrained local weaver, Cowell. Moreover, it was preferable to portray Slackbridge as the quintessential union extremist – in reality an outmoded figure whose tenets belonged more to earlier decades of the nineteenth century (Carnall 40) – than to present him as an unsettling mixture of firm leader and kind man. If, as Dickens believed, the middle classes were responsible for the improvement of working-class life, then to present Slackbridge as other than reprehensible would be to sanction workers' initiatives. Dickens did maintain, however, that in the case of sanitation and decent housing workers could take the initiative only if they united with 'the whole powerful middle-class of this country' who were 'ready to join them' ('To Working Men', *HW* 10.169–70). For an explanation of Dickens's equivocal treatment of the union in *HT*, see note to book 2, chapter 1, pp. 161–2 (Carnall, 1964, 31–48; Smith, 1973, 153–62; Fraser, 1974, 200–1; Dutton and King, 1981, 4–5, 46–50, 59–61, 184, 193–4; *Letters* 7.479, 485).

'Oh my friends and fellow-men!' said Slackbridge

he who sold his birthright for a mess of pottage]   In Genesis, Esau sold his birthright to his twin brother Jacob in return for some bread and soup (25.29–34). The seventeenth report and balance-sheet of 18 December 1853, issued by the Central Committee of the Preston power-loom weavers, contained a caveat in verse about the mill-owners' recent offer to striking operatives. Entitled 'The New Dodge', it ran:

> Ye weavers all of Preston,
>   I warn you to take care;
> The cotton lords are trying hard,
>   To draw you in a snare.
>
> Two and sixpence they will give,
>   Besides a mess of stew,
> If you will SIGN and go to work
>   But don't or you will rue.
>
> Let them sup their stew themselves;
>   Tell them you want it not;
> Christmas time will soon be here,
>   With beef and puddings hot.
>
> Sell your BIRTH-RIGHT for their SLOPS
>   No! No! you will not do;
> While you can get four shillings a week,
>   You do not need THEIR STEW.
>   (Harris Library, Preston)

One placard, which Dickens quoted in full in 'On Strike', asserted that 'it is against nature to believe, that those who plant and reap all the grain, should not have enough to make a mess of porridge' (*HW* 8.555).

Judas Iscariot]   The disciple who betrayed Jesus for thirty pieces of silver (Matthew 26.14–16). At a large open-air meeting of Blackburn and Preston cotton operatives on 11 March 1854, Robert Worswick, the Padiham delegate, praised 'the noble-hearted men and women of Preston' and was convinced that they 'were not going to act the part of a Judas and sell the interests of the working classes of this country' (*Preston Guardian*, 18 March 1854). Biblical allusion was a common component of speeches, ballads and poems during the Preston campaign for a 10 per cent wage-increase. The strike motto, 'Ten per cent. and no surrender', according to the *Annual Register*, 'seemed to have possessed the minds of the working classes, in some districts, *as a religious faith; nay, in one place, the people assembled in a chapel and sung a hymn to Ten per Cent.!*' (May 1854, 79).

Castlereagh]   Robert Stewart, 2nd Viscount Castlereagh (1769–1822), British Foreign Secretary from 1812 until 1822, was an austere and unpopular politician unjustly regarded by the working class as an oppressive tyrant. He was held responsible for the repressive measures carried out by the Liverpool ministry following the Napoleonic Wars, and in particular he was blamed for the reactionary decision taken to send in troops during a peaceful parliamentary reform meeting of 80,000 people at St Peter's Fields, Manchester, on 16 August 1819, when 11 people were killed and 400 injured. The 'Peterloo Massacre' led to the restrictive 'Six Acts' or 'gag acts' which severely curtailed the freedom of the press and the right to hold public meetings. Castlereagh committed suicide in August 1822, and his funeral was cheered through the London streets (Palmer, 1962, 71).

'My brothers,' said Stephen, whose low voice

Strike o' day] Daybreak. In Lancashire it is termed 'skrike o' dey' (Bobbin). The phrase may also be a veiled allusion to a workers' strike, one which Stephen envisages if he continues to work in Bounderby's factory.

I know weel that if I was a lyin' parisht i' th' road, yo'd feel it right to pass me by, as a forrenner and stranger.] A reference to the parable of the Good Samaritan, Luke 10.29–37. Dickens later applies the biblical story to Gradgrind's politico-economic doctrines (in book 2, chapter 12, and, indirectly, in book 3, chapter 8).

There was an universal murmur

There was an universal murmur . . . fellow-labourer could.] This whole paragraph is written on the verso of the MS leaf – and is apparently an afterthought.

'Haply,' he said, turning his furrowed face

there'll be a threat to turn out if I'm let to work among yo.] One of the strike issues in the engineering dispute of 1852 was the demand that 'illegal' men – unskilled employees – who worked on the self-acting machines should be dismissed and replaced by skilled mechanics. In the public consciousness, the 'closed shop' policy dominated the other issues of piece-work and overtime. The weekly levy paid by non-striking operatives to support those on strike in Preston in 1853–4 became a mark of solidarity among the cotton-workers who, in the majority of cases, donated willingly. The subscriptions were crucial for the continuance of the campaign, thus failure to pay the levy was considered treacherous. For such disloyalty, veiled threats were published in the weekly balance-sheet and report of the Central Committee, which was posted throughout the district. Claims of intimidation, widely publicized in the local and national press, ranged from being 'sent to Coventry' (see note below at p. 184) to losing one's job. Dickens's 'On Strike' quotes three typical threats of physical violence (8.556). A Blackburn weaver who said he could not afford to pay the weekly levy alleged that delegates persuaded mill-workers to strike against those who had not subscribed to the fund: 'that is the only reason why I have been turned into the streets, with a wife and family' (letter to the Editor, *Blackburn Standard*, 25 January 1854). Other allegations related to the treatment of blacklegs, or 'knobsticks'. One 'sufferer' claimed to have been 'literally hunted out of the shop' for offering to work at the old five-shilling rate: 'I am now, no doubt, what is so much dreaded by all my class – a marked man' (*The Times*, 10 October 1853; Dutton and King, 1981, 64–5, 173).

turn out]   To strike. The word 'strike' – in the sense of the cessation of work for certain concessions from an employer – had been used from around 1810, although the term 'to strike work' was a phrase employed occasionally in the eighteenth century and probably derived from the maritime term 'to strike sail' (Pelling 19). Harriet Martineau's short story, which attempted to illustrate the detrimental effects of strikes and to condemn the pernicious influence of trade unions, is called *The Turn Out* (1829).

There is no strike in *HT* and little evidence to suggest that Dickens meant to portray one. He vehemently denied claims that his journalistic observations of the Preston strike had either informed the story or his choice of title (see Dickens's letter to Peter Cunningham, 11 March 1854, *Letters* 7.290–1), and his denial is partially borne out by a comment made to Angela Burdett Coutts on 23 January 1854, the day he started writing *HT*: 'The main idea of [the story] is one on which you and I . . . have often spoken' (*Letters* 7.256). If Dickens had a strike in mind when he went to view the dispute in Preston in late January 1854 (he remarked to Forster that 'I am afraid I shall not be able to get much here': *Letters* 7.260), by 21 April he was fully resolved as to the novel's concerns: 'I have no intention of striking,' he assured Mrs Gaskell, who had begun writing her industrial novel *North and South* in mid-January 1854:

> The monstrous claims at domination made by a certain class of manufacturers, and the extent to which the way is made easy for working men to slide down into discontent under such hands, are within my scheme. (*Letters* 7.320)

Three days earlier, Forster had also written to Mrs Gaskell with less certain conviction that Dickens's material would not clash with her plans, but he reassured her that 'with what a different purpose and subsidiary to what quite opposite manifestations of character and passion *your* strike will be introduced and I am your witness . . . that your notion in this matter existed before and quite independently of his' (*Letters* 7.320, note 7). Mrs Gaskell's *North and South* was serialized in *HW* from 2 September 1854 until 27 January 1855. Despite the absence of an actual strike in *HT* and Dickens's firm refutation of thematic links with Preston, it is certain that he used the topicality of the campaign and adapted events and characters to focus his past experience of the negative effects of industrialization.

As a young reporter, Dickens had taken part in two disputes: the first with the *True Sun* in 1832 when he acted as spokesman for striking reporters, and the second while working for the *Morning Chronicle* in 1836 (Forster 1.4.75–6; *Letters* 1.122–3; Mott, 1984, 9, 234–5). Nevertheless, he perceived such action as undermining the mutual relationship between employer, employee and the community as a whole.

(See Dickens's HW articles, 'Railway Strikes', 2.361–4, and 'On Strike', 8.553–9.) Another article by William Duthie and Henry Morley, 'The French Workman' (8.199–204), is a veiled criticism of the English worker: French workmen 'can ill afford the interference of any small crisis in the shape of a strike' (8.203). However, two other articles by Morley – 'The Good Side of Combination' (4.56–60) and 'The Manchester Strike' (13.63–6) – modify Dickens's opinion on the subject. For Dickens's editorial changes to 'The Manchester Strike', see *Letters* 8.9–10.

I who ha worked sin I were no heighth at aw] Stephen would have been 5 years old when the 1819 Factory Act made illegal the employment in cotton-factories of children under 9 years of age, but the provisions of the Act were frequently ignored by mill-owners. However, the Factory Acts of 1833 and 1844 extended the legal requirements for the textile industry, which included some elementary education for factory children and, significantly, introduced a factory inspectorate.

Thomas Banks, who became Secretary of the Spinners' Union after the Preston strike of 1853–4, gave a description of the life of a typical 7-year-old factory boy in 1821:

> starting work before six o'clock in the morning; trotting on through the long day till nearly eight o'clock at night, and the same time on Saturday nights, with little time allowed for meals. A rope hung up in every wheel-house, for what purpose we will leave you to judge. . . . All this time and labour for 2s. 1d. a week. (1888, 1)

Then Slackbridge, who had kept his

Had not the Roman Brutus . . . condemned his son to death] Lucius Junius Brutus (*fl.* late sixth century BC) is said to have founded the Roman Republic after ousting the tyrannical Lucius Tarquinius Superbus in 509. As first Consul he condemned his two sons to death for entering into a conspiracy against the Roman state to restore the Tarquins. His action demonstrated the priority of state over individual interest.

had not the Spartan mothers . . . driven their flying children on the points of their enemies' swords?] Spartans were known for their bravery and strength in battle, and were trained not to retreat under any circumstances. A Spartan mother would give her son his shield before he went off to fight and declare that he was to come back with it or on it (*Brewer*).

Slackbridge acted as fugleman

fugleman] A soldier especially expert and well drilled, who marched in front of a regiment or company as an example and model to the others.

He had been for many years

He had never known before, the strength of the want in his heart for the frequent recognition of a nod, a look, a word]   Nicholas Higgins, the weaver in *North and South*, succinctly describes what happens when a worker refuses to join his union:

> them as works next looms has orders not to speak to him – if he's sorry or ill it's a' the same; he's out o' bounds; he's none o' us. I' some places them's fined who speaks to him . . . try living a year or two among them as looks away if yo' look at 'em; try working within two yards o' crowds o' men, who, yo' know, have a grinding grudge at yo' in their hearts – to whom if yo' say yo'r glad, not an eye brightens, nor a lip moves, – to whom if your heart's heavy, yo' can never say nought, because they'll ne'er take notice on your sighs or sad looks.
> (2.3; *HW* 10 [2 December 1854] 381)

Later, Higgins admits that a

> man leads a dree life who's not i' th' Union. But once i' th' Union his interests are taken care on better nor he could do it for himsel, or by himsel, for that matter. It's the only way working men can get their rights by all joining together. . . . Government takes care o' fools and madmen; and if any man is inclined to do himsel or his neighbour a hurt, it puts a bit of a check on him, whether he likes it or no. That's all we do i' th' Union. We can't clap folk into prison; but we can make a man's life so heavy to be borne, that he's obliged to come in, and be wise and helpful in spite of himself.
> (2.11; *HW* 10 [30 December 1854] 470)

'You are the Hand they have sent to Coventry

sent to Coventry]   Excluded from social intercourse; alienated from a social circle or community. The origin of the term is uncertain. One possible explanation is that in ancient times Coventry was a town where the practice of most trades was confined to a privileged number of townspeople. Thus, an outsider wishing to set up in business had little hope of custom. In addition, the phrase might have an association with Coventry Gaol, where Royalists were imprisoned during the Civil War. Coventry was also a garrison town, and its inhabitants detested the army presence to the extent that no intercourse was allowed between soldiers and citizens. Any woman seen conversing with a soldier was immediately in disgrace and socially ostracized (Hotten; *Brewer*).

Book 2, Chapter 5						Eleventh weekly part
								Saturday, 10 June 1854

MEN AND MASTERS

'Though he knows,' said Mr Bounderby

transportation]   The practice of sending convicts to British penal colonies originated in the late sixteenth century but increased considerably in the early seventeenth century when prisoners condemned to death were instead transported to plantations and settlements in America. Transportation was not only a convenient way to banish criminals from Britain and so obviate the expense of housing them in gaols, but it also provided a substantial and cheap workforce for the new settlements throughout the burgeoning British Empire. However, the American War of Independence (1775–83) stopped this transportation channel, and from 1776 prisoners awaiting transportation were kept in overcrowded hulks – old carrier and naval ships – until another penal colony could be found. In January 1788 the First Fleet of eleven British ships under the leadership of Captain Arthur Phillip arrived in Botany Bay with 696 convicts to establish the first penal settlement in Australia. Australian penal colonies were still in place during the 1850s and 1860s. The practice was discontinued in 1868 (Hughes, 1987, 40–2, 71, 83).

'How 'tis, ma'am,' resumed Stephen

what is best in us fok, seems to turn us most to trouble an misfort'n an mistake]   This was Dickens's conviction about the cotton-factory workers during the Preston strike: 'their mistake is generally an honest one, and . . . is sustained by the good that is in them and not by the evil' ('On Strike', *HW* 8.557).

'Sir, I were never good at showin o't

to card]   Raw cotton from Egypt, India and America was first cleaned and broken up by a machine called a scutcher which produced rolls of fleece, or laps, ready for carding. The carding process extracted impurities from the cotton such as seeds or stalks left from the previous cleaning methods and raked the lap into a loose rope of parallel fibres known as a sliver, ready for drawing out into a coil of cotton sufficiently fine to spin into yarn. Until the introduction of Arkwright's carding engine (first used in his Cromford Mill in 1775), the cotton was combed using hand cards – brushes with wire bristles. Carding engines contained millions of needle-pointed teeth which, in the early years of industrialization, were set in leather by children who received a penny for every three thousand. It is estimated that it took them four hours to earn a penny. For the lung complaint which could affect workers in carding-rooms, see note to book 2, chapter 1, p. 165 (Aspin, 1981, 5–7; Chapman, 1904, 72–3).

Look how you considers of us, an writes of us, an talks of us, and goes up wi' yor deputations to Secretaries o' State 'bout us] An allusion to the deputation of mill-owners and manufacturers who protested to the Home Secretary, Lord Palmerston, against an order in January 1854 to fence every industrial shaft regardless of size or height. In this passage, Dickens returns, albeit in a modified form, to the issues raised in a cancelled passage in book 1, chapter 13 (see note at pp. 143–6).

Look how this ha growen and growen, sir, bigger an bigger, broader an broader, harder an harder, fro year to year, fro generation unto generation.] Stephen's observations echo Carlyle's remarks on the Chartist cause: 'The matter . . . is weighty, deep-rooted, far-extending; did not begin yesterday; will by no means end this day or tomorrow' (*Chartism*, 1839, 1). Oddie points out that Stephen's views, taken as a whole and expressed most fully in this second interview with Bounderby, 'form an interdependent and distinctively Carlylean corpus of ideas' (1972, 49).

'I'll tell you something towards it

'We will make an example of half a dozen Slackbridges. We'll indict the blackguards for felony, and get 'em shipped off to penal settlements.'] This was not an idle threat. In 1834 six labourers from the Dorset village of Tolpuddle, accused of practising trade-union rituals, were charged under the 1797 Act against Unlawful Oaths and sentenced to seven years' transportation to Australia. Two years later, the 'Tolpuddle Martyrs' were pardoned and allowed to return home. In 1837 several union members were transported for intimidation of strike-breakers ('knobsticks') during the Glasgow cotton-spinners' strike in which one strike-breaker was murdered. The violence of the Glasgow dispute and the subsequent trial resulted in the establishment of a Select Committee on Combinations in 1838, and their damning revelations about union activity over the previous twenty years influenced Victorian attitudes for the next decade. The Committee's report on the violence of the strike and the secret union rituals and oaths was a major source for Dickens's portrayal of the 'Prentice Knights in *BR*. In the present passage, Dickens may have had in mind more recent events in Preston: in March 1854, at the climax of the Preston strike, eleven weavers' delegates – including two of the chief strike leaders, George Cowell and Mortimer Grimshaw – were arrested on charges of conspiracy. They were accused of persuading 'knobsticks' (mostly unskilled Irish immigrants), brought in by the mill-owners, to leave the town. The trial at Liverpool assizes was adjourned until the following August, and the charges were subsequently dropped (*HN* 1854–5, 89; Pelling, 1976, 41–2; Brantlinger, 1969, 37–52; Dutton and King, 1981, 128, 181–3).

'Sir,' returned Stephen, with the quiet confidence

'if yo was t' tak a hundred Slackbridges . . . an was t' sew 'em up in separate sacks, an sink 'em in the deepest ocean . . . yo'd leave the muddle just wheer 'tis.] Compare Carlyle's comments in *Chartism* (1839):

What will execration; nay at bottom, what will condemnation and banishment to Botany Bay do for it? Glasgow Thuggery, Chartist torch-meetings, Birmingham riots, Swing conflagrations, are so many symptoms on the surface; you abolish the symptom to no purpose, if the disease is left untouched. (1)

See Oddie (52–3) for a discussion of the differences between a Carlylean perception of cause and effect and Dickens's distinctive view.

'when ha we not heern . . . o' th' mischeevous strangers! 'Tis not by *them* the trouble's made, sir. 'Tis not wi' *them* 't commences. I ha no favour for 'em . . . but 'tis hopeless an useless to dream o' takin' them fro their trade, 'stead o' takin their trade fro them!] At their first meeting since the lock-out of the Preston operatives on 15 October 1853, the Masters' Association referred to the 'interference of . . . mischievous and irresponsible parties who have been the cause of all the distress brought upon the town'. The Association resolved that the mills would remain closed unless the masters were 'satisfied that the general body of operatives [were] prepared to emancipate themselves from the dictation of parties who have an interest in prolonging the unfortunate dispute'. In their reply, the operatives insisted that their leaders were 'but our servants, rendered necessary by the position you [the masters] have placed us in. If any of those servants be either strangers to the town, or trades in agitation, [the masters should] come to an honourable arrangement, and their occupation is gone' (*Preston Guardian*, 5 November 1853, 3–4). James Lowe's objective account of the Preston strike assessed the role of the agitators during the dispute and came to a similar conclusion:

> speeches of the agitators began to breathe a sterner spirit of hostility against the employers. It is, indeed, greatly to be feared that much of the subsequent evil is to be traced to these crude speeches at the outset of the dispute; it is to be feared that the unconsidered declamations of these men . . . were accepted as the earnest utterances of the people. If so, we can scarcely wonder at the position subsequently taken by the employers . . . [but] we cannot help thinking that the employers made a great mistake in taking these utterances for the real sentiments of the operatives; for . . . they forced them to act them out. They forgot that the agitators arose from the agitation, and not the agitation from the agitators.
>
> (1860, 212)

For Dickens's views about agitators, see note to book 2, chapter 4, pp. 177–9.

Norfolk Island] An Australian territory in the south-west Pacific Ocean, Norfolk Island served as a British penal colony from 1788 to 1813 and again from 1825 to 1855. For a contemporary account of convict life on Norfolk Island, see the *HW* article, 'Norfolk Island', 5.73–7. An earlier article had described the famous pine trees of Norfolk Island as having 'a drooping sadness of look worthy of their origin' ('The Palace of Flowers', *HW* 3.117–20).

'Sir, I canna, wi' my little learning

The strong hand will never do't. . . . Agreeing fur to mak one side unnat'rally awlus and for ever right, and toother side . . . for ever wrong, will never, never do't. Nor yet lettin alone will never do't. . . . Not drawin' nigh to fok, wi' kindness and patience an cheery ways . . . will never do't] Compare Dickens's concluding paragraph of 'On Strike':

> in its encroachment on the means of many thousands who are laboring from day to day, in the gulf of separation it hourly deepens between those whose interests must be understood to be identical or must be destroyed, it is a great national affliction. But, at this pass, anger is of no use, starving out is of no use . . . political economy is a mere skeleton unless it has a little human covering and filling out, a little human bloom upon it, and a little human warmth in it. . . . I would entreat both sides now so miserably opposed, to consider whether there are no men in England, above suspicion, to whom they might refer the matters in dispute. . . . Masters right, or men right; masters wrong, or men wrong; both right, or both wrong; there is a certain ruin to both in the continuance or frequent revival of this breach. And from the ever-widening circle of their decay, what drop in the ocean shall be free! (HW 8.558–9)

till th' Sun turns t' ice.] This is more likely to be Stephen's version of 'when Hell freezes over' than Dickens's allusion to the theory of the entropy of the universe. The concept of 'heat death' was definitively described only in 1867 (by the physicist Clausius in a lecture in Frankfurt) and was not widely discussed until the late nineteenth century (Brush, 1986, 1.577–8; see also Fielding, 1996, 200–16).

Book 2, Chapter 6   Twelfth weekly part
                                                                              Saturday, 17 June 1854

FADING AWAY

'Why, I come to be with this good lass

the Travellers' Coffee House down by the railroad] By the 1840s refreshment-rooms and waiting-rooms in railway stations had displaced the familiar coaching inns, and neighbourhood taverns and eating-houses provided further rest and sustenance for the rail traveller. In *DS*, Dickens described the adaptation of the old with the new establishments during the construction of the railway at Staggs's Gardens in Camden Town:

A bran-new Tavern, redolent of fresh mortar and size, and fronting nothing at all, had taken for its sign The Railway Arms; but that might be rash enterprise – and then it hoped to sell drink to the workmen. So, the Excavators' House of Call had sprung up from a beer-shop; and the old-established Ham and Beef Shop had become the Railway Eating House, with a roast leg of pork daily, through interested motives of a similar immediate and popular description. Lodging-house keepers were favourable in like manner; and for the like reasons were not to be trusted. (6)

For an excellent account of the culinary – and other – drawbacks of a railway refreshment-room, see Dickens's tale, 'Main Line: The Boy at Mugby', in 'Mugby Junction' (*AYR* 17 [Christmas 1866] 1–48; see also 'Chips: Railway Comfort', *HW* 1.449) (Dodds, 1953, 219).

He lighted a candle, set out his little tea-board

the sugar lump, of course] White sugar, purer and more expensive than less refined brown sugar, was sold in conical loaves a yard or so in length. Owing to the introduction of a lower tariff on sugar, consumption increased dramatically from 1845. The belief that it was indulgent for the working class to have such luxuries as sugar is borne out by G. R. Porter's remark in *The Progress of the Nation* (1847):

> The consumption of this class of articles affords a very useful test of the comparative conditions at different periods of the labouring classes. If by reason of the cheapness of provisions, the wages of the labourer afford means for indulgence, sugar, tea, and coffee are the articles to which he earliest has recourse.
>
> (Quoted in Burnett, 1989, 15)

(Freeman, 1989, 91; Burnett, 1989, 14–15.)

She was fain to take up the note again,

his manner . . . had a grace in it that Lord Chesterfield could not have taught his son in a century.] The politician and diplomat Philip Dormer Stanhope, 4th Earl of Chesterfield (1694–1773), wrote a series of letters to his illegitimate son which were published posthumously in 1774. In the letters, Lord Chesterfield instructed his son in how to succeed in the world by flattery and pretence. He laid stress on the acquisition of all the social graces, and dwelt on the importance of appearing to be highly moral and righteous in order to gain respect and win courtly favour. Dickens detested Chesterfield's hypocrisy and satirized him frequently in his works. In 'The Boarding-House' (*SB*), 'Mr. Hicks and the ladies discoursed most eloquently about poetry, and the theatres, and Lord Chesterfield's Letters'. The socially polished but cold-hearted John Chester in *BR* praises the *Letters*, for 'in every page of this enlightened writer, I find some captivating hypocrisy which has never occurred to me before, or some superlative piece of selfishness to which I was utterly a stranger' (23). In *BH* the selfish elderly dandy Mr Turveydrop is partly modelled on Lord Chesterfield. See also *AN* (3), *LD* (1.19), and *Letters* 6.741.

It was but a hurried parting

the poor you will have always with you.]   Matthew 26.11: 'For ye have the poor always with you'.

Then came the lamplighter, and two lengthening

the lamplighter]   A man employed to light and extinguish the street gas-lamps. The rapidity with which lamplighters executed this task gave rise to the expression 'off like a lamplighter' (c.1840).

By the place where Rachael lived

by the railway, where the danger-lights were waning]   Lights were placed at both ends of the railway station to signal approaching problems on the railway line – a white light for 'safety', green to 'use caution' and red signalling 'danger':

> On a train stopping, or travelling slowly through an intermediate station, the signal which was painted red on one side was shown for five minutes in the direction from which the train had come, so as to stop any following train; the green signal, on the shorter post, was then turned on for five minutes, to complete the ten minutes' precautionary signal. (Williams, 1968, 275)

More sophisticated signalling systems were used at main stations and where there were level crossings and junctions: see note to book 2, chapter 11, p. 208 (Williams, 1968, 276). Also see note to book 2, chapter 2, pp. 166–7, about the introduction of an automatic signalling system to prevent serious railway accidents.

by the railway's crazy neighbourhood, half pulled down and half built up]   The disruptive effect of the railway system on communities was fully felt by the time railway-building reached its peak between 1844 and 1848. Dickens, an advocate of technological progress but also a critic of its negative impact, was swift to respond in his fiction and in *HW*. The depiction of Staggs's Gardens in *DS* (transformed by the demolition of Camden Town to accommodate the London-to-Birmingham railway) represents a neighbourhood in physical and psychological flux (see chapters 6 and 15). A casualty of the same railway line was Wellington House Academy, Dickens's old school (*HW* 4.49). A later article, 'An Unsettled Neighbourhood' (10.289–92), articulated Dickens's misgivings about the disadvantages of such advances: 'what I do complain of, and what I am distressed at, is, the state of mind – the moral condition – into which the neighbourhood has got. It is unsettled, dissipated, wandering' (10.290). Dickens applied this confusion and disorientation to railway travel itself. The waiter attending Carker in *DS* remarks how it was 'Very confusing. . . . Not much in the habit of travelling by rail myself, Sir, but gentlemen frequently say so' (55). And in a *HW* article of 1856, 'Railway Dreaming', Dickens admitted that he was 'never sure of time or place upon a Railroad. . . . Rattling along in this railway carriage in a state of luxurious confusion, I take it for granted I am coming from somewhere, and going somewhere else. I seek to know no more' (13.385).

Book 2, Chapter 7   Thirteenth weekly part
                                             Saturday, 24 June 1854

GUNPOWDER

Towards what? Step by step

Gorgon] Medusa, the best-known of the three Gorgons in Greek mythology, was a female monster whose head was covered with live serpents in place of hair. Those who looked at her were turned to stone, but Perseus, by reflecting her image using Athene's mirror-like shield, cut off Medusa's head.

He was quick enough to observe

depth answers unto depth]   Psalms 42.7: 'Deep calleth unto deep at the noise of thy waterspouts: all thy waves and thy billows are gone over me'.

Mr Bounderby had taken possession of a house

by a railway striding on many arches over a wild country, undermined by deserted coal-shafts, and spotted at night by fires and black shapes of stationary engines at pits' mouths.]   Compare Dickens's description of the winter landscape between Birmingham and Wolverhampton:

> Now, a smoky village; now, a chimney; now, a dormant serpent [windlass] who seems to have been benumbed in the act of working his way for shelter into the lonely little engine-house by the pit's mouth; now, a pond with black specks sliding and skating . . . now, a cold white altar of snow with fire blazing on it; now, a dreary open space of mound and fell, snowed smoothly over, and

closed in at last by sullen cities of chimneys. Not altogether agreeable to think of crossing such space without a guide, and being swallowed by a long-abandoned, long-forgotten shaft. Not even agreeable . . . to think of half-a-dozen railway arches with the train upon them, suddenly vanishing through the snow into the excavated depths of a coal-forest. (*HW* 8.481)

by one of the Coketown magnates, who . . . overspeculated himself by about two hundred thousand pounds . . . but the bankrupts had no connexion whatever with the improvident classes.] 'City Spectres', a *HW* article of 1852, relates the unfortunate histories of prosperous merchants and speculators whose bankruptcies have made them 'gaunt men, with haggard countenances' (4.481). Another article, 'The Ruined Potter', which appeared in the same number as the present chapter, relates the story of a potter who was imprisoned for debts accumulated during a long bout of cholera which had left him and his wife weak and penniless. The piece, although sympathetic towards the potter's plight, is pessimistic about the possibility of rehabilitation after such financial ruination: 'a thoroughly fallen man seldom rights himself, and bankruptcy is a break-up for life in the constitution of successful industry' (9.441). Bankruptcy law at this time applied to traders only; non-traders who found themselves in debt appeared before the Insolvent Debtors' Court (see note to book 1, chapter 7, pp. 105–6).

accidents did sometimes happen in the best-regulated families] A proverb which originates from the farce, *The Deuce is in Him* (1763), by George Colman the Elder: 'Accidents, accidents will happen – No less than seven brought into our infirmary yesterday' (1.22). Scott modified the phrase in *Peveril of the Peak* (1822): 'Had your ladyship any reason to suspect . . . any improper intimacy between Master Peveril and this same female attendant? . . . such things will befall in the best-regulated families' (3.19). Another variation appeared in one of Christopher North's *Noctes Ambrosianae* papers for *Blackwood's Magazine*: 'Such accidents will happen in the best-regulated families' (August 1834). Variations of the proverb occur in *PP* (2), *DS* (2), and *DC* (28). (Hill, 1952, 179.)

It afforded Mr Bounderby supreme satisfaction

with demonstrative humility to grow cabbages in the flower-garden.] Only people of modest means, living in cottages with small gardens, planted their vegetables among their flowers.

'gave seven hundred pound for that Sea-beach.] English landscape paintings were highly valued in the British art world, but this might possibly be a particular reference to Dickens's close friend, the marine and landscape artist Clarkson Stanfield (1793–1867). The Royal Academy exhibition of 1852, which Dickens attended, had three of Stanfield's works including 'Port of La Rochelle'. In 1853 two paintings were exhibited there – 'Affray in the Pyrenees, with Contrabandistas' and his highly acclaimed 'HMS Victory (with the body of Nelson on board) towed into Gibraltar after the Battle of Trafalgar'. Four of Stanfield's works were shown at the Royal Academy from May 1854. In 1853 his 'The Lake and Town of Lugano' was sold for 332 guineas (£348.60); at the same sale, a seascape by Turner, 'A Seashore, with a Fishing Boat pushing off', fetched 1250 guineas (£1312.50) (*Annual Register*, May 1852, 72–3, April 1853, 54–5, May 1853, 58–9; *Letters*, 1.553, 6.670; The Royal Academy Library, London).

the engravings of a man shaving himself in a boot, on the blacking bottles] One of the advertisements depicted on a label of shoe-polish as a sign of its effectiveness. Such engravings were also placed in newspapers and periodicals and posted on walls throughout London (see Langton, 1883, 75, for three of the most popular engravings at the time). This is one of the many allusions in Dickens's fiction to his work as a boy at Warren's blacking factory, from February 1824 until March or April 1825. He had to 'cover the pots of paste-blacking; first with a piece of oil-paper, and then with a piece of blue paper; to tie them round with a string; and then to clip the paper close and neat' and finally 'to paste on each a printed label' (Forster 1.2.31–2; Langton, 1883, 72–5; Allen, 1988, 81, 102–3).

'Harthouse, you have a couple of horses

Went to Westminster School as a King's Scholar] Westminster School dates from the Reformation when Henry VIII turned the Benedictine Abbey of St Peter into the College of St Peter. By 1553 'grammar children' were known as King's Scholars, receiving an annual stipend of £3 6s 8d. The scholarship system became part of the annual Election, a three-day ceremony of oral examinations for potential scholars, new boys and for at least six reserved places for Westminster pupils at Christ Church, Oxford, and Trinity College, Cambridge. Successful King's scholars received free education inclusive of board and lodging, and the rest remained 'Town Boys' (scholarships were opened to 'Town Boys' in 1873). Those candidates with an annual inheritance of £10 or more were not eligible for scholarship election (Field, 1987, passim).

sleeping in market baskets] In *UT* Dickens recollects that 'one of the worst night sights' in London was that of the homeless children in Covent Garden market 'who prowl about this place; who sleep in the baskets, [and] fight for the offal' ('Night Walks'). See also 'Covent Garden Market' (*HW* 7.505–11), which reports that sleeping 'upon a heap of baskets' is now 'trusting to a tradition of other times, that here the unfortunate might find a sure sleeping-place, without fear of disturbance' (508).

used to act in Latin, in the Westminster School plays, with the chief-justices and nobility of this country applauding him] The annual Westminster Latin Play originated in the early fifteenth century when the Abbot was entertained with a Christmas performance. The tradition continued into the twentieth century, and performances were attended by royalty, foreign dignitaries, High Churchmen, and politicians (Field, 1987, 13, 25, 51).

Tom to rob Bounderby?   Yes.

Louisa to be acted on by Harthouse, through Tom ?   Yes.

Louisa's danger slowly drawn about her.   Yes.

Sissy ?   No

Rachael ?   No.
Bring her with Louisa again   ?
Stephen ?   No

To shew Louisa, how alike in their creeds, her father and

Harthouse are ? - How the two heartless things come to the

same in the end ?
                        Yes. But almost imperceptibly.

Louisa

"You have brought me to this, father. Now, save me!"

(Hard Times. ——————————————————————— Nº: IV.)

Weekly Nº 13

Chapter XVIII

Country house — Bounderby <fore> has foreclosed a mortgage on it

James Harthouse

Undermines her through Tom

Scene with Tom

Plucking rosebuds

Tom softens to his sister. "So much the less is the whelp the only creature she cares for".

Weekly Nº 14

Chapter XXIV.

Take up from last chapter

Account of the Robbery

" Bitzer and Mrs Sparsit: Bounderby made by that good lady to feel as if he had been crossed in something though he has no idea in what."

Scene with Tom and Louisa.   Tom in bed.   Dogged and hard <No> "What can I say? I don't know what you mean."

Weekly Nº 15

Chapter XXV.

Take up Mrs Sparsit again - Mrs Gradgrind dies.   "Mr Gradgrind must have forgotten some Ology.   Can't have <had> had them all taught. Something wanting in Louisa   surely."

chapter XXVI.

" Mrs Sparsit's Giant staircase. Louisa always coming Down, Down, Down.

Weekly Nº 16

chapter XXVII.

Mrs Sparsit watching her staircase.   Overhears them together -

Follows Louisa.   <Louis> Loses her.   Wet night picture

She seems to have eloped

chapter XXVIII.

The National Dustman in his study - Another scene between them - Companion to the former   "you have brought me to this, father. Now save me!"

in a fifth floor, up a narrow dark back street in Antwerp.'] English bankrupts often decamped to the Continent, where they could live cheaply and anonymously. Until 1859, Antwerp was a fortified city of narrow, labyrinthine streets. In Dickens's next novel, *LD*, Rigaud meets Ephraim Flintwinch 'in the Cabaret of the Three Billiard Tables, in the little street of the high roofs, by the wharf at Antwerp!'. Like Nickits, Ephraim lives in a fifth-floor apartment (2.30). Dickens first visited Antwerp in July 1837; and in 1841, faced with the problem of his father's mounting debts, he suggested to his father that he should move 'to Calais, Boulogne, or Antwerp. The last, I think, is the best place, but let him please himself' (*Letters* 2.225; Johnson, 1986, 182).

'Mrs Bounderby, though a graceless person

of the world worldly] A variation of 1 Corinthians 15.47: 'The first man is of the earth, earthy'. Dickens adapted the phrase earlier at book 1, chapter 6.

Book 2, Chapter 8   Fourteenth weekly part
                         Saturday, 1 July 1854

EXPLOSION

And yet he had not, even now

that he and the legion of whom he was one] That is, devils. See Mark 5.9: 'My name is Legion: for we are many'.

When the Devil goeth about like a roaring lion

When the Devil goeth about like a roaring lion . . . the kindling of red fire] This passage incorporates two biblical quotations: 'Be sober, be vigilant; because your adversary, the devil, as a roaring lion, walketh about, seeking whom he may devour' (1 Peter 5.8); and 'But the fearful, and unbelieving, and . . . whoremongers, and sorcerers, and idolators, and all liars, shall have their part in the lake which burneth with fire and brimstone' (Revelation 21.8).

red tape] A rigid or mechanical adherence to rules and regulations. The term derives from the pinkish-red tape used to secure legal documents and governmental papers giving them a firmly parcelled appearance (*OED*). Carlyle popularized the term, and in a '*Speech of the British Prime-Minister to the floods of Irish and other*

Beggars . . .' ('The Present Time') he described the Prime Minister, Lord John Russell, as 'little other than a redtape Talking-machine, and unhappy Bag of Parliamentary Eloquence' (*Latter-Day Pamphlets*). Dickens's eponymous HW article condemned the Red Tapist for tying up 'public questions, great and small, in an abundance of this official article – to make the neatest possible parcels of them, ticket them, and carefully put them away on a top shelf out of human reach' ('Red Tape', 2.481–4).

the very Devil] It has been suggested (by Oddie, 1972, 58) that the ideas of the previous two paragraphs derive from book II of Carlyle's *Sartor Resartus*:

> Some comfort it would have been, could I, like Faust, have fancied myself tempted and tormented of the Devil; for a Hell, as I imagine, without Life, though only diabolic Life, were more frightful: but in our age of Down-pulling and Disbelief, the very Devil has been pulled down, you cannot so much as believe in a Devil. (2.7)

'A hundred and fifty-four, seven

'A hundred and fifty-four, seven, one,'] That is, £154 7s 1d.

'Sir,' returned Mrs Sparsit, 'I cannot say

sounds of a nature similar to . . . Dutch clocks] Popular and inexpensive wooden striking wall-clocks with brass mechanisms, made in the Black Forest of Germany, were misnamed 'Dutch' instead of 'Deutsch'. The reference is to the distinctive loud sound the clocks made before striking the hour. Many lower-class homes had a Dutch clock – for instance, the Peggotty family in *DC* (3) and the Gargery household in *GE* (2). For other references, see *PP* (28) and (40). A Dutch clock appears in an illustration for *PP* (40), 'Mr. Pickwick sits for his Portrait', and in the illustration of the Peggotty home in *DC* (3).

'You can recall for yourself, Harthouse

Having come to the climax, Mr Bounderby, like an oriental dancer, put his tambourine on his head.] Many street and theatre performers used a tambourine in their acts (see Mayhew 3.190–1). As an indication that the entertainment had come to an end, they would hit their heads with the tambourine and subsequently hand it round the audience as a collection-dish (Easson 68).

'I think so, sir,' said Bounderby

all sorts of defects are found out in the stable door after the horse is stolen]   From the proverb 'to lock the stable door after the horse is stolen'.

'Of course, they will be punished

they will be punished with the utmost rigour of the law, as notice-boards observe,']   Parish authorities often erected notice-boards to warn vagrants and beggars that they faced up to a year's hard labour if they remained in the parish. In fact, magistrates were only empowered to send vagabonds to prison for one month. Oliver sees such painted boards in the villages he passes through on his way to London (*OT* 8) (Paroissien, 1992, 88–9).

It soon appeared that if Mrs Sparsit

the mangle in the laundry]   A two-cylindered rolling-press used to dry and press cotton and linen after washing.

'wait for the simple mutton.']   Although not as cheap as beef, mutton was by far the most popular meat enjoyed by the middle class. Victorian cookery-books and women's periodicals contain an abundance of recipes for mutton dishes (Freeman, 1989, 193–4). The mutton supplied to the London markets was generally that of crossbred sheep. According to Mrs Beeton, 'if care is taken not to purchase it too fat, it will be found the most satisfactory and economical mutton that can be bought' (333).

But Mrs Sparsit's greatest point

'Alas poor Yorick!']   *Hamlet* 5.1: 'Alas, poor Yorick. I knew him, Horatio, a fellow of infinite jest, of most excellent fancy' (178–9). Although this was a familiar quotation in the nineteenth century, it is nevertheless interesting to note that Dickens went to see *Hamlet* at the Theatre Royal in Preston on 28 January 1854, but he was unimpressed by the production (*Letters* 7.261).

When candles were brought, Mrs Sparsit

backgammon]   Backgammon, an ancient board game dating from around 3000 BC, was a popular Victorian pastime.

When the time drew near for retiring

sherry warm, with lemon-peel and nutmeg?']   This is negus, a sweet beverage which can be made with sherry, sweet white wine or port. Mrs Beeton's recipe allows one quart of boiling water, a quarter-pound of sugar, one lemon and grated nutmeg, to every pint of wine (Beeton 890).

She waited yet some quarter of an hour

went out of her room] Louisa and Bounderby apparently sleep in different rooms. In 1857, Dickens made arrangements for separate bedrooms in Tavistock House for himself and Catherine (see note to book 1, chapter 11, pp. 134).

'My dear brother:' she laid her head down

her hair flowed over him] The display of flowing, abundant hair in many ancient, religious and literary traditions can be a sign of female sexuality, sexual availability, subjection or unchastity. St Paul entreated that a woman's head should be covered: 'For if the woman be not covered, let her also be shorn: but if it be a shame for a woman to be shorn or shaven, let her be covered' (1 Corinthians, 11.6). St Paul further compounds the symbolism by alluding to the beauty and mystery of women's hair: 'if a woman have long hair, it is a glory to her: for her hair is given her for a covering' (11.15). Inherent in Paul's directive is the dual, and ambivalent, notion of female subjection and male glorification – a concept which would have been familiar to the Victorian mind. For the nineteenth-century imagination, women's hair was a symbolic conflation of sex and worship. Moreover, a literary heritage of fairy-tales, ballads and classical myths which stressed the magical quality of long and preferably golden hair (the colour added the suggestion of wealth) gave complex meaning to fictional references (Gitter, 1984, 936–54; Fabrizio, 1987, 78, 90).

'Another person may seem to you dishonest

'Another person may seem to you dishonest, and yet not be so.'] A variation of Iago's view of Othello: 'The Moor is of a free and open nature/That thinks men honest that but seem to be so;/And will as tenderly be led by th' nose/As asses are' (*Othello* 1.3.397–400).

Book 2, Chapter 9   Fifteenth weekly part
                                      Saturday, 8 July 1854

HEARING THE LAST OF IT

MRS SPARSIT, *lying by to recover*

her eyes, like a couple of lighthouses on an iron-bound coast, might have warned all prudent mariners]   The 1840s and 1850s were the heyday of lighthouse construction in the British Isles on account of advances in civil engineering and refinements in the production of reflector lamps. Prior to the mid-1780s, most of the 135 lighthouses in the world were lit by coal-fires, and the minority used either oil-lamps or crude reflectors. But in 1786 and 1787 a lighthouse near Lynn in Norfolk and four lighthouses on remote Scottish coasts were erected using a new device: an oil-lamp surrounded by a glass chimney with a reflector behind which focused the light into a beam. The lighthouses were praised by sailors for their brilliance and visibility from great distances; and, with the increase in shipping caused by the Industrial Revolution, demand grew for the construction of new lighthouses. A major advance in the nineteenth century was the individual identification of lighthouses. For example, the St Agnes light off the Scilly Isles identified itself by a revolving light with three sides which produced three flashes of different intensity, and the two lighthouses at Portland produced a distinctive combination of beams that enabled mariners to tell them apart and to recognize clearly the location of their ship (Mair, 1978, passim).

   A *HW* article of 1851, 'Lighthouses and Light-Boats', based substantially on Alan Stevenson's *A Rudimentary Treatise on . . . Lighthouses* (1850), comments that the British coast 'is so well furnished with lighthouses, that this is the first of our arrangements which strikes foreigners with admiration' (2.373). The report discusses the manufacture of reflectors and provides the architectural histories of the Tour de Corduan, the Eddystone, the Carlington and the Skerryvore lighthouses (2.373–9).

an iron-bound coast]   The earliest printed usage is William Falconer's *An Universal Dictionary of the Marine* (1769): 'Terres hautes, high land on the sea-shore; a bold, or iron-bound coast' (1780 edn, 405) (*OED*). Frequently reprinted in the nineteenth century, the dictionary was widely read, so it is likely that Dickens either knew it or had come across a later book which used Falconer's image. One such book was George B. Earp's *The Gold Colonies of Australia* (1852), which describes 'a survey of the iron-bound coast of Australia' (ch. 30).

smoothing her uncomfortable . . . mittens (they were constructed of a cool fabric like a meat-safe)]   Probably home-made mesh mittens netted with a netting-needle and a mesh-stick. A meat-safe is a ventilated cupboard usually made of wire-gauze or perforated zinc, for the storage of meat (*OED*; Brittain, 1979, 186).

'A singular world, I would say, sir,'

dulcet tones] Compare *The Merchant of Venice* 3.2.48–53:

> Then music is
> Even as the flourish, when true subjects bow
> To a new-crowned monarch: such it is,
> As are those dulcet sounds in break of day,
> That creep into the dreaming bridegroom's ear,
> And summon him to marriage.

'Offence!' repeated Bounderby.

beating about for side-winds.'] In sailing, this means altering course to take advantage of the winds. (This nautical imagery seems out of character for Bounderby.)

Mr Bounderby had not been long gone

over the long line of arches that bestrode the wild country of past and present coal pits] See note to book 2, chapter 7, pp.191–2.

She had seldom been there, since her marriage.

sifting and sifting at his parliamentary cinder-heap in London (without being observed to turn up many precious articles among the rubbish), and was still hard at it in the national dust-yard.] On account of the high consumption of coal in London, ashes and cinders from household fires had to be regularly removed in order to reduce the amount of accumulated rubbish and filth in the streets. Each parish commissioned dust contractors to remove such refuse to dust-yards around the outskirts of the city. There the dust was piled into volcano-like heaps of various heights, ready for sifting with iron sieves by an army of low-paid women and old men. Mayhew lists the constituents and uses of such a dust-heap:

1. "Soil," or fine dust, sold to brickmakers for making bricks, and to farmers for manure, especially for clover.
2. "Brieze," or cinders, sold to brickmakers, for burning bricks.
3. Rags, bones, and old metal, sold to marine-store dealers.
4. Old tin and iron vessel, sold for "clamps" to trunks, &c., and for making copperas.
5. Old bricks and oyster shells, sold to builders, for sinking foundations, and forming roads.
6. Old boots and shoes, sold to Prussian-blue manufacturers.
7. Money and jewellery, kept, or sold to Jews. (2.171)

A *HW* article of 1850, 'Dust; or Ugliness Redeemed', describes the 'soft-ware' section of a dust-heap: 'all vegetable and animal matters – everything that will decompose. . . . Under this head . . . the dead cats are comprised' (1.380). Dickens's image of parliamentary rubbish is similar to that used by Carlyle in his *Latter-Day Pamphlets* (1850):

> it is felt that 'reform' in that Downing-Street department of affairs is precisely the reform which were worth all others; that those administrative establishments in Downing Street are really the Government of this huge ungoverned Empire; that to clean-out the dead pedantries, unveracities, indolent somnolent impotences, and accumulated dung-mountains there, is the beginning of all practical good whatsoever. Yes, get down once again to the actual pavement of that; ascertain what the thing is, and was before dung accumulated in it; and what it should and may, and must, for the life's sake of this Empire, henceforth become. ('Downing Street')

One of the proposed titles for *HT* was 'Rust and Dust'. In *OMF* the dust-heaps at Belle Isle, near Battle Bridge, form a literal and symbolic backdrop to the novel (see Cotsell, 1986, passim).

Neither, as she approached her old home now

suffering little children to come into the midst of it] Mark 10.14–15: 'Suffer little children to come unto me, and forbid them not: for of such is the kingdom of God. . . . Whosoever shall not receive the kingdom of God as a little child, he shall not enter therein.'

not a grim Idol, cruel and cold, with its victims bound hand to foot, and its big dumb shape set up with a sightless stare, never to be moved by anything but so many calculated tons of leverage] Dickens probably had in mind the huge stone bas-reliefs, statues of gods, warriors and kings, the gigantic human-headed winged lions and the famous Nineveh bull which the archaeologist Austen Henry Layard (1817–94) brought back to England from his Mesopotamian excavations of Nineveh (Kuyunjik) and at Nimrud between 1845 and 1851. Layard published several accounts of his explorations and travels: *Nineveh and its Remains* (1848–9); *Nineveh and Babylon* (1853); and *A Popular Account of Discoveries at Nineveh* (1851). Copies of the last sold at railway bookstalls for five shillings (Waterfield, 1963, 228).

Nineveh and its Remains includes illustrations from the sculptures of Khorsabad and Kuyunjik showing manacles for the feet and hands used for captured 'inferior prisoners' (376), and in his description of tortured captives depicted in the Kuyunjik bas-reliefs Layard graphically notes that 'Two were stretched naked at full length on the ground, and whilst their limbs were held apart by pegs and cords they were being flayed alive' (*Nineveh and Babylon*, 456–7). In *Nineveh and its Remains*, Layard describes the strenuous task of moving the colossal winged bull of Nineveh (one of a pair) for transport to England. The operation involved many men lowering the bull on to wooden rollers using a system of ropes and supporting beams: 'Several of the strongest Chaldaeans placed thick beams against the back of the bull, and were directed to withdraw them gradually, supporting the weight of the slab, and checking it in its descent, in case the ropes should give way' (2.80–1). During the serialization of HT, a HW article about Layard's travels, 'Under Canvas', recalled the discovery of the Nineveh bull and the Arabs' reaction to it, quoted from Layard: ' "Walleh! it was not the work of men's hands, but of those infidel giants of whom the Prophet . . . has said that they were higher than the tallest date-tree; it was one of the idols which Noah . . . cursed before the flood" ' (9.368).

Layard was a friend of Dickens, who had recently joined him in November 1853 on an ascent of Vesuvius during Dickens's trip to Switzerland and Italy. A radical who entered politics after 1852, Layard was supported by Dickens in 1855 when he took a stand in the House of Commons against government maladministration of the Crimean War (*Letters* 7.189, 624; Waterfield, 1963, 272–3; *Speeches* 191).

The golden waters were not there. They were flowing for the fertilization of the land where grapes are gathered from thorns, and figs from thistles.] In the *Arabian Nights* 'Tale of the three sisters who envied their sister', Parizade successfully finds the golden waters which will bring her petrified brothers back to life and so enable them all to be reunited with their father. The allusion becomes ironic when conflated with the paraphrase from Luke 6.44: 'For every tree is known by his own fruit. For of thorns men do not gather figs, nor of a bramble bush gather they grapes'.

Her feeble voice sounded so far away

she might have been lying at the bottom of a well. The poor lady was nearer Truth than she ever had been] From the proverb, 'Truth lies at the bottom of a well', attributed to a saying of the Greek philosopher Democritus: 'We know nothing certainly, for truth lies in the deep.'

On being told that Mrs Bounderby was there

an unobjectionable name] In MS, CP and *HW*. The one-volume first edition and CD read 'objectionable name' – doubtless a typographical error. 'Unobjectionable name' makes sense in terms of Mrs Gradgrind's timidity.

She fancied, however, that her request

emerged from the shadow in which man walketh and disquieteth himself in vain] An allusion to the service for the Burial of the Dead in BCP (from Psalms 39.6): 'For man walketh in a vain shadow, and disquieteth himself in vain'.

Book 2, Chapter 10   Fifteenth weekly part
Saturday, 8 July 1854

MRS SPARSIT'S STAIRCASE

MRS SPARSIT'S nerves being slow to recover

feeding on the fat of the land]   From Genesis 45.18: 'And take your father and your households, and come unto me: and I will give you the good of the land of Egypt, and ye shall eat the fat of the land'.

Mr Bounderby, having got it into his explosive

Mrs Sparsit returned . . . though not of the Mahommedan persuasion: 'To hear is to obey.']   Scheherazade's frequent response to her sultan husband in the *Arabian Nights* is 'To hear you is to obey'.

'In a similar manner, ma'am,' said Bounderby

If Romulus and Remus could wait]   According to legend, Romulus and Remus were the founders of Rome. The abandoned baby twin brothers were left to drown in the River Tiber, but both survived and were suckled by a she-wolf downstream at the place where Rome now stands. The legendary brothers waited for many years before the city was built on the site.

Alderney]   A breed of dairy-cow originally from Alderney, one of the Channel Islands.

'No, ma'am,' continued Bounderby

under the rose]   'Secretly' – a translation of the Latin phrase *sub rosa*. In Roman mythology, Cupid gave a rose as a bribe to Harpocrates, the god of silence, so that he would not disclose Venus' love-affairs. Thus the rose came to represent silence and secrecy (Hotten).

Mrs Sparsit saw James Harthouse come

Giants' Staircase]   A reference to the ancient staircase found in the courtyard of the Doges' Palace in Venice, which Dickens visited on his tours of Italy in 1844 and 1853 (see *Letters* 7.215). The name of the steps derives from the huge statues of Mars and Neptune which stand guard at the top. Dickens's image of steady descent alludes to his comments made on his first sight of the staircase in 1844: 'Descending from the palace by a staircase, called, I thought, the Giant's – I had some imaginary recollection of an old man abdicating, coming, more slowly and more feebly, down it, when he heard the bell proclaiming his successor' ('An Italian Dream', *PI*). (He was thinking about the forced abdication of the Venetian leader Francesco Foscari in 1457.) Dickens's recollections of Foscari are from Byron's *The Two Foscari* (1821), a tragedy which also formed the basis of a Verdi opera. Byron's other Venetian drama of the same year, *Marino Faliero: Doge of Venice*, relates the tragic events leading up to the assassination of the fourteenth-century doge, Marin Falier (1274–1355). Byron's Faliero is beheaded on the Giant's Staircase.

Book 2, Chapter 11   Sixteenth weekly part
Saturday, 15 July 1854

LOWER AND LOWER

In the meantime, Mrs Sparsit kept unwinking

iron road]   A popular term for the railway. The name was used as the title of an important contemporary history of the railways by F. S. Williams, *Our Iron Roads: Their History, Construction, and Administration* (1852).

'Bitzer,' said Mrs Sparsit that afternoon

walnut ketchup]   Mrs Beeton gives the ingredients for this full-flavoured sauce: '100 walnuts, 1 handful of salt, 1 quart of vinegar, ¼ oz. of mace, ¼ oz. of nutmeg, ¼ oz. of cloves, ¼ oz. of ginger, ¼ oz. of whole black pepper, a small piece of horseradish, 20 shalots, ¼ lb. of anchovies, 1 pint of port wine.' Walnut ketchup was usually made in the first two weeks of July when walnuts are perfect for pickling (Beeton 255).

India ale]   This was India Pale Ale (IPA), specially brewed in England from the 1780s for the Indian market. British colonization had created a growing demand for home-brewed beer, since tropical climates and inadequate brewing facilities ruled out the possibility of local production. English brewers, however, faced a multiplicity of transportation problems, including the high cost of shipping non-returnable glass bottles abroad and ensuring the good quality of the exported ale. As a result, many brewing firms concentrated on the home market and left the export of ales to a few breweries. One London establishment, Abbot & Hodgson's Bow Brewery, had virtually all the India ale export trade, conducted through the East India Company until 1822, when two Burton upon Trent brewers, Bass and Allsopp, entered the market.

With the advantage of the high mineral content of Burton water (and later, in the 1840s, with their union system of fermentation, which 'cleansed' the ales in large casks during the fermentation process) they produced a superior, clear pale ale which could travel well. Ten years later, Bass were shipping one-third more barrels of IPA than Hodgson. Moreover, the Burton breweries had established a home trade among the middle classes in London and the North – a domestic market which was to expand dramatically over the next twenty years as a direct result of the railways (Gourvish and Wilson, 1994, passim).

'Where may he be at present?' Mrs Sparsit asked

Furies] The Roman name for the Eumenides (or Erinyes), the Greek goddesses of vengeance. According to legend, they ascended from the underworld to pursue wicked mortals.

'He is shooting in Yorkshire,'

'He is shooting in Yorkshire,' said Tom. 'Sent Loo a basket half as big as a church, yesterday.'] Large estates provided sport for landowners and their friends, and the expansion of the railways made it easier to travel to shoots in remote counties such as Yorkshire. But shooting was an expensive sport which engendered hostility and alienation in rural society. Unlike fox-hunting – which was enjoyed by farmers, estate tenants and landowners alike – shooting was the preserve of the gentry and aristocracy, for farmers' leases usually specified that game could be shot only by the landlord. The 'guns' customarily sent gifts of game to their friends, and Harthouse's basket would most likely have comprised grouse – who are partial to the heather-covered, uncultivated Yorkshire moors – rather than partridge or pheasant, who thrive in lowland areas having ploughland and grain crops (Thompson, 1981, 459–65; Carr, 1981, 482–5).

It was the conception of an inspired moment

as if she had been caught up in a cloud and whirled away.] Reminiscent of several biblical allusions: 'Elijah went up by a whirlwind into heaven' (2 Kings 2:11), and 'Then we which are alive and remain shall be caught up together with them in the clouds' (1 Thessalonians 4:17). See also Revelation 11:12.

All the journey, immovable in the air

electric wires] Electric telegraph wires literally and metaphorically paralleled the revolutionary progress of the railway system. They were first patented in 1837 by the physicist Sir Charles Wheatstone, and by 1840 the wires were evident along the side of the railways as far north as Glasgow. Telegraph poles were not introduced until 1843. The Railway Act of 1844 made provision for the extensive establishment of electrical telegraphs on all railway lines, and in 1846 the first Electric Telegraph Company was set up. In 1851, 99,216 messages were transmitted; by 1855 the number had soared to 745,880.

Dickens was fascinated by the electric telegraph. Writing to Mark Lemon in 1856, he gave an account of the use of the telegraph in a play he had seen in Paris: 'There is nothing in the piece, but it was impossible not to be moved and excited by the telegraph part of it' (*Letters* 8.11–12). A *HW* article of 1850 which discussed the technicalities of the telegraph also eulogized its invention: 'In our fast days, we have one thing, above all others, the fastest; in our generation of marvels, we have one thing of all others the most marvellous' ('Wings of Wire', 2.241–5). See also 'Wire-Drawing', *HW* 9.217–21; and 'House-Top Telegraphs', *AYR* 2.106–9 (Dodds, 1953, passim; Briggs, 1988, 377).

She went up to the house, keeping

all the creeping things that be.]   In Acts 10.12, Peter saw in a vision 'all manner of four-footed beasts of the earth, and wild beasts, and creeping things, and fowls of the air'. One of many biblical references to the Creation and, by implication, the Fall of man. See also Genesis 1.26, Psalms 104.25, Romans 1.23. The passage would seem to suggest that Mrs Sparsit has herself become 'a snake in the grass'.

Bending low among the dewy grass

like Robinson Crusoe in his ambuscade against the savages]   An allusion to Daniel Defoe's novel in which Robinson Crusoe and Friday attack the cannibals from the corner of a wood.

When she stopped to close the side-gate

ascended the wooden steps to the railroad.]   The description of the railway station and the roar of the train which follows this sentence is similar to Dickens's account of his impending train journey from Wolverhampton to Birmingham in 'Fire and Snow':

> Come we at last to the precipitous wooden steps by which we are to be mast-headed at a railway station. . . . Station very gritty, as a general characteristic. Station very dark, the gas being frozen. Station very cold, as any timber cabin suspended in the air with such a wind making lunges at it, would be. Station very dreary, being a station. Man and boy behind money-taking partition. . . . Shivering porter going in and out, bell in hand, to look for the train, which is overdue, finally gives it up for the present, and puts down the

bell. . . . In our own innocence we repeatedly mistake the roaring of the nearest furnace for the approach of the train, run out, and return covered with ignominy. Train in sight at last – but the other train – which don't stop here – and it seems to tear the trembling station limb from limb, as it rushes through. Finally, some half-an-hour behind its time through the tussle it has had with the snow, comes our expected engine, shrieking with indignation and grief.

(HW 8.483)

The seizure of the station with a fit of trembling

red light] 'Auxiliary' or 'distant' signals were operated in most main railway stations at this time. The signals, which worked on a wire system, could be erected at some distance from the signal box. The arrangement proved to be extremely effective in bad weather conditions when the train driver could not clearly see the station lights. The auxiliary signals had 'only the green or "caution," and the "all right" signals: the former intimating that the red signal was turned on at the station' (Williams, 1968, 276).

Book 2, Chapter 12   Sixteenth weekly part
Saturday, 15 July 1854

DOWN

THE national dustmen, after entertaining

THE national dustmen] That is, Members of Parliament. Mayhew observed that 'dustmen, scavengers and nightmen are, to a certain extent, the same people . . . the men who collect the dust on one day may be cleaning the streets on the next, especially during wet weather, and engaged at night, perhaps, twice during the week, in removing nightsoil' (2.172). They

> perambulate the streets with a heavily-built high box cart, which is mostly coated with a thick crust of filth, and drawn by a clumsy-looking horse. These men used, before the passing of the late Street Act, to ring a dull-sounding bell so as to give notice to housekeepers of their approach, but now they merely cry, in a hoarse unmusical voice, "Dust oy-eh!"

(2.175)

For a discussion of cinder- and dust-heaps, see note to book 2, chapter 9, pp. 201–2.

He sat writing in the room

the Good Samaritan was a Bad Economist.] In the biblical parable, the Samaritan, after binding up the wounds of a man who has been robbed, takes the stranger to an inn and pays for his care and accommodation, with no desire for recompense (Luke 10.29–37).

'How could you give me life

what have you done, with the garden that should have bloomed once, in this great wilderness here!'] An account of the damage done to olive trees and crops on the Greek islands, caused by a long and severe winter, appeared a few pages later in the same number of *HW*:

> When the hurricanes ceased at last, and the July sun blazed out in all its deadly heat, the olive trees, instead of presenting their usual dark luxuriant foliage and ripening crops, looked as if they had been burnt, and were naked of both leaves and fruit. They had indeed withered away. All the life and sap had been burnt out of them.
> ('The Roving Englishman: Village Diplomatists', 9.510)

'When I was irrevocably married

the secrets of my soul.'] Compare *2 Henry VI* (3.2.374–6):

> sometimes he calls the King
> And whispers to his pillow, as to him,
> The secrets of his overcharged soul.

BOOK THE THIRD.

GARNERING.

GARNERING] There are many biblical references to garnering, but two are particularly apt: Psalms 144.12-13 – 'That our sons may be as plants grown up in their youth; that our daughters may be as corner stones. . . . That our garners may be full'; and Joel 1.17 – 'The seed is rotten under their clods, the garners are laid desolate, the barns are broken down; for the corn is withered'. See also Matthew 3.12.

Book 3, Chapter 1   Seventeenth weekly part
Saturday, 22 July 1854

ANOTHER THING NEEDFUL

LOUISA awoke from a torpor

the shadows of a dream] From Keats's *Endymion*: 'A hope beyond the shadow of a dream' (I.857).

He said it earnestly, and to do him justice

excise-rod] A measuring-stick used by a tax official for taking samples of certain goods to determine what excise duty to impose on them. Excise tax was charged either during the process of manufacture or before sale to home consumers. Dickens may have had in mind the exciseman's gauging-stick for spirits. Dodd provides a detailed account of the governmental powers given to an exciseman in a spirit-producing distillery:

> he has keys to most of the vessels and stills; he gauges and measures whenever he pleases; he knows and marks every vessel throughout the establishment; he, or his co-officers, are constantly within the premises day and night . . . in short, the exciseman is virtually the master within the distillery.
> (1856, 477–8)

'O my child, my child!' he said

'O my child, my child!'] Perhaps an allusion to King David's cries on hearing of his son's death: 'O my son Absalom, my son, my son Absalom! would God I had died for thee, O Absalom, my son, my son!' (2 Samuel 18.33).

that what the Head had left undone and could not do, the Heart may have been doing silently.] Compare part of the general confession recited at Morning Prayer: 'We have left undone those things which we ought to have done; And we have done those things which we ought not to have done' (BCP).

In the innocence of her brave affection

shone like a beautiful light upon the darkness of the other.] Compare Isaiah 9.2: 'The people that walked in darkness have seen a great light: they that dwell in the land of the shadow of death, upon them hath the light shined'. See also Luke 1.79: 'To give light to them that sit in darkness'.

'O lay it here!' cried Sissy.

'Lay it here, my dear.'] After these words, the MS has the following passage that was deleted in CP: 'Louisa's tears fell like the blessed rain after a long drought. The sullen glare was over, and in every drop there was a germ of hope and promise for the dried-up ground.'

Book 3, Chapter 2 Seventeenth weekly part
Saturday, 22 July 1854

VERY RIDICULOUS

MR JAMES HARTHOUSE passed a whole night

glass in its eye] A single eye-glass: a monocle.

In these circumstances he had nothing

griffin!] Or gryphon. A mythical animal with a lion's body and the head and wings of an eagle. The Greeks believed that griffins inhabited the ancient region of Scythia and protected that country's gold, just as Mrs Sparsit had 'watch[ed] over the treasures of' Bounderby's bank. For an earlier comparison between Mrs Sparsit and the dragon Ladon, see note to book 2, chapter 1, p. 160 (OED).

(Weekly N^{os}: to be enlarged to 10 of my sides each -about)

Sissy and Louisa. ✓

Sissy with James Harthouse. ✓

       to
Stephen Blackpool ⌐disappear<s>

           Rachael ✓   ⎛ Tom, and his discovery
                                        ⎜   (Bitzer)
Stephen Blackpool to be found   ⎝   Mrs Pegler.

  His wife?   No.
                        Sleary's Horsemanship and Sissy's
                              father - Merrylegs.

Slackbridge.

  Bounderby and Mrs Sparsit.

(Hard Times. ——————————— Nos: V. & VI.

Weekly No: 17.

chapter XXIX.

Sissy and Louisa. Head and heart - "O lay your head here my dear, lay it here!"

chapter XXX.

—Sissy and James Harthouse

Goes in for camels

He goes away. One of the best actions of his life, quite a silent sorrow to him afterwards.

Weekly No: 18.   chapter XXXI.

Bounderby and Mrs Sparsit together   -   Separation scene with Mr Gradgrind

chapter XXXII.

Pursue the robbery - disappearance of Stephen

Rachael

Tom plucking up a spirit, because   -
   Still no Stephen.

Weekly No: 19.   Chapter XXXIII.   The great effect.

Still No Stephen   Mrs Sparsit fearfully energetic
   Mrs Pegler Bounderby's mother - Excellent woman. Brought him up capitally

Still no Stephen.
                        Chapter XXXIV.
                     Coal pit & death.
"I leave 't to yo to clear my good name. Ask   Stephen and Rachael
     yor son Sir.   The Star that leads
Stephen found and Tom vanishes.   Bear and forbear   the way

Weekly No: 20.   chapter XXXV.

            Louisa
Sissy and <Rachael> pursue Tom

                         — "Comic Livery"
Find him <wit> with travelling riders ₁ and <xxxx xx> so work round Sissy's own

story.   chapter XXXVI.
      Bitzer true to his bringing-up.   Tom saved by Sleary — Finish Sissy here

Weekly No: 21.   Conclusion.
                            Dispose of Mrs Sparsit.

Wind up —
            The ashes of our fires grown grey and cold

'So, whether I am waiting for a hostile message

wrestle . . . in the Lancashire manner] A particularly vicious style of wrestling which required a man to hold his opponent's shoulders on the ground for two seconds. It is described by a nineteenth-century expert as

> the most barbarous of the English systems, and more nearly approaches the French dog-fighting and tumbling than any other.... Open competitions such as take place in Cumberland and Westmoreland and in Cornwall and Devon are almost unknown in Lancashire, contests there being mostly confined to matches under the 'gaffer' system. A local writer delivers himself to the following effect: 'A Lancashire wrestling-match is an ugly sight: the fierce animal passions of the men which mark the struggles of maddened bulls, or wild beasts, the savage yelling of their partisans, the wrangling, and finally the clog business which settles all disputes and knotty points, are simply appalling.'
> (Beaufort, 1890, 230)

The Lancashire style developed into the catch-as-catch-can style which gave rise to such moves as the Half Nelson and the more dangerous manoeuvre, the Double Nelson (Camaione and Tillman, 1980, 7; Beaufort, 1890, 230–3).

However, he took affairs as coolly

'Or a fellow of about thirteen or fourteen stone] Between 182 and 196 pounds. One stone is the British standard weight of 14 pounds.

It was impossible, even before dinner

'like the Holy Office and slow torture.'] Barbaric tortures were carried out by the Holy Inquisition of the Roman Catholic Church in fifteenth-century Spain. In *A Child's History of England* (1851–3), Dickens called the Holy Inquisition 'the most unholy and the most infamous tribunal that ever disgraced mankind, and made men more like demons than followers of Our Saviour' (20).

A general recollection that

the swell mob] The 'swell mob' was a common nineteenth-century colloquialism for better-dressed thieves and pickpockets. The swell-mobsman was the aristocrat of the thief world, the pickpocket was next in rank, followed by the 'sneak' who went into shops and snatched from the till. Those who stole goods displayed outside shops, or who took food, came last in the thieves' hierarchy (Paroissien, 1992, 249). In 'The Artful Touch', the second of Dickens's 'Three "Detective" Anecdotes', Inspector Wield (Scotland Yard's Inspector Charles Field and the model for Mr Bucket in *BH*) describes the *modus operandi* of the swell mob (*HW* 1.577–80).

Giving the waiter to the personage

hurried into the gallery.]   A common feature of a coaching inn was a long, balustraded balcony which surrounded the inn-yard. The Bull and Royal Hotel, where Dickens stayed during his visit to Preston at the end of January 1854, had such an open gallery which was still extant in the 1940s (Sartin). A local historian, J. H. Spencer, writing in the *Preston Herald* of 27 June 1941, referred to the hotel's former importance as the 'centre for connection with other coaches to the north, and many travellers put up at the Bull. A relic of those days still survives, for as you enter the courtyard you will notice on the right, part of the old gallery, now boarded up.' Dickens was not impressed with the hotel and described it to Forster as an 'old, grubby, smoky, mean, intensely formal red brick house with a narrow gateway and a dingy yard' (*Letters* 7.261).

'The drowning man catches at the straw.

'The drowning man catches at the straw.]   A well-known proverb meaning that a person in desperation will grab at the slightest chance when all hope is slipping away.

He was touched in the cavity where his heart

in the cavity where his heart should have been – in that nest of addled eggs]   This is reminiscent of *Henry V* (2.Chorus, 20–2):

> But see, thy fault France hath in thee found out,
> A nest of hollow bosoms, which he fills
> With treacherous crowns. . . .

Book 3, Chapter 3 Eighteenth weekly part
Saturday, 29 July 1854

VERY DECIDED

The indefatigable Mrs Sparsit

St James's Street]   In the fashionable West End of London, connecting Pall Mall with Piccadilly. Many celebrated gaming clubs and coffee-houses were established here from the seventeenth century onwards.

Mr Bounderby's first procedure was

screwing the patient's thumbs] A thumb-screw was a medieval instrument of torture by which one or both thumbs were compressed (*OED*).

'Well, ma'am,' said Bounderby

a glass of scalding rum and butter] An alcoholic restorative, hot spiced rum:

> Combine in a tumbler one or two lumps of sugar, half a teaspoonful of mixed allspice, one wineglass of Jamaica rum, and a piece of fresh butter as large as a chestnut. Fill the tumbler with hot water and grate a little nutmeg on top before serving. (Hewett and Axton, 1983, 116)

'There you hit it,' returned Bounderby.

I'll tell you what education is – To be tumbled out of doors, neck and crop, and put upon the shortest allowance of everything except blows.] This attitude was expressed by Bendigo Buster, the pugilistic character based on the boxer William 'Bendigo' Thompson in Dickens's and Morley's *HW* article, 'Mr. Bendigo Buster on our National Defences against Education':

> Schools are intolerable follies. . . . England is acting, in regard to schools, as becomes her practical good sense. Her boys are in the gutters, growing up to manly independence; they swear well, fight like bricks, and have game in 'em. By her boys, I mean the multitude, the children of the people. I know that in the upper classes there are children more or less demoralized by education, and that the same evil influence is sometimes brought to bear upon the poor. But, England, as a nation, don't trouble herself much about the education of the masses; something like forty-five out of a hundred of 'em can't read and write. That's what I call being practical. (2.313)

He discharged this, like a Rocket

He discharged this, like a Rocket, at his father-in-law's head.] A 'behind the scenes' account of a firework display in Vauxhall Gardens described the pyrotechnics of a variety of fireworks including rockets, and listed some popular types:

> First there is the Sky-rocket . . . a cylindrical case intended to ascend to a

great height, give out a profusion of sparks during its ascent, and spread a brilliant shower of coloured stars when it explodes, high up in the skiey regions. A *Tourbillon* is a sort of double rocket . . . [which] revolves and ascends at the same time. . . . A *Saucisson* is compounded of a brilliant fire and a bounce, and is discharged out of a mortar fixed on the ground. A Scroll is a kind of *tourbillon* on a small scale, provided with a rotatory motion.

(HW 8 [10 September 1853] 47)

Of the many proposed titles which Dickens had thought about for what eventually became *Household Words* in 1850, one was 'The Rocket' (*Letters* 6.26).

Book 3, Chapter 4   Eighteenth weekly part
Saturday, 29 July 1854

LOST

THE robbery at the Bank had not

Venus, who had risen out of the . . . sea] Venus, or Aphrodite, the goddess of love and beauty, is said to have sprung to life from the sea's foam. A copy of the two pieces of the original statue of the Venus de Milo was exhibited at the Great Exhibition in the Crystal Palace. (The originals were found in 1820 and exhibited in the Louvre.) (Cotsell, 1986, 70.)

The factory-bells had need to ring their loudest

the groups of workers . . . collected round the placards, devouring them with eager eyes.] When Dickens arrived in Preston in the afternoon of Saturday, 28 January 1854, to view the cotton workers' strike in its twenty-third week, he was surprised to find the town relatively quiet and free from disturbance:

> except for the cold smokeless factory chimnies, the placards at the street corners, and the groups of working people attentively reading them, nor foreigner nor Englishman could have had the least suspicion that there existed any interruption to the usual labours of the place.
>
> ('On Strike', HW 8 [11 February 1854] 554)

Dickens wrote to Forster of his disappointment at finding Preston so uneventful: 'I am afraid I shall not be able to get much here. Except the crowds at the street-corners reading the placards pro and con; and the cold absence of smoke from the mill-chimneys; there is very little in the streets to make the town remarkable' (*Letters* 7.260). Dickens's Preston article also contains a complete bill issued by the operatives' committee on 24 January 1854.

that would have been half ludicrous if] After 'half ludicrous if' MS and CP read: 'such a picture of a Country as a suicidal idiot with its sword of state ∧POINTED∧ at its own heart could ever be otherwise than wholly shocking'.

Slackbridge, the delegate, had to address

Slackbridge unfolded what he called 'that damning document,' and held it up to the gaze, and for the execration, of the working-man community!] At a contentious delegate meeting held in the Preston Cock-pit on Sunday, 29 January 1854, which Dickens attended for a brief time, Mortimer Grimshaw was accused by Warrington delegates of placarding their town with libellous bills. Grimshaw responded by pouring out 'vials of his wrath upon the committee and the operatives of that town, who he said had sent only £11, £12, and £13 a week to Preston, a mere trifle for such a town as Warrington' (*Manchester Guardian*, 1 February 1854). Dickens reported the altercation in 'On Strike', and presented the Warrington – 'Throstletown' – delegate holding up 'an offensive bill' to the assembled crowd (8.557). It would appear that Dickens loosely based the placard scenes in the novel on both his general observations of the Preston strikers' eagerness to read the varied bills posted throughout the town, and on the specific incident of the aggrieved Warrington delegate. Ironically, it is Slackbridge who now holds 'this blighting bill'.

my band of brothers] From *Henry V* (4.3.60): 'We few, we happy few, we band of brothers'.

Since his sheet-anchor had come home

sheet-anchor] Formerly, the largest of a ship's anchors which was used only in an emergency. Figuratively, someone or something on which one relies when all else has failed (*OED*).

'It goes against me,' Rachael answered

'It goes against me,' Rachael answered. . . . and not near it.'] These passages are written on the verso of the MS leaf.

Book 3, Chapter 5   Nineteenth weekly part
                                     Saturday, 5 August 1854

FOUND

Although Mr Bounderby carried it off

the Slough of Despond]   From John Bunyan's *Pilgrim's Progress* (1678), one of the books most frequently referred to in Dickens's writings. Christian falls into this deep bog of despair, but Help lifts him out (1.57–8).

Book 3, Chapter 6   Nineteenth weekly part
                                     Saturday, 5 August 1854

THE STARLIGHT

As Coketown cast ashes not only

cast ashes not only on its own head but on the neighbourhood's too – after the manner of those pious persons who do penance for their own sins by putting other people into sackcloth]   An allusion to Sabbatarian prohibition of recreations and entertainment on a Sunday (see notes to book 1, chapter 5, pp. 85 and 88). The image derives from the Roman Catholic practice during Lent of sprinkling ashes on the heads of penitents who had confessed on the day (Ash Wednesday).

to get a few miles away by the railroad]   Apart from the cheap parliamentary trains (see note to book 1, chapter 12, p. 139), inexpensive excursion trains were run on most lines. Their popularity is recorded in 'Chips: Excursion Trains':

> On the Great Western line the results of excursion trains were beyond all expectation. On the occasion of the first cheap Sunday trip to Bath and Bristol, although the advertised time for starting was eight o'clock, the excursionists had arrived in such large numbers, long before that time, that two immense trains were despatched by half-past seven, and a third at eight o'clock. Each of these trains comprised about twenty-five of the company's large carriages, the number of persons conveyed by them being nearly six thousand. The profit netted by the company was very considerable. (HW 3.355)

The demand for excursion trains continued to rise throughout the century.

They walked on across the fields

Mounds where the grass was rank and high . . . they always avoided; for dismal stories were told in that country of the old pits hidden beneath such indications.] Dickens had had similar thoughts about the snow-covered area of mound and fell outside Wolverhampton: '[it is] Not altogether agreeable to think of crossing such space without a guide, and being swallowed by a long-abandoned, long-forgotten shaft' ('Fire and Snow', *HW* 8.481). See also 'The King of the Hearth', *HW* 2.229–33.

First to wake them, and next to tell them

Old Hell Shaft] Although Dickens uses Stephen's fall into the disused pit to criticize mine-owners' disregard for safety, Old Hell Shaft may be an indirect allusion to factory shafts which, until January 1855, manufacturers were not compelled by law to fence, despite calls for safety legislation from factory inspectors. (See note to book 1, chapter 13, pp. 143–6, about the severe injuries caused by unprotected factory shafts; also see note to book 2, chapter 1, p. 158, which discusses the fierce resistance of manufacturers to government interference and Palmerston's equivocal role in the issue.)

Every sound of insects in the air

there was a surgeon, who brought some wine and medicines.] It is likely that a *HW* article entitled 'Sharpening the Scythe' informed many details of Stephen's short deliverance from the pit. See pp. 223–4 below.

The sun was four hours lower

a candle was sent down to try the air] Colliery explosions caused by underground combustible gases were frequent (see notes following, pp. 221–2).

The consultation ended in the men returning

a hurdle] A portable, rectangular frame with horizontal bars supported by one diagonal bar. Hurdles can be used to form sheep enclosures and act as temporary fences. Traitors for high treason were carried through the streets to execution on a sledge-like hurdle. This was a statutory requirement up until 1870 (*OED*). Dickens may well have been aware of the ironic relevance the latter meaning had for the condemned Stephen.

They gave him drink, moistened

drops of cordial] Alcoholic cordials were sweetened or spiced spirits. Whisky cordial, for example, included currants, lemon, ginger and sugar. Used medicinally, they were believed to aid digestion and stimulate the heart (Beeton 892).

'I ha' fell into th' pit, my dear

Fire-damp] A highly explosive gas, formed by the combination of methane and air, which gave rise to many pit disasters. The safety lamp, invented by Sir Humphry Davy in 1815, greatly reduced the incidence of coal-mine explosions by means of its two-layer metal gauze chimney which conducted heat away from the fire-damp. The flame of a safety lamp also elongates in the presence of this gas. The dangers caused by coal mines were described in a *HW* article of 1850:

> A sudden death, and a violent is often our fate. We may fall down a shaft; something may fall upon us and crush us; we may be damped to death; we may be drowned by the sudden breaking in of water; we may be burned up by the wild-fire, or driven before it to destruction.
> ('The True Story of a Coal Fire', 1.72)

The following footnotes, relatively rare for *HW*, explained the terms 'damped' and 'wild-fire': '*The choke-damp,* carbonic acid gas./*Fire-damp,* also called *the sulphur* – hydrogen gas.' 'Wire-Drawing' (*HW* 9.217–21) discusses the importance of the iron-wire gauze used in Davy's safety lamp and reports that 'Even while we now write, public attention is directed to a dread calamity whereby nearly a hundred human creatures in one pit have been destroyed by an explosion of fire-damp' (220).

I ha' read on't in the public petition, as onny one may read, fro' the men that works in pits, in which they ha' pray'n and pray'n the lawmakers for Christ's sake not to let their work be murder to 'em] 'A Coal Miner's Evidence' relates the cause of one colliery explosion and implicitly criticizes government inertia:

> We think the explosion was caused by the gas from the old working, now opened after being closed thirteen years. Some noise made the undergoer go to this place, and instead of taking his Davy lamp, he ran there with a lighted candle in his hand. He, and the man who was at work there, we found near each other all black and mutilated. . . . The Queen's gentlemen, when they came down here among us, said they could mend these things; but they hav'nt, [sic] you see. We think the Queen was'nt told. (*HW* 2.249)

See also 'Chips: A Remedy for Colliery Explosions' (*HW* 2.323–5) and 'Preventible Accidents' (*HW* 9.105–6). In 1842, Dickens had fervently supported Lord Ashley's 'Act to prohibit the Employment of Women and Girls in Mines and Colleries, to regulate the Employment of Boys, and make Provisions for the Safety of Persons working therein'. Dickens's letter to the *Morning Chronicle* about the proposed bill attacked negligent mine-owners who considered the measure as 'an interference with the rights of labour', and he also called for the provision of greater safety measures for miners whose lives 'must be fraught with danger, toil, and hardship' (*Letters* 3.278–85).

'Thy little sister, Rachael, thou hast not

and how she died, young and misshapen, awlung o' sickly air] Rachael's sister was originally to have died from the results of a factory accident (see note to book 1, chapter 13, pp. 143–6).

'It ha' shined upon me,' he said reverently

'It ha' shined upon me,' he said reverently, 'in my pain and trouble down below.] Reminiscent of Dickens's short story, 'A Child's Dream of a Star', in which a star guides and comforts a boy from childhood to old age through a recurrent vision of the star as a heavenly receptacle for the departed, including the souls of his sister, baby brother, mother and daughter. On his deathbed, he cries

> "I see the star! . . . My age is falling from me like a garment, and I move towards the star as a child. And O, my Father, now I thank thee that it has so often opened, to receive those dear ones who await me!"
> And the star was shining; and it shines upon his grave.
> (HW 1.25–6)

The article draws heavily on Dickens's memory of his childhood experiences at Chatham with his sister, Fanny, who died of tuberculosis on 2 September 1848 at the age of 38. Forster notes that Dickens and Fanny 'used to wander at night about a churchyard near their house, looking up at the stars; and her early death . . . had vividly reawakened all the childish associations which made her memory dear to him' (2.19.424–5). Dickens was prompted to write the *HW* story in response to his uneasiness about 'there being a want of something tender' in the second number of the periodical. During his railway journey back to London from Brighton in March 1850, he 'was looking at the stars, and revolving a little idea about them' (*Letters* 6.65). Before and during the serialization of *HT*, other *HW* pieces appeared which have associations with stars and starlight. See 'Starlight in the Garden', 8.108–9; 'Exiled', 9.440–1, 'The Ruined Potter', 9.441–4; and the poem 'Shining Stars', 9.536–7.

that aw th' world may on'y coom toogether more, an get a better unnerstan'in o' one another] A sentiment which Dickens had frequently reiterated in his writings and speeches, which was a principal aim of *Household Words* (see 'A Preliminary Word', *HW* 1.1), and which was uppermost in his mind at this time. On 30 December 1853 he prefaced his reading of *A Christmas Carol* (in aid of the newly formed Birmingham and Midland Institute) with some advice:

> If there ever was a time when any one class could of itself do much for its own good, and for the welfare of society – which I greatly doubt – that time is unquestionably past. It is in the fusion of different classes, without confusion; in the bringing together of employers and employed; in the creating of a better common understanding among those whose interests are identical, who depend upon each other, and who can never be in unnatural antagonism without deplorable results, that one of the chief principles of a Mechanics' Institution should consist. In this world a great deal of the bitterness among us arises from an imperfect understanding of one another. (*Speeches* 167)

Over a month later, Dickens expressed similar views, specifically aimed at both sides of the industrial conflict in Preston:

> I believe ... that into the relations between employers and employed, as into all the relations of this life, there must enter something of feeling and sentiment ... otherwise those relations are wrong and rotten at the core. (*HW* 8.553)

He believed that the strike and lock-out was 'a deplorable calamity ... in the gulf of separation it hourly deepens between those whose interests must be understood to be identical or must be destroyed, it is a great national affliction' ('On Strike', 8.553–9). Dickens was soon reminded of these words when, on 13 March 1854, his close friend Mr Justice Talfourd died suddenly on the Bench at Stafford Assizes. Talfourd had been addressing the court on the causes of an increase in crime throughout the district: 'I cannot help thinking that it may, in no small degree, be attributed to that separation between class and class which is the great curse of British society ... that reciprocation of kind words and gentle affections' (*Law Magazine*, 1854, NS 20). Dickens's tribute to Talfourd in *HW* acknowledged his last utterances 'of Christian eloquence, of brotherly tenderness and kindness towards all men, yet unfinished on his lips' (9.117–18). The dying words of a destitute potter in a *HW* story of 24 June 1854 also echo Stephen's plea: 'bid the rich folk consider the labourer ... an' England will be right' ('The Ruined Potter', 9.444).

Numerous *HW* articles over a wide range of subjects mirrored Dickens's criticism of a divided nation. See: 'Some Account of an Extraordinary Traveller', 1.73–7; 'Supposing!', 1.96; 'Cheerful Arithmetic', 1.531–4; 'Lively Turtle', 2.97–9; 'Views of the Country', 2.169–72; 'Human Brotherhood', 2.229; 'The Grave of Faction', 3.60–1; 'The Claims of Labour', 3.356; 'Gunpowder', 4.457–65; 'Chip: Corporation Dreams', 7.512–13; 'Locked Out', 8.345–8; 'Nobody's Story', 8 [Christmas 1853] 34–6; 'The Quiet Poor', 9.201–6; 'Ground in the Mill' 9.224–7; 'Death's Doors', 9.398–402. See also a later article by Henry Morley, 'The Manchester Strike' (13.63–6), which cites an enlightened Preston manufacturer's pamphlet written at the time of the Preston strike.

They carried him very gently along

Rachael always holding the hand in hers. Very few whispers broke the mournful

silence. It was soon a funeral procession.] Elements of Stephen's rescue bear a passing similarity to those found in an earlier *HW* story about scythe-stone cutters and the hazards of mining. The tale, 'Sharpening the Scythe', which appeared in the same number as the first instalment of *HT* (1 April 1854), relates the fate of a certain scythe-stone cutter, John Drewit, who, along with his eldest son, became trapped when an unpropped passage leading into a cliff collapsed. The alarm is raised and

> in an incredibly short space of time the labourers from field and cave came hurrying up to the rescue. Two only could dig together, two more propped the way behind them foot by foot; relays eagerly waited at the entrance; and not an instant was lost in replacing the exhausted workmen. Everything was done as quickly, and, at the same time, as judiciously as possible; the surgeon had at the first been ridden for, at full speed, to the neighbouring town; brandy and other stimulants, a rude lancet . . . bandages and blankets were all placed ready at hand. . . . Those who were not actively engaged about the cave, were busy in the construction of a litter – perhaps a bier – for the unhappy victims. (9.151–2)

When the son is 'delivered, pale and corpse-like, but alive . . . a shout as of an army was set up by all the men'. It is well after sunset before John's body is 'placed upon the litter, and taken, under the soft evening sky, down through the beech wood home. Alice [his wife] walked by its side, holding its hand in hers, speechless, and with dry eyes' (152).

Book 3, Chapter 7 — Twentieth weekly part
Saturday, 12 August 1854

WHELP-HUNTING

In the morning, he went down

swelling like an immense soap-bubble, without its beauty.] Michael Faraday (1791–1867), the distinguished physicist and chemist, used soap-bubbles to determine the magnetic property of gases. Writing to the geologist and Dean of Westminster, the Rev. William Buckland, Faraday described a soap-bubble as 'a beautiful and wonderful thing' (12 January 1848). Dickens first wrote to Faraday on 28 May 1850 to ask if he could borrow the notes for six lectures Faraday had given at the Royal Institution of Electrical Engineers. Two *HW* articles by Percival Leigh, 'The Chemistry of a Candle' (1.439–44) and 'The Mysteries of a Tea-Kettle' (2.176–81), were based on Faraday's notes (Williams, 1971, 513; *Letters* 6.105–6, 108, 110, 230).

A *HW* article of 24 August 1850 entitled 'A Shilling's Worth of Science', which reported on the exhibition of models and objects at the Royal Polytechnic Institution in London, might also have informed Dickens's comment. As an introduction, the article related the observations of Sir Isaac Newton's neighbour, who watched Newton sit for hours on a stool blowing soap-bubbles. The neighbour was informed that, far from being a lunatic, Newton was 'studying the refraction of light upon thin plates, a phenomenon which is beautifully exhibited upon the surface of a common soap-bubble' (1.507–8).

But, in the morning he appeared at breakfast

Aged and bent he looked, and quite bowed down; and yet he looked a wiser man, and a better man, than in the days when in this life he wanted nothing but Facts.] Compare the final lines of Coleridge's *The Rime of the Ancient Mariner* (1798):

> He went like one that hath been stunned,
> And is of sense forlorn:
> A sadder and a wiser man,
> He rose the morrow morn.

It was the more hopeful as the town

Mr Bounderby ... might play a Roman part] That is, like Lucius Junius Brutus, he would have no qualms about sacrificing family in the name of state justice (see note to book 2, chapter 4, p. 183).

The two travelled all night, except when

down wells] Stairwells – shafts containing flights of stairs to enable passengers to cross underneath a railway track.

a fly] A one-horse covered carriage for hire.

smuggled into the town by all the back lanes where the pigs lived: which, although not a magnificent or even savoury approach, was, as is usual in such cases, the legitimate highway.] To enter a town by this route was by no means uncommon. The omnibus which brings Helena, Neville and Mr Honeythunder to Cloisterham has come the way of all traffic which 'deserting the high road, came sneaking in from an unprecedented part of the country by a back stable-way' (*MED* 6).

A Grand Morning Performance by the Riders

Grand Morning Performance]   In the now obsolete sense of the word, 'morning' meant that part of the day which extended to the fashionable dinner-time. A morning show in theatrical or musical terms meant an afternoon performance. Matinée, from the French *matin*, now always means an afternoon production.

The Emperor of Japan, on a steady

The Emperor of Japan]   At the time when Dickens was writing *HT*, the majority of the British public had never seen a Japanese person and, until 1858, neither the national press nor the House of Commons was remotely interested in Anglo-Japanese affairs, minimal as they were. Japan's cultural mystique and self-imposed seclusion were therefore perfect ingredients for exotic and imaginative equestrian acts (Fox, 1969, 534–6). An act called 'The Emperor of Japan' had been performed by John or Anthony Bridges during the week of 24 January 1853, and a 'Popular Scene' in the 1850s was the 'Juggler of Japan', performed frequently by Anthony Bridges (Astley's playbills for 8 December 1851 and 11 October 1852, Theatre Museum, London; Schlicke, 1985, 161).

on a steady old white horse stencilled with black spots]   In October 1856, when Dickens was preparing for a private amateur production of Wilkie Collins's play, *The Frozen Deep*, he consulted Astley's manager, William Cooke, for advice concerning the seating and staging arrangements. Dickens described Cooke's arrival at Tavistock House as 'one of the finest things' he had ever seen in his life. Cooke appeared 'in an open phaeton drawn by two white ponies with black spots all over them (evidently stencilled), who came in at the gate with a little jolt and a rattle, exactly as they come into the Ring when they draw anything' (Forster 3.6.141; see the Astley's programme for 28 February 1854 [Plate 18] which features many members of the Cooke family). Dickens's extensive familiarity with circus techniques was noted in 1868 by Mrs Annie Fields during his reading tour in America: 'Last night we went to the circus together. . . . I was astonished at the knowledge C.D. showed of everything before him. He knew how the horses were stenciled, how tight the wire bridles were, etc.' (Howe, 1922, 178).

Mr Sleary had only made one cut

Mr Sleary had only made one cut at the Clown with his long whip-lash]   This was a usual comic routine between the riding master and the clown, one which Dickens described in 'Astley's' (*SB*).

an ingenious Allegory relating to a butcher, a three-legged stool, a dog, and a leg of mutton]   The clown's conundrum belongs to a group of 'leg riddles' similar to the one posed by the Sphinx to Oedipus: 'What is the being that has one name, but first

ASTLEY'S ROYAL AMPHITHEATRE.

Lessee and Manager . . Mr. WILLIAM COOKE

PROGRAMME

OF THE

ROYAL EQUESTRIAN ENTERTAINMENT.

By Command

ON TUESDAY, FEBRUARY 28, 1854.

COMMENCING WITH

Miss AVERY, & Mr. W. BARLOW,

IN A CLASSICAL SCENE ON TWO HORSES, AS
"FLORA AND ZEPHYR."

Miss KATE COOKE,

AND HER MILK WHITE CHARGER,
"SNOWDROP,"
IN THE HIGH SCHOOL OF THE MANÈGE.

Mr. WILLIAM COOKE,

WILL INTRODUCE HIS PET PONIES,
"BLUE BELL" AND "VESTA."

Programme continued.

Miss EMILY COOKE,

THE EQUESTRIAN WONDRESS'

FLIGHT THROUGH SIXTEEN BALOONS!

Mr. JAMES BARLOWS

THE EXTRAORDINARY FEATS
OF THE

PERFORMING ELEPHANTS

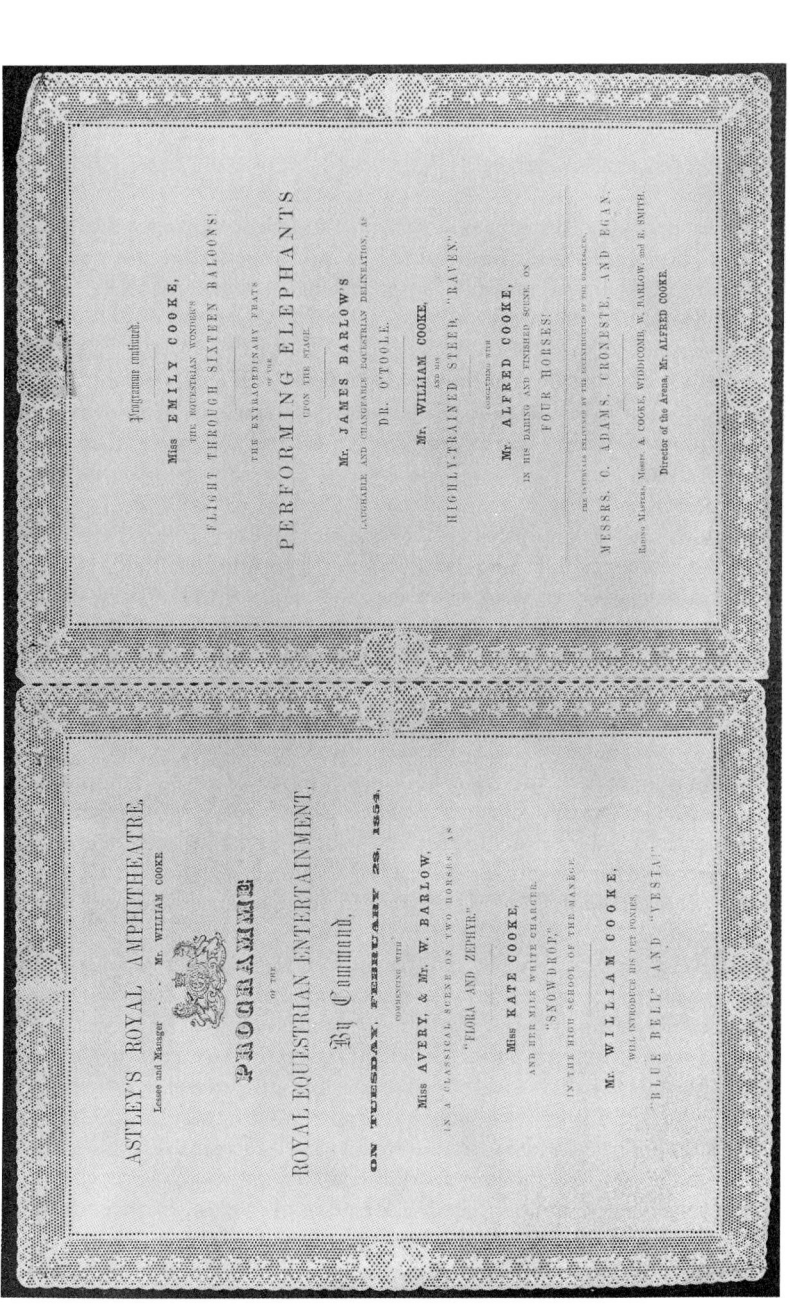

UPON THE STAGE.

LAUGHABLE AND CHAMPAGNE EQUESTRIAN DELINEATION, AS
DR. O'TOOLE.

Mr. WILLIAM COOKE,

AND HIS

HIGHLY-TRAINED STEED, "RAVEN."

CONCLUDING WITH

Mr. ALFRED COOKE,

IN HIS DARING AND FINISHED SCENE, ON

FOUR HORSES.

THE ACTING DRAWN BY THE DIRECTION OF THE COMPLIES.

MESSRS. C. ADAMS, CRONESTE, AND EGAN.

Band Master, Messrs A. COOKE, WIDDCOMB, W. BARLOW and E. SMITH.
Director of the Arena, Mr. ALFRED COOKE.

18 A lace-edged Astley's programme for 28 february 1854 (by courtesy of the Board of Trustees of the Victoria and Albert Museum)

four feet, then two feet, and then three feet?' Oedipus replies 'Man' (he crawls on all fours, then walks with two legs, then needs an extra 'leg'– a stick – as he gets old) (Róheim, 1934, 21).

She took Louisa with her; and they

brandy]   This was probably 'British brandy', a favourite working-class drink made from malt spirit and other secret additives. It was claimed that the spirit was distilled from substandard ingredients such as 'spoilt wine and damaged grain' (Beeton 668; Freeman, 1989, 97).

The Little Wonder Of Thcolathtic Equitation]   Dickens's title for the infant Childers is similar to the name Philip Astley gave to his performing horse in 1768 – the 'Little Military Learned Horse'. Astley's rival, Charles Hughes, had a 'Horse of Knowledge' (Disher, 1937, 24–6, 30–1).

Athley'th]   Astley's Royal Amphitheatre was the most famous English circus theatre of the nineteenth century. It was first established in a field called Halfpenny Hatch near Westminster Bridge by a former sergeant-major, Philip Astley, in 1768, and the following year it moved to a corner site at Westminster Bridge Road. A drawing of Astley's Riding School by William Capon in 1777 shows an open-air arena, 60 feet in diameter, with one jump, a semi-circle of stands and stables, and the rest enclosed by a deal board fence. There is no stage, but one was set up at the front of the main stand for non-equestrian acts. Astley added a permanent stage to his ring in 1783. The arena was partially roofed in 1779 and renamed Astley's Amphitheatre Riding House. From 1783 until it burnt down in August 1794, it was known as the Royal Grove Theatre (it was painted inside like a grove of trees). Astley's re-opened in 1795 as the Amphitheatre of Arts, but after 1798 retained the name Astley's Royal Amphitheatre until it closed in 1893. The Amphitheatre burnt down three times – in 1794, 1803 and 1841.

Astley chose 'Amphitheatre' (occasionally nicknamed by visitors 'Ample-theatre'), not because he associated it with the large Roman arenas which served up rather more gory animal entertainments but probably because he made a connection between his ring and the boxing amphitheatres which thrived in the eighteenth century.

Astley's importance lay in how he developed the forms of amusement he knew so well, and how he turned disparate, unconnected entertainments into an art form which straddled the theatrical and equestrian worlds. He had a strong sense of theatricality early fostered in an age of fairs where tumblers, strongmen, clowns, equilibrists and the star attraction, rope dancers, jostled for audiences along with performing animals, puppeteers and actors.

Astley's influential managership lasted forty-five years (1769–1814), to be matched only by Andrew Ducrow's gifted direction and spectacular shows from 1825 until 1841. *HT* was written during William Cooke's proprietorship at Astley's, a reign which lasted from 1853 until 1861. A play which depicts some characters based on *HT*, *Under the Earth; or, The Sons of Toil*, by W. H. C. Nation, was performed at

Astley's on 22 April 1867 (Speaight, 1980, passim; Disher, 1937, 25; Saxon, 1978, 21, 27; Manning, 1984, 23).

you'll hear of him at Parith.]   The circus would have been either the Cirque d'Été, Champs Élysée, or the Cirque d'Hiver, boulevard des Filles du Calvaire, both managed at the time by Louis Dejean and Adolphe Franconi. Both the Franconi family and Dejean greatly influenced the development of the French circus during the nineteenth century. Astley's circus in Paris, Amphithéâtre Astley, established in 1783, had to be abandoned by 1791 because of the war between England and France. After serving as a barracks for a time, the building was taken over by Antonio Franconi under the new name Amphithéâtre Franconi. From 1817 to 1826 it was known as Cirque Olympique (Speaight, 1980, 196, 156; Disher, 1937, 165).

Children in the Wood]   Sleary's description of the horseback version of this well-known English ballad is an exact account of the traditional story. The poem was frequently and variously adapted for pantomime throughout the nineteenth century (Disher, 1925, passim). Wallett, the Shakespearian clown, called it 'the great and irresistible attraction – the Babes in the Wood, the cruel uncle, and the blessed birds, their undertakers' (49). Dickens intended to write a version of the pantomime for his son Charley's eighteenth birthday. He instead adapted J. R. Planche's *Fortunio* (*Letters* 7.454).

a Overtheer]   An overseer or supervisor. From the late sixteenth century until 1834, the unpopular and unpaid office of parish overseer entailed the annual assessment, collection and distribution of funds for the destitute of each parish. On the recommendations of the 1832–3 Royal Commission on the Poor Laws, overseers were replaced by government- paid supervisors (Paroissien, 1992, 38).

'That'h Jack the Giant Killer

'That'h Jack the Giant Killer. . . . There'th a property-houthe . . . there'th my Clown with a thauthepan-lid and a thpit, for Jack'th thervant . . . and the Giant (a very ecthpenthive bathket one)]   Wallett recalled a performance of this popular equestrianized fairy-tale as an after-piece at the Brooklyn Circus in New York, in which he played the comic role:

> We had a splendidly modelled castle, single-headed and double-headed giants, male giants and female giantesses that swallowed live children. . . . After dressing for my part I was furnished with a huge wooden sword. I had no rehearsal, and was therefore ignorant of the action of the drama. On the entrance of a ponderous giant with his massive club I stood upon my defence, and fought him like a man and a hero. With the first blow I scalped him; my sword then went through his eye, and out at the back of his head. The next severed the head from his shoulders, and sent his trunk rolling in the sawdust. I then belaboured his body with my sword till the basket work flew in a thou-

sand pieces, and then in great terror appeared "Snug the joiner," a canvas man called Long Jem, who crept from the interior of the giant to the extreme delight of the audience, and made rapid tracks towards the dressing room. The other giants shared the same fate one by one, without the slightest assistance from my friend Jack the Giant Killer. (1870, 102–3)

Props of houses – Sleary's 'property-houthe' – animals, birds, monsters and humans were constructed of wood, straw, pasteboard, papier-mâché, canvas or wickerwork. Many of the human props were used either when the circus company ran out of live actors (see Wallett, 1870, 49), or as substitutes for perilous roles – 'wooden children to be tossed over battlements, straw heroes and heroines to be hurled down a precipice' (Disher, 1937, 60). For the dangerous mountain ascents – raised platforms – in the equestrian adaptation of Byron's *Mazeppa*, a dummy was strapped to the horse until the occasion when the American equestrienne Adah Isaac Menken momentously performed the entire ride herself at Astley's in 1864. Many proprietors went to great lengths to achieve the verisimilitude they thought necessary for their productions. According to Disher, the Drury Lane Theatre 'brought realism and mechanism to the limit of costliness. Giants for "Jack the Giant Killer" were recruited from the Basque country among the farmers who spent their lives on stilts' (61). Other human 'giants' did not need such aids: the strongman Belzoni, 6 feet 7 inches tall and known as the 'Patagonian Sampson', played the giant in an 1803 production. For a short account of Belzoni's life and work, see 'The Story of Giovanni Belzoni', *HW* 2.548–52 (Disher, 1925, 97; Disher, 1937, 233–6).

They all three went in

the Clown's performing chair] The circus historians Arthur Saxon and George Speaight offer two possible explanations. Saxon suggests that the chair 'was manipulated by an invisible wire and was pulled out from under the Clown or someone else when he went to sit on it'. Speaight adds another possibility: a collapsing chair.

> When I performed a clowning act I used to start off by settling comfortably into a chair, which collapsed beneath me. . . . I used one of those wicker chairs that were designed to fold up; the seat hinged down to be supported in the front by a solid bamboo bar; with the arm-rests on hinged sides. I cut away the projections which fitted the seat on to the front bamboo bar, and left the seat resting and just balanced on this front bar. When I sat down with a sigh of contentment, the seat slid off the bar, the seat folded down, and I was left with my legs in the air and my bottom almost on the ground. I was careful to have my arms firmly on the sides, which were enough to keep me from actually hitting the floor.

The laughter in both examples comes from the unexpected humiliation and helplessness of the recipient (letters to the author from A. H. Saxon and George Speaight).

In a preposterous coat, like a beadle's

so grimly, detestably, ridiculously shameful . . . the whelp in his comic livery] In 'The Pantomime of Life' (1837), Dickens compared pantomime characters with 'those of every-day life'. The description of the pantaloon's pantomime role is similar to Tom's dual fraudulence as real-life thief and disguised performer:

> he is a treacherous, worldly-minded old villain, constantly enticing his younger companion, the clown, into acts of fraud or petty larceny, and generally standing aside to watch the result of the enterprise. If it be successful, he never forgets to return for his share of the spoil; but if it turn out a failure, he generally retires with remarkable caution and expedition, and keeps carefully aloof until the affair has blown over.

'A Jothkin – a Carter. Make up your mind quick

I've never met with nothing but beer ath'll ever clean a comic blackamoor.'] Burnt cork and beer were the usual 'blacking-up' ingredients for 'negro minstrels' in the nineteenth century, and in America burnt cork was still being used by clowns in the late 1960s. According to the statement of one Ethiopian serenader in 1851, bootblacking had been used in the past for face make-up, and 'burnt cork and beer wasn't so popular then' (Mayhew 3.192; Disher, 1925, 193).

Book 3, Chapter 8 Twentieth weekly part
Saturday, 12 August 1854

PHILOSOPHICAL

'The circulation, Sir,' returned Bitzer

facts established by Harvey relating to the circulation of the blood] William Harvey (1578–1657) discovered the circulation of the blood and the function of the heart. His book, *On the Motion of the Heart and Blood in Animals*, was published in 1628.

It was a fundamental principle of the Gradgrind

It was a fundamental principle of the Gradgrind philosophy, that everything was to be paid for.] The Rev. Richard Dawes, Dean of Hereford and original proponent of the movement for the teaching of common things in schools, gave a paper to the Society of Arts on 27 April 1853 on the subject of schools for the industrial classes with particular emphasis on the great need for schools to be self-supporting:

> One good school on self-supporting principles, or on principles which will eventually lead to this, is worth any number of gratuitous ones in a public point of view. We cannot educate a nation by charity; and we ought not to teach the people that it is possible. (38)

Later in his address he reiterated his view that a free education system would not work:

> In a social point of view, it would not have that elevating tendency in rearing up an industrious race depending in after-life upon themselves; which would arise out of a system, where all classes were obliged to pay in proportion to their means; and when school expenses were made a part of the family expenditure. (45)

A letter which Dawes had received from an Inspector of Schools agreed with the proposal to raise rather than lower the payments made by parents: 'To say that a parent has a right to expect the free education of his child from the state, I believe to be neither more nor less than communism, little better than the doctrine that he has a right to food at the hands of the state' (26).

Dickens himself approved of fee-paying schools. In a letter of 1852 he praised a number of manufacturers who had established 'decent houses, paying schools, savings banks, little libraries, &c.' (*Letters* 6.645).

'I'm bletht if I know what to call it,'

whether that dog hadn't gone to another dog, and thed] The intelligence and language of animals were popularly discussed topics. Animal communication was addressed in a *HW* article of 1852, by R. H. Horne, 'More Dumb Friends'. In relation to dogs, he observed that:

> We once saw a large stranger dog trotting through a village, who was assailed by the yelpings of a number of curs, of whom he took no notice, but ran on with perfect good temper, even though some of them almost flew at his hind legs. At length, happening to stop and look around him, one cur, of a most insolent physiognomy, quickly tripped up to him, and appeared to whisper something (though we could hear no sound of it) in his ear. In an instant the large stranger pounced upon him – flung him sprawling on his back – gave him a tremendous shaking – rolled his howling body over and over in the dust – and then drove him yelping away as fast as his legs could carry him. What word or sound of the canine language was uttered is forbidden knowledge to us, but the insult conveyed was obviously of the most gross and intelligible kind to the individual most concerned. (5.124)

Horne concluded that all creatures of the earth 'have "a mother-tongue" of their own, which answers all their purposes' (127). Timbs noted that 'We know that some animals – the dog especially – understand many words that we employ . . . but if we do not understand what one dog says to another, whose fault is it – ours or the dog's?' (1872, 2). He also relates two anecdotes on the subject: 'Leibnitz bears witness to a hound, in Saxony, that could speak distinctly thirty words'; and 'Pliny [in his *Natural History*] tells that a dog spoke when Tarquin was driven from the throne' (1866, 20; 1872, 4).

Book 3, Chapter 9   Twentieth weekly part
Saturday, 12 August 1854

FINAL

Into how much of futurity?

this same precious will was to begin its long career of quibble, plunder, false pretences, vile example, little service and much law?]   A reference to the dilatory nature of the Chancery Court, a scandal which formed the thematic nucleus of *BH*. The expense and delays of Chancery suits were decreased by a series of significant Chancery reforms from 1850 to 1854 which amended and regulated the procedure of the court (see Shatto, 1988, 28–30).

Here was Mr Gradgrind on the same day

Faith, Hope, and Charity]   From 1 Corinthians 13.1–13: 'And now abideth faith, hope, charity, these three; but the greatest of these is charity' (13).

an abstraction called a People]   In a speech during his final visit to Birmingham in January 1870, Dickens remarked: 'I have very little faith in the people who govern us – please to observe "people" there will be with a small "p" . . . but that I have great confidence in the People whom they govern: please to observe "People" there with a large "P".' Dickens then quoted from Buckle's *History of Civilization in England* (2 vols, 1857 and 1861): 'lawgivers are nearly always the obstructors of society, instead of its helpers . . . they always should be, the mere servants of the people, to whose wishes they are bound to give a public and legal sanction' (*Speeches* 411).

But, happy Sissy's happy children loving her

the Writing on the Wall]   An allusion to the portent of disaster written by the hand of God on the plaster of King Belshazzar's wall (Daniel 5.5–31).

APPENDIX A

Glossary of Lancashire Dialect Words Used in *Hard Times*

Dickens's major source for dialect forms in the novel was the extensive glossary of Lancashire words and phrases in *A View of the Lancashire Dialect* (1746) by 'Tim Bobbin' (the pseudonym of John Collier). Dickens owned a copy of the 1818 edition (Stonehouse 111). Words not listed by Bobbin are indicated by an asterisk. Variations from Bobbin are given in parentheses.

ahind or *ahint* (*behint, behunt, behund*)	behind
aw	all
awlung	because
awlus	always
awmust*	almost
brigg	bridge
chilt	child
dree	tedious, long
dunnot (*dunnaw*)	do not
een	eyes
eern (*years*)	ears
eigh	yes
enow (*onough*)	enough
ett'n	eaten
fair faw 'em a'	wish them all well
faw'en (*fawn* or *foan*)	fallen
fawt	fault
fewtrils	little things, small items of furniture
fratch	quarrel
fro or *fra*	from
Gonnows*	God knows
gowd	gold
ha'	have
haply	perhaps
har-stone or *harston*	hearthstone, fireplace
hed	heeded, minded
heern (*hear'n*)	heard
hetter	eager, keen

hey-go-mad	excited, enthusiastic
hottering mad	very mad, or ill-vexed
howd	hold
Hummobee	the humming bee or bumble-bee
leefer or *liefer*	rather
leetsome	cheerful, glad
licker	more likely
lickly	very likely
monny	many
moydert	puzzled or confused
mun	must
nobbut*	only
nowt	nothing
onny	any
owd	old
parisht	starving, or extremely cold
reek	vapour, steam, or smoke
riven	torn apart, split
seet'n	sat
sen	say
seln	self
sin	since
sitch	such
Strike o' day (skrike o' dey)	daybreak
thowt	thought
towd	told
year	hear or ear

APPENDIX B

Glossary of Slang Terms Used in *Hard Times*

Works of reference used to annotate slang terms and phrases:
  John Camden Hotten, *A Dictionary of Modern Slang, Cant, and Vulgar Language . . . by a London Antiquary* (1859), 1887 edition reprinted as *The Slang Dictionary* (Wakefield: EP Publishing, 1972)
  Eric Partridge, *A Dictionary of Slang and Unconventional English* (1937), 1961 edition abridged as *The Penguin Dictionary of Historical Slang* (Harmondsworth: Penguin, 1972)
  Brewer's Dictionary of Phrase and Fable
  The Oxford English Dictionary

Book 1, Chapter 4

sop — a piece of bread soaked in liquid, usually milk (*milksop*). The word also applies to a soft or foolish person.

strollers — vagabonds, itinerant beggars, pedlars, wandering actors and players

Book 1, Chapter 5

larruped — flogged, beaten or thrashed

Book 1, Chapter 6

stow that — leave off, or stop it

cheeking — addressing a person saucily. To irritate by impudence.

ochre — money, specifically applied to gold coin

missed his tip — failed to jump over the garters and banners

garters — narrow bands

banners — bordered cloths held horizontally during an equestrian performance

loose in his ponging	a bad performance
bespeak	a benefit performance, also termed a 'ben'
Tight-Jeff	tight-rope
goosed	hissed at by the audience
cackler	an actor or performer who has a speaking part
give it mouth	a graceless request for an actor to speak up
cut away	to run away, or move off quickly
Lord Harry!	or 'Old Harry', the Devil
morrithed	'morrised' or 'morriced' – run away, or decamped. The word is connected with the Morris dance.
I'll pound it	'I'll bet a pound on it', or 'I'll guarantee it'
pursy	short-winded

Book 1, Chapter 7

Mr Bounderby's car	a 'bounder' in the 1850s was a four-wheeled cab or trap
blind-hookey	a card game in which bets are placed 'blind', that is, before the players have seen their cards. The term is therefore slang for 'a great risk'. The game was also called 'Wilful Murder'. An alternative meaning is 'non-aristocratic'.
Scadgers	'Scadger' or 'cadger' is common slang for an artful beggar
clap-trap	cheap, showy sentiment; nonsense, rubbish. An old theatrical term meaning a trick, device, or language designed to catch applause – 'to trap a clap'. Also, a mechanical contrivance which made a clapping noise in theatres and street shows.

shake-down	an improvised bed; an eighteenth-century phrase originally meaning a temporary bed made over straw on the floor
little puss	a term of affection sometimes used with a sexual connotation; a hare
cramming	acquiring knowledge quickly, or preparing for an examination
maw	the mouth
crack	first-class, excellent or fashionable

Book 1, Chapter 11

played old Gooseberry	played the devil; upset or spoilt; defeated without delay

Book 2, Chapter 3

as flat as a warming-pan	inexperienced, dull or silly

Book 2, Chapter 4

sent to Coventry	excluded from any social intercourse; alienated from a social circle or community

Book 2, Chapter 8

mealy	mealy-mouthed; soft-spoken, plausible, deceitful

Book 2, Chapter 10

under the rose	secretly

Book 3, Chapter 2

the swell mob	better-dressed thieves and pickpockets

Book 3, Chapter 7

jothkin   a joskin; a country bumpkin. Also thieves' cant for a clown or yokel.

Book 3, Chapter 8

the drag   a cart or a private vehicle like a stage coach, usually drawn by four horses

Luth   'Lush': slang for alcoholic drinks, usually applied to beer

APPENDIX C

Table of Factory Accidents, 1852–4

All factory accidents for the two years from 1 May 1852 to 30 April 1853 and 1 May 1853 to 30 April 1854*

	By machinery 1852/3	By machinery 1853/4	Not by machinery 1852/3	Not by machinery 1853/4	Total 1852/3	Total 1853/4
Deaths	42	42	8	19	50	61
Amputations	554	595	3	2	557	597
Fractures	439	525	34	46	473	571
Injuries to head and face	177	225	45	27	222	252
Other injuries	2811	2657	177	119	2988	2776
	4023	4044	267	213	4290	4257

*Based on the *Returns of the Numbers Reported by the Inspectors in the Factory Districts to have been Killed or Injured in those Districts during the Years from 30 April 1845 to 30 May 1854* (BPP 1854, 65.497–504).

APPENDIX D

Table of the *Household Words* Articles Relevant to Topics in *Hard Times*

Household Words, Volume 9, 18 February – 12 August 1854

Date	Article	Its relevance to Hard Times
18 February	'A Dish of Fish'	galvanic battery
25 February	'Jack and the Union Jack'	national and naval banner
	'For the Benefit of the Cooks'	the fair teaching of 'Common Things'
4 March	'The Secrets of the Gas'	gaslight
11 March	'The Bottle of Hay'	public houses teetotallers
18 March	'Shadows of Dark Days'	fairy- and ghost-stories
	'Preventible Accidents'	railway and mining accidents
25 March	'The Late Mr. Justice Talfourd'	mutual understanding between classes
	'Plant Architecture'	fairy palace
	'Deaf Mutes'	need for a national system of education

(HT starts serialization in HW from 1 April to 12 August 1854)

Date	Article	Its relevance to Hard Times
1 April	'Oranges and Lemons'	oranges for the theatres
	'Sharpening the Scythe'	an industrial accident and rescue
	'Rights and Wrongs of Women'	marriage laws
8 April	'Goblin Life'	folk-lore and superstitions

	'A Call upon Sophy'	ballooning
	'Behind the Louvre'	street-performer and his dog strongman act
15 April	'The Quiet Poor'	circuses and the need for amusement housing and sanitary conditions
	'Legs'	character and legs legs and circus performers modesty and legs
22 April	'Wire-Drawing'	nature imagery in cotton manufacture telegraph wires coal-pit explosions
	'Ground in the Mill'	factory accidents
29 April	'Busy with the Photograph'	the 'man in the moon'
	'Paris with a Mask On'	popular entertainment
	'A Canny Book'	humorous books
	'One of Our Legal Fictions'	marriage laws
6 May	'A Manchester Warehouse'	the cotton trade
13 May	'Tattyboys Rents'	performing dog and absent owner and performer
20 May	'The Cankered Rose of Tivoli'	unhappy marriage lack of understanding between father and daughter
27 May	'Brother Mieth and his Brothers'	education of the head and the heart cultivation imagery
3 June	'Under Canvas'	giant stone statues of idols

		the Nineveh bull
Austen Henry Layard
	'Strollers at Dumbledowndeary'	travelling actors
circus and theatrical entertainment
10 June	'The Sailor'	disparity in age between husband and wife
	'Chip: A Lesson in Multiplication'	rise in population
	'Death's Doors'	housing conditions
need for wholesome amusement
17 June	'Man as a Monster'	ghost-stories
dwarfs, giants and heroes
24 June	'Done to a Jelly'	Professor Richard Owen
	'Exiled'	exile
starlight
	'The Ruined Potter'	need for understanding between rich and poor
starlight
	'The War with Fever'	disease
sanitary reform
1 July 1854	'Smoke or No Smoke'	smoke pollution
	'Our Sister'	the cotton trade
prosperous merchants
fairy palaces
8 July 1854	'A Good Brushing'	brushes and brooms
15 July 1854	'The Roving Englishman: Village Diplomatists'	images of withered and lifeless crops
22 July 1854	'Shining Stars'	starlight
29 July 1854	'The Musical World'	the Italian Opera

APPENDIX E
Ballads of the Preston Strike, 1853–4

The Preston steam-loom weaver (1853)

(From: *Poverty Knock*. Palmer, ed. 1974: 22–3)

In the morning just at six o'clock the engine does begin;
You must set off a-running, for a prize you have to win,
For should it happen that you be ten minutes there too late,
You must give in your number and twopence they will bate.

And while the engine's running, oh, I'm sure it's very hard:
There's threepence more if you should chance to go out in the yard.
If anything about your looms should chance to break that day,
There's no excuse, they'll tell you plain, you will get off for pay.

Four shillings for a temple box and eight pence for a stud,
Six or eightpence for a fork, they'll suck your very blood;
Two shillings for a driving wheel, two pence for one day's waste,
Three pence for a gold bobbin if it does not run its race.

Should sickness overtake you and you stay away one day,
Two shillings they will fine you, or else they'll stop your pay;
And should you never mend again, it's true what I have said,
You must go and serve your notice out, boys, after you are dead.

The engineers of England are doing all they can
And standing up in every town to help their fellowman.
Then Preston weavers do the same and stand firm every one,
And other towns will back you up, assist you all they can.

Now to conclude and make an end, let's all unite, and quick,
And never cease to labour till we drive *him* to old Nick;
For these have always been his plans, both town and country knows;
The devil his rights will never have till he's got him in his claws.

bate: deduct

temple: instrument for stretching cloth on loom

stud: support

him: the employer

The Cotton Lords of Preston (1853–4)

(From: A *Touch on the Times*. Palmer, ed. 1974: 313–15)

Have you not heard the news of late
About some mighty men so great?
I mean the swells of Fishergate,
The Cotton Lords of Preston.
They are a set of stingy blades,
They've locked up all their mills and shades,
So now we've nothing else to do
But come a-singing songs to you.
So with our ballads we've come out
To tramp the country round about,
And try if we cannot live without
The Cotton Lords of Preston.

Chorus

Everybody's crying shame
On these gentlemen by name,
Don't you think they're much to blame,
The Cotton Lords of Preston?

The working people such as we
Pass their time in misery,
While they live in luxury,
The Cotton Lords of Preston.
They're making money every way
And building factories every day,
Yet when we ask them for more pay,
They had the impudence to say:
'To your demands we'll not consent;
You get enough, so be content' –
But we will have the ten per cent
From the Cotton Lords of Preston.

Our masters say they're very sure
That a strike we can't endure;
They all assert we're very poor,
The Cotton Lords of Preston.
But we've determined every one
With them we will not be done,
And we will not be content

Until we get the ten per cent.
The Cotton Lords are sure to fall,
Both ugly, handsome, short and tall;
For we intend to conquer all
The Cotton Lords of Preston.

So men and women, all of you,
Come and buy a song or two,
And assist us to subdue
The Cotton Lords of Preston.
We'll conquer them and no mistake,
Whatever laws they seem to make,
And when we get the ten per cent
Then we'll live happy and content.
Oh then we'll dance and sing with glee
And thank you all right heartily,
When we gain the victory
And beat the Lords of Preston.

SELECT BIBLIOGRAPHY

The manuscript, corrected proofs and work plans of *Hard Times* are in the Forster Collection of the Victoria and Albert Museum, London.

With the exception of *Household Words* and *All the Year Round*, articles in contemporary periodicals (*Bentley's Miscellany*, *Eliza Cook's Journal*, *The Illustrated London News*, etc.) are not listed because complete bibliographical information is given in the text.

(i) Works by Dickens

The Clarendon Dickens. Oxford: Clarendon Press, 1966–. Edition cited in quotations from
    David Copperfield. Ed. Nina Burgess. 1981
    Dombey and Son. Ed. Alan Horsman. 1974
    Great Expectations. Ed. Margaret Cardwell. 1993
    Little Dorrit. Ed. Harvey Peter Sucksmith. 1979
    Martin Chuzzlewit. Ed. Margaret Cardwell. 1982
    The Mystery of Edwin Drood. Ed. Margaret Cardwell. 1972
    Oliver Twist. Ed. Kathleen Tillotson. 1966

The Penguin English Library. Harmondsworth: Penguin. Edition cited in quotations from
    Barnaby Rudge. Ed. Gordon Spence. 1973
    Bleak House. Ed. Norman Page. 1971
    The Christmas Books. Ed. Michael Slater. 2 vols, 1971
    Hard Times. Ed. David Craig. 1969
    Nicholas Nickleby. Ed. Michael Slater. 1978
    The Old Curiosity Shop. Ed. Angus Easson. 1972
    Our Mutual Friend. Ed. Stephen Gill. 1971
    The Pickwick Papers. Ed. Robert L. Patten. 1972
    A Tale of Two Cities. Ed. George Woodcock. 1970

The Oxford Illustrated Dickens. 21 vols. London: Oxford UP, 1947–58. Edition cited in quotations from
    American Notes and *Pictures from Italy*
    Master Humphrey's Clock (includes *A Child's History of England*)
    Sketches by Boz (this volume includes *Sketches of Young Gentlemen*, *Sketches of Young Couples*, *The Mudfog Papers* and 'The Pantomime of Life')
    The Uncommercial Traveller and Reprinted Pieces (this volume includes *Sunday under Three Heads*, *To Be Read at Dusk*, *Hunted Down*, *Holiday Romance* and *George Silverman's Explanation*)

Memoirs of Joseph Grimaldi, edited by Dickens. Ed. Richard Findlater. London: MacGibbon & Kee, 1968.

Miscellaneous Papers. Vol. 22 of the Universal Edition of the Works of Charles Dickens. Ed. B. W. Matz. 22 vols. London: Chapman & Hall, 1914.

The Letters of Charles Dickens. Pilgrim Edition. 8 vols to date. Oxford: Clarendon, 1965– . Vols 1 and 2. Ed. Madeline House and Graham Storey. Vol. 3. Ed. Madeline House, Graham Storey and Kathleen Tillotson. Vol. 4. Ed. Kathleen Tillotson. Vol. 5. Ed. Graham Storey and K. J. Fielding. Vol. 6. Ed. Graham Storey, Kathleen Tillotson and Nina Burgis. Vol. 7. Ed. Graham Storey, Kathleen Tillotson and Angus Easson. Vol. 8. Ed. Graham Storey and Kathleen Tillotson.

The Letters of Charles Dickens. Ed. Walter Dexter. Nonesuch Edition. 3 vols. London: Nonesuch Press, 1938.

Letters from Charles Dickens to Angela Burdett-Coutts, 1841–1865. Ed. Edgar Johnson. London: Jonathan Cape, 1953.

The Letters of Charles Dickens. Edited by his Sister-in-law and his Eldest Daughter. Vol. 1. 1833–1856. London: Chapman & Hall, 1880.

Charles Dickens as Editor: Being letters written by him to William Henry Wills his sub-editor. Ed. R. C. Lehmann. London: Smith, Elder, 1912.

The Speeches of Charles Dickens. Ed. K. J. Fielding. 2nd edn. Hemel Hempstead: Harvester, 1988.

(ii) Articles in 'Household Words'

Allingham, William. 'The Sailor.' 9 (10 June 1854): 393.
Buckland, Francis Trevelyan. 'A Dish of Fish.' 9 (18 February 1854): 16–17.
Buckley, Theodore. 'The Babbleton Book Club.' 6 (23 October 1852): 129–33.
Capper, John. 'British Cotton.' 5 (3 April 1852): 51–4.
Capper, John. 'The Great Yorkshire Llama.' 6 (27 November 1852): 250–3.
Capper, John. 'Lancashire Witchcraft.' 8 (4 February 1854): 549–51.
Capper, John. 'The Northern Wizard.' 8 (5 November 1853): 225–8.
Capper, John. 'Oranges and Lemons.' 9 (1 April 1854): 145–50.
Capper, John. 'Our Sister.' 9 (1 July 1854): 471–4.
Capper, John. 'The Wonders of Mincing Lane.' 5 (5 June 1852): 273–6.
'Chips: A Remedy for Colliery Explosions.' 2 (28 December 1850): 323–5.
Cole, Charles Augustus, and W. H. Wills. 'The Adventures of the Public Records.' 1 (20 July 1850): 396–9.
Dickens, Charles. 'The Amusements of the People.' 1 (30 March 1850): 13–15; 1 (13 April 1850): 57–60.
Dickens, Charles. 'Betting-Shops.' 5 (26 June 1852): 333–6.
Dickens, Charles. 'A Child's Dream of a Star.' 1 (6 April 1850): 25–6.
Dickens, Charles. 'A December Vision.' 2 (14 December 1850): 265–7.
Dickens, Charles. 'A Detective Police Party.' 1 (27 July 1850): 409–14; 1 (10 August 1850): 457–60.
Dickens, Charles. 'Fire and Snow.' 8 (21 January 1854): 481–3.
Dickens, Charles. 'A Flight.' 3 (30 August 1851): 529–33.

Dickens, Charles. 'Frauds on the Fairies.' 8 (1 October 1853): 97–100.
Dickens, Charles. 'From the Raven in the Happy Family.' 1 (8 June 1850): 241–2.
Dickens, Charles. 'The Great Baby.' 12 (4 August 1855): 1–4.
Dickens, Charles. 'Home for Homeless Women.' 7 (23 April 1853): 169–75.
Dickens, Charles. 'The Household Narrative.' 1 (13 April 1850): 49.
Dickens, Charles. 'It Is Not Generally Known.' 10 (2 September 1854): 49–52.
Dickens, Charles. 'The Last Words of the Old Year.' 2 (4 January 1851): 337–9.
Dickens, Charles. 'The Late Mr. Justice Talfourd.' 9 (25 March 1854): 117–18.
Dickens, Charles. 'Lively Turtle.' 2 (26 October 1850): 97–9.
Dickens, Charles. 'Lying Awake.' 6 (30 October 1852): 145–8.
Dickens, Charles. 'Mr. Booley's View of the Last Lord Mayor's Show.' 2 (30 November 1850): 217–19.
Dickens, Charles. 'The Murdered Person.' 14 (11 October 1856): 289–91.
Dickens, Charles. 'The Noble Savage.' 7 (11 June 1853): 337–9.
Dickens, Charles. 'Nobody's Story.' 8 (Christmas 1853): 34–6.
Dickens, Charles. 'On Duty with Inspector Field.' 3 (14 June 1851): 265–70.
Dickens, Charles. 'On Strike.' 8 (11 February 1854): 553–9.
Dickens, Charles. 'Our School.' 4 (11 October 1851): 49–52.
Dickens, Charles. 'Our Watering Place.' 3 (2 August 1851): 433–6.
Dickens, Charles. 'Pet Prisoners.' 1 (27 April 1850): 97–103.
Dickens, Charles. 'A Poor Man's Tale of a Patent.' 2 (19 October 1850): 73–5.
Dickens, Charles. 'A Preliminary Word.' 1 (30 March 1850): 1–2.
Dickens, Charles. 'Railway Dreaming.' 13 (10 May 1856): 385–8.
Dickens, Charles. 'Railway Strikes.' 2 (11 January 1851): 361–4.
Dickens, Charles. 'Red Tape.' 2 (15 February 1851): 481–4.
Dickens, Charles. 'A Sleep to Startle Us.' 4 (13 March 1852): 577–80.
Dickens, Charles. 'Some Account of an Extraordinary Traveller.' 1 (20 April 1850): 73–7.
Dickens, Charles. 'The Sunday Screw.' 1 (22 June 1850): 289–92.
Dickens, Charles. 'Supposing!' 1 (20 April 1850): 96; 1 (10 August 1850): 480; 3 (7 June 1851): 264; 3 (6 September 1851): 576; 11 (10 February 1855): 48.
Dickens, Charles. 'Things That Cannot Be Done.' 8 (8 October 1853): 121–3.
Dickens, Charles. 'Three "Detective" Anecdotes.' 1 (14 September 1850): 577–80.
Dickens, Charles. 'To Working Men.' 10 (7 October 1854): 169–70.
Dickens, Charles. 'Trading in Death.' 6 (27 November 1852): 241–5.
Dickens, Charles. 'An Unsettled Neighbourhood.' 10 (11 November 1854): 289–92.
Dickens, Charles. 'Whole Hogs.' 3 (23 August 1851): 505–7.
Dickens, Charles, and Henry Morley. 'Boys to Mend.' 5 (11 September 1852): 597–602.
Dickens, Charles, and Henry Morley. 'H.W.' 7 (16 April 1853): 145–9.
Dickens, Charles, and Henry Morley. 'Mr. Bendigo Buster on Our National Defences against Education.' 2 (28 December 1850): 313–19.
Dickens, Charles, and Henry Morley. 'Our Wicked Mis-statements.' 13 (19 January 1856): 13–19.
Dickens, Charles, Henry Morley, and W. H. Wills. 'In and Out of Jail.' 7 (14 May 1853): 241–5.

Dickens, Charles, and W. H. Wills. 'Chips: Small Beginnings.' 3 (5 April 1851): 41–2.
Dickens, Charles, and W. H. Wills. 'The Metropolitan Protectives.' 3 (26 April 1851): 97–105.
Dickens, Charles, and W. H. Wills. 'The Old Lady in Threadneedle Street.' 1 (6 July 1850): 337–42.
Dickens, Charles, and W. H. Wills. 'Received, a Blank Child.' 7 (19 March 1853): 49–53.
Dickens, Charles, and W. H. Wills. 'Spitalfields.' 3 (5 April 1851): 25–30.
Dixon, Edmund Saul. 'Domestic Pets.' 7 (14 May 1853): 248–53.
Dixon, Edmund Saul. 'Holiday Times.' 7 (4 June 1853): 329–32.
Dixon, Edmund Saul. 'The Mind of Brutes.' 7 (13 August 1853): 564–9.
Dodd, George. 'A Brilliant Display of Fireworks.' 8 (10 September 1853): 45–8.
Dodd, George. 'Busy with the Photograph.' 9 (29 April 1854): 242–5.
Dodd, George. 'Done to a Jelly.' 9 (24 June 1854): 438–40.
Dodd, George. 'A Good Brushing.' 9 (8 July 1854): 492–5.
Dodd, George.'Opium.' 16 (1 August 1857): 104–8; 16 (22 August 1857): 181–5.
Dodd, George. 'Wallotty Trot.' 6 (5 February 1853): 499–503.
Dodd, George. 'Wire-Drawing.' 9 (22 April 1854): 217–21.
Dodd, George, and Henry Morley. 'Accommodation for Quidnuncs.' 8 (24 September 1853): 88–91.
Duthie, William. 'Licensed to Juggle.' 7 (20 August 1853): 593–4.
Duthie, William, and Henry Morley. 'The French Workman.' 8 (29 October 1853): 199–204.
Forster, John. 'The Power-Loom.' 7 (9 July 1853): 440–5.
Hannay, James. 'Lambs to be Fed.' 3 (30 August 1851): 544–9.
Hannay, James. 'The Palace of Flowers.' 3 (26 April 1851): 117–20.
Harper. 'The Claims of Labour.' 3 (5 July 1851): 356.
Harper. 'The Grave of Faction.' 3 (12 April 1851): 60–1.
Harper. 'Human Brotherhood.' 2 (30 November 1850): 229.
Harris. 'Exiled.' 9 (24 June 1854): 440–1.
Hart, Ernest Abraham. 'Plant Architecture.' 9 (25 March 1854): 129–32.
Hogarth, George and W. H. Wills. 'Heathen and Christian Burial.' 1 (6 April 1850): 43–8.
Horne, Richard H. 'Ballooning.' 4 (25 October 1851): 97–105.
Horne, Richard H.'The Cattle-Road to Ruin.' 1 (29 June 1850): 325–30.
Horne, Richard H. 'A Coal Miner's Evidence.' 2 (7 December 1850): 245–50.
Horne, Richard H. 'Dust; or Ugliness Redeemed.' 1 (13 July 1850): 379–84.
Horne, Richard H. 'Father Thames.' 2 (1 February 1851): 445–50.
Horne, Richard H. 'Gunpowder.' 4 (7 February 1852): 457–65.
Horne, Richard H. 'Household Crime.' 4 (13 December 1851): 277–81.
Horne, Richard H. 'Lighthouses and Light-Boats.' 2 (11 January 1851): 373–9.
Horne, Richard H. 'More Dumb Friends.' 5 (24 April 1852): 124–7.
Horne, Richard H. 'The Pen and the Pickaxe.' 3 (24 May 1851): 193–6.
Horne, Richard H. 'The True Story of a Coal Fire.' 1 (13 April 1850): 68–72.
Horne, Richard H. 'A Witch in the Nursery.' 3 (20 September 1851): 601–9.
Hunt, Frederick Knight. 'Greenwich Weather-Wisdom.' 1 (1 June 1850): 222–5.

Hunt, Frederick Knight. 'A Visit to the Registrar-General.' 2 (30 November 1850): 235–40.
Hunt, Frederick Knight. 'What a London Curate Can Do If He Tries.' 2 (16 November 1850): 172–6.
Hunt, Frederick Knight. 'Wings of Wire.' 2 (7 December 1850): 241–5.
Irwin, and Henry Morley. 'Norfolk Island.' 5 (10 April 1852): 73–7.
Jerrold, William Blanchard. 'Behind the Louvre.' 9 (8 April 1854): 185–8.
Jerrold, William Blanchard. 'Food for the Factory.' 2 (30 November 1850): 225–9.
Jerrold, William Blanchard. 'For the Benefit of the Cooks.' 9 (25 February 1854): 42–4.
Jerrold, William Blanchard. 'Paris with a Mask On.' 9 (29 April 1854): 245–8.
Jerrold, William Blanchard. 'Pipe-Clay and Clay Pipes.' 4 (21 February 1852): 526–8.
Jerrold, William Blanchard. 'Protected Cradles.' 2 (26 October 1850): 108–12.
Knight, Charles. 'Three May-Days in London.' 3 (3 May 1851): 121–4.
Leigh, Percival. 'Address from an Undertaker to the Trade.' 1 (22 June 1850): 301–4.
Leigh, Percival. 'The Chemistry of a Candle.' 1 (3 August 1850): 439–44.
Leigh, Percival. 'The Chemistry of a Pint of Beer.' 2 (15 February 1851): 498–502.
Leigh, Percival. 'The Mysteries of a Tea-Kettle.' 2 (16 November 1850): 176–81.
Lewis, John Delaware. 'City Graves.' 2 (14 December 1850): 277.
Lowe, James. 'Locked Out.' 8 (10 December 1853): 345–8.
Lowe, James. 'A Manchester Warehouse.' 9 (6 May 1854): 268–72.
Lynn, Eliza. 'Marriage Gaolers.' 13 (5 July 1856): 583–5.
Lynn, Eliza. 'One of Our Legal Fictions.' 9 (29 April 1854): 257–60.
Lynn, Eliza. 'Rights and Wrongs of Women.' 9 (1 April 1854): 158–61.
Lynn, Eliza. 'Under Canvas.' 9 (3 June 1854): 368–73.
Mackay, Alexander. ' "The Devil's Acre." ' 1 (22 June 1850): 297–301.
Macpherson, Ossian. 'Chips: Excursion Trains.' 3 (5 July 1851): 355–6.
Martineau, Harriet. 'An Account of Some Treatment of Gold and Gems.' 4 (31 January 1852): 449–55.
Martineau, Harriet. 'Birmingham Glass Works.' 5 (27 March 1852): 32–8.
Martineau, Harriet. 'Butter.' 6 (25 December 1852): 344–50.
Martineau, Harriet. 'Deaf Mutes.' 9 (25 March 1854): 134–8.
Martineau, Harriet. 'Flower Shows in a Birmingham Hot-House.' 4 (18 October 1851): 82–5.
Martineau, Harriet. 'Guns and Pistols.' 4 (13 March 1852): 580–5.
Martineau, Harriet. 'The Magic Troughs at Birmingham.' 4 (25 October 1851): 113–17.
Martineau, Harriet. 'Malvern Water.' 4 (11 October 1851): 67–71.
Martineau, Harriet. 'The Miller and His Men.' 4 (24 January 1852): 415–20.
Martineau, Harriet. 'Needles.' 4 (28 February 1852): 540–6.
Martineau, Harriet. 'The New School for Wives.' 5 (10 April 1852): 84–9.
Martineau, Harriet. 'Rainbow Making.' 4 (14 February 1852): 485–90.
Martineau, Harriet. 'Time and the Hour.' 4 (6 March 1852): 555–9.
Martineau, Harriet. 'Tubal-Cain.' 5 (15 May 1852): 192–7.
Martineau, Harriet. 'What There is in a Button.' 5 (17 April 1852): 106–12.
Martineau, Harriet. 'The Wonders of Nails and Screws.' 4 (1 November 1851): 138–42.
Maxwell, H. H. 'An Opium Factory.' 6 (16 October 1852): 118–20.

Mayhew, Horace. 'Chips: Corporation Dreams.' 7 (30 July 1853): 512–13.
Morley, Henry. 'Brother Mieth and his Brothers.' 9 (27 May 1854): 344–9.
Morley, Henry. 'A Call upon Sophy.' 9 (8 April 1854): 174–6.
Morley, Henry. 'The Cankered Rose of Tivoli.' 9 (20 May 1854): 314–17.
Morley, Henry. 'Chips: Deadly Shafts.' 11 (23 June 1855): 494–5.
Morley, Henry. 'Chip: A Lesson in Multiplication.' 9 (10 June 1854): 398.
Morley, Henry. 'Commission and Omission.' 10 (18 November 1854): 319–24.
Morley, Henry. 'Constitutional Trials.' 5 (17 July 1852): 423–6.
Morley, Henry. 'Conversion of a Heathen Court.' 10 (16 December 1854): 409–13.
Morley, Henry. 'Death's Cyphering Book.' 11 (12 May 1855): 337–41.
Morley, Henry. 'Death's Doors.' 9 (10 June 1854): 398–402.
Morley, Henry. 'Fencing with Humanity.' 11 (14 April 1855): 241–4.
Morley, Henry. 'Goblin Life.' 9 (8 April 1854): 174–6.
Morley, Henry. 'The Good Side of Combination.' 4 (11 October 1851): 56–60.
Morley, Henry. 'Ground in the Mill.' 9 (22 April 1854): 224–7.
Morley, Henry. 'A Home Question.' 10 (11 November 1854): 292–6.
Morley, Henry. 'A House Full of Horrors.' 6 (4 December 1852): 265–70.
Morley, Henry. 'Jack and the Union Jack.' 9 (25 February 1854): 32–3.
Morley, Henry. 'The King of the Hearth.' 2 (30 November 1850): 229–33.
Morley, Henry. 'The Labourer's Reading-Room.' 3 (13 September 1851): 581–5.
Morley, Henry. 'Little Red Working-Coat.' 4 (27 December 1851): 324–5.
Morley, Henry. 'Man as a Monster.' 9 (17 June 1854): 409–14.
Morley, Henry. 'Manchester Men at their Books.' 8 (17 December 1853): 377–9.
Morley, Henry. 'The Manchester Strike.' 13 (2 February 1856): 63–6.
Morley, Henry. 'Modern Human Sacrifices.' 8 (11 February 1854): 561–4.
Morley, Henry. 'More Grist to the Mill.' 11 (28 July 1853): 605–6.
Morley, Henry. 'Mr. Bendigo Buster on the Model Cottages.' 3 (5 July 1851): 337–41.
Morley, Henry. 'Need Railway Travellers Be Smashed?' 4 (29 November 1851): 217–21.
Morley, Henry. 'Our Last Parochial War.' 7 (21 May 1853): 265–70.
Morley, Henry. 'Piping Days.' 10 (14 October 1854): 196–9.
Morley, Henry. 'Preventible Accidents.' 9 (18 March 1854): 105–6.
Morley, Henry. 'The Quiet Poor.' 9 (15 April 1854): 201–6.
Morley, Henry. 'School-Keeping.' 8 (21 January 1854): 499–504.
Morley, Henry. 'Science and Sophy.' 8 (28 January 1854): 505–8.
Morley, Henry. 'Shadows of Dark Days.' 9 (18 March 1854): 93–8.
Morley, Henry. 'The Two Guides of the Child.' 1 (7 September 1850): 560–1.
Morley, Henry. 'Two Shillings per Horse-Power.' 12 (8 September 1855): 130–1.
Morley, Henry. 'Views of the Country.' 2 (16 November 1850): 169–72.
Morley, Henry. 'The War with Fever.' 9 (24 June 1854): 447–9.
Morley, Henry. 'The Water-Drops. A Fairy Tale.' 1 (17 August 1850): 482–9.
Morley, Henry. 'What Is Not Clear about the Crystal Palace.' 3 (19 July 1851): 400–2.
Morley, Henry. 'Your Very Good Health.' 8 (28 January 1854): 524–6.
Morley, Henry, and Lynn. 'Free Public Libraries.' 3 (19 April 1851): 80–3.
Morley, Henry, and W. H. Wills. 'Rational Schools.' 6 (25 December 1852): 337–42.
Murray, Grenville. 'The Roving Englishman: Village Diplomatists; The Schoolmaster and his Lesson.' 9 (15 July 1854): 510–13.

Murray, Grenville, and W. H. Wills. 'Cheap Pleasures – A Gossip.' 3 (24 May 1851): 201–3.
Ollier, Edmund. 'Starlight in the Garden.' 8 (1 October 1853): 108–9.
Owen, Richard. 'Justice to the Hyaena.' 6 (1 January 1853): 373–7.
Owen, Richard. 'A Leaf from the Oldest of Books.' 13 (7 June 1856): 500–2.
Owen, Richard. 'Poisonous Serpents.' 6 (6 November 1852): 186–8.
Payn, James. 'Sharpening the Scythe.' 9 (1 April 1854): 150–2.
Peppé. 'The Crocodile Battery.' 2 (1 March 1851): 540–3.
Peppé. 'A Fuqueer's Curse.' 3 (21 June 1851): 310–12.
Procter, Adelaide Anne. 'Shining Stars.' 9 (22 July 1854): 536–7.
Sala, George Augustus. 'The Bottle of Hay.' 9 (11 March 1854): 69–75.
Sala, George Augustus. 'Bullfrog.' 10 (18 November 1854): 333–6.
Sala, George Augustus. 'A Canny Book.' 9 (29 April 1854): 249–53.
Sala, George Augustus. 'Case of Real Distress.' 8 (14 January 1854): 457–60.
Sala, George Augustus. 'City Spectres.' 4 (14 February 1852): 481–5.
Sala, George Augustus. 'Getting Up a Pantomime.' 4 (20 December 1851): 289–96.
Sala, George Augustus. 'Legs.' 9 (15 April 1854): 209–12.
Sala, George Augustus. 'Little Children.' 8 (26 November 1853): 289–93.
Sala, George Augustus. 'The Musical World.' 9 (29 July 1854): 561–7.
Sala, George Augustus. 'Open-Air Entertainments.' 5 (8 May 1852): 165–9.
Sala, George Augustus. 'Phases of "Public" Life.' 5 (22 May 1852): 224–30; 5 (29 May 1852): 250–5.
Sala, George Augustus. 'The Secrets of the Gas.' 9 (4 March 1854): 45–8.
Sala, George Augustus. 'The Sporting World.' 6 (23 October 1852): 133–9.
Sala, George Augustus. 'Strollers at Dumbledowndeary.' 9 (3 June 1854): 374–80.
Sala, George Augustus. 'Sunday Morning.' 6 (9 October 1852): 81–4.
Sala, George Augustus. 'Sunday Out.' 10 (9 September 1854): 73–7.
Sala, George Augustus. 'Sunday Tea-Gardens.' 10 (30 September 1854): 145–8.
Sala, George Augustus. 'Tattyboys Rents.' 9 (13 May 1854): 297–304.
'Smoke or No Smoke.' 9 (1 July 1854): 464–6.
Stone, Thomas. 'Dreams.' 2 (8 March 1851): 566–72.
Stone, Thomas. 'A Shilling's Worth of Science.' 1 (24 August 1850): 507–10.
Thomas, William Moy. 'Covent Garden Market.' 7 (30 July 1853): 505–11.
Thornbury, George Walter. 'Sherry.' 18 (13 November 1858): 508–14.
Wills, W. H. 'Cheerful Arithmetic.' 1 (31 August 1850): 531–4.
Wills, W. H. 'Chips: Clean Water and Dirty Water.' 6 (5 February 1853): 496–7.
Wills, W. H. 'Chip: The Crimes of Cotton.' 6 (6 November 1852): 188–9.
Wills, W. H. 'Chips: Sabbath Pariahs.' 1 (13 July 1850): 378–9.
Wills, W. H. 'A Good Plain Cook.' 1 (4 May 1850): 139–41.
Wills, W. H. 'Health by Act of Parliament.' 1 (10 August 1850): 460–3.
Wills, W. H. 'A Legal Fiction.' 11 (21 July 1855): 598–9.
Wills, W. H. 'Poison Sold Here!' 2 (9 November 1850): 155–7.
Wills, W. H. 'The Private History of the Palace of Glass.' 2 (18 January 1851): 385–91.
Wills, W. H. 'The Troubled Water Question.' 1 (13 April 1850): 49–54.
Wills, W. H., and Mrs Hoare. 'The Story of Giovanni Belzoni.' 2 (1 March 1851): 548–52.

Wills, W. H., and Grenville Murray. 'Chips: Railway Comfort.' 1 (3 August 1850): 449–50.
Wills, W. H., and George Augustus Sala. 'Fairyland in Fifty-four.' 8 (3 December 1853): 313–17.
Wood. 'The Ruined Potter.' 9 (24 June 1854): 441–4.

(iii) *Articles in 'All the Year Round'*

Dickens, Charles. 'Mugby Junction.' 17 (Christmas 1866): 1–48.
'House-Top Telegraphs.' 2 (26 November 1859): 106–9.
Paterson, Peter [James Glass Bertram]. 'Town and Country Circus Life.' 6 (16 November 1861): 181–6.

(iv) *Other Material*

Ackroyd, Peter. *Dickens*. 1990. London: Minerva, 1991.
Adamson, John William. *English Education, 1789–1902*. Cambridge: Cambridge UP, 1930.
Allen, Michael. *Charles Dickens' Childhood*. Basingstoke: Macmillan, 1988.
Altick, Richard D. *The English Common Reader: A Social History of the Mass Reading Public, 1800–1900*. Chicago, Ill.: U of Chicago P, 1957.
Altick, Richard D. *The Shows of London*. Cambridge, Mass.: Harvard UP, 1978.
Anderson, B. L., and P. L. Cottrell. 'Another Victorian Capital Market: A Study of Banking and Bank Investors on Merseyside.' *Economic History Review* 2nd ser. 28 (1975): 598–615.
Anderson, Michael. *Family Structure in Nineteenth Century Lancashire*. Cambridge: Cambridge UP, 1971.
Andrews, Malcolm. 'A Note on Serialisation.' *Reading the Victorian Novel: Detail into Form*. Ed. Ian Gregor. London: Vision, 1980. 243–7.
Appleby, Louis. *A Medical Tour through the Whole Island of Great Britain*. London: Faber, 1994.
Ashburton [William Bingham Baring]. *Ashburton Prizes for the Teaching of 'Common Things'*. London: Groombridge, 1854.
Ashworth, Henry. *The Preston Strike, An Enquiry into its Causes and Consequences*. Manchester: Simms; London: W. & F. G. Cash, 1854.
Aspin, Chris. *The Cotton Industry*. Princes Risborough: Shire, 1981.
Bailey, Peter. *Leisure and Class in Victorian England*. London: Routledge, 1978.
Baines, Edward. *History of the Cotton Manufacture in Great Britain*. London: Fisher, 1835.
Baird, John D. ' "Divorce and Matrimonial Causes": An Aspect of "Hard Times".' *Victorian Studies* 20 (1977): 401–12.
Baker, William J. '*Hard Times* and Orr's Circle of the Sciences.' *Dickens Studies Newsletter* 8 (1977): 78.
Banks, Thomas. *A Short Sketch of the Cotton Trade of Preston for the last 67 Years*.

Preston: Spinners' Institute, 1888.

Bartrip, Peter W. J. 'Household Words and the Factory Accident Controversy.' Dickensian 75 (1979): 17–29.

Beaufort, Henry Charles FitzRoy, 8th Duke of, ed. The Badminton Library of Sports and Pastimes: Fencing, Boxing, Wrestling. 2nd edn. London: Longmans, 1890.

Beeton, Isabella, Mrs Beeton's Book of Household Management. Enlarged edn. London: Chancellor, 1982. Reprint. of The Book of Household Management. 1861.

Belcher, Margaret E. 'Bulwer's Mr Bluff: A Suggestion for Hard Times.' Dickensian 78 (1982): 105–9.

Belden, Mary Megie. The Dramatic Works of Samuel Foote. Hamden, Conn.: Archon, 1969.

Bell, Quentin. The Schools of Design. London: Routledge, 1963.

Bentham, Jeremy. An Introduction to the Principles of Morals and Legislation. 1789. Oxford: Clarendon Press, 1907.

Bentley, Nicolas, Michael Slater, and Nina Burgis. The Dickens Index. Oxford: Oxford UP, 1988.

Bernard, Catherine A. 'Dickens and Victorian Dream Theory.' Victorian Science and Victorian Values: Literary Perspectives. Eds James Paradis and Thomas Postlewait. New York: NY Acad. of Sciences, 1981.

Berridge, Virginia. 'Victorian Opium Eating: Responses to Opiate Use in Nineteenth-Century England.' Victorian Studies 21 (1978): 437–61.

Berridge, Virginia, and Griffith Edwards. Opium and the People: Opiate Use in Nineteenth-Century England. 1981. New Haven: Yale UP, 1987.

Best, Geoffrey. Mid-Victorian Britain, 1851–75. 1971. London: Fontana, 1990.

Binfield, Clyde. So Down to Prayers: Studies in English Nonconformity, 1780–1920. London: Dent, 1977.

Blyth, Edmund Kell. Life of William Ellis. London: Kegan Paul, 1889.

Brailsford, Dennis. Sport, Time, and Society: The British at Play. London: Routledge, 1991.

Brantlinger, Patrick. 'The Case Against Trade Unions in Early Victorian Fiction.' Victorian Studies 13 (1969): 37–52.

Brantlinger, Patrick. 'Dickens and the Factories.' Nineteenth-Century Fiction 26 (1971): 270–85.

Brantlinger, Patrick. Spirit of Reform: British Literature and Politics 1832–1867. Cambridge, Mass.: Harvard UP, 1977.

Brattin, Joel. 'Recent Norton Critical Editions.' Review. of Charles Dickens's Hard Times. Eds George Ford and Sylvère Monod. Dickens Quarterly 8 (1991) 182–7.

Briggs, Asa. The Age of Improvement, 1783–1867. London: Longman, 1959.

Briggs, Asa. Victorian Cities. 1963. Harmondsworth: Penguin, 1990.

Briggs, Asa. Victorian Things. 1988. Harmondsworth: Penguin, 1990.

British and Foreign School Society, Forty-Eighth Report. London: Rider, 1853.

Brittain, Judy. Assisted by Sally Harding. Good Housekeeping Step-by-Step Encyclopaedia of Needlecraft. London: Ebury, 1979.

Brook, G. L. The Language of Dickens. London: André Deutsch, 1970.

Brush, Stephen G. The Kind of Motion We Call Heat: a History of the Kinetic Theory of Gases in the 19th Century. 2 vols. Amsterdam: North Holland Personal Library,

1986.

Buchan, William. *Complete Domestic Medicine*. Otley: Walker, 1830.

Buckler, William E. 'Dickens's Success with *Household Words*.' *Dickensian* 46 (1950): 197–203.

Buckley, Jerome Hamilton. *The Triumph of Time: A Study of the Victorian Concepts of Time, History, Progress, and Decadence*. Cambridge, Mass.: Belknap-Harvard UP, 1966.

Bulwer-Lytton, Edward. *England and the English*. 1833. London: Routledge, 1876.

Burnett, John. *Plenty and Want: A Social History of Food in England from 1815 to the Present Day*. 1966. 3rd edn. London: Routledge, 1989.

Burnett, John. *A Social History of Housing 1815–1985*. 2nd edn. London: Routledge, 1986.

Butt, John, and Kathleen Tillotson. *Dickens at Work*. 1957. London: Methuen, 1982.

Butwin, Joseph. '*Hard Times*: The News and the Novel.' *Nineteenth-Century Fiction* 32 (1977): 166–87.

Buzard, James. *The Beaten Track: European Tourism, Literature, and the Ways to Culture, 1800–1918*. Oxford: Clarendon, 1993.

Camaione, David N., and Kenneth G. Tillman. *Teaching and Coaching Wrestling: A Scientific Approach*. 2nd edn. New York: Wiley, 1980.

Carlyle, Thomas. *The Ashburton Edition of Thomas Carlyle's Works*. 17 vols. London: Chapman & Hall, 1885–9.

Carnall, Geoffrey. 'Dickens, Mrs Gaskell, and the Preston Strike.' *Victorian Studies* 8 (1964): 31–48.

Carr, Raymond. 'Country Sports.' *The Victorian Countryside*. Vol. 2. Ed. G. E. Mingay. London: Routledge & Kegan Paul, 1981. 475–87.

Cazamian, Louis. *The Social Novel in England, 1830–1850*. Trans. Martin Fido. London: Routledge, 1973. Trans. of *Le Roman social en Angleterre*. 1903.

Chapman, S. J. *The Lancashire Cotton Industry*. Manchester: Manchester UP, 1904.

Chedzoy, Alan. *A Scandalous Woman: The Story of Caroline Norton*. London: Allison & Busby, 1992.

Clay, Walter Lowe. *The Prison Chaplain: A Memoir of the Rev. John Clay, B.D.* Cambridge: Macmillan, 1861.

Collins, Philip. 'Dickens and Adult Education.' *British Journal of Educational Studies* 3 (1955): 115–27.

Collins, Philip. *Dickens and Crime*. 3rd edn. Basingstoke: Macmillan, 1994.

Collins, Philip, ed. *Dickens: The Critical Heritage*. London: Routledge, 1971.

Collins, Philip. *Dickens and Education*. London: Macmillan, 1963.

Collins, Philip. 'Dickens and Industrialism.' *Studies in English Literature* 20 (1980): 651–73.

Combe, George. *Lectures on Phrenology*. New York: Colman, 1839.

Cook, E. T., and Alexander Wedderburn. *The Works of John Ruskin*. Vol. 5. London: Allen, 1904.

Cotsell, Michael. *The Companion to 'Our Mutual Friend'*. London: Allen & Unwin, 1986.

Crouzet, François. *The Victorian Economy*. Trans. Anthony Forster. 1982. London: Routledge, 1990.

Cunningham, Valentine. *Everywhere Spoken Against: Dissent in the Victorian Novel.* Oxford: Clarendon, 1975.

Davies, John D. *Phrenology, Fad and Science: A 19th-Century American Crusade.* 1955. Hamden, Conn.: Archon, 1971.

Davis, Nuel Pharr. *The Life of Wilkie Collins.* Urbana, Ill.: U of Illinois P, 1956.

Dawes, Richard. *Schools and Other Similar Institutions for the Industrial Classes: Remarks on the importance of giving them . . . a self-supporting character, and the means of doing so.* London: Groombridge, 1853.

Dawes, Richard. *Suggestive Hints Towards Improved Secular Instruction.* 1847. 6th edn. enlarged and improved. London: Groombridge, 1853.

Dennis, Barbara and David Skilton, eds. *Reform and Intellectual Debate in Victorian England.* London: Croom Helm, 1987.

Dickens, Charles. *Hard Times.* 1854. Ed. George Ford and Sylvère Monod. 2nd edn. New York: Norton, 1990.

Dickens, Charles. *Hard Times.* 1854. Ed. Paul Schlicke. World's Classics edn. Oxford: Oxford UP, 1989.

Disher, M. Willson. *Clowns and Pantomimes.* 1925. New York: Blom, 1968.

Disher, M. Willson. *Greatest Show on Earth.* London: G. Bell, 1937.

Dodd, George. *Curiosities of Industry and the Applied Sciences . . . Supplement to the National Cyclopaedia.* London: Knight, 1854.

Dodd, George. *Dictionary of Manufacturing, Mining, Machinery and the Industrial Arts.* London: Virtue, 1869.

Dodd, George. *The Food of London.* London: Longman, 1856.

Dodds, John W. *The Age of Paradox.* London: Gollancz, 1953.

Dubbey, J. M. *The Mathematical Work of Charles Babbage.* Cambridge: Cambridge UP, 1978.

Dunbar, Janet. *The Early Victorian Woman: Some Aspects of Her Life, 1837–57.* London: Harrap, 1953.

Dutton, H. I., and J. E. King. *'Ten Per Cent and No Surrender': The Preston Strike, 1853–1854.* Cambridge: Cambridge UP, 1981.

Easson, Angus. *Hard Times: Critical Commentary and Notes.* London: U of London P, 1973.

Edwards, Clive D. *Victorian Furniture: Technology and Design.* Manchester: Manchester UP, 1993.

Ellis, Ethel E. *Memoir of William Ellis.* London: Longmans, 1888.

Ellis, William. *Progressive Lessons in Social Science.* 1850. 2nd edn. London: Smith, 1862.

Engels, Friedrich. *The Condition of the Working Class in England.* 1845. Revised edn. Harmondsworth: Penguin, 1987.

The Etiquette of Modern Society: a guide to good manners in every possible situation. London: Ward, Lock, 1882.

Evans, Eric J. *The Forging of the Modern State: Early Industrial Britain, 1783–1870.* London: Longman, 1983.

Evers, C. R. *Rugby.* London: Blackie, 1939.

Fabrizio, Richard. 'Wonderful No-Meaning: Language and the Psychopathology of the Family in Dickens' *Hard Times.*' *Dickens Studies Annual* 16 (1987): 61–94.

Falconer, William. *An Universal Dictionary of the Marine*. London: T. Cadell, 1769; 1780. Reprinted Newton Abbot: David & Charles, 1970.
Fawkes, Richard. *Dion Boucicault: A Biography*. London: Quartet, 1979.
Field, John. *The King's Nurseries: The Story of Westminster School*. London: James, 1987.
Fielding, Kenneth J. 'Carlyle and Dickens or Dickens and Carlyle?' Review of *Dickens and Carlyle, The Question of Influence*, by William Oddie, and *Carlyle and Dickens*, by Michael Goldberg. *Dickensian* 69 (1973): 111–18.
Fielding, Kenneth J. 'Charles Dickens and the Department of Practical Art.' *Modern Language Review* 48 (1953): 270–7.
Fielding, Kenneth J. 'Dickens and Science?' *Dickens Quarterly* 13 (1996): 200–16.
Fielding, Kenneth J. 'Hard Times and Common Things.' *Imagined Worlds: Essays on some English Novels and Novelists in Honour of John Butt*. Eds Maynard Mack and Ian Gregor. London: Methuen, 1968. 183–203.
Fielding, Kenneth J. 'The Weekly Serialisation of Dickens's Novels.' *Dickensian* 54 (1958): 134–41.
Fielding, Kenneth J., and Anne Smith. '*Hard Times* and the Factory Controversy: Dickens vs. Harriet Martineau.' *Nineteenth-Century Fiction* 24 (1970): 404–27.
Fitzgerald, Percy. *Memories of Charles Dickens*. Bristol: Arrowsmith, 1913.
Flint, Kate, ed. *The Victorian Novelist: Social Problems and Social Change*. London: Croom Helm, 1987.
Ford, George H. 'Stern Hebrews Who Laugh: Further Thoughts on Carlyle and Dickens.' *Carlyle Past and Present: A Collection of New Essays*. Ed. K. J. Fielding and Rodger L. Tarr. London: Vision, 1976.
Forster, John. *The Life of Charles Dickens*. 3 vols. London: Chapman & Hall, 1872–4.
Fox, Grace. *Britain and Japan, 1858–1883*. Oxford: Clarendon, 1969.
Fraser, W. Hamish. *Trade Unions and Society: The Struggle for Acceptance, 1850–1880*. London: Allen & Unwin, 1974.
Freeman, Sarah. *Mutton and Oysters: The Victorians and their Food*. London: Gollancz, 1989.
Frost, Thomas. *Circus Life and Circus Celebrities*. London: Tinsley Brothers, 1875.
Gadd, W. Laurence. 'Coketown.' *Dickensian* 36 (1940): 85–7.
Gaskell, William. *Two Lectures on the Lancashire Dialect*. London: Chapman & Hall, 1854.
Gilmour, Robin. 'Dickens and the Self-Help Idea.' *The Victorians and Social Protest: A Symposium*. Eds J. Butt and I. F. Clarke. Newton Abbot: David & Charles; Hamden, Conn.: Archon, 1973.
Gilmour, Robin. 'The Gradgrind School: Political Economy in the Classroom.' *Victorian Studies* 11 (1967): 207–24.
Gitter, Elisabeth G. 'The Power of Women's Hair in the Victorian Imagination.' *PMLA* 99 (1984): 936–54.
Goldberg, Michael. *Carlyle and Dickens*. Athens, Ga: U of Georgia P, 1972.
Goldstine, Herman H. *The Computer from Pascal to von Neumann*. Princeton, NJ: Princeton UP, 1972.
Goldwater, Leonard J. *Mercury: A History of Quicksilver*. Baltimore, Md: York, 1972.
Gomme, G. Laurence. *London in the Reign of Victoria (1837–1897)*. London: Blackie,

1898.

Gourvish, T. R., and R. G. Wilson. *The British Brewing Industry, 1830–1980*. Cambridge: Cambridge UP, 1994.

Graveson, R. H., and F. R. Crane, eds. *A Century of Family Law, 1857–1957*. London: Sweet & Maxwell, 1957.

Green, J. A., ed. *Pestalozzi's Educational Writings*. London: Arnold, 1916.

Hall, James, ed. *Dictionary of Subjects and Symbols in Art*. 1974. Revised edn. London: Murray, 1979.

Hammond, J. L., and Barbara Hammond. *The Age of the Chartists, 1832–1854*. London: Longmans, 1930.

Hardwick, Charles. *History of the Borough of Preston and its Environs in the County of Lancaster*. Preston: Worthington; London: Simpkin, 1857.

Harrison, Brian. *Drink and the Victorians: The Temperance Question in England, 1815–1872*. London: Faber, 1971.

Hempton, David. 'Popular Religion and Irreligion in Victorian Fiction.' *The Writer as Witness: Literature as Historical Evidence*. Ed. Tom Dunne. Historical Studies 16. Cork: Cork UP, 1987. 177–96.

Hewett, Edward, and W. F. Axton. *Convivial Dickens: The Drinks of Dickens and His Times*. Athens, Ohio: Ohio UP, 1983.

Hewitson, Anthony. *Our Churches and Chapels, their Parsons, Priests, and Congregatioñs; being a critical and historical account of every place of worship in Preston*. Reprinted from *Preston Chronicle*. Preston: 'Chronicle' Office, 1869.

Hill, Nancy K. *A Reformer's Art: Dickens' Picturesque and Grotesque Imagery*. Athens, Ohio: Ohio UP, 1981.

Hill, T. W. 'Notes on *Hard Times*.' *Dickensian* 48 (1952): 134–41, 177–85.

Hobhouse, Hermione, ed. *Survey of London*. Vol. 42. London: Athlone, 1986.

Hobsbawm, E. J. *Industry and Empire: An Economic History of Britain since 1750*. London: Weidenfeld, 1968.

Holcombe, Lee. *Wives and Property: Reform of the Married Women's Property Law in Nineteenth-Century England*. Toronto: U of Toronto P, 1983.

Holdsworth, Sir William. *A History of English Law*. 17 vols to date. London: Methuen, 1903– .

Hopkins, Eric. *A Social History of the English Working Classes, 1815–1945*. 1979. London: Hodder & Stoughton, 1990.

Horn, Pamela. *The Rise and Fall of the Victorian Servant*. Dublin: Gill, 1975.

Horstman, Allen. *Victorian Divorce*. London: Croom Helm, 1985.

Hotten, John Camden. *The Slang Dictionary*. Wakefield: EP Publishing, 1972. Reprint of 1887 edn. *A Dictionary of Modern Slang, Cant, and Vulgar Language . . . by a London Antiquary*. 1859.

Houghton, Walter E. *The Victorian Frame of Mind, 1830–1870*. New Haven, Conn.: Yale UP, 1957.

Howe, M. A. DeWolfe, ed. *Memories of a Hostess: A Chronicle of Eminent Friendships Drawn Chiefly from the Diaries of Mrs. James T. Fields*. Boston, Mass.: Atlantic Monthly Press, 1922.

Howell, Peter, and Ian Sutton, eds. *The Faber Guide to Victorian Churches*. London: Faber, 1989.

Hughes, Robert. *The Fatal Shore: A History of the Transportation of Convicts to Australia, 1787–1868.* London: Collins Harvill, 1987.
Hyman, Anthony. *Charles Babbage: Pioneer of the Computer.* Oxford: Oxford UP, 1982.
Ingham, Patricia. 'Dialect as "Realism": *Hard Times* and the Industrial Novel.' *Review of English Studies* 37 (1986): 518–27.
Inglis, K. S. *Churches and the Working Classes in Victorian England.* London: Routledge; Toronto: U of Toronto P, 1973.
James, M. H. 'Bentham and Legal Theory – Introduction.' *Northern Ireland Legal Quarterly* 24 (1973): 267–74.
Jeffs, Julian. *Sherry.* London: Faber, 1961.
Johnson, Edgar. *Charles Dickens: His Tragedy and Triumph.* 1952. Revised and abridged. Harmondsworth: Penguin, 1986.
Kaplan, Fred. *Dickens: A Biography.* London: Hodder & Stoughton, 1988.
Kaplan, Fred. *Dickens and Mesmerism.* Princeton, NJ: Princeton UP, 1975.
Kay, James Phillips. *The Moral and Physical Condition of the Working Classes.* 1832. Didsbury: Morten, 1969.
Kay-Shuttleworth, James. *Four Periods of Public Education as Reviewed in 1832, 1839, 1846, 1862.* 1862. Brighton: Harvester, 1973.
Kelly, Thomas. *George Birkbeck: Pioneer of Adult Education.* Liverpool: Liverpool UP, 1957.
Klingender, Francis D. *Art and the Industrial Revolution.* London: Curwen, 1947.
Knight, Charles. *Knight's Cyclopaedia of London 1851.* London: Charles Knight [1851].
Knight, Charles. *Passages of a Working Life.* 3 vols. London: Bradbury & Evans, 1865.
Kovačević, Ivanka. *Fact into Fiction: English Literature and the Industrial Scene, 1750–1850.* Leicester: Leicester UP; Faculty of Philology, U of Belgrade, 1975.
Langton, Robert. *The Childhood and Youth of Charles Dickens.* Manchester: Langton, 1883.
Larwood, Jacob [pseud.], and John Camden Hotten. *The History of Signboards from Earliest Times to the Present Day.* London: Hotten, 1866.
Layard, Austen Henry. *Nineveh and Babylon.* London: Murray, 1853.
Layard, Austen Henry. *Nineveh and its Remains.* 2 vols. London: Murray, 1849.
Le Roux, Hugues, and Jules Garnier. *Acrobats and Mountebanks.* London: Chapman & Hall, 1890.
Lohrli, Anne, ed. *Household Words: A Weekly Journal, 1850–1859, Conducted by Charles Dickens. A Table of Contents, List of Contributors and Their Contributions Based on the 'Household Words' Office Book . . .* Toronto: U of Toronto P, 1973.
Longrigg, Roger. *The History of Horse Racing.* London: Macmillan, 1972.
Love and Barton. *Manchester As It Is.* Manchester: Love & Barton, 1839.
Lowe, James. *An Account of the Strike in the Cotton Trade at Preston in 1853.* London: Parker, 1860.
Lubbock, Jules. *The Tyranny of Taste: The Politics of Architecture and Design in Britain, 1550–1960.* New Haven, Conn., and London: Yale UP, 1995.
Lux, Kenneth. *Adam Smith's Mistake: How a Moral Philosopher Invented Economics and Ended Morality.* Boston, Mass.: Shambhala, 1990.
M'Culloch, J. R. *The Principles of Political Economy.* 1830. 4th edn. Edinburgh: Black, 1849.

Macdonald, Stuart. *The History and Philosophy of Art Education.* London: U of London P, 1970.

MacKeith, Margaret. *The History and Conservation of Shopping Arcades.* London: Mansell, 1986.

MacKeith, Margaret. *Shopping Arcades: A Gazetteer of Extant British Arcades, 1817–1939.* London: Mansell, 1985.

McKendrick, Neil. 'Josiah Wedgwood and Factory Discipline.' *Historical Journal* 4 (1961): 30–55.

Mair, Craig. *A Star for Seamen: the Stevenson Family of Engineers.* London: John Murray, 1978.

Malcolmson, Robert W. *Popular Recreations in English Society, 1700–1850.* London: Cambridge UP, 1973.

Malthus, Thomas. *An Essay on the Principle of Population,* and *A Summary View of the Principle of Population.* 1798 and 1830. Ed. Antony Flew. Harmondsworth: Penguin, 1985.

Manning, Sylvia. *'Hard Times': An Annotated Bibliography.* New York: Garland, 1984.

Marindin, G. E., ed. *A Smaller Classical Dictionary.* New edn. 1898. 6th impression 1947. London: John Murray, 1948.

Marshall, John, and Ian Willox. *The Victorian House.* London: Sidgwick, 1986.

Martindale, William. *The Extra Pharmacopoeia of Unofficial Drugs and Chemical and Pharmaceutical Preparations.* 3rd edn. London: Lewis, 1884.

Martineau, Harriet. *The Factory Controversy; A Warning against Meddling Legislation.* Manchester: Ireland, 1855.

Maunder, E. W. *The Royal Observatory, Greenwich: a Glance at its History and Work.* London: Religious Tract Society, 1900.

Mayhew, Henry. *London Labour and the London Poor.* 3 vols and an 'Extra Volume'. London: Griffin, Bohn, 1861–2.

Melada, Ivan. *The Captain of Industry in English Fiction, 1821–1871.* Albuquerque, N. Mex: U of New Mexico P, 1970.

Mill, John Stuart. *Autobiography.* 7th edn. London: Longmans, 1882.

Mill, John Stuart. 'Bentham.' *Mill on Bentham and Coleridge.* Introduction by F. R. Leavis. London: Chatto & Windus, 1950.

Mill, John Stuart. *Utilitarianism.* 1861. Ed. [with critical essays] Samuel Gorovitz. Indianapolis, Ind.: Bobbs-Merrill, 1971.

Montague, Charles W. *Recollections of an Equestrian Manager.* London: Chambers, 1881.

Morgan, Nigel. *Vanished Dwellings: Early Industrial Housing in a Lancashire Cotton Town. Preston.* Preston: Mullion, 1990.

Morus, Iwan Rhys. 'Marketing the Machine: the Construction of Electrotherapeutics as Viable Medicine in Early Victorian England.' *Medical History* 36 (1992): 34–52.

Mott, Graham. ' "I Wallow in Words": Dickens, Journalism and Public Affairs, 1831–1838.' Diss. Leicester U, 1984.

Mugglestone, Lynda. *'Talking Proper': The Rise of Accent as Social Symbol.* Oxford: Clarendon, 1995.

Murphy, P. J. 'The Origins of the 1852 Lock-Out in the British Engineering Industry Reconsidered.' *International Review of Social History* 23 (1978): 242–66.

Murray, John. 'The Origin and History of Murray's Handbooks for Travellers.' *Murray's Magazine* 6 (1889): 623–9.
Neiman, Fraser, ed. *Essays, Letters, and Reviews by Matthew Arnold*. Cambridge, Mass.: Harvard UP, 1960.
Norman, E. R. *Church and Society in England, 1770–1970*. Oxford: Clarendon, 1976.
Oddie, William. *Dickens and Carlyle: The Question of Influence*. London: Centenary, 1972.
Old Yarns Respun: The Story of Preston and the Cotton Industry, 1791–1991. Booklet produced in conjunction with the exhibition 'Old Yarns Respun' organised by the Harris Museum and Art Gallery, 1991.
Opie, Iona, and Peter Opie, eds. *The Oxford Dictionary of Nursery Rhymes*. Oxford: Oxford UP, 1951.
Oppenheim, Janet. *'Shattered Nerves': Doctors, Patients, and Depression in Victorian England*. Oxford: Oxford UP, 1991.
Page, Norman. ' "Ruth" and "Hard Times": A Dickens Source.' *Notes & Queries* 216 (1971): 413.
Page, Norman. *Speech in the English Novel*. London: Longman, 1973.
Palmer, A. W. *A Dictionary of Modern History, 1789–1945*. 1962. Harmondsworth: Penguin, 1976.
Palmer, Roy, ed. *Poverty Knock: a Picture of Industrial Life in the Nineteenth Century through Songs, Ballads and Contemporary Accounts*. Cambridge: Cambridge UP, 1974.
Palmer, Roy, ed. *A Touch on the Times: Songs of Social Change, 1770–1914*. Harmondsworth: Penguin, 1974.
Parker, Langston. *The Modern Treatment of Syphilitic Diseases, both Primary and Secondary*. London: John Churchill, 1854.
Paroissien, David. *The Companion to 'Oliver Twist'*. Edinburgh: Edinburgh UP, 1992.
Partridge, Eric. *The Penguin Dictionary of Historical Slang*. London: Penguin, 1972. Abr. of 1961 edn. *A Dictionary of Slang and Unconventional English*. 1937.
Patten, Robert L., ed. *George Cruikshank: A Revaluation*. 1974. Princeton, NJ: Princeton UP, 1992.
Pattison, Iain. *The British Veterinary Profession 1791–1948*. London: Allen, 1984.
Pelling, Henry. *A History of British Trade Unionism*. 1963. 3rd edn. Harmondsworth: Penguin, 1976.
Perkin, Harold. *The Origins of Modern English Society 1780–1880*. London: Routledge, 1969.
Peyrouton, N. C. 'Boz and the American Phreno-Mesmerists.' *Dickens Studies* 3 (1967): 38–50.
Pike, E. Royston. *Human Documents of the Industrial Revolution in Britain*. London: Allen & Unwin, 1966.
Pimlott, Ben, and Chris Cook, eds. *Trade Unions in British Politics: the First 250 Years*. 1982. 2nd edn. London: Longman, 1991.
Piper, David. *London: An Illustrated Companion Guide*. London: Collins, 1980.
Plamenatz, John. *The English Utilitarians*. Oxford: Blackwell, 1966.
Poovey, Mary. *Uneven Developments: The Ideological Work of Gender in Mid-Victorian England*. 1988. London: Virago, 1989.
Pope, Norris. *Dickens and Charity*. London: Macmillan, 1978.

Price's Patent Candle Company Limited. *Special Report by the Directors to the Proprietors*. London, 1852.

The Queen's Beasts. [account of heraldic animals]. Norfolk Herald Extraordinary and Garter King of Arms. London: Newman Neame [n.d. c.1955].

Redgrave, Richard. 'On the Methods Employed for Imparting Education in Art to All Classes.' *Addresses of the Superintendents of the Department of Practical Art*. London: Chapman & Hall, 1853.

Rich, R. W. *The Training of Teachers in England and Wales during the Nineteenth Century*. Cambridge: Cambridge UP, 1933.

Róheim, Géza. *The Riddle of the Sphinx or Human Origins*. Trans. R. Money-Kyrle. London: Hogarth, 1934.

Rowell, Geoffrey. 'Nineteenth-century Attitudes and Practices.' *Dying, Death, and Disposal*. Ed. Gilbert Cope. London: SPCK, 1970. 49–56.

Rubin, Isaac Ilyich. *A History of Economic Thought*. Trans. 2nd revised Russian edn. 1929. London: Pluto, 1979.

Sartin, Stephen. *The People and Places of Historic Preston*. Preston: Carnegie, 1988.

Saxon, A. H. *The Life and Art of Andrew Ducrow and the Romantic Age of the English Circus*. Hamden, Conn.: Archon, 1978.

Schlicke, Paul. *Dickens and Popular Entertainment*. 1985. London: Unwin Hyman, 1988.

Shanley, Mary Lyndon. *Feminism, Marriage, and the Law in Victorian England, 1850–1895*. London: Tauris, 1989.

Shatto, Susan. *The Companion to 'Bleak House'*. London: Unwin Hyman, 1988.

Shatto, Susan. ' "A complete course, according to question and answer".' *Dickensian* 70 (1974): 113–20.

Shiman, Lilian Lewis. *Crusade against Drink in Victorian England*. New York: St Martin's, 1988.

Showalter, Elaine. *The Female Malady: Women, Madness and English Culture, 1830–1980*. 1985. London: Virago, 1987.

Simmons, Jack. *The Railway in England and Wales, 1830–1914*. Leicester: Leicester UP, 1978.

Slater, Michael. 'Carlyle and Jerrold into Dickens: A Study of *The Chimes*.' *Nineteenth-Century Fiction* 24 (1970): 506–26.

Slater, Michael. *Dickens and Women*. London: Dent, 1983.

Sloane, David E. E. 'Phrenology in *Hard Times*: A Source for Bitzer.' *Dickens Studies Newsletter* 5 (1974): 9–12.

Smith, Anne. '*Hard Times* and *The Times* Newspaper.' *Dickensian* 69 (1973): 153–62.

Smith, F. B. *The People's Health 1830–1910*. 1979. London: Weidenfeld, 1990.

Smith, Frank. *A History of English Elementary Education, 1760–1902*. London: U of London P, 1931.

Smith, Frank. *The Life and Work of Sir James Kay-Shuttleworth*. London: Murray, 1923.

Smith, Morris Brooke. 'The Growth and Development of Popular Entertainment and Pastimes in the Lancashire Cotton Towns 1830–1870.' Diss. Lancaster U, 1970.

Smith, Sheila M. 'Blue Books and Victorian Novelists.' *Review of English Studies* 21 (1970): 23–40.

Smith, Sheila M. *The Other Nation: The Poor in English Novels of the 1840s and 1850s.* Oxford: Clarendon, 1980.
Somervell, D. C. *English Thought in the Nineteenth Century.* London: Methuen, 1929.
Speaight, George. *A History of the Circus.* London: Tantivy Press; San Diego, Calif., and New York: Barnes, 1980.
Speaight, George. 'Some Comic Circus Entrées.' *Theatre Notebook* 32 (1978): 24–7.
Steig, Michael. '*Dombey and Son* and the Railway Panic of 1845.' *Dickensian* 67 (1971): 145–8.
Stetson, Dorothy. *A Woman's Issue: The Politics of Family Law Reform in England.* Westport, Conn.: Greenwood, 1982.
Stone, Harry, ed. *Dickens' Working Notes for His Novels.* Chicago, Ill. : U of Chicago P, 1987.
Stone, Harry, ed. *The Uncollected Writings of Charles Dickens: Household Words, 1850–1859.* 2 vols. London: Allen Lane, Penguin, 1968.
Stone, Lawrence. *Road to Divorce: England, 1530–1987.* 1990. Oxford: Oxford UP, 1992.
Stonehouse, J. H. *Catalogue of the Library of Charles Dickens from Gadshill . . .* London: Piccadilly Fountain, 1935.
Stow, David. *Supplement to Moral Training and The Training System, with Plans for Erecting and Fitting up Training Schools.* 1839. Didsbury, Manchester: Morten, 1971.
Sturt, Mary. *The Education of the People: A History of Primary Education in England and Wales in the Nineteenth Century.* London: Routledge, 1967.
Summerson, John. *Architecture in Britain 1530–1830.* 1953. 4th edn. Harmondsworth: Penguin, 1963.
Svilpis, J. E. ' "The Sultan Who Put His Head in the Pail of Water": A Possible Addison Allusion in *Hard Times.*' *Dickens Quarterly* 8 (1991): 177–8.
Szirotny, J. S. 'A Classical Reference in "Hard Times" and in "Middlemarch".' *Notes & Queries* 213 (1968): 421–2.
Thompson, E. P. 'Time, Work-Discipline, and Industrial Capitalism.' *Past and Present* 38 (1967): 56–97.
Thompson, F. M. L. 'Landowners and the Rural Community.' *The Victorian Countryside.* Vol. 2. Ed. G. E. Mingay. London: Routledge & Kegan Paul, 1981. 457–74.
Thorne, James. *Handbook to the Environs of London.* 1876. Bath: Adams, 1970.
Timbs, John. *Curiosities of Animal and Vegetable Life.* London: Charles Griffin, 1872.
Timbs, John. *Curiosities of London.* London: Longmans, 1868.
Timbs, John. *Strange Stories of the Animal World.* London: Griffith & Farran, 1866.
[Timbs, John]. *The Year-book of Facts in Science and Art.* London: Charles Tilt, 1840.
Tomalin, Claire. *The Invisible Woman: The Story of Nelly Ternan and Charles Dickens.* New York: Viking-Penguin, 1990.
Turner, E. S. *Taking the Cure.* London: Michael Joseph, 1967.
Walkingame, Francis. *The Tutor's Assistant.* London: Richardson [n.d. c.1850].
Wallett, W. F. *The Public Life of W. F. Wallett, The Queen's Jester: An Autobiography.* Ed. John Luntley. London: Bemrose; London: Lacey; Edinburgh: John Menzies, 1870.
Walmsley, Thomas. *Reminiscences of the Preston Cockpit and the Old Teetotallers.* Preston: Guardian, 1892.

Walvin, James. *Leisure and Society 1830–1950*. London: Longman, 1978.

Waterfield, Gordon. *Layard of Nineveh*. London: Murray, 1963.

Wheeler, Michael. *The Art of Illusion in Victorian Fiction*. London and Basingstoke: Macmillan; New York: Barnes, 1979.

Whittock, N., J. Bennett, J. Badcock, C. Newton, et al. *The Complete Book of Trades, or the Parents' Guide and Youths' Instructor*. London: Bennett, 1837.

Wigley, John. *The Rise and Fall of the Victorian Sunday*. Manchester: Manchester UP, 1980.

Williams, Frederick, S. *Our Iron Roads: Their History, Construction and Administration*. 1852. New impression 2nd edn. 1883. London: Frank Cass, 1968.

Williams, L. Pearce, ed. *The Selected Correspondence of Michael Faraday*. Vol 1. 1812–1848. Cambridge: Cambridge UP, 1971.

Wohl, Anthony S. *Endangered Lives: Public Health in Victorian Britain*. London: Dent, 1983.

Woodward, Sir Llewellyn. *The Age of Reform, 1815–1870*. 2nd edn. Oxford: Clarendon, 1962.

Wright, Lawrence. *Clean and Decent: The Fascinating History of the Bathroom and the Water Closet*. London: Routledge, 1960.

Yate-Lee, Lawford, and Henry Wace. *The Law and Practice of Bankruptcy and the Bills of Sale Acts*. 3rd edn. London: Sweet & Maxwell, 1887.

INDEX

Abbot & Hodgson's Bow Brewery, 205–6
Abercrombie, Dr John, *Inquiries Concerning the Intellectual Powers*, 141
Abolition of Slavery Act (1833), 170
accidents: circus, 58, 89; factory, 5, 118, 143–5, 221, 241; mining, 220, 221, 224; railway, 166; at sea, 119
Acts of Parliament, *see under title of Act*
Addison, Joseph, 2; *Turkish Tales*, 165
adult education, *see* education; libraries; mechanics' institutes
adultery: biblical allusion, 139–40; and Mrs Blackpool, 128, 130–1; as commonplace, 134–5; 'criminal conversation', 132–3, 136–7; and Frederick Dickens, 130; as grounds for divorce, 131–2, 134–5, 136–7; *see also* marriage and divorce; married women's property laws
Aeschylus, *Agamemnon*, 148
African 'natives', 6; *see also* savages; imagery
agitators: George Cowell, 117–18, 171, 179, 186, (illus.) 178; Dickens's attitude towards, 179; Mortimer Grimshaw, 6–7, 171, 172, 177–8, 186, (illus.), 176; millowners' attitude towards, 187; rhetoric of, 171, 177–8; role of, 187; *see also* industrial relations; Preston strike and lock-out; trade unionism
Airy, George Biddell, 148
alcohol: gauging stick for, 210; medicinal liquors, 103; and opium, 86; prohibition of the sale of, 52; as restorative, 5–6, 216, 221; *see also* drinks; drunkenness; gin-palaces; temperance movement
Alderney, 204
All England Rules, 43
All the Year Round: anonymity of articles in, 4; and Dickens's attitude towards amusements, 88; *Great Expectations* serialized in, 11; Sala contributor to, 35; *Tale of Two Cities* serialized in, 11; *see also Household Words*; *Household Narrative of Current Events*
Allestree, Richard, *The Whole Duty of Man*, 6, 163
Allsopp Brewery, 205
allusions, literary, *see under author of work referred to*; for books of the Bible, *see under* Bible; for anonymous works, *see* title. *See also* classical allusions; emblematic figures; gods and goddesses
Amalgamated Association of Cotton Operative Spinners, 175

Amalgamated Committee of Trades and Factory Operatives, 175
Amalgamated Society of Engineers, 162, 175, 179
American Indians, 6
American Notes, 78, 87, 189
American War of Independence, 129, 185
Amphithéâtre Astley, 229
Amphithéâtre Franconi, 229
Analytical Engine, *see* calculating machines
animal communication, 9, 232; *see also* animals: dogs
animals: cows, 38, 204; crocodiles, 36; dogs, 9, 62–4, 91, 104, 121, 232; dormice, 10, 122; elephants, 6, 44, 79; frogs, 35; horses, 36, 37–8, 89, 92–3, 226, 228; ill-treatment of, 62, 121; lions, 92; serpents, 6, 79, 191; sheep, 38, 220; *see also* birds; fish
Annual Register, 39, 180
annulments: of marriage 135; of factory school certificates, 154
Anti-Slavery Society, 171
Antwerp, 196
apprenticeships: circus, 97–8; *see also* education: teachers and teaching
Arabian Nights, 51, 109, 111, 121, 203, 204
arcades: Burlington, 108; Royal Opera, 108
architectural design. *For specific buildings, see under the name of the building. See also* churches
architecture: 'Dissenting Gothic', 82; 'florid Gothic', 82; Georgian, 56; Gothic, 58, 82–3; 'romantic Gothic', 56
Arkwright, Richard, carding engine, 185
Arnold, Matthew, 'On the Modern Element in Literature', 70
Arnold, Dr Thomas, 123
art: classical, 151; laws of colour, 46; marine and landscape paintings, 192; Renaissance, 151; technical, 43; transparencies, 74; *see also* Department of Practical Art; Department of Science and Art
Ashburton, Lord, *see* Baring, William Bingham
Ashley, Lord, *see* Cooper, Anthony Ashley, 7th Earl of Shaftesbury
Ashworth, Henry, 177
Astley, Philip, 36, 64, 68, 91, 100, 228
Astley's Royal Amphitheatre: adaptation of *HT* performed at, 228; balloon ascensions, 71; Tom Barry 60; Andrew Ducrow, 62; John Ducrow, 62; equestrian performances at, 64–6,

93; 'Flying Childers', 93; former names of, 228; history of, 228; 'Lottery Ticket', 108; managers of, 66, 226, 228; Adah Menken at, 230; in Paris, 229; 'à la Perche', 98, (illus.) 99; performing dogs at, 62–4; playbills, 60, 62, 108; ringmaster of, 96; Louisa Woolford, 60; see also circus; circuses; popular entertainment; sport
astronomy, 52, 53; 'Great Bear', 53; observatories, 148; 'Plough', 53; and time, 148; see also stars and starlight
Auriol, Jean-Baptiste, 100, (illus.) 101
Austin, Henry, 79
Australia: penal colonies in, 185; transportation to, 186; Norfolk Island, 187

Babbage, Charles, 40
backgammon, 198
ballooning, 71
Bank Charter Act (1844), 146
Bank of England, 160
Bank Holidays Act (1871), 130
Bank Reform Acts: (1826), 146; (1833), 146
bankers, 55, 71
bankruptcy and debt, 106, 192, 193
banks: joint-stock, 71, 146; opening hours of, 160; private, 146; savings, 72, 86, 232; security in, 160
Banks, Thomas, 183
barbers and barbers' shops, 10, 76
Baring, William Bingham, 2nd Baron Ashburton, *Ashburton Prizes for the Teaching of 'Common Things'*, 30–1
Barnaby Rudge, 2, 3, 162, 186, 189
barragon jackets, 125
Barry, Thomas, 62, 92, (illus.) 65
Bass Brewery, 205–6
Bassle, Master, 39–40
baths: shower, 165; vapour, 140
Battersea Training College, 28, 48, 50
Battle Bridge, 202
Batty's circus, 64, 89
beds, truckle, 160
Bee, The, 2
beef, 129, 198
beer: and burnt cork for 'blacking up', 231; India Pale Ale, 205; Select Committee on Public Houses and the Sale of Beer (1853), 87
beer-houses, 86
Beeton, Isabella, *Household Management*, 198, 205
beggars and vagrants, 66, 68, 76, 198; see also strollers
Belcher, Jim, 'belcher handkerchief', 97
Bell, Rev. Andrew, 27

Bellinck, Juan, 64
bells, factory, 125
Belzoni, Giovanni, 230
Bentham, Jeremy: 'greatest happiness' principle, 33–4, 118; ideology of, 147; *Introduction to the Principles of Morals and Legislation*, 40; legal theory of, 131; and poetry, 75; see also laissez-faire; political economy; Utilitarianism
Bertram, James Glass, alias Peter Paterson, 98
Bethnal Green, 122, 159
Bible
 Old Testament, 139
 books: Genesis, 125, 129, 139, 158, 180, 204, 209; Deuteronomy, 142; 2 Samuel, 210–12; 2 Kings, 206; Job, 24; Psalms, 24, 151, 191, 209, 210; Proverbs, 151; Isaiah, 211; Ezekiel, 146; Daniel, 234; Joel, 210; Matthew, 24, 33, 117, 138, 143,180, 190, 210; Mark, 196, 202; Luke, 24, 143, 181, 204, 208, 211; John, 35, 139–40; Acts, 140, 209; Romans, 167, 209; 1 Corinthians, 95, 196, 199, 233; Galatians, 26, 154; 1 Thessalonians, 206; Hebrews, 81; 1 Peter, 196; Revelation, 43, 89–91, 148, 150, 196, 206
 see also biblical; Christianity
biblical: allusion during the Preston strike, 180; figures, 140; names, 35, 125; nursery tale, 53; phraseology, 25, 81, 117, 139–40, 143, 145, 149, 167, 179, 189, 191, 193–5, 201, 203, 206, 233; scriptural stance on divorce, 135–6
Bidder, George Parker, 39, 152
bigamy and bigamists, 131, 134, 136
'Billy Button': possible origin of name, 66; see also circus: circus acts
birds: grouse, 206; partridge, 206; peacocks (feathers), 92; pheasant, 206; see also animals
Birkbeck, George, 116–17
Birkbeck schools, 31, 38–9, 52, 116–17; see also education; political economy; mechanics' institutes
Birmingham, 5, 50, 54, 191, 207, 233; and Coketown, 78; Dickens's description of, 55; hardware, 55; hucksters' shops in, 74; Polytechnic Institution, 24–5
Birmingham and Midland Institute, 222
Bitzer: characterization of, 7, 38–40; and Malthusian population theory, 7, 164
Black Country, 5, 78
Black Forest, 197
Blackfriars Road, 91
blacklegs ('knobsticks'), 181, 186
Blackpool, Stephen: age of, 124; biblical allusion, 140; and child labour, 183; and Dickens's marriage, 130, 142; and Frederick

Dickens, 130; and Lancashire dialect, 126; and mesmerism, 142–3; and 'Sharpening the Scythe', 5–6, 220, 224
Blackwood's Magazine, 192
Bleak House, 1–2, 28, 40, 71, 72, 75, 78, 105, 106, 113, 139, 147, 190, 214, 233
Blue Beard, 147
blue books, 86, 118, 147, 167, 168
Board of Trade, 43, 83
Bolton, 55, 79
book clubs, 111
Book of Common Prayer, 7; Burial Service, 203; Catechism, 117; Evening Prayer, 84, 146; Litany, 135; Morning Prayer, 84, 146, 211; Solemnization of Matrimony, 69, 97, 132
Botany Bay, 185
Boucicault, Dion, *The Long Strike*, 78
Boulogne, 24–5, 193
Bounderby, Josiah: and Bulwer's Mr Bluff, 73; characterization of, 72–3; and Thomas Miller, Jnr, 73; and self-help theory, 71–2
boxing and wrestling, 43, 88, 216, 228; Lancashire wrestling, 214; see also popular entertainment; sports
Bradbury & Evans, publishers, 1–2
Bradford, 55
Brentford, 64–6
breweries, 205
Bridges, Anthony, 226
Bridges, John, 226
British Army Board of General Officers, 36
'British brandy', 228
British Constitution, 106
British Museum, 108
British national anthem, 106–7
British nationalism, 106
Broadstairs, Albion Hotel, 165
Brontë, Charlotte, *Shirley*, 162
Brook Field fair, 109
Brooklyn circus, 229
'Brothers Siegrist', 98
Broughton, Jack, 42
brushes and brooms, 57
Brutus, Lucius Junius, 183, 225
Buchan, William, *Complete Domestic Medicine*, 42
Buckland, Rev. William, Dean of Westminster, 224
Buckle, Henry Thomas, *History of Civilization in England*, 35, 233; Dickens' description of, 35
Bull, Dr John, 107
Bull Inn and Royal Hotel, 91; gallery of, 215
Bulwer, Sir Edward Lytton, *England and the English*, 25, 34, 42, 73
Bunyan, John, *Pilgrim's Progress*, 116, 219
Burchett, Richard, 44

burial clubs, 127–8
burial grounds, 127
Burke, James, 42
Burke, William, 142
Burke's *Peerage*, 105
Burlington arcade, 108
Burnley, 158
Bury, 79
butter, 87
Byron, George Gordon, 6th Baron: *Marino Faliero*, 205; *Mazeppa*, 230; *Two Foscari*, 205

Calais, 106, 193
'calculating boys', 38–40
calculating machines, 40
Cambridge, 193
Campbell, Lord John, 136–7
candles, 92
Capon, William, *Astley's Riding School*, 228
Carey, Henry, 107
Carlyle, Thomas, 22–3, 147; 'Characteristics', 22; Chartism, 22, 84, 127, 147, 186–7; *Critical and Miscellaneous Essays*, 75; *French Revolution*, 22; *Latter-Day Pamphlets*, 22, 196, 202; *Past and Present*, 22, 25, 70, 73, 148, 167; *Sartor Resartus*, 22, 30, 197; 'Signs of the Times', 22
carpets, designs of, 44–5
Cartwright, Edmund, 124
Castlereagh, Robert Stewart, 2nd Viscount, 180
Central Committee of the Preston power-loom weavers, 180, 181
Chadwick, Edwin, *Report on the Sanitary Condition of the Labouring Population*, 79
Chalk Farm fair, 88
champagne, 151
Champs Élysées, 98
Chancery Court, 233
Chancery Lane, 116
chandler's shops, 74
characterization in HT, *see under individual characters*
Charing Cross Road, 74
Charles II, 148
Charles II Street, 108
chartists and chartism, 116, 162, 172, 179, 186
Chatham, 92, 222
Chelsea, 22
chemical processes, 113
Chesterfield, 4th Earl of, *see* Stanhope, Philip Dormer, 4th Earl of Chesterfield
Cheyne Row, 24
chicory, 87
child labour, 154, 183, 185
Childers, E. W. B.: appearance, 93; name, 93

Childers, Colonel Leonard, 93
children: child labour, 154, 183, 185; Children Employment Commission (1843), 147; in circuses, 93, 97–8; cruelty to, 121, 183; custody of, 132–3; and factory schools, 154; in factories, 154, 183; illegitimacy, 134; Infant Custody Act (1839), 133; infant mortality, 123, 127; *see also* education
Child's History of England, A, 1, 214
Chimes, The, 22, 35, 72, 147, 164
Christianity: church attendance, 82, 84, 86; lack of faith, 70; Lord's Day Observance Society, 85; political economy and, 6–7; religious worship, 84; sanctity and indissolubility of marriage, 134–6; see also Church of England; nonconformists; Roman Catholic Church; sabbatarianism
Christmas Carol, A, 222
Church of England: Church Calendar, 32; 'Church and State', 107; 'Commissioners' Churches', 82; ecclesiastical courts, 131, 132, 134, 136, 137; Lord's Day Observance Society, 85; marriage and divorce, 131–2; pew rent system, 84; and religious instruction, 28; and religious worship, 84; *see also* Christianity; nonconformists; Roman Catholic Church; sabbatarianism
churches: Old Lambeth church, 103; St Giles's, 74; St Paul's cathedral, 137; St Peter's, Preston, 82
circulating libraries, 110
circus, 5, 6, 9–10, 88, 91–3
 accidents and injuries, 58, 89
 acrobats and equilibrists: Jean-Baptiste Auriol, 100, (illus.) 101; Juan Bellinck, 64; Brothers Siegrist', 98; 'Herr Diavolo Buffo', 62; Lee Lavater, 98; Louisa Woolford, 60, 97–8
 admission, 68
 'blacking-up', 231
 buildings, 58
 clowns: Jean-Baptiste Auriol, 100, (illus.) 101; Tom Barry, 62, 92, (illus.) 65; costumes, 92; John Ducrow, 62, 104; Joseph Grimaldi, 62; Charles Marsh, 64; 'performing chair', 230; W. F. Wallett, 64, 89, 92, 95, 96, 102–3, 229
 cruelty to: animals in, 62, 121; children in, 121
 dual nature of, 92
 eating fruit in, 92
 equestrians: Philip Astley, 36, 66, 68, 91, 98, 229; Anthony Bridges, 226; John Bridges, 226; Jack Clarke, 103; Andrew Ducrow, 62, 91, 93, 97, 121, 228; 'Mademoiselle Ella', 60, (illus.) 61; Adah Isaac Menken, 230; Eaton Stone, 93; Tourniaire, 92; Louisa Woolford, 60, 97–8
 Italianizing names, 62
 lighting in, 92
 matinées, 226
 parades, 100
 performers: apprenticeships of, 97–8; characteristics of, 102; children, 93, 97–8; earnings of, 102; formal education and, 97–8, 102; immodesty of, 9, 100; off-stage dress of, 100–2; pantaloon, 231; 'tip-toppers', 102
 playbills, 60, 64, 108, (illus.) 63
 props, 229
 slang, 96, 237–40
 titles of acts: 'Billy Button's Ride to Brentford', 62, 66, (illus.) 67; 'Bouquet de L'Amour', 93; 'Children in the Wood', 93, 229; 'Dog of the Château', 62; 'Dog of Montargis', 62; 'Dog of the Pyrenees', 62; 'Egyptian Pyramids', 98; 'Emperor of Japan', 226; 'Flower Girl', 58–60; 'Flying Mercury', 93; 'Harlequin Tam O'Shanter', 62; 'Indian of the Far West or the Wild Horse of the Prairie', 93; 'Jack the Giant Killer', 229; 'Jockeis anglais, aux courses de Newmarket', 92; 'Juggler of Japan', 226; 'Jupiter's Decree and the Fall of Phaeton', 93; 'à la Perche', 98, (illus.) 99; 'Rosière', 58–60; 'Tyrolean Shepherd and Swiss Milk Maid', 60, (illus.) 59; 'Wild Indian Hunter', 93, (illus.) 94
 trainers: animal, 62, 104, 121
 travelling, 58, 93
 treatment for bruises 89
circuses: Amphithéâtre Astley, 229; Amphithéâtre Franconi, 229; Batty's, 64, 89; Brooklyn, 229; Cirque D'Été, 2268; Cirque D'Hiver, 229; Cirque Olympique, 229; Holloway's Amphitheatre, 89; Royal, 62, 91; Wallett's, Kidderminster, 95; *see also* Astley's Royal Amphitheatre; popular entertainment; sports
Cirque D'Été, 229
Cirque D'Hiver, 229
Cirque Olympique, 229
Clarke, Jack: Sleary's characterization, 103
classical allusions: Horae, 152; Ladon, 160, 211; lares and penates, 168; Lernean hydra, 52; Medusa, 191; Oedipus, 226–7; Pegasus 91; *see also* gods and goddesses
Clausius, Rudolf, 'heat death', 188
Clay, Rev. John, 86–7
clocks: 'Dutch', 197
clogs, 125
coal-mining: blue books about, 147; colliery

explosions, 221; Davy's safety lamp, 221; mine owners, 222; pits and shafts, 191, 220; safety in mines, 220–1
coats of arms, 91, 105, 106
Cocker, Edward, *Cocker's Arithmetic*, 113
coffee, 87, 151
Coke, Sir Edward, 107
Coketown, 6, 55, 149–50; creation of, 77–9
Colburn, Zerah, 39
Cole, Henry, 43, 45; characterization of 'third gentleman', 41–2, 43, 45, 46
Coleridge, Samuel Taylor: 'Devil's Thoughts', 713; *Rime of the Ancient Mariner*, 225
Collier, John ('Tim Bobbin'), *A View of the Lancashire Dialect*, 126; glossary of Lancashire dialect words 235–6
Collins, Wilkie: *Frozen Deep*, 226; *Hide and Seek*, 104
Colman the Elder, George, *The Deuce Is in Him*, 192
Combination Acts: (1799), 161; (1800), 161
Combination of Workmen Act (1825), 161
combinations, *see* trade unionism
comic books, 108–9
Committee of Council, *see* Committee of the Privy Council on Education
Committee of the Privy Council on Education, 28, 36, 42, 44, 49; *see also* education
composition of *HT*, 77–8, 103–4, 109: Agreement for, 1–2; cancelled passage in, 5, 143, 185; characterization revisions: 'third gentleman' 41–2, 43, 45, 46; Forster's review of, 5; one-volume edition, 9, 19, 23, 24, 45, 203; and the Preston strike, 78, 182; serialization within *HW*, 1–11, 132, 135; time-scheme, 130; titles of books, 8, 24; *see also All the Year Round*; Coketown; Dickens, Charles: autobiographical elements in *HT*; *Household Words*; Lancashire dialect; titles of *HT*
Congreve, William, *The Way of the World*, 140
contagion: theories of, 56
Cooke, William, 66, 226, 228
cookery books, 198
Cooper, Anthony Ashley, 7th Earl of Shaftesbury, Lord Ashley, 221
Copley, John Singleton, the younger, 1st Baron Lyndhurst, 133
Cornet of Dragoons, 167
cosmetics, 95, 231
costume and appearance
  clothing
    clogs, 125
    coats: Newmarket, 92; sealskin, 102
    gloves, 76
    handkerchiefs: belcher, 97
    jackets: barragon, 125
    mittens, 76, 200
    caps: night, 91–2; tasselled, 91–2
    vests: velvet, 102
  eye-glasses: monocles, 211
  hair
    peacocks' feathers in, 91
    pigtails, 91
  jewellery: chains, 102
cotton industry
  carding, 165, 185
  cotton pod, 88
  'Cottonopolis' (Manchester), 78
  factories: accidents in, 5, 118, 143–5, 222, 241; bells, 125; blue books about, 147; children in, 154, 183; description of, 81; environment of, 159; gas lighting in, 125; library collections in, 110; Horrockses & Miller, 73, 81; inspectors, 129, 154, 158, 183, 220; insurance premiums for, 124; night work, 124; Swainson & Birley, 81, (illus.) 80
  hours of work, 111
  occupational diseases, 159, 165
  operatives, 6, 78, 81, 88, 124, 137, 158, 171, 172, 174, 175, 180, 181; age of 123, 125
  piece-work and piece-rate lists, 138, 162
  power-loom weaving, 124
  process of cotton manufacture, 79–81, 165, 185
  results of cotton manufacture, 81
  see also factory safety; industrialization; industrial processes; industrial relations; manufacturers and merchants; Preston strike and lock-out; spinners and spinning; trade unionism; weavers and weaving
courts: Chancery, 233; civil, 131, 132, 135, 137; Doctors' Commons, 137; ecclesiastical, 131, 132, 134, 136, 137; Insolvent Debtors', 106
Coutts, Angela Burdett, 1, 78, 182; *Summary Account of Prizes for Common Things*, 50; Urania Cottage, 109
Covent Garden: opera house and theatre, 108; market, 193
Coventry, 184
coverture, 133, 151
Cowell, George, 117–18, 171, 179, 186, (illus.) 178
Cranworth, Lord, *see* Rolfe, Robert Monsey, Baron Cranworth
Crimean War, 202
crossing-sweepers, 107
cruelty: to animals, 62, 121; to children, 121, 183; marital, 131, 134, 135

Cruikshank, George, 52, 54
Crystal Palace, 217; as 'fairy palace', 125; see also Great Exhibition
Cunningham, Peter, 182

Dante, 53
Davenport, Jean Margaret, 95
David Copperfield, 28, 40, 91, 106, 192, 197
Davy, Sir Humphry, 221
Dawes, Rev. Richard, 231; *Suggestive Hints*, 38, 75
de la Rue, Augusta, 143
De Quincey, Thomas, 86
deal boards, 68
death-rates, 83, 124; infant mortality, 123, 127
Debrett's *Peerage*, 105
Debtors Act (1869), 106
Defoe, Daniel: *Moll Flanders*, 111, 116; *Robinson Crusoe*, 111, 113, 207
Dejean, Louis, 229
Department of Practical Art: aims of, 43–4: and Henry Cole, 40; becomes Department of Science and Art, 43; James Kay-Shuttleworth and, 34; and national education, 41, 43; principles satirized, 43; and Utilitarianism, 41; visiting art master from, 41, 43; and the laws of colour, 46; see also education; Marlborough House
Department of Science and Art, see Department of Practical Art
depression, 69–70, 86, 113; see also diseases; Victorian perceptions of; women
desertion: marital, 131, 134
Dewhurst, circus clown, 64
dialect: Lancashire, 126, 131, 235–6
Dick, William, 37
Dickens, Anna Weller, 130
Dickens, Catherine, 130, 134, 142
Dickens, Charles
 attitudes towards: agitators, 179; Birmingham, 55, 78; charity schools, 28; Lord Chesterfield, 189; design reformers, 44; Doctors' Commons, 137; dreams, 141, 142; education, 25, 31, 40, 43–4, 49–51, 216; electric telegraph, 206–7; employment and safety in mines, 221; factory safety, 5, 143–5, 158; fairy tales, 52; fee-paying schools, 232; funeral practices, 127; genealogy, 105; girls' education, 50–1; government, 233; homeless and fallen women, 108; industrial relations, 83, 182, 187, 223; industrialization, 4, 78, 128, 145; James Kay-Shuttleworth, 34, 50; laissez-faire, 127; learning by rote, 40; libraries, 110; marriage laws, 8–9, 132, 136; mechanics' institutes, 111; mechanization, 10; phrenology, 31–2; political economy, 4, 6–7, 117, 145, 147; Preston, 217; Preston Masters' Association and lock-out, 163; Preston strikers, 174, 185; ragged school movement, 28; rail travel, 54, 190; railway construction, 190–1; railway engine drivers, 54; recreations and popular entertainment, 85, 88, 121; Sabbatarianism, 85; sanitary reform and sanitation, 25, 79, 179; savages, 6, 79; self-help, 72; self-made industrialists, 72; 'separate system', 87; social division, 222; social engineering, 44, 116, 164; statistics, 83, 129, 147; Stow's 'training system', 47; strikes, 182, 223; temperance movement, 85; trade unionism 161, 162, 163; Utilitarian educationalists, 35; women's legal inequalities, 8–9, 134–5; working-class initiatives 179
 autobiographical elements in HT
 blacking bottles, 193
 Fanny Dickens and starlight, 222
 Dickens's marriage: time of, 130, 142; unhappiness of, 130
 homes, see Boulogne; Chatham; Tavistock House
 knowledge and experience: Birmingham, 78; Calais, 106; church architecture, 82–3; circus acts, 9; circus slang, 96; circus techniques, 226; dream theories, 140–2; editing, 3–5; engineers' strike, 175; exploitation of workers, 147; factory safety legislation, 5, 143–5; industrial life, 77–8, 182; Insolvent Debtors' Court, 106; Lancashire dialect, 126, 131; legal procedure for divorce, 136–7; Lyons, 152–3; Manchester, 77–8; marital breakdown, 130; mesmerism 142–3; patent law, 41; phrenology, 31–2, 39; Preston strike, 175, 182; Preston Temperance Hall, 6, 174; shower-baths, 165; striking, 182; weekly serialization 2–4
 relationships: Charles Babbage, 40; William Bradbury, 1–2; Thomas Carlyle, 22–3; Rev. John Clay, 86–7; Henry Cole, 41–2, 45; Wilkie Collins, 104; William Cooke, 226; Angela Burdett Coutts, 1–2, 50, 78, 108, 182; George Cruikshank, 52; Peter Cunningham, 182; Augusta de la Rue, 143; Anna Weller Dickens, 130; Catherine Dickens, 130, 133–4, 142; Charles Dickens, Jnr, 229; Edward Bulwer Lytton ('Plorn') Dickens, 1; Fanny Dickens, 222; Frederick Dickens, 130; Henry Fielding Dickens, 54; John Dickens, 105, 193;

Index

Alfred, Count D'Orsay, 153; Dr John Elliotson, 32, 142–3; Frederick Mullett Evans, 1–2; Michael Faraday, 224; Charles Fechter, 78; Annie Fields, 226; Percy Fitzgerald, 4; John Forster, 1, 2, 4, 6, 19, 22, 35, 53, 68, 182, 215, 217; Elizabeth Gaskell, 184; Sir James Kay-Shuttleworth, 34; Austen Henry Layard, 202–3; Mark Lemon, 91, 96, 207; Eliza Lynn, 8–9; Harriet Martineau, 4, 145–6, 155; Henry Morley, 8, 145; Sir Richard Owen, 53; George Augustus Sala, 35; Clarkson Stanfield, 192; Dr Thomas Stone, 141; Serjeant Thomas Noon Talfourd, 133, 223; Nelly Ternan, 149; W. H. Wills, 1, 3, 7, 49, 144
  visit to Preston 6, 58, 78, 91, 118, 159, 174, 177–8, 182, 198, 215, 217; and strike article, 6, 47, 58, 83, 145, 163, 171, 172–3, 177, 179, 180, 181, 185, 187, 217, 223
  writings, see under individual titles
Dickens, Charles, Jnr, 229
Dickens, Edward Bulwer Lytton, 'Plorn', 1
Dickens, Fanny, 222
Dickens, Frederick, 130–1
Dickens, Henry Fielding, 55
Dickens, John, 105
disease: asthma, 42; carder's cough, 165; colds, 42, 86; coughs, 42, 86, 165; depressive illness, 69–70, 86; diarrhoea, 86; emphysema, 165; epilepsy, 142; fever, 83; haemorrhage, 42; headaches, 86, 150; hypochondria, 42, 69; insomnia, 86; jaundice, 113; mulespinner's cancer, 159; rheumatic complaints, 42, 86; sepsis, 83; skin disorders, 42, 140; syphilis, 140; theories of contagion 56
Disraeli, Benjamin, *Sybil*, 162
divorce, *see* marriage and divorce
Divorce Act (1857), 131, 132, 133, 136
Doctors' Commons, 137
Dodd, George, 81
Dodd's *Dictionary of Manufactures*, 55
dogs: animal communication, 9, 232; cruelty to, 62, 121; performing, 9, 62–4, 91, 104, 119, 121, (illus.) 120; training of, 62, 104; *see also* animals; circus: circus acts
Dombey and Son, 2, 28, 35, 36, 40, 47, 78, 96–7, 103, 188, 191, 192
domestic science, in schools, 50
domestic servants: housekeepers, 106; housemaids, 57, 160
dormice, 10, 122
D'Orsay, Alfred, Count, 153
dream theories, 140–2
dreams, 141, 142, 222

drinks: adulteration of, 47; beer, 86, 205, 231; bitters, 103; 'British brandy', 228; champagne, 151, 152; coffee, 87, 151; cordials, 221; gin, 88–9; India Pale Ale, 205; negus, 198; port, 152, 198, 205; punch, 129; rum (hot spiced), 216; sherry, 103, 152, 198; tea, 151; whiskey, 221; wine, 198; *see also* alcohol; drunkenness; gin-palaces; temperance movement
drugs, 47; opium 86
drunkenness, 86, 88; *see also* alcohol; drinks; gin-palaces; temperance movement
Drury Lane Theatre, 60, 92, 93, 98, 230; 'Lottery Ticket', 108
Ducrow, Andrew, 62, 91, 92, 98, 121, 228; 'Swiss Maid and Tyrolean Shepherd', 60, (illus.) 59; 'Wild Indian Hunter', (illus.) 94
Ducrow, John, 62, 91, 104
Ducrow, Peter, 121
dust-heaps, 201–2; contents and use of, 201–2; parliament as, 201–2
dustmen: Members of Parliament as, 208
Dutch clocks, 197
Duthie, William, 183
dwarfs, 109

Earp, George B., *The Gold Colonies of Australia*, 200
East India Company, 205
Edinburgh Veterinary School, 37
education, 5, 34–5, 47
  adult, 50, 110, 116
  blue books about, 147
  Henry Cole and, 41–2
  Committee of Council, 28, 30, 36, 44
  Department of Practical Art, 41–2, 43–4
  Department of Science and Art, 43–4
  Dickens's attitude towards, 26–7, 28, 31, 39–40, 43–4, 49–51, 216, 232
  educationalists: Andrew Bell, 25; William Ellis, 7, 38, 52, 116–17, 119, 164; Friedrich Froebel, 48; Sir James Kay-Shuttleworth, 25–8, 30, 34, 48, 50, 116, (illus.) 29; Joseph Lancaster, 25, 30; Elizabeth and Charles Mayo, 37, 48; Johann Pestalozzi, 37, 48; Johann and Bertha Ronge, 48; David Stow, 30, 46, 47, 48; Samuel Wilderspin, 28–30, 40–1
  establishment of elementary education, 25–30
  examinations: in art, 42; on Euclid, 113; for pupil-teachers, 30, 48, 49; subjects 49, 51
  of girls, 49, 50
  political economy in schools, 7, 38, 52, 116, 118–19, 164
  school buildings and classrooms: early Birkbeck schools, 31; lay-out of classrooms,

31, 36; slates as writing material, 77; standard of 30
school inspectors, 42, 116, 232; annual teaching examinations and, 48; criticism of training colleges, 51; establishment of, 28; Rev. Henry Moseley, 37–8, 51
schoolchildren: class size, 31, 36; factory children, 154, 183; monitorial system and, 27, 36; numbering of, 36
schools and colleges: Battersea Training College, 28, 48; Birkbeck schools, 31, 38–9, 52, 116–17; British and Foreign, 116; charity, 28; Glasgow Normal Seminary, 30, 46, 48; infant, 28; Manchester Lancasterian, 36; model, 28, 31, 52; monitorial, 25; Moravian 31; Normal, 28, 52; Norwood, 28; Orphan and Normal (Switzerland), 48; Padiham 34; ragged, 28; Rugby, 123; self-supporting, 232; Schools of Art, 45; Wellington House Academy, 190; Westminster, 193; Wood's Sessional, 30, 46, 48; workhouse, 30
standard of instruction, 25
teachers and teaching, 48, 49–51, 75, 116; 'common things', 30, 38, 50, 232; Queen's Scholars (pupil-teacher system), 25, 30, 49, 113; science, 44; standard of, 30, 52; visiting art masters, 41, 43
teaching methods, 48, 49–51; etymological memorizing, 40; gallery system, 30, 47; latinate and scientific definitions, 37–8, 40–1; learning by rote, 37, 39; monitorial system, 25, 30, 36; object lessons, 7, 37–8, 48, 116; Pestalozzian system, 48; 'progressive lessons', 7, 116, 118, 164
textbooks and manuals, 7, 37–8, 42, 44–5, 47, 69, 111, 116, 163
see also libraries; mechanics' institutes
Edwards, Edward, 110
electric telegraph, 206–7
Electric Telegraph Company, 206
electricity: galvanic, 36; static, 35–6; telegraph wires, 206–7
elephants, 6, 44, 79
elevators, *see* lifts
Elliotson, Dr John, 32, 142–3; *Human Physiology*, 141
Ellis, William, (illus.) 112; Birkbeck schools, 31, 52, 116–17; and Lloyd's, 119; 'progressive lessons' in social economy, 7, 38, 116–17, 119, 164; *see also* education; political economy
emblematic figures: dormice, 122; Graces, 166; Horae, 152; Wild Man, 52; *see also* gods and goddesses
Engels, Friedrich, 55, 79, 125

engineers' strike, 162, 175, 179, 181
ennui, *see* depression
Euclid, 113
Eumenides, 206
Examiner, The, 5; 'Demoralisation and Total Abstinence', 85
excavations: coal-mining, 191, 220; Layard's Mesopotamian, 202–3; scythe-stone cutting, 5–6, 224; *see also* coal-mining; accidents
excise-rod, 210
excursion trains, 219
exhibitions: cabinets, 57; Great Exhibition, 43, 44, 125, 217; of ornamental art, 44, 46; *see also* Marlborough House; museums

factories, *see* cotton industry
Factory Acts: (1819), 183; (1833), 183; (1844), 144, 154, 183; (1847), 88, 111; (1853), 111
factory safety, 5, 118, 144–5, 155–7, 159, 166, 185, 220; *see also* accidents; coal-mining; cotton industry; industrial relations; manufacturers and merchants
fairs: booths at, 92; Brook Field, 109; Chalk Farm, 88; and holidays, 130; London, 102; performers at, 228; during public hangings, 88
Falconer, William, *An Universal Dictionary of the Marine*, 200
Falier, Marin, 205
Faraday, Michael, 224
farriers, *see* veterinary surgeons
Fechter, Charles, 78
Field, Charles, 75
Fielding, Henry: *Jonathan Wild*, 116; *Tom Jones*, 116; *Tom Thumb*, 54
Fields, Annie, 226
fireworks: displays, 79; types of, 216
fish: torpedo fish, 36
Fitzgerald, Percy, 4
flowers: in carpet designs, 45; vegetables grown with, 192
'Flying Childers, The', 93
food: adulteration of, 47; beef, 198; butter, 87; chicory, 87; coffee, 87, 189; cookery books, 198; mutton, 198; oranges, 92; pineapples, 44; sausages (polonies and saveloys), 169; steak 129; storage (meat-safe), 200; sugar, 189; sweetbreads (lamb and veal), 151; tea, 151, 189; turtle soup, 130; venison, 130; walnut ketchup, 205
Foote, Samuel, *The Maid of Bath*, 66
Forster, John, 1, 2, 5, 6, 19, 22, 35, 53, 64, 68, 182, 215, 222
Foscari, Francesco, 205
Fowler, Lorenzo Niles, 32
fox-hunting, 206

Franconi, Adolphe, 229
Franconi, Antonio, 229
Frankfurt, 188
French Revolutionary Wars, 124, 129, 161, 229
friendly societies, 161
Friendly Societies Act (1793), 161
Froebel, Friedrich, 48
fruit
  oranges, 92
  pineapples: on wallpaper, 44; in carpet designs, 44
fugleman, 183
funerals: and black ladders, 127; burial clubs, 127–8; Dickens's attitude towards, 127; dying request, 104; practices, 127; processions, 6; wakes, 130; working-class, 127
furnishings: carpets, 44; 'Dutch' clocks, 197; floor-cloth, 76; wallpaper, 44
furniture: truckle bed, 160; mechanized wood-turning of, 10, 49

Galvani, Luigi, 36
galvanism, 36
gambling: betting shops, 88; casinos, 86; and factory workers, 87; horse races, 88; lotteries, 108
games: backgammon, 198; *see also* circus; popular entertainment; sports
gas
  for cooking, 56
  lighting, 56, 108; for circuses, 118; in factories, 125
gases, 224; fire-damp, 221
Gaskell, Elizabeth: and Lancashire dialect, 126; *Mary Barton*, 126, 143, 162; *North and South*, 73, 109, 126, 155, 165, 170, 184; *Ruth*, 35, 56
Gaskell, Rev. William, *Two Lectures on the Lancashire Dialect*, 126, 131
genealogy, 104–5
General Association of Power Loom Weavers of Great Britain and Ireland, 175
Genoa, 143
giants, 109, 202, 229; Giant's Staircase, 204; 'Jack the Giant Killer', 229
gin-palaces, 85, 89
Glasgow, 55, 79, 206; cotton spinners' strike, 186; Educational Society, 30; Normal Seminary, 30, 47, 48
Gloucester Crescent, 133–4
gloves, 76
gods and goddesses: Furies, 206; Graces, 166; Harpocrates, 204; household gods, 168; Mars, 204; Muses, 91; Neptune, 204; Venus, 204, 217; *see also* classical allusions; emblematic figures

Goethe, Johann Wolfgang von, *Faust*, 169
Goldsmith, Oliver: *Bee*, 2; *Deserted Village*, 107; *Vicar of Wakefield*, 113
government, 107, 161, 196, 210, 221, 229
  Board of Trade, 43, 83
  Dickens's attitude towards, 233
  Home Office, 158
  Home Secretary (Palmerston), 158, 175, 186, 220
  Public Record Office, 41, 105
  state grants for: Anglican churches, 82; pupil-teacher system, 30
  see also blue books; Department of Practical Art; education; House of Commons; House of Lords; Parliament
Gradgrind, Louisa: characterization of, 10; choice of name, 60, 68; and depression, 69–70; and marital breakdown, 148
Gradgrind, Mrs: and married women's property law, 75; resemblance to a dormouse, 10, 122; Victorian invalid wife, 74
Gradgrind, Thomas: characterization of, 25, 33–5; and James Kay-Shuttleworth, 33–5; and phrenology, 31–2
Gradgrind, Tom, 146, 231
Grammar of Ornament, The, 45
Great Eastern railway: Welwyn Viaduct, 139
Great Exhibition, 43, 45, 125, 217; *see also* Crystal Palace; exhibitions; museums
Great Expectations, 10, 72, 197
Great Harwood, 177
Great Western Railway, 125, 219
Greek islands, 208
Greenwich, 148
Grey Horse and Seven Stars, 91
griffins, 160, 211
Grimaldi, Joseph, 62; *Memoirs*, 50
Grimshaw, Mortimer, 6–7, 171, 172, 186, 218, (illus.) 176; model for Slackbridge, 171, 177–8
grouse, 206
Grundy, Mrs, 71
guidebooks, 55
guilds, 161; *see also* trade unionism
gypsies, *see* beggars and vagrants

hair: and female sexuality, 199; pigtail, 92; *see also* barbers; hairdressers
hairdressers and hairdressers' shops, 77
Hall, Thomas, 136
hard labour, 134, 136, 197
Hard Times, *see* *All the Year Round*; Coketown; composition of *HT*; Dickens, Charles: autobiographical elements in *HT*; *Household Words*; Lancashire dialect; titles of *HT*
hardware, description of, 55

Hardwick, Charles, 58, 155, 177
Harthouse, James, 167
Harvey, William, 231
Haymarket, 108
Helps, Arthur, 25
Henry VIII, 193
Her Majesty's Theatre: Italian Opera House, 108; Royal Opera Arcade, 108
Hercules, 53
'Hercules Hall', 100
Hogarth, Georgina, 104
Hogarth, William: *Harlot's Progress*, 116; *Rake's Progress*, 116
Holborn, 117
holidays, 87–8, 130; public, 88, 130
Holloway's Amphitheatre, 89
Holy Innocents' Day, 33
Holy Inquisition, 214
Home and Colonial Infant School Society, 48
Homer: *Iliad*, 152; *Odyssey*, 152
Horne, Richard H., 81, 232
Horner, Leonard, 128, 154
Horrockses & Miller, 73, 81
horse-breaker, *see* horses
horse slaughterhouse, 169
horses: breaker, 36; embrocation for, 89; farriery, 36–7; 'Flying Childers', 93; 'Horse of Knowledge', 228; 'Little Military Learned Horse', 228; stencilled, 226; *see also* animals; circus: circus acts; equestrians
hospitals: lying-in, 83
hotels: Albion, Broadstairs, 165; Bull and Royal Hotel, Preston, 91, 215
house construction: 'back-to-backs', 81; damp-proof course, 73; *see also* architecture; housing and housing conditions; red bricks
House of Commons, 66, 136, 202; Anglo-Japanese affairs, 226; MPs, 166, 208
House of Correction, 68; at Preston, 68, 86
House of Lords, 132, 136, 166
Household Narrative of Current Events, 148, 166
Household Words: articles for working class, 4; articles relevant to topics in HT, 241–3; circulation during serialization of HT in, 3; Dickens's literary and social vision, 3–4; Dickens's use of articles in, 5–10; Dickens's views about popular amusements, 88; factory safety and, 144–5; flagging sales of, 1; footnotes in, 143, 221; interdependency of HT and, 4–5, 132, 135; middle-class readership, 4; proposed titles for, 3–4, 217; serialization of HT in, 1–11, 132, 135; success of, 4; *see also* All the Year Round; composition of HT; *Household Narrative of Current Events*. Complete information on all HW articles cited is given in the Select Bibliography
housemaids, 57, 160
housekeepers, 106
housing and housing conditions: alienation, 84; 'back-to-backs', 81; of bankers, 55; of manufacturers and merchants, 55; slums, 56, 123, 159; ventilation, 56, 122, 159; *see also* architecture; gas; house construction; plumbing; sanitary reform and sanitation; water-systems
hucksters' shops, 74
Hughes, Charles, 228
Hunt, Robert, *The Poetry of Science*, 44
hurdles, 220

illegitimacy, 134
Illustrated London News, The, 66, 92, 174
imagery: of cultivation and growth, 7–8, 24, 116, 180, 208; hair, 198; industrial, 5, 79, 149–50; nautical, 200; and the railway, 79; savages, 6, 79; serpents, 6, 79, 191; Shakespearian, 159
imperial weights and measures, 32, 214
incest: grounds for divorce, 131–2, 135–6
Indemnity Mutual Marine Assurance Company (Lloyd's), 119
industrial diseases: carder's cough, 165; emphysema, 165; mulespinner's cancer, 159; *see also* disease; medicine
industrial processes: books about, 110; carding, 165, 185; chemical manufacture, 6, 79; dyeing, 170; Tom Gradgrind likened to, 145; Harriet Martineau's HW articles about, 146; mechanized cotton manufacture, 81; mechanized wood-turning, 10, 49; water pollution and, 79, 170
industrial relations: Dickens's attitude towards, 83, 182, 187, 223; factory safety legislation and, 144–5, 158, 185; Preston Masters' Association, 158, 162, 187; during the Preston strike, 83, 145, 158, 162, 187; trade unions and, 161; *see also* manufacturers and merchants; Preston strike and lock-out; trade unionism
industrialization, 5, 7, 78; Dickens's attitude towards, 5, 78, 129, 145; housing conditions, 55, 56–7, 81, 122–3; life expectancy, 124, 150; population growth, 81, 82, 131; red bricks, 58, 83; steam power, 128; *see also* cotton industry; Factory Acts; industrial processes; industrial diseases; mechanization; working class
Infant Custody Act (1839), 133
infant mortality, 123, 127
'infant phenomenon', 95

Infant School Society, 30
inns, *see* public houses
insects: butterflies, 46
Insolvent Debtors' Court, 106, 192
insurance: Lloyd's, 119; premiums for mills, 124
Irk River, 79
Italian Opera House, 108
Italy, 1; Genoa, 143; Venice, 205; Vesuvius 203

jails, *see* hard labour; House of Correction; prisons; transportation
Jacquard, Joseph-Marie, 152–3
Japan, 226
jaundice, 113
Jews: money-lenders, 105
Jones, Ernest: Labour Parliament, 172, 179
Jones, Owen, 44–5
Jupe, Cecilia (Sissy): alternative Christian names, 45–6; and Wilkie Collins's Hide and Seek, 104
Jupe, Signor: clowns' costumes, 92; Italianizing English names, 62; possible models for, 62

Kalmucks, 149
Kay, James Phillips, *see* Kay-Shuttleworth, Sir James Phillips
Kay-Shuttleworth, Sir James Phillips, (illus.) 29; Battersea training college, 48, 50; and Dickens, 34; approach to education, 34; 'Educational Grand Tours', 25–9; and Gradgrind's characterization, 34; and the Jacquard loom, 152–3; and mechanization, 81; *Moral and Physical Condition of the Working Classes*, 81, 165; and Pestalozzian methods, 48; and political economy, 34–5, 116; criticism of the Preston strike, 34; pupil-teacher scholarships, 25, 30; teaching methods, 48; visits Whitelands College, 50; *see also* education; political economy; Utilitarianism
Keats, John, *Endymion*, 210
Kensington Court, 57
Kidderminster, Worcestershire, 96
kindergarten movement, 48
King's Scholars, 193
Kingsley, Charles, *Alton Locke*, 162
Knight, Charles, 122–3

Labour Parliament, 172
Ladon, 160, 211
laissez-faire, 22, 33, 47, 52, 71, 77, 84, 110, 118, 127, 161, 163; Dickens's attitude towards, 126, 127; *see also* political economists; political economy; Utilitarianism
Lamb, William, 2nd Viscount Melbourne: and Caroline Norton, 132
lamplighter, 190
Lancashire dialect, 126, 131, 181; glossary of, 235–6
Lancashire wrestling, 214; *see also* boxing and wrestling
Lancaster, Joseph, 25, 30
Landon, Letitia, 68
law: bankruptcy laws, 106, 192; Benthamite legal theory, 131; Bill of Rights, 107; canon law, 136, 137; cost of legal proceedings, 134; Dickens's knowledge and experience of, 5, 41, 105; Doctors' Commons, 137; factory safety legislation, 5, 144–5, 158, 220; those fleeing from, 105; Habeas Corpus, 107; inadequacy of, 131, 134, 136; legal system, 34, 131, 134; Magna Carta, 107; marriage and divorce, 8–9, 126, 131–3, 134–8; patent, 41; probate, 137; red tape, 196; *see also* courts
Law Amendment Society, 131
Layard, Austen Henry: *Nineveh and Babylon*, 202–3; *Nineveh and its Remains*, 202–3; *Popular Account of Discoveries at Nineveh*, 202–3
Lee, Lavater, 64, 98
Leeds, 55; mechanics' institution, 111
Leeds Mercury, 170
legs, 9, 97, 100; pianoforte legs and mechanization, 10, 49; riddles, 226
Leibniz, Gottfried Wilhelm, 40
'Leibniz wheel', *see* calculating machines
Leigh, Percival, 224
Lemon, Mark, 55, 91, 96, 207
Lever, Charles, *A Day's Ride: A Life's Romance*, 11
libraries, 72, 110, 232; Dickens's attitude towards, 110; Manchester Free, 78, 110; *see also* adult education; mechanics' institutes
life expectancy: middle class, 150; working class, 124, 150; *see also* death-rates; infant mortality
lifts: dumb-waiters, 57
light porters, 160
lighthouses, 200: Carlington, 200; Eddystone, 200; Lynn, Norfolk, 199; Portland, 200; St Agnes, Scilly Isles, 200; Skerryvore, 200; Tour de Corduan, 200
lighting: candles, 92; Davy's safety lamp, 221; gas, 56, 92, 108, 125, 190; links, 108; naphtha flare lamps, 92; tallow, 124; whale-oil, 124
links and linkboys, 108
Little Dorrit, 1, 106, 139, 167, 189, 193, 196
Liverpool, 53, 55, 82: assizes, 186; mechanics' institution, 51, 111
Liverpool and Manchester railway, 54
London: balloon flights in, 71; Battle Bridge,

202; Bethnal Green, 122, 159; Blackfriars Road, 91; Bridewell, 66; Chancery Lane, 116; Charing Cross Road, 74; Charles II Street, 108; Chelsea, 24; Cheyne Row, 24; Gloucester Crescent, 134; Greenwich, 148; Haymarket, 108; Holborn, 117; lying-in hospitals in, 83; Mayfair, 109; mechanics' institution, 38–9, 116; New Oxford Street, 75; Oxford Street, 109; Pall Mall, 108, 215; Park Lane, 109; Piccadilly, 109, 216; Prize Ring rules, 42; rail journey to Paris, 54; Regent Street, 109; Regent's Park, 134; St Giles's, 75; St James's Street, 215; St Philip's, Shoreditch, 123; Seven Dials, 75; Shaftesbury Avenue, 74; Shepherd's Bush, 109; street architecture of, 56; train service to Birmingham, 54, 190; Vauxhall Gardens, 216; Veterinary College, 37; Wapping, 97; Westminster Bridge, 108, 228; Westminster Bridge Road, 68, 91; *see also* churches; circuses; observatories; theatres

Lord's Day Observance Society, 85

lotteries, 108

'Lottery Ticket, The', 108

Loutherbourg, Philippe Jacques de, 74

Lowe, James, 124, 162, 187

Lunardi, Vincenzo, 71

Lyceum Theatre, 78

Lyndhurst, Lord, *see* Copley, John Singleton, the younger, 1st Baron Lyndhurst

Lynn, Eliza, 8–9, 126, 134

Lyons, 152–3

Lytton, Sir Edward, *see* Bulwer, Sir Edward Lytton

M'Choakumchild: characterization of, 47; and the pupil-teacher system, 48

M'Culloch, J. M., *A Series of Lessons in Prose and Verse*, 47

M'Culloch (McCulloch), J. R., 33, 47, 118; *Dictionary, Practical, Theoretical, and Historical of Commerce*, 47; *Principles of Political Economy*, 47

MacNish, Robert, *Philosophy of Sleep*, 141

'Mademoiselle Ella', 60, (illus.) 61

Malt Shovel Inn, 91

Malthus, Rev. Thomas, 7, 33, 77, 164

Manchester: Athenaeum, 111; chemical manufacturing industry in, 79; and Coketown, 78; Dickens's description of, 55; Free Library, 78, 110; Institutional Association of Lancashire and Cheshire, 129; Lancasterian School, 36; and *The Long Strike*, 77; and opium, 86; railway, 54; rivers and canals of, 79; St Peter's Fields ('Peterloo'), 181; 'school of ethics', 78; Statistical Society, 28, 34, 83

Manchester Spinners and Manufacturers' Association, 162

mangle, 198

Mangnall, Richmal, *Historical and Miscellaneous Questions*, 37

manufacturers and merchants: attitude towards agitators, 187; and banking, 55, 71; and child labour, 183; and the education of factory children, 154; employers' unions, 73, 158, 162, 187; and factory safety legislation, 143–5, 155–7, 166, 185, 220; houses, 55, 73; Thomas Miller, Jnr, 73; and Palmerston, 158, 186; and the Preston strike and lock-out, 158, 162, 187, 223; and smoke pollution, 154–6; *see also* cotton industry; industrial relations; Preston strike and lock-out; trade unionism

market baskets, 193

markets: booths, 92; Covent Garden, 193; London, 198; street, 85

Marlborough House, 42, 43, 44, 45; *see also* Department of Practical Art; exhibitions; museums

Marlowe, Christopher, *Dr Faustus*, 169

marriage and divorce: adultery, 128, 131, 132, 134, 136; age difference in marriage, 149; bigamy, 132, 134, 136-7; civil ceremonies, 132, 136-7; cost of divorce, 134–5, 136-7; Dickens and Stephen Blackpool, 131, 142; Dickens's separation, 133–4; Frederick Dickens's separation, 130–1; grounds for divorce, 131–2, 134–5; history of divorce, 134-7; legal procedure for divorce, 132–3, 134–5, 135–6; Eliza Lynn's articles on, 8–9, 126, 134; marriage laws, 126, 132–3, 136–7; Norton divorce case, 134; separation, 131, 132–3, 133–5, 136–7; wedding breakfasts, 152; *see also* courts; married women's property laws; women

Married Women's Property Act (1870), 151; second reading of Bill (1868), 137

married women's property laws, 8, 132–3, 136; coverture 133, 151; Dickens's attitude towards, 8, 136; Married Women's Property Act (1870), 151; *see also* marriage and divorce; women

Marshalsea Debtors' Prison, 106

Marston, John, *The Patrician's Daughter*, 24

Martin Chuzzlewit, 77, 103, 105, 169

Martineau, Harriet 4, 74; *Factory Controversy*, 144, 155; *Illustrations of Political Economy*, 110; *Turn Out*, 182

Master Humphrey's Clock, 2, 3, 77

matinées, 226

Maudsley, Henry, 70
Maule, Sir William, 136
Mayfair, 109
Mayhew, Henry, 108, 201, 208
Mayo, Dr Charles, 48
Mayo, Elizabeth, 48; *Lessons on Objects*, 37; *Lessons on Shells*, 37
meat-safe, 200–1
mechanics' institutes: Birmingham and Midland, 222; Chatham, 111; Dickens's attitude towards, 111; Leeds, 111; libraries in, 111; Liverpool, 51, 111; London, 38–9, 116; Manchester, 129
mechanization: in cotton manufacture, 81; Dickens's attitude towards, 10; effects of, 81; wood-turning, 10, 49
medicine: anthelmintics (for intestinal worms), 103; bismuth, 95; bitters, 103; boluses (pills), 42; mercury treatments, 140; nine oils, 89, (illus.) 90; opium, 86; restoratives, 6, 150, 216, 221; stomachics, 103; *see also* disease; drugs; hospitals; industrial disease; surgeons
Medusa, 191
megaphone, 73
Melbourne, Lord, *see* Lamb, William, 2nd Viscount Melbourne
Melton Mowbray, 93
Memoirs of Joseph Grimaldi, 58
Menken, Adah Isaac, *Mazeppa*, 230
mental illness, 133, 135; depression, 69–70
Mercier, Charles, 70
Merrylegs, 9, 62–3; dog act, 121, (illus.) 120
Mesmer, Franz Anton, 142
mesmerism, 142–3
Metropolitan Interments Act (1850), 79, 128
Milan, 1
Mill, James, 33
Mill, John Stuart, 33; *Utilitarianism*, 118
Miller, Thomas, Jnr, 73
Mines and Collieries Bill, 221
Mitford, John Thomas Freeman, Earl of Redesdale, 135
mittens, 76, 200
money-lenders: Jewish, 105
monocles, 211
Montague, Charles, 103
Montgolfier brothers, 71
Morley, Henry, 8, 31, 42, 43, 44, 45, 69, 71, 79, 123, 145, 155, 183, 216
Morning Chronicle, 78, 133, 182, 222
Morton, Thomas, *Speed the Plough*, 71
Moseley, Rev. Henry, 37–8, 51
mottos, 168, 170, 180
Mudfog Papers: 'Full Report of the First Meeting of the Mudfog Association', 147

Murdock, William, 124
Murray, John, 56; *Handbook for Shropshire, Cheshire, and Lancashire*, 56
Museum of Ornamental Art, *see* Marlborough House
museums: establishment of, 44, 57; Hunterian, 53; Ornamental Art, 44, 46; private, 57–8; Sunday opening of, 85; Victoria and Albert, 44; *see also* exhibitions; Marlborough House
musical instruments: tambourines, 197
mutton, 197
Mystery of Edwin Drood, The, 24, 225

names
 biblical: Rachael, 125; Thomas, 35
 popular, 35, 125
 For other characters' names, see under the surname, e.g. Gradgrind, Louisa
Napoleonic Wars, 124, 129, 181
Nash, John, 108
Nation, W. H. C., *Under the Earth; or, The Sons of Toil*, 228
national anthem, British, 106–7
National Association of Factory Occupiers, 145
National Association for Promoting the Political and Social Improvement of the People, 116
National Association of United Trades for the Protection of Labour, 161
National Debt, 129
National Society for Promoting the Education of the Poor in the Principles of the Established Church, 31
needlework: needlepoint, 151; netting, 130, 200; work-box, 150
negus, 198
netting, *see* needlework
neurasthenia, *see* depression
'New Dodge, The', 179–9
New Oxford Street, 75
Newcastle, 54
Newcastle Commission (1861), 51
Newmarket race-course: coat, 92
newspapers and periodicals (only if specifically mentioned): advertisements in, 192; and the engineers' strike, 175; *Bee*, 2; *Examiner*, 5, 85; *Illustrated London News*, 66, 92, 174; *Leeds Mercury*, 170; *Morning Chronicle*, 78, 133, 182, 222; *Preston Guardian*, 118, 163; *Preston Herald*, 215; and the Preston strike, 6–7, 162, 179; *Punch*, 76; *Spectator*, 2, 165; *Tatler*, 2; *Times*, 39, 167, 175, 179; *True Sun*, 182; *see also All the Year Round*; *Household Words*
Newton, Sir Isaac, 225
New York, 229
Nicholas Nickleby, 40, 41, 58, 60, 62, 76, 88, 95,

103, 105
night-cap, 91
nine oils, 89, (illus.) 90
Nineveh bull, 202
nonconformists: and Anglican privilege, 131; architecture of, 82; Calvinism, 96; church attendance and, 82, 84; church-building and, 82, 84; church services, 84; growth of sects, 84; the New Church, 83; Norfolk Island, 187; religious instruction, 28; and trade, 83; *see also* Christianity; Church of England; Roman Catholic Church; sabbatarianism
North, Christopher, *see* Wilson, John
Norton, Caroline Sheridan, 8–9, 134
Nottingham, 55
nursery rhymes and stories: Blue Beard, 147; editing fairy stories, 52, 54; fairy stories, 109, 199; folk lore, 109; ghost stories, 109; 'House that Jack Built', 54; 'man in the moon', 53; 'Peter Piper', 57; 'There was an old woman', 87; 'Tom Thumb, 52, 54; Turkish Tales, 165; 'Twinkle, twinkle, little star', 53; *see also* Arabian Nights; songs and ballads

Oastler, Richard, 170
observatories: Kew Gardens, 148; Royal Greenwich, 148
Oedipus, 226
Old Cockpit, *see* Preston: Temperance Hall
Old Curiosity Shop, The, 2, 3, 78, 88
Old Lambeth Church, 104
Oliver Twist, 97, 147, 197
opium, *see* drugs
Orr, William Somerville, *Orr's Circle of the Sciences*, 69
Our Mutual Friend, 5, 47, 97, 106, 167, 202
overseers and supervisors, 229
overtime, 175, 181
Owen, Sir Richard, 53
Oxford, 193
Oxford Street, 109

Padiham, 34
Pall Mall, 108, 215
Palmerston, Lord, *see* Temple, John Henry, 3rd Viscount Palmerston
'Pantomime of Life, The', 231
Paris, 9, 54, 71, 100, 206, 217, 229
Park Lane, 109
Parliament, 85
    Bill of Rights, 107
    divorce, 131–3, 135–8
    as dust-heap, 201–2
    House of Commons, 136, 202, 226; MPs, 166, 208

House of Lords, 132, 136, 166
    see also blue books; government
parliamentary trains, 138, 219
partridge, 206
Pascal, Blaise, 40
Patent Act (1852), 41
Paterson, Peter, *see* Bertram, James Glass
Payn, James, 'Sharpening the Scythe', 5–6, 220, 224
Pedder family, 55
Pegasus, 91
Pegasus's Arms: possible sources for, 91; signboard, 91
Perrault, Charles, *Contes du temps passé*, 147
Pestalozzi, Johann, 37, 47–8
'Peter Piper' (tongue-twister), 58
'Peterloo Massacre', 181
Pharmacy Act (1868), 86
pheasant, 205
Phillip, Captain Arthur, 185
phraseology: biblical, 24, 81, 117, 139, 142, 145, 149, 167, 179, 189, 191, 196, 202, 202, 203, 206, 233, 234; boxing, 42; colloquialisms, 137, 170, 188, 207, 214; commonplaces, 111, 184; Latin, 204; nautical, 182, 200, 218; in Renaissance drama, 42; slang, 130, 214; synecdoche, 123; *see also* glossary of slang, 237–40; proverbs
phrenology, 31–2, 39
Piccadilly, 109, 216
Pickwick Papers, 78, 88, 106, 134, 192, 197
Pictures from Italy, 152, 204
piece-rate price lists, 137
piece-work, 138, 175, 181
pipe-clay, 77
pipes, 77
Planche, J. R., *Fortunio*, 229
playbills, 60, 76, 108
Playfair, Lyon, 43, 158
'Plorn', *see* Dickens, Edward Bulwer Lytton
Plug Plot riots, 175
plumbing, 56–7; *see also* gas; housing; lighting; sanitary reform and sanitation; shower-baths; ventilation
poetry: and Bentham, 75; during the Preston strike, 172, 179; *see also* Arabian Nights; nursery rhymes and stories; songs and ballads
political economists: J. R. M'Culloch, 33, 47, 118; Thomas Malthus, 7, 33, 77, 164; James Mill, 33; John Stuart Mill, 33, 118; David Ricardo, 33; Adam Smith, 33, 77
political economy: principles criticized in *The Chimes*, 22; Christianity and, 7; Dickens's attitude towards, 5, 7, 117, 145, 147; laissez-faire, 22, 33, 47, 52, 71, 77, 84, 110, 118,

127, 161, 163; Malthusian population theory, 7, 33, 77, 164; Harriet Martineau and, 110, 145; Preston strike and, 6, 34–5, 118, 126; in schools, 7, 38, 52, 116, 118, 164; and trade unionism, 6-7, 162; Utilitarianism, 35, 83, 116
pollution: smoke, 154–5, 167; water, 79, 170
polonies, 169
Poor Law Amendment Act (1834), 34
popular entertainment
  attitudes towards, 68, 87, 96
  ballooning, 71
  boxing, 42, 88
  in 'Chadwick's Orchard', 58
  Dickens's attitude towards, 85, 88, 122
  gambling, 87, 88
  mummers' plays, 92
  places of: betting-shops, 88; boxing amphitheatres, 228; casinos, 86; concert rooms, 86; dancing rooms, 86; fairs, 88, 108; gin-palaces, 85, 89; saloons, 86, 88
  prize fights, 88
  Punch and Judy show, 98
  sabbatarianism and, 85
  wrestling, 42, 214
  see also circus; fairs; public-houses; sports; theatres
port, 152; in negus, 198; in walnut ketchup, 205
Porter, G. R., *The Progress of the Nation*, 189
power-looms, 124, 180; *see also* cotton industry; silk-weaving; weavers and weaving
Preston: bankers, manufacturers and merchants of, 55, 71, 72; Banking Company, 71; Bull Inn and Royal Hotel, 91, 215; 'Chadwick's Orchard', 58; and Coketown, 79, 182; cotton factories in, 73, 81, 159; death-rate, 124; Dickens's attitude towards, 217; Grey Horse and Seven Stars Inn, 91; House of Correction, 66, 86; the Marsh, 58; Miller Park, 73; New Jerusalem Church, 83; Ribble River, 58; St Peter's Church, 82; smoke pollution in, 155; Temperance Hall, 6, 174, 218, (illus.) 173; and the temperance movement, 86; Temperance Society, 172–3; Theatre Royal, 198; University of Central Lancashire, 82; Winckley Square, 73; *see also* cotton industry; Dickens, Charles: visit to Preston; Preston strike and lock-out
Preston Guardian, 118, 163
Preston Herald, 215
Preston Masters' Association, 73, 158, 162, 187
Preston strike and lock-out, 6, 34–5, 78, 145, 162, 174, 185, 187, 223; arrests for conspiracy, 186; ballads, poems and songs of, 126, 174, 179, 245-6; biblical allusion, 180; bills and placards, 6, 180, 217; blacklegs, 181, 186; chartism, 172; and the composition of *HT*, 78, 182; Dickens attitude towards industrial relations during, 83, 145, 159, 163, 187; intimidation, 182; Irish immigrants and, 186; Labour Parliament, 174; lock-out, 162, 163, 175, 187; Masters' Association, 73, 158, 162, 187; meetings during, 6, 58, 174, 180, 218; Thomas Miller, Jnr, 73; Palmerston, 158, 175; piece-rate lists, 137–8; political economy and, 6, 34–5, 116, 126; the press and, 6, 162, 179; speeches during, 174; strike leaders, 6, 118, 174, 177–8, 186, 218; trade unionism and, 6, 162, 163, 174; weekly levy and payments, 174, 182; *see also* Coketown; Dickens, Charles: visit to Preston and strike article; industrial relations; Preston; trade unionism
prisons: Coventry Gaol, 184; Eastern Penitentiary, Philadelphia, 87; Pentonville, 87; Preston House of Correction, 66, 86; reports and blue books about, 86, 147; *see also* hard labour; transportation
professionalization: veterinary surgeons, 37
props, 229
proverbs, 168, 192, 197, 203, 215
Public Health Act (1848), 79
public houses: Bull Inn and Royal Hotel, 91, 215; factory workers and, 88; Flying Childers, 93; 'Free and Easies', 88; Grey Horse and Seven Stars, 91; Malt Shovel, 92; railway taverns, 189; Select Committee on Public Houses and Sale of Beer (1853), 87; signboards, 91; Sunday closing of, 85; theatrical, 60, 62, 91; turtle soup and venison in, 130; *see also* alcohol; beer-houses; saloons; hotels; drinks; drunkenness; gin-palaces
Public Libraries Act (1850), 111
Public Record Office, 41, 105
Pugin, Augustus Welby Northmore, 44
Punch, 76
Punch and Judy show, 98

Queensberry rules, 42
Queen's Scholars, 30, 49, 113

Rachael: as angel, 142; name, 125; and marriage laws, 126; speech of, 125
Ragged Churches, 85
Ragged School movement, 28
Railway Act (1844), 139, 166, 206
railways
  accidents, 166
  arches, 139, 191
  construction, 53–4, 190, 206–7
  Dickens's attitude towards, 54, 190

electric telegraph and, 207–8
engine drivers, 54
excursion trains, 219
fares, 138
Great Eastern, 139
Great Western, 125, 219
Liverpool and Manchester, 54
locomotive speeds, 53, 124
parliamentary trains, 138, 219
signals and signalling systems, 166, 190, 207
South Eastern, 54
stations: bookstalls, 202; Dickens's description of, 207; refreshment and waiting rooms, 188; stairwells, 225; term for, 206–7; viaducts, 139
travel: Brighton to London, 222; to Birmingham and Wolverhampton, 5, 78, 207; London to Birmingham 53–4, 190; London to Exeter, 125; London to Paris, 54
recreations, see popular entertainment
red bricks, 58, 83
red tape, 196
Redesdale, Lord, see Mitford, John Thomas Freeman, Earl of Redesdale
Redgrave, Richard, 43–4, 46
Redruth, Cornwall, 124
reflector lamps, see lighthouses
Regent Street, 109
Regent's Park, 134
Registration of Births, Deaths, and Marriages Act (1836), 131
Repton, George, 108
Ribble River, 58
Ricardo, David, 33
Rochdale, 79
Rolfe, Robert Monsey, Baron Cranworth, 132, 133
Roman Catholic Church: Ash Wednesday, 219; Holy Inquisition, 214; see also Church of England; Christianity; nonconformists
Romulus and Remus, 204
Ronge, Johann and Bertha, 48
Roos, Philip, 149
Royal Academy, 51, 192
Royal Arms, 106; see also coats of arms; genealogy
Royal Circus, 91
Royal College of Veterinary Surgeons, 37
Royal Commission on Poor Laws (1832), 229
Royal Institution of Electrical Engineers, 224
Royal Observatory, Greenwich, 148
Royal Opera Arcade, 108
Royal Polytechnic Institution, 225
Royal Society of Arts, 41
Royal Statistical Society, 83

Royton, Oldham, 177
Rugby School, 123
rum (hot spiced), 216
Rüntz, John, 31
Ruskin, John, *Modern Painters*, 70
Russell, Lord John, 1st Earl Russell, 30, 168, 197

sabbatarianism
  Lord's Day Observance Society, 85
  Sunday: as holiday, 88; postal collections and deliveries on, 85; recreations on, 85, 219; trading on, 85; travel on, 85
St Giles's, 75
St Giles's rookery, 75
St James's Street, 215
St Paul's cathedral, 137
St Peter's, Preston, 82
Sala, George Augustus, 9, 35, 64, 76, 91, 97, 100
Salford, 79
saloons, 86, 88
sanitary reform and sanitation: Acts of Parliament associated with, 79; blue books and reports about, 79, 147; in circuses, 92; Dickens's attitude towards, 25, 79, 179; in factory towns, 55; overcrowding, 159; sewage disposal, 56, 159; water pollution, 79; see also disease; housing; plumbing; pollution; ventilation
sausages: polonies and saveloys, 169
savages: Dickens's dislike of, 6, 79; see also imagery
saveloys, 169
sawdust, 92
Saxon, Arthur, 'Clown's performing chair', 230
School of Design, 41, 43, 44; see also Department of Practical Art; education; Marlborough House
Scott, Sir Walter: *Ivanhoe*, 111; *Peveril of the Peak*, 192
seals (document), 161
sealskin: coat, 102
self-help, 71; and the trade union movement, 161
Seneca, 84
separation, see marriage and divorce
serpents, 6, 79, 191; see also imagery
Seven Dials, 75
Shaftesbury Avenue, 74
Shakespeare, William, 53, 64–6, 152; *As You Like It*, 105; *Comedy of Errors*, 160; *Coriolanus*, 106, 164; *Hamlet*, 103, 198; *Henry V*, 215, 218; *2 Henry VI*, 209; *King John*, 159; *Love's Labour's Lost*, 160; *Measure for Measure*, 107; *Merchant of Venice*, 201; *Othello*, 199; *Rape of Lucrece*, 160; *Titus Andronicus*, 160

sheep, 38, 220
Shelley, Mary, *Frankenstein*, 121
Shepherd's Bush, 109
sherry, 130; in negus, 198
ships: 'bottoms', 152; First Fleet, 185; *see also* lighthouses
shipwrecks, *see* accidents
shooting, 206
shops: barbers', 10, 76; betting, 88–9; chandler's, 74, 86; chemist, 86; hairdressers', 76; hucksters', 74; stealing from, 214; in Royal Opera arcade, 108
Shoreditch, Bethnal Green, 123
shower-baths, 165
signboards, 91
silk-weaving, 82, 111; Jacquard loom, 152–3; *see also* cotton industry; weavers and weaving
simoom, 159
Simplon Pass, 1
'Six Acts', 180
Sketches by Boz, 88, 106; 'Astley's', 60, 95, 100, 226; 'Boarding-House', 189; 'Doctors' Commons', 137; 'Gin-Shops', 85, 89; 'Meditations in Monmouth Street', 74; 'Seven Dials', 74; 'Vauxhall Gardens by Day', 71
Sketches of Young Couples, 77
Slackbridge, *see* Grimshaw, Mortimer
slang: circus, 96; glossary of, 235–9; theatrical, 96; thieves', 214
slates: for school use, 77
slavery, 170; and industrial workers, 170; and the Preston strike, 174
Sleary: characterization of, 60, 103
Sleary, Josephine: and Louisa Woolford, 58–60
smelling-salts, 151
Smiles, Samuel: *Life and Labour*, 72; *Life of George Stephenson*, 72; *Lives of the Engineers*, 72; *Self-help*, 71
Smith, Adam, *Wealth of Nations*, 33, 77
soap-bubbles, 224
social division, 125, 223; *see also* industrial relations
Society for the Diffusion of Useful Knowledge, 122
Somerset House, 43
songs and ballads, 199; 'Children in the Wood', 229; of the Preston strike, 126, 245–6
South Eastern railway, 54
Southey, Robert, 'The Devil's Thoughts', 73
Sparsit, Mrs: and *Coriolanus*, 105, 164; age disparity of marriage, 149
Spartans, 183
Speaight, George, 'Clown's performing chair', 230
special effects: transparencies, 74

Spectator, The, 2; *Turkish Tales* in, 165
Spencer, J. H., 215
Sphinx, 226–7
spinners and spinning: occupational disease, 159; pay, 168; unions, 174, 182; working conditions of, 159; *see also* cotton industry; Preston strike and lock-out; trade unionism; weavers and weaving
sports: boxing, 42, 88; cricket, 167; fox-hunting, 206; horse-racing, 88; shooting, 206; wrestling, 42, 214; *see also* circus; popular entertainment
stairwells, 225
Stanfield, Clarkson, 192
Stanhope, Philip Dormer, 4th Earl of Chesterfield, 189
stars and starlight, 142, 222; *see also* astronomy
statistical science
 blue books, 86, 118, 147, 167, 168
 Dickens's attitude towards, 83–4, 147
 growth of, 83
 societies: Manchester, 28, 34, 83; Royal, 83
 tabular reports, 87, 147
steam-engines, 128
steak, 129
Steele, Richard, 2
Stephenson, George, the *Rocket*, 54
Stephenson, Robert, 54
Stevenson, Alan, *A Rudimentary Treatise on . . . Lighthouses*, 200
Stewart, Dugald, *Elements of the Philosophy of the Human Mind*, 141
Stockport, 55, 177
Stone, Eaton, 93
Stone, Dr Thomas, 141
Stow, David, 'training system', 30, 47–8; Glasgow Educational Society, 30; Glasgow Normal Seminary, 30, 47, 48
strikes, 78, 161, 162, 163, 175; Dickens's attitude towards, 182, 223; engineers', 162, 175, 179, 181; Glasgow spinners', 186. For the Preston strike and lock-out see individual entry
strollers, 68, 75–6; *see also* beggars and vagrants
sugar, 189
Sunday under Three Heads, 85
superstitions, 138
surgeons, 6, 224; veterinary, 36–7
Swainson & Birley, 81, (illus.) 80
Swedenborg, Emanuel, 83
sweetbreads, 151
Swift, Jonathan, *Gulliver's Travels*, 116
Switzerland: Dickens's trip to, 1, 203; Orphan and Normal schools, 48
syphilis, 140

Tale of Two Cities, A, 10, 22
Talfourd, Serjeant Thomas Noon, 133, 223
tallow, 124
tambourines, 197
Tatler, The, 2
taverns, *see* public houses
Tavistock House, 54, 134, 199, 226
Taylor, Jane, 53
tea, 151
teetotalism, *see* temperance movement
temperance movement, 52, 86; badges and regalia, 86; Rev. John Clay and, 110; Dickens's attitude towards, 85; teetotalism and Preston, 86; Preston Temperance Hall, 172, (illus.) 173; Preston Temperance Society, 172–3; *see also* alcohol; beer-houses; drinks; drunkenness; gin-palaces; public-houses; saloons
Temple, John Henry, 3rd Viscount Palmerston, 158, 175, 186, 220
Ten Hours Act (1847), 88; *see also* Factory Acts
Ten Hours movement, 111, 170, 179
Tennyson, Alfred, 1st Baron, *In Memoriam*, 140
Ternan, Ellen Lawless (Nelly), 149
theatre visits: by Dickens, 198; by factory operatives, 88
theatres: Covent Garden, 108; Drury Lane, 60, 92, 93, 98, 108, 230; Lyceum, 77; Her Majesty's, 107; Theatre Royal, Preston, 198; *see also* circuses; popular entertainment
theatrical slang, 96
thermodynamics: entropy theory, 188
thieves' slang, 214
Thompson, William ('Bendigo'), 42, 216
thumb-screw, 216
time: amusements as a waste of, 68, 87, 95; and astronomy 148; clocking-in, 95; holidays, 88, 129–30; hours of work, 111; and idleness, 68, 95; regulation of, 87, 95; 'short Saturday', 88, 111
Times, The, 39, 167, 175, 179
titles of HT, 19, 35, 111–13, 148, 201
tobacco: pipes, 77; types of, 169
'Tolpuddle Martyrs', 186
Tourniaire (equestrian), 92
Toussenel, Alphonse, *L'Esprit des Bêtes*, 122
'Town Boys', 193
Towns Improvement Clauses Act (1847), 79, 154, 167
trade unionism 5, 6–7; agitators, 6–7, 117, 171, 174; 'closed shop' policy, 181; cotton industry and, 175; Dickens's attitude towards, 161, 162, 163; history of, 161; rituals and oaths, 186; Tolpuddle Martyrs, 186; transportation and, 186; Select Committee on Combinations, 186; *see also* guilds; industrial relations; manufacturers and merchants; Preston strike and lock-out; unions
transport: 'bounder', 105; fly, 225; omnibus 225; *see also* railways
transportation: to Australia, 186, 187; for bigamy, 134; to Norfolk Island, 187; penal colonies, 185, 187; and trade unionism, 186; *see also* hard labour; prisons
treadwheel, 66
True Sun, 182
tumblers, 107
Turner, Joseph Mallord William, 192
turtle soup, 130

Uncommercial Traveller, The: 'Arcadian London', 108; 'Bound for the Great Salt Lake', 169; 'Calais Night Mail', 106; 'Dullborough Town', 111; 'Little Dinner in an Hour', 32; 'Medicine Men of Civilization', 127; 'Night Walks', 193
undertakers and undertaking, 127
Union Jack, 107
unions, 161, 170, 172; employers', 73, 158, 162, 187; engineering, 162; refusal to join, 184; spinners', 175, 183; weavers', 175; workers', 162; *see also* guilds; trade unionism
University of Central Lancashire, 82
Unlawful Oaths Act (1797), 186
Urania Cottage, 109
Utilitarianism, 25, 40, 41, 52, 56, 75, 111, 118; Jeremy Bentham and, 33, 40, 75, 118; industrialism and, 78; James Kay-Shuttleworth and, 34; political economy and economists, 35, 83, 116; *see also* Department of Practical Art; education; laissez-faire; political economists; political economy

Vagrancy Act (1824), 68
vagrants, *see* beggars and vagrants
Vauxhall Gardens, 216
venereal disease, *see* disease; medicine; syphilis
Venice, Doges' Palace, 205
venison, 130
ventilation, 56, 122–3, 159; *see also* gas; housing; plumbing; pollution; sanitary reform and sanitation
Venus, 204, 217
veterinary medicine: nine oils, 89, (illus.) 90; *see also* disease; medicine
veterinary surgeons, 36–7
Veterinary Surgeons Act (1881), 37
viaducts: Welwyn, 139
Victoria, Queen, 107, 108
Victoria and Albert Museum, 45
Victorian perceptions of: dreams, 141; education

as social control, 113–16; laissez-faire, 126; legal reform, 126; marriage and divorce, 132, 134–6; poverty, 72; time, 68, 95; trade unionism, 161, 186; women, 10, 69–70

wafers (document), 161
wakes, 130
Walkingame, Francis, *Tutor's Assistant*, 32
Wallett, W. F., 64, 89, 91, 96, 97, 102–3, 229
wallpaper, 44
walnut ketchup, 205
Wapping, 97
warming-pan, 170
Warren's blacking factory, 193
Warrington, 6, 172, 218
water-systems, 56–7; *see also* plumbing; sanitary reform and sanitation; shower-baths
weavers and weaving: age of, 124; hand-loom, 66, 82, 124; hours of work, 113; Jacquard loom, 152–3; pay, 168; power-loom, 124, 158, 179; respiratory disorders of, 165; unions, 175; women 124, 168; *see also* cotton industry; Preston strike and lock-out; spinners and spinning; trade unionism
wedding breakfasts, 152
Wedgwood, Josiah, 95, 170
Welwyn Viaduct, 139
Westminster Bridge, 108, 228
Westminster Bridge Road, 68, 91, 228
Westminster School, 193; Latin Play, 193
whale-oil, 124
Wheatstone, Sir Charles, 206
Whitelands College, 50
Whole Duty of Man, The, 7, 163
Widdicombe, John Esdaile, 96
Wild Man (*Homo silvestris*), 53
Wilderspin, Samuel, 28–30, 40–1
Wilkes, John, 66
William III, 129
Williams, F. S., *Our Iron Roads*, 205
Wills, W. H., 1, 3, 7, 49, 144
Wilson, John (Christopher North), *Noctes Ambrosianae*, 192
wine: port ,152, 198; sherry, 103, 152, 198; sweet white, 198
Wolverhampton, 5, 78, 79, 150, 191, 207, 220; black ladder, 127
women: adult education and, 50–1; cruelty to, 130, 134; and depression, 69–70; and divorce, 131–6; factory workers, 74, 82, 124, 125, 168; and hair, 199; homeless, 108; legal inequalities and, 8–9, 12–13, 134–5; married women's property law, 8–9, 75, 132–3; in mines, 221; and power-loom weaving, 124; pregnancy and childbirth, 83; Victorian

ideology and, 10, 69, 199; Victorian invalid wife, 73; wilfulness and subservience of, 69
Wood's Sessional School, 30, 46, 48
Woolford, Louisa, (illus.) 59; model for Josephine Sleary, 60; and Louisa Gradgrind, 68; *see also* circus acts
Worcester, Connecticut, 32
work-box (needlework), 150
working class: 'British brandy', 228; Castlereagh and, 180; church attendance of, 84; Dickens's attitude towards, 179; funeral practices, 127; gin and gin-palaces 85, 89; HW articles written for, 4; housing, 56, 81, 85, 122–3, 159; libraries for, 110; life expectancy of, 124, 150; and marriage laws, 132; mechanics' institutes and, 111; opium-eating, 86; paternalistic attitude towards, 109; reading habits of, 110, 122; teaching political economy to, 116; temperance and, 85; trade unionism and, 161; *see also* cotton industry; education; industrial relations; industrialization; marriage and divorce; political economy; popular entertainment; sports; trade unionism; women
Worswick, Robert, 180
Wren, Sir Christopher, 148
wrestling, *see* boxing

Yorkshire: woollen industry of, 79; shooting on the moors, 206